THE
LONGEST
VOYAGE

THE
LONGEST
VOYAGE

Circumnavigators

in the

Age of Discovery

ROBERT SILVERBERG

OHIO UNIVERSITY PRESS

ATHENS

Ohio University Press, Athens, OH 45701
© 1972 by Robert Silverberg
All rights reserved
Printed in the United States of America

First printed in 1972 by The Bobbs-Merrill Company
First paperback edition printed by
Ohio University Press in 1997

03 02 01 00 99 98 97 5 4 3 2 1

Library of Congress Cataloging-in-Publication Data
Silverberg, Robert.
    The longest voyage : circumnavigators in the age of discovery /
Robert Silverberg.
        p.   cm.
    Originally published : Indianapolis : Bobbs-Merrill, 1972.
    Includes bibliographical references and index.
    ISBN 0-8214-1192-6 (pbk. : alk. paper)
    1. Voyages around the world. 2. Explorers. I. Title.
G419.S55   1997
910.4'1—dc21   97-1812
                                                        CIP

This book is printed on acid-free paper ∞

Contents

Illustrations

(MAPS)

THE
LONGEST
VOYAGE

THE ROUND WORLD'S
IMAGINED CORNERS

A T ANCHOR IN A SPANISH RIVER, FIVE SHIPS, waiting. Old ships, patched, small, untrustworthy. Aboard them 948 cheeses, 1,512 pounds of honey, 3,200 pounds of raisins, much pickled pork, a two-year supply of biscuits. Wine, rice, lentils, flour, provisions for a long journey. A mingled crew, Spaniards, Italians, Frenchmen, Basques, Greeks, a Malayan, an Englishman. For a Spanish fleet, a Portuguese commander: Fernão de Magalhães, called Hernando de Magallanes by the Spaniards, Ferdinand Magellan by posterity. Under harsh September sunlight Magellan readies his vessels for departure. The year is 1519. The destination is the Moluccas, the islands where spices are grown, a cluster of fragrant isles in a distant sea.

Grim, limping, austere Magellan expects it to be a long voyage. He goes westward into the Atlantic to seek the Spice Islands, though he knows they lie in other waters. The damnable massive continents of Columbus stand between Magellan and the Moluccas like high green walls cutting ocean from ocean. Never mind; he will find a sea route westward to the Indies, a strait to take him past those two slabs of land. He knows the strait is there, just as he knows that Jesus and the Virgin guide him, that the King of Portugal loathes him, and that the throbbing in his wounded leg will not leave him. For God, for Spain, and for his own private profit and glory, the little Portuguese will find that strait. And traverse it. And leave his body beyond it on the shores of a strange sea, though that is no part of his plan.

Sailing around the world is likewise no part of Magellan's plan. He believes that the circumnavigation is possible, of course, or he would never lift anchor in the first place. But the homeward leg of that voyage, past the Spice Islands, would take him through waters where only Portuguese ships lawfully might sail. Magallanes is no longer Magalhães; a Spaniard now, he has no wish to trespass on the seas of his former country. That is the whole point of this enterprise: to reach the Moluccas without trespass, by a new route, to lead Spain to the source of spices and to return the way he came, snatching cloves and peppers away from Lisbon by brilliant geographical achievement. So this is not to be a world-girdling voyage—not as of September 1519.

Plans change. Men die. Most of those who wait here, at anchor by the mouth of the Guadalquivir river, will never see Spain again. Some will return in cowardice to their starting point, timidly resigning from the grandest maritime adventure in human history. The others, those who from stubbornness or foolishness or luck or greed see the mission to its end, will make the longest voyage of all, to the ends of the Earth and back. A trespass, a calamity, a circumnavigation—a miracle of seamanship.

The port of departure is Sanlúcar de Barrameda, 75 miles downriver from Seville. The castle of the Duke of Medina Sidonia guards the river's mouth. The farewell parties there have been going on for weeks; the wives and mistresses of the officers gather in the castle, in the guest chambers of the monastery, in the inns; wine flows freely; there is laughter, gambling, talk of fortunes to be won in the Spice Islands. Now the month of final preparations ends. The voyagers kneel, accept the wafer and the wine, hear the Kyrie, the Credo, the Sanctus. Confession and communion behind them, they go to their ships; figures wave from shore; guns are sounded; sails are raised. Captain-General Magellan stands apart, a small and lonely figure. A commander must always create a distance between himself and his men, but for Magellan that is no task: this private man is accessible to few, alone even in the midst of his men. He is iron, jacketed in ice, and his sailors will follow him out of fear, not out of love. He has powerful enemies among the captains of his own fleet; there are whispers of mutiny even here at the moment of leave-taking.

Tuesday, September 20, 1519. The sails fill with breeze. The wives weep and contemplate their likely widowhood. The Atlantic swallows Magellan's vessels. The round world awaits its conqueror. He will reveal to man the nature of man's planet; he will perish; he will live forever.

2

Only a spherical planet can be circumnavigated. But that medieval aberration, the concept of a flat Earth, had long since gone into the discard heap. Columbus, we like to say, proved that the world was round, though all he did was scratch a short track over a small part of its circumference. It was Magellan's fearful voyage, and not Columbus' swift five-week cruise, that confirmed the obvious and made the world unarguably a globe.

Primitive man, seeing the ground flat beneath his feet, extended that datum to the horizon and imagined the world as a flat disk with edges over which unwary travelers might tumble. But such an image suits only the very simple and the very sophisticated, such as cloistered scholastics. Early man, though he depended on common sense, did not have the wit to comprehend the implications of what he saw; scholastics of any period do not bother to see at all, but spin theories to suit prior concepts. Neither the Neanderthal nor the absentminded professor could properly evaluate the shape of his planet, but almost any fisherman or sailor of antiquity was capable of deciding that the thing must be a sphere.

Babylonian court theologians taught that the Earth was a hollow mountain, floating on the waters of the deep. Egyptian priests saw it as the floor of a box, with a goddess—the sky—bending over it and supporting herself on elbows and knees. Neither Egyptians nor Babylonians were known as seafarers, and doubtless those who did go to sea had other ideas. They knew that when they stood in harbor and observed a ship approaching shore from far out at sea, the top of the mast appeared first, then the upper part of the sails, then the hull of the ship, as though the vessel were moving along a curved surface. The Mycenaeans and Minoans who sailed the Mediterranean before 1200 B.C. did not show much fear of falling off the world's edge; and their successors, the Greeks of post-Homeric times, argued clearly and convincingly against the flat-Earth theory.

True, the first Greek philosopher whose name we know —Thales of Miletus, who lived in the sixth century B.C.— seems to have believed that the world was a flat disk floating on water. Thales was a clever man, but he lived in a time when speculative theorists were often too fertile with ideas. After him came Anaximander, who said that the Earth had the shape of a cylinder, with a height one-third its diameter. That at least accounted for the obvious curvature of the surface. Two generations later, Pythagoras of Samos, having studied the mysteries of Egypt and Babylonia, announced that the world was a sphere. Though he had traveled abroad, Pythagoras was no empiricist; searching for underlying mathematical laws to explain the universe, he worked from mystical premises and gave the Earth that shape because a sphere, a perfect geometrical figure, was the only form the Earth *deserved* to have. Following the same notion of the necessity of a perfect universe, he put the planets into circular orbits. Pythagoras was more nearly right than anyone before him, but for the wrong reasons.

Plato, another mystic, accepted Pythagoras' theories. He regarded cosmological questions of this sort as far less important than such matters as the search for truth and justice, but he did speak of a spherical Earth. At least, Plato said, in an ideal universe the world could have no other shape. His pupil Aristotle, a man of tauter mind, gave reasons for the sphericity of the planet. He observed that the Earth cast a circular shadow on the moon during an eclipse, and cited the experience of travelers to prove the impossibility of the Earth's flatness. By the third century B.C., matters had advanced to the point where Eratosthenes, a member of the brilliant Hellenistic band of scientists in the Egyptian city of Alexandria, was able to compute the circumference of the Earth with impressive success. Eratosthenes measured the height of the noontime sun at Alexandria and at Aswan, figured the distance between those two points, and, with two angles and a known base, achieved a figure of 25,000 miles for the entire sphere of which he had surveyed an arc. That was extraordinarily close to the truth; but, unfortunately for Columbus and Magellan, later Alexandrian mathematicians revised Eratosthenes' figures to make the world seem much smaller than it really is.

The size and shape of the world thus were revealed by a progression of clever men. By 300 B.C. no educated person seriously doubted the sphericity of the Earth. Finding out

[7]

what that Earth contained, though, was a different matter. One could, like Aristotle or Eratosthenes, perform wonders of intellection without leaving home; but to know what lay beyond the horizon, one had to go and look. The Greeks spoke of their familiar Mediterranean world as the *oikoumene*, by which they meant the known or inhabited part of the Earth. (Our word "ecumenical," meaning "universal," is derived from this.) Though the limits of the *oikoumene* were unknown, it was assumed that a single world-girdling ocean bounded it.

We sometimes tend to think of discovery as something that began with Columbus, but the Greeks were considerable explorers and gradually pushed the borders of the *oikoumene* outward, as did their commercial rivals, the Carthaginians, who lived on the North African coast. For Homer, writing perhaps in 800 B.C., the world began somewhere in the hazy east, beyond Egypt, beyond Assyria, and ended in the misty west, at the Pillars of Hercules, which we call the Straits of Gibraltar. Nothing of Africa was known but its northern coast; Europe north of Greece was a wild forest; everything was surrounded by the "girdling river of Ocean." Then the world widened. A Carthaginian captain named Himilco may have passed through the Pillars of Hercules about 500 B.C., spending four months on a reconnaissance that took him to Brittany and perhaps to Cornwall. More reliably documented is the voyage of his brother Hanno down the western coast of Africa, far enough south to have had a glimpse of gorillas in Guinea or the Cameroons. If we can believe Herodotus, a Phoenician expedition a century before Hanno actually circumnavigated Africa from east to west. This was done, so we are told, at the instigation of Necho, Pharaoh of Egypt from 610 to 594 B.C. Looking for a maritime link between the Red Sea and the Mediterranean, Necho hired a fleet of Phoenicians and sent them south, thinking that all they need do was go around Libya to find a route. To their surprise they found that Africa extended vastly beyond all expectations. Herodotus relates that "the Phoenicians took their departure from Egypt by way of the Red Sea, and so sailed into the southern ocean. When autumn came, they went ashore, wherever they might happen to be, and having sown a tract of land with corn, waited until the grain was fit to cut. Having reaped it, they again set sail; and thus it came to pass that two whole years went by, and it was not till the third year that they doubled the Pillars of Hercules, and made good their voyage home. On their return they declared—I for my part do not believe them, but perhaps others may—that in sailing around Libya they had the sun upon their right hand."

The story is vague, but that last detail rings true. Libya here means the whole of Africa; and what Herodotus is saying is that the Phoenicians, as they proceeded southward and then westward beyond the equator, noticed the sun always in the north. This would be contrary to the experience of Mediterranean peoples, but it is what would be expected in navigation of the southern hemisphere. Possibly rumor or even guesswork could have led the Egyptians to the correct picture, but it is much more likely that an actual venture below the equator yielded this knowledge. The sun indeed would stand on the right hand as voyagers from Egypt rounded Africa.

It was a journey of some 13,500 miles—taken unhurriedly, with long spells ashore for rest and reprovisioning. Unhappily, the great fact it yielded—that Africa was a gigantic peninsula surrounded by water to the south—was lost soon after Herodotus' time. Ultimately, geographers decided that Africa stretched off infinitely to the south, connected to an unknown southern land, *Terra Australis Incognita*. It remained for Portuguese navigators twenty centuries later to repeat the work of the Phoenicians, coming around this time from west to east, and restore the knowledge that Necho's sailors had won so dearly.

Herodotus, who was a fair traveler himself—leaving his home in Asia Minor to visit Egypt, fallen Babylon, the Phoenician cities, all of the Greek world, and even the Scythian barbarians north of the Black Sea—tells of another expedition sent out by the Persian ruler Darius about 510 B.C., commanded by a Greek named Scylax. Wishing to know where the Indus river flowed to the sea, Darius sent Scylax eastward from Persia to enter the Indus via the Kabul river, follow it along its course to the sea, and return by coasting the shores westward around Arabia to Egypt. Thus India became part of the *oikoumene*.

Another of the ancient voyagers was Pytheas, a Greek born in the Greek colony of Massilia, now Marseilles, about 360 B.C. Carthage then controlled the Straits of Gibraltar and monopolized such traffic as there was between the Mediterranean and the Atlantic; but while Carthage was temporarily preoccupied with a war against the Sicilian city of Syracuse about 320 B.C., the merchants of Massilia sent Pytheas through the straits and into the North Atlantic to blaze a sea route linking them to the chief sources of those valuable commodities, amber and tin. He coasted western Spain and Portugal, took regular observations of latitude, reached the tin mines of Cornwall, and evidently circumnavigated Britain. His latitudes were expressed in the Greek fashion, in terms of a calculation of how long the longest day of the year would be at a given distance from the equator. In the northernmost part of Britain, he said, the longest day has eighteen hours, which corresponds to a latitude of 57°58′N. in Scotland. He sailed at least as far north as a place where the longest day was nineteen hours long; this would be at 61°N. at the northernmost of the Shetland

Islands. Here he heard about a land called Thule, six days' sail to the north: the northern termination of the world, beyond which no man could go. The narrative of his voyage is ambiguous, but some modern partisans of Pytheas, notably the explorers Fridtjof Nansen and Vilhjalmur Stefansson, feel that he actually went in quest of Thule, entering the frozen sea above the Arctic Circle.

Through these and other journeys, most of them unrecorded for reasons of commercial security, the Greeks and their contemporaries extended the *oikoumene* from Gibraltar to the Ganges, from the Baltic to the southern reaches of Africa. All this comprised a single continuous land mass attainable by coastal sailing. They did not often venture into the open sea—at any rate, most of those who went beyond sight of land did not return to tell the tale—but their caution stemmed from deficiencies in their ships and their navigational abilities, not from any dread of sailing over the world's edge. The existence of some other *oikoumene* across the ocean had to remain a matter for speculative thinking, no more.

There were many theories. Aristotle argued for a single *oikoumene*, bordered by ocean. He allowed for the possibility of huge extensions of the land in the directions of Africa and India, but insisted that there was only one continent. On a spherical Earth, then, the western and eastern shores of the one *oikoumene* must converge, and Aristotle did not think they would be separated by an ocean of any great size. His authority was invoked much later to show that it would be an easy matter to reach India by sailing westward from Spain.

In the second century B.C., Crates of Mallus postulated *four* continents, separated by two river-like oceans, one running from east to west, the other from north to south, crossing at right angles. Though the symmetry of this system, with its neatly balanced northern and southern hemispheres separated by water and an impassable zone of fire, had a certain appeal to the Greeks, only one aspect of it had any lasting geographical significance: the suggestion that below the equator lay the antipodes, a continent or continents that balanced the known land of the north.

Greek theorists also divided the world into varying climatic zones, usually five in number. At each of the two poles was a frigid zone, eternally icebound, everlastingly dead. Round the middle of the world lay the blazing tropics, a torrid zone of terrible heat. Between the frigid and the torrid were two temperate zones, a northern and a southern one. The northern temperate zone included the familiar Mediterranean *oikoumene;* its southern counterpart might well be equally favorable to human life, but no one in the north would ever know, for it was impossible to survive a crossing of the frightful equatorial zone. (That mariners had penetrated the tropics as early as 600 B.C. was somehow overlooked in these hypotheses.)

The climactic figure of Greek geography was Ptolemy of Alexandria, who lived in the second century after Christ. What journals of explorers were available to him in Alexandria's vanished library we cannot even guess, but Ptolemy had only to walk down to his city's flourishing docks to talk to men who had seen distant wonders. Alexandria was a great nexus of seaborne trade; in its harbor Ptolemy could find sailors who had gone via the Red Sea to Arabia, and on to the Persian Gulf and the coasts of India. Certainly there was traffic in Ptolemy's time from Egypt to the Indian Ocean ports of Africa—possibly even to Zanzibar, five degrees south of the equator. From these seafarers and his own studies and intuitions, Ptolemy derived a picture of the world superior in detail to anything previously conceived.

On home grounds he was superb. His maps of the

Mediterranean area were accurate for latitudes and even for longitudes, which were less easy to calculate. Europe, Asia, and Africa were well portrayed; but when he got beyond his knowledge, he simply invented. It was Ptolemy who concocted *Terra Australis Incognita*, tacking that mythical southern continent to the lower part of Africa and carrying it far to the east, where it joined Asia. This converted the Indian Ocean into a wholly enclosed sea similar to the Mediterranean and made unthinkable any hope of circumnavigating Africa. Reaching the great southern continent was impossible because of the intervening zone of burning tropics. *Terra Australis* was Ptolemy's only major geographical blunder, but it was a cruel heritage to leave.

3

After him came darkness. Rome, which had swallowed Greece, was devoured by barbarians, and out of the chaos arose Christianity to make a cult out of sacred ignorance. The early Christians, with justifiable pessimism, believed that their crumbling world was soon to pass away and that it was futile and even blasphemous to probe its secrets; the proper occupation of men was to prepare their souls for the coming City of God. Three centuries after Ptolemy, St. Augustine was warning against the "mere itch to experience and find out," and protesting that "men proceed to investigate the phenomena of nature—the part of nature external to us—though the knowledge is of no value to them; for they wish to know simply for the sake of knowing." Augustine gave thanks to God, who had freed him from the sin of curiosity! "What concern is it to me whether the heavens as a sphere enclose the Earth in the middle of the universe or overhang it on either side?"

In this era of deliberate rejection of knowledge, Greek learning was jettisoned and Biblical texts became the foundation of all theory. On the first page of Genesis was a statement borrowed from the Babylonians and now thrust forth as unassailable doctrine: "And God said, Let there be a firmament in the midst of the waters, and let it divide the waters from the waters. And God made the firmament, and divided the waters which were under the firmament from the waters which were above the firmament." A flat terrestrial disk, sandwiched between water and water. If there had to be a description of the world at all, said the churchly fathers, this was quite good enough; but most shared the attitude of St. Basil, who asked in the fourth century, "Of what importance is it to know whether the Earth is a sphere, a cylinder, a disk, or a concave surface? What is of importance is to know how I should conduct myself towards myself, towards my fellow man, and towards God."

A few Christian philosophers succumbed to the temptation to embroider and embellish the permissible concepts of this epoch of institutionally exalted nonsense. A sixth-century monk, Cosmas of Alexandria, produced a bizarre work called *Christian Topography* in which he described the universe as a huge box having a curved lid, with a partition across the middle of the box to divide it into upper and lower sections. This is the "firmament" of Genesis. It serves as the floor for the upper section, which is heaven, and as the ceiling of the lower section, which is man's world. The sun, moon, and stars are carried by angels just below the ceiling of the lower section. The Earth lies at the bottom of the box, not flat, but slanting sharply upward from the south and east so that the sun can go down each night in the west. At the northwest corner rises a great mountain behind which the sun disappears at nightfall. One lengthy section of the work is devoted to proving that the sun is small enough to fit entirely behind this mountain.

What makes all this shameful rather than merely

quaint is that Cosmas had himself been a mariner, nick-named *Indicopleustes*, "the Indian traveler." He had visited India, Ceylon, and Ethiopia; but in his long voyages over the Indian Ocean he had learned nothing of the world about him, though he had been privileged to see more of it than most men of his time.

It is wrong, though, to assume that the medievals were unreconstructed flat-Earthers until Columbus dramatically shattered their fantasy. The flat-Earth hypothesis won general support among the Christian fathers no earlier than the fifth century A.D., was under serious attack by the seventh, and had fairly well been abandoned except by the ignorant and the reactionary before the end of the period we call the Dark Ages. Certainly by Columbus' time, at least three centuries had passed since any reputable scholar had upheld the churchly cosmology.

Even those Christians who accepted the idea of a spherical Earth tended to incline toward Aristotle's old concept of a single continent, though this was purely a coincidence, since Aristotle went unread in Europe until the twelfth century. The Scriptures declared, "Thus saith the Lord, This is Jerusalem: I have set her in the midst of the nations and countries that are round about." Thus Jerusalem had to be the central point of the whole Earth, and in the early Christian era a pillar was erected in the holy city to mark the fact. If there were other continents beyond the sea, could Jerusalem still be said to have a central location? The notion seemed unappealing. In any event, if other continents lay beyond the tropics, they could in no circumstance be habitable. St. Augustine, who was no flat-Earther, had sharply attacked "the fable, that there are antipodes—that is to say, that on the opposite side of the Earth, where the sun rises when he sets to us, men plant their footsteps opposite to our feet—it is by no means to be believed." There had been only one human creation, had there not? How, then, could mortal men have crossed the uncrossable tropics to reach the supposed lands of the southern hemisphere?

Quietly the Greek geographical ideas reasserted themselves. At the beginning of the seventh century Isidore of Seville assembled an omnibus of the arts and sciences in twenty sections, which included some cogent views from the writers of antiquity. St. Isidore's book, *Etymologies*, remained the basic source for geographers for several centuries, and helped to disseminate the concept of a spherical world, though it seems that Isidore himself tended to the orthodox churchly view. No ambiguities at all surround the teachings of the Venerable Bede, that learned English churchman of the eighth century who fully accepted the Earth's sphericity. Casting aside the picture of a one-continent world with Jerusalem at its center, Bede revived the ancient five-zone theory of geography: a northern zone, "uninhabitable by reason of cold"; a temperate zone; a tropic, "torrid and uninhabitable"; a southern temperate zone, habitable; and finally "the austral [southern] zone around the southern turning point [the south pole] which is covered with land and is uninhabitable by reason of the cold."

This was the intelligent speculation of an armchair geographer; but meanwhile other men, unfettered by Christian prejudices, were going to sea and making significant discoveries. They were Arab Moslems, propelled by the astonishing impetus of their religion's dynamic founder. While carrying Islam to the far regions of the Earth, they became not only sword-bearing missionaries, but also mariners, geographers, and scientists. During Bede's lifetime Arab sailors reached the coast of China, and soon there were regular voyages between the ports of the Persian Gulf and such international depots as Canton. China had been in contact with Western nations previously, for several centuries

beginning about 100 B.C. But that had been strictly an overland connection by caravan westward out of China along
the line of the Great Wall through Central Asia, and it had
ended by A.D. 200 with the decline of Rome and the virtually
simultaneous collapse of China's great Han Dynasty. The
Arab-Chinese sea trade of the eighth century and afterward
led to a marvelous flowering of both cultures through cross-
fertilization; Chinese junks now called at the ports of the
Bay of Bengal, the Arabian Sea, and the Persian Gulf, and
Arab ships, ever more skillfully managed, were common in
the South China Sea. Vessels in both directions circulated
through the harbors of the Malay Peninsula and the Indonesian islands, since these lay like buoys across the water
between China and the Moslem west.

This Arab seafaring produced major changes in the
design of sailing ships and in the techniques of navigation.
During Greek and Roman times the special conditions of
Mediterranean shipping had exerted a negative influence on
the evolution of seacraft. The Mediterranean is tideless
and is relatively free from rough weather, and the abundance
of good ports made it possible to travel in a series of short
hops, rarely losing sight of land. Mycenaeans of Homer's
day had already arrived at a satisfactory vessel for such a
sea, and the Phoenicians, Greeks, Carthaginians, and Romans who followed merely elaborated on the basic model
without making fundamental changes. In classical times the
Romans built large, unwieldy cargo vessels, slow and heavily
timbered, which used square sails; these were good enough
for hauling grain about the Mediterranean but had little of
the maneuverability needed for voyages in the open sea.
Roman ships of war were much lighter and were propelled
by oars; they were speedy and maneuverable, but their range
was held down by the limitations of human brawn. Galley
slaves could not take a ship across an ocean.

[*17*]

The chief Arab contribution was the versatile lateen sail. This triangular sail, probably an Arab invention though also known to the Polynesian seafarers, is laced to a long yard hoisted obliquely to a forward-raked mast. Unlike the clumsy square-rigged sail of the Romans, the lateen sail permits swift adjustment to meet a variety of wind conditions; a ship under lateen rig can sail closer to the wind—that is, make use of breezes even when they happen not to be blowing in the direction the ship is supposed to be going—and can cope with sudden changes in wind direction. Though it has disadvantages, mainly in the limit it places on the size of a vessel, the lateen rig made it feasible for the Arabs to challenge the open waters of the Indian Ocean with great success.

Of course they needed to find their bearings. We know from the account of Pytheas' voyage that the Greeks had rough but serviceable ways of calculating latitudes, and that they were able to guess at longitudes. To find latitude they measured the height of the sun at noon; for longitude, they employed an involved method of computing by comparing observations made at two different points of the time of a lunar eclipse. This was hardly feasible aboard a ship, and so ancient seamen worked on a dead-reckoning basis most of the time, trying to keep track of longitude by totaling the distance covered from the home port. It rarely worked well, but that was not of immense concern in the Mediterranean, where a seaman could discover his longitude simply by putting in at the nearest port and asking where he was.

Arab skippers guided themselves with a variety of devices borrowed from landside astronomers. One of the first was the *kamal*, a series of small wooden boards, each representing a specific altitude, strung on a cord. The navigator, gripping the end of the cord between his teeth, drew it taut and placed the boards against the sky, lining up the polestar or some other heavenly body with a particular altitude-board. The height of the guide star above the horizon gave him his latitude. A simpler and more reliable form of this instrument was the cross-staff, a rod three or four feet long with a sliding crosspiece; holding it upright, the navigator squinted at his guide star through an opening, and moved the crosspiece to determine the star's altitude. The astrolabe and the quadrant, more complex devices working on the same principle of visual sighting, were perfected by the Arabs by the thirteenth or fourteenth century. Thus they coped with latitude. Longitude was more of a puzzle for them, but solving it was not urgent for Indian Ocean navigation. The one instrument that the Arabs made little use of was the magnetic compass, an invention of their Chinese friends; it seems to have come to them from China by way of Europe rather than by direct transmission, and during their greatest seafaring years they got along without it quite satisfactorily.

Thus pursuing geography with such ardor, the Arabs came to know the world well while Europeans still engaged in pious speculations. The Arabs had no fear of the supposedly burning tropics and sailed far south down Africa's eastern coast, at least to Zanzibar and probably well beyond. To the east they went as far as the South China Sea; possibly they ventured on occasion past the wall of islands, Philippine and Indonesian, that separates that sea from the Pacific Ocean, but they could not have entered the Pacific often or gone very deeply into it. They called it "the Sea of Darkness" and spun fables about it. The twelfth-century Arab geographer al-Edrisi wrote, "No one has been able to verify anything concerning it, on account of its difficult and perilous navigation, its great obscurity, its profound depth and frequent tempests; through fear of its mighty fishes and its haughty winds; yet there are many islands in it, some peopled, others uninhabited. There is no mariner who dares to enter into its deep waters; or, if any have done so, they have merely kept along its coasts, fearful of departing from them. The waves of this ocean, although they roll as high as mountains, yet maintain themselves without breaking; for if they broke, it would be impossible for a ship to plough them."

At least the Arabs knew the Pacific was there. Europe remained locked in ignorance. Some of the new nautical skills of Islam filtered into Europe through that remarkable funnel, Byzantium, where Orient and Occident met; but though lateen sails appeared on Byzantine ships in the eastern Mediterranean by the ninth century A.D., western Europe remained a region of timid landlubbers who if they went to sea at all stayed close to home. Conspicuous exceptions were the Norsemen, who built a series of stepping-stones that took them all the way across the Atlantic: to Iceland by A.D. 870, to Greenland about a century later, and, beyond much doubt, to North America by the year 1000. Of their navigational methods little is known; they evidently relied on keen observation, intuition, and courage, and in any event were never very far from land, for their route lay around the northern edges of the Atlantic rather than straight through its heart.

Aside from the Vikings, Europeans had no firsthand experience with the outer world until the beginning of the Crusades at the end of the eleventh century, and even the Crusaders went no farther than the eastern end of that familiar lake, the Mediterranean. So the learned theorists, working by guesswork, divine inspiration, and echoes out of Byzantium, continued to construct images of the world in their land-bound studies. The Crusaders brought home news of the Arab discoveries and also manuscripts of Arab translations of Greek scientific works. The Arabs had made a specialty of finding and translating into their own tongue the forgotten works of Aristotle, Ptolemy, and the other great men of antiquity; these now began to seep into Europe.

Ptolemy became available again when the monk Gerardus of Cremona translated him from Arabic to Latin in 1175. Euclid, Archimedes, the many volumes of Aristotle—all these came by way of Islam and created a revolution in Europe's long-stagnant intellectual life.

Thus William of Conches, in the middle of the twelfth century, argued mathematically for a spherical Earth. If the world were flat, he said, it would be day at the same time everywhere, which is not the case. Certain stars are visible in one latitude and not another, indicating curvature of the planet. His contemporary, Lambert of Saint-Omer, agreed that the world was round and revived the Ptolemaic notion of *Terra Australis Incognita*, an antipodal continent, "temperate in climate but unknown to the sons of Adam, having nothing which is related to our race. . . . When we are scorched with heat [the Antipodes] are chilled with cold; and the northern stars which we are permitted to discern are entirely hidden from them." John of Holywood, in the thirteenth century, adapted Arab ideas to prove the roundness of the Earth by the difference in the time of eclipses between places in the east and in the west; his great contemporaries Albertus Magnus and Roger Bacon, accepting the spherical Earth without question, devoted attention to the problem of the southern hemisphere and concluded that it must be habitable. Albertus, writing about 1260, even declared that the torrid zone was peopled, a fact that the Arabs had already removed from the realm of speculation so far as they were concerned.

Despite this rush of new thought, European seafaring remained almost entirely confined to the Mediterranean; even the Vikings went no more a-roving by the fourteenth century. The Italian cities—first Amalfi and Pisa, then Genoa and Venice—replaced Byzantium as the chief maritime powers; the magnetic compass came into use; charts and maps appeared; ship design improved vastly as clever combinations of lateen and square rig were devised; and still no Europeans left their safe inland sea. The most famous of medieval travelers, Marco Polo, reached China by land, taking the old silk road of Han Dynasty days.

Marco's journey was made possible by grace of the Mongol conquerors of Asia who under Genghis Khan had come spilling out of their bleak steppes to batter at the gates of Europe. By the middle of the thirteenth century the Mongols controlled the largest empire the world had ever known, encompassing everything from Russia and Persia to the Chinese coast. With a single family ruling—surprisingly well—the vast region from the Mediterranean to the South China Sea, the overland route from Europe to China became safe and accessible to travelers, and contact between the two continents was restored after a lapse of centuries. The Polo family had two predecessors, a pair of astonishing monks named John of Plano Carpini and William of Rubruck, who made successive journeys to the Mongol domain in 1245 and 1253 respectively. Marco's father and uncle were next, arriving at the court of Kublai Khan in 1265; they had not meant to go to China, but only to Mongol-occupied Russia, and made the long trek eastward when a quarrel between two grandsons of Genghis Khan disturbed the western part of the Mongol empire and cut off their homeward route. They returned to their native Venice in 1269 and set out for China again two years later, this time accompanied by seventeen-year-old Marco. Arriving at Kublai's capital of Shang-tu or Xanadu, just north of the Great Wall, they received a warm welcome and remained in positions of high trust in Mongol-held China until 1292. During those years Marco attained important responsibilities in Kublai's government and traveled from Tibet to Burma. He was the first European to have any knowledge of the great ocean that lies east of China. He did not see the Pacific proper, only its westernmost limb, the South China Sea; but he brought back tales of its wonders that had a good deal to do with shaping the future course of world history.

For Marco told of the splendor of the spice-rich, gold-rich islands of that sea; it contained, he said, "no fewer than seven thousand four hundred islands, mostly inhabited." He spoke of the island of Cipangu—Japan—east of China, "rich in gold, pearls, and gems; the temples and palaces are roofed with solid gold." On their homeward journey from China the Polos went by sea as far as Persia and saw Java and the other Indonesian islands; there Marco heard of another golden kingdom nearby, known as Locach, and the readers of his book misinterpreted an ambiguous passage and placed Locach south of Java, regarding it as the *Terra Australis Incognita*. Thus, with the best of intentions, Marco became a snare for ambitious voyagers. Columbus, who knew Marco's book well, persuaded himself that Cipangu and the shores of Cathay—China—lay only a short distance west of Spain, washed by the familiar Atlantic; and later travelers searched south of Java for the glittering phantom of Locach.

4

The trade between East and West in the days of the Mongols was rich and fabulous. By caravan out of China came silks and incense, gems, spices, jade. At the western end of the trade routes, in the Levant and along the Black Sea, enterprising Italian merchants following in the tradition of the Polos established depots where Oriental goods were received and shipped on, via the Mediterranean, to the cities of Europe. Strange and gaudy new delights reached Paris and London and Rome: rhubarb and emeralds, rubies and pepper, sapphires, ivory, cinnamon, dyes, perfumes.

With the collapse of the Mongol empire in the middle

of the fourteenth century, contact between Europe and eastern Asia again was lost. The xenophobic Ming Dynasty rulers shrouded China in a bamboo curtain. Central Asia dissolved in anarchy, making the caravan route to the Orient unsafe. The last grip of the Crusaders on the Near East was dislodged, and now the increasingly more menacing Turks, replacing the Arabs as Islam's chief standard-bearers, sealed the eastern end of the Mediterranean as they encroached on tottering Byzantium.

Though European merchants could no longer go far into Asia, the export of Oriental goods persisted. Chinese and Persian silks still came overland to Tabriz and Trebizond, and on to Byzantium for distribution to Europe; jewels and ivory and jade still trickled westward somehow. But the most important, and thus the most carefully organized, of the commercial links between East and West was the spice trade. "Spice," to the medievals, meant many things: not merely condiments for seasoning and preserving foods, but also dyes, drugs, perfumes, cosmetics, and other exotic goods. Francesco Pegolotti, a Florentine merchant of the fourteenth century whose handbook on Oriental trade was indispensable to his contemporaries, compiled a list of 288 "spices," including eleven kinds of sugar, a variety of waxes and gums, and even glue. The core of the spice trade lay in true spices, however: pepper, nutmeg, mace, cinnamon, and cloves.

Europe, with its botanical sparseness, depended wholly on the fertile tropics for these delights. The craze for spices grew so intense that moralists assailed it, protesting, as did the early sixteenth-century scholar Ulrich von Hutten, that Europeans had become "slaves to their stomachs." Hutten, looking testily at such fads as mixing sugar and pepper to sprinkle on toast, declared: "I wish to mention the life of my grandfather, Lorenz Hutten, as a glowing example of a simple life. He was a rich man and held the highest offices in both the civil and military services. But pepper, ginger, saffron, and other foreign spices never crossed his threshold, and he only wore coats of German wool."

Spices were much more than fads for the flighty, though. They were necessities for medieval Europe. Lacking fodder to see their livestock through the winter, European farmers slaughtered most meat animals as the cold weather approached. This produced a great surplus of meat in autumn, which had to be consumed gradually over the long winter months. The rich could experiment with ice cellars, but most people made do with smoked or pickled meat for seven or eight months of the year. Spices were essential to cure and preserve the stored meat; spices also disguised the flavor of the meat as it spoiled. Pepper, the master spice, was most useful, and Europe's appetite for pepper was insatiable, but cloves and cinnamon and nutmeg were also highly prized, and harder to obtain.

An elaborate mercantile chain brought these spices to Europe in the fourteenth and fifteenth centuries. The raw materials came from countries at the eastern edge of the known world—that is to say, from countries bordering on the Pacific Ocean. Cloves grew only in the Moluccas, the original Spice Islands: five small isles, Tidore, Motir, Makian, Bachan, and Ternate, clustered about a much larger island, Gilolo, or Halmahera, on which the peoples of the other five depended for their food supply. Nutmeg and its allied spice, mace, originated in the Banda Islands; other important spices came from the Amboina group. All of these islands are now included in the Republic of Indonesia. The source of cinnamon was Ceylon; pepper, the fruit of *Piper nigrum*, grew in western India, but the choicest came from the Indonesian island of Sumatra. (White and black pepper were made from the same plant; if the shell was left on while the berries were being dried in the sun, black pepper was produced, and the milder white pepper was obtained by removing the shell before drying.)

The berries, nuts, roots, leaves, and pieces of bark from which spices were made were gathered cheaply by humble native laborers in the islands. Chinese and Malayan merchants made regular tours of these islands, collecting the baled produce and carrying it to the great port of Malacca near the tip of the Malay Peninsula. On this voyage the cargoes received their first thinning at the hands of the Chinese and Malay pirates who infested the Java Sea. Whatever spices got through to Malacca were sold at good profits to Hindu traders from India after the Sultan of Malacca had collected his heavy customs duties. The Hindus shipped their merchandise across the Bay of Bengal through a second gauntlet of Malay pirates, and realized their profits in the ports of India's Malabar Coast—Calicut, Cochin, Cannanore, and Goa. Arab merchants were the next purchasers. Loading their vessels with precious cargoes, they set sail for Persia, Arabia, or East Africa, traveling in convoys to escape the depredations of Indian buccaneers.

From the Indian Ocean to the Mediterranean there were many possible routes of access. One was via the Red Sea; the cargo could be landed at the Ethiopian port of Massawa and fetched inland by caravan to Egypt, thence up the Nile to Alexandria. Another Red Sea route necessitated transferring the cargo at the Gulf of Aden; the spices were taken from the big oceangoing ships and placed aboard small Egyptian coasting vessels that threaded the hazardous path to Suez, the harbor for Cairo and the Nile delta. An alternate route, via Jidda in Arabia, required a lengthy desert trek to Syria. Or the Red Sea could be avoided altogether and the spices taken up the Persian Gulf to Ormuz, and by the Euphrates to Baghdad, and from there to Aleppo or Damascus or Beirut. One way or another, the valuable goods at last reached the ports of the eastern Mediterranean. Now for the first time they passed into Christian hands. Italians, mostly Venetians, collected the spices from Byzantium, Alexandria, Antioch, Tripoli, or Beirut. Though relations between Christians and Moslems were bitter in the late Middle Ages, these pragmatic merchants were shrewd in their ability to maintain their trading concessions in hostile cities. They paid for the spices with Europe's woolen and linen textiles, with arms and armor, with copper, lead, and tin from European mines, with amber, and with gold and silver bullion; they also did a retail trade in slaves from the Caucasus and coral from the depths of their own Mediterranean.

To Venice and Genoa, at last, came the harvest of Asia —mainly to Venice. Dealers in spices crowded the Rialto to buy what the spice fleets brought. The markups were immense—since the goods reaching Venice had survived the repeated raids of pirates—and not only reflected the built-in profits of countless middlemen but also bore the burden of all the steep duties and taxes exacted by princes along the route. A bale of dried leaves purchased for a ducat in Ternate or Amboina sold for a hundred ducats in Venice. Then came the final distribution from Venice to the ultimate recipients all over Europe, and one final round of profit before the pickling and preserving could begin.

The canny Genoese and Venetians knew quite well how the world was shaped, at least that part of the world along which their spices were shipped. They even made a few tentative ventures beyond their immediate Mediterranean world. From bases in North Africa they penetrated the Sahara and got into black Africa as far as Timbuktu; they went up the Nile into the Sudan; they even peered into the Atlantic, which except for the Viking ships of A.D. 1000 had seen few vessels. In 1291 the Genoese brothers Guido and

Ugolino Vivaldo, guessing that they might reach India by sailing around Africa, went boldly off into the Atlantic and were never heard from again. Other Genoese two or three generations later, their names lost to us, discovered Madeira and the Azores, necessary island outposts in any Atlantic exploration. But these were isolated instances. Well into the fifteenth century, Europe stayed locked in geographical ignorance, deluded by inherited myths. To seek the Indies by way of Africa seemed hopeless, for the burning tropics blocked the path; and, in any case, what of Ptolemy's *Terra Australis*, making the Indian Ocean a landlocked sea? The maps of the unexplored regions were thick with legendary monsters and dragons, which terrified the innocent as effectively as considerations of high commercial risk terrified the clever.

These medieval geographical delusions—and a fair amount of sensible geography as well—were most attractively expressed in the remarkable work *Travels of Sir John Mandeville*, written about 1370. This purported to be the memoir of an authentic traveler but actually was a compilation of other men's writings, liberally padded with fantasies dating to classical times. "In a certain isle toward the south," Mandeville declared, "dwell folk of foul stature and of cursed kind that have no heads, and their eyes be in their shoulders. . . . And in another isle be folk of foul fashion and shape that have the lip above the mouth so great that when they sleep in the sun, they cover all the face with that lip." Amid the lively portraits of monstrosities and chimeras, though, was an intelligent discussion of the sphericity of the Earth and the possibility of a voyage of circumnavigation. Noting the fact that the constellations of the northern hemisphere were different from those visible in that part of the southern hemisphere known to Europeans, Mandeville declared: "Men may well perceive that the land and the sea be of round shape and form, for the part of the firmament that showeth in one country, showeth not in another country. And men may well prove by experience and subtle compassment of wit that if a man found passages by ships that would go to search the world, men might go by ship all about the world above and beneath. . . ."

Early in the fifteenth century the learned Cardinal Pierre d'Ailly (1350–1420) codified most existing knowledge of the world, hypothetical and factual, into a series of valuable treatises. He had ransacked the works of antiquity —Aristotle, Ptolemy, Pliny—as well as the Arab writings of more recent times; reconciling their differences, rejecting discrepancies and improbabilities, he produced a shrewd, judicious image of the world. His essays—the *Imago Mundi* of 1410 and the *Compendium Cosmographiae* of 1413— circulated widely in manuscript all during the century and finally were printed at Louvain about 1480; Christopher Columbus owned a copy of the published volume, and it still exists in a library at Seville, its margins crammed with comments in the explorer's hand.

D'Ailly was both the last of the medievals and the first of the modern geographers. He was capable of writing such things as, "At the Poles there live great ghosts and ferocious beasts, the enemies of man. Water abounds there, because those places are cold, and cold multiplies vapors." But he also declared plainly, "The earth is spherical, and the western ocean is relatively small." Discarding Ptolemy's idea of a landlocked Indian Ocean, d'Ailly used other classical authorities to bolster his belief in a short westward passage by sea to Asia. "The west coast of Africa cannot be far removed from the east coast of India," he wrote, following Aristotle, "for in both those countries elephants are found." In another place he repeated the Aristotelian assertion that "the extent of sea is small between the coast of Spain in the West and the shores of India in the East." And he added, "Pliny teaches us that ships from the Gulf of Arabia can arrive in a short time at Gades [Cádiz] in the south of Spain." D'Ailly adopted the pre-Ptolemaic belief that one could go either way to the Indies: eastward around Africa, or westward across the unknown sea. Neither burning tropics nor an obstinate southern continent would block mariners. Columbus, when his time came to test d'Ailly's ideas, chose the westward route, but by then he had no option, for the eastward track was no longer a matter of theory. It had been found, and it belonged to the Portuguese.

5

The era that one recent historian has aptly called the "Age of Reconnaissance" was dawning in Europe as Cardinal d'Ailly wrote. Why did the European discovery of the world begin in the fifteenth century, one wonders, and not in the third or sixth or twelfth? What mysterious signal was given to usher in the epoch of maritime adventure? Actually, a combination of forces—commercial, political, geographical, and technological—served to send Europe into that frenzy of exploration that transformed the world. It was a cumulative process, an accretion of necessary factors.

Global discovery was impossible without ships that could survive in the open sea. In theory, a Phoenician or a Roman galley might have reached the Americas, and perhaps a few did; but the vessels used by the Mediterranean seafaring nations were unsuited for Atlantic conditions, and only the evolution of ships that were both sturdy and maneuverable made the long voyages worth attempting. The exploring impulse was not unknown prior to the fifteenth century, but those rash men who sailed into the Atlantic did not return.

The arts of navigation and cartography had to develop.

Each voyage had to build on previous knowledge, which meant there had to be ways of charting that knowledge, and ways of determining one's position so charts could be followed. The Viking method of guesswork navigation would not do for systematic martime exploitation; only after the nautical science of the Arabs—derived as it was from ancient Greece and Rome—began to seep into the Mediterranean was Europe ready to chance long journeys by sea.

A motive for voyaging, other than pure curiosity, was needed. The spice trade supplied it. Europe had become dependent on the treasures of the Indies; and the sources of those precious goods were in the hands of Europe's enemies, the Moslems. Merely by courtesy of Islam did pepper and cloves trickle into Europe, and at any moment the trickle might be cut off by the whim of some distant sultan or pasha. With Turks and Arabs strangling the land routes to the Orient, there was good reason to seek the Indies by sea.

The Venetians and the Genoese, Europe's dominant mariners in the early medieval period, were best equipped to undertake that quest, but they saw no point in tackling it. They had insinuated themselves into the terminal stations of the spice trade, and their positions seemed secure. So long as they could hop across the Mediterranean to Alexandria or Beirut to pick up cargoes of spices, why bother to look for a long way around? In the twelfth, thirteenth, and fourteenth centuries they were the only ones capable of making the attempt—but they lacked motive. So, while the necessary resources of navigation and shipbuilding and cartography accumulated, what remained missing was a nation hungry enough to want to steal the spice trade from the Italians and determined enough to accept the risks and costs of exploration. Such a nation did not emerge until the fifteenth century —the century of Portugal.

Portugal till then had been an unimportant strip of

rocky coast on the Iberian Peninsula, an insignificant appendage to Spain. The Romans had given that coastal strip its name when they anchored their ships in its one good harbor at the mouth of the Douro river; they called their anchorage "Portus Cale," "the hot harbor," and the name came to include the entire coast. (The settlement at that harbor is known today as Oporto.) Before the Romans penetrated the Iberian Peninsula, the Carthaginians were there; if there is a genetic predisposition to the maritime life, those heirs of the Phoenicians transmitted it, making the Portuguese seafarers by first nature. Their small, poor country looks toward the sea anyway, with nothing behind it but bleak Spain, hostile through most of history and walling Portugal off from Europe. So the Portuguese went to sea, first as fishermen, then as merchants plying familiar routes to Brittany, Flanders, and England.

The country's progress was hampered by war. For centuries there was the struggle against the Moors, who came out of North Africa in A.D. 711 to seize most of Spain and all of Portugal. Gradually the Moors were pushed out, but still Portugal had no independent existence, being merely a district of the Spanish kingdom of León, distinct only in its dialect. Through a long and intricate struggle, the Portuguese detached themselves from León in the twelfth century and preserved their independence through a series of shifting alliances with the numerous kingdoms and principalities of which Spain was then composed. The most important of these alliances, though a troubled one, was with Castile, the leading power of medieval Spain after the expulsion of the Moors.

During the fourteenth century Castile made several attempts to absorb Portugal; with English help, the Portuguese resisted invasion and managed to strike costly truces. The situation was complicated by intricate dynastic struggles both in Portugal and in Castile. One claimant to the Castilian throne had murdered the other, who was the father-in-law of John of Gaunt, son of England's King Edward III. John of Gaunt then claimed the throne of Castile himself and welcomed the Portuguese alliance as a way of unseating the usurper. Meanwhile, the Portuguese dynasty had become extinct in 1383, and the throne was claimed both by the King of Castile and by João of Aviz, the illegitimate half-brother of the late king.

John of Gaunt backed João of Aviz, to whom he was related by marriage. In 1385 the outnumbered Portuguese withstood a Castilian thrust and whipped the Spaniards decisively in the battle of Aljubarrota; soon afterward, João of Aviz became King João I of Portugal and cemented his English alliance by marrying Philippa of Lancaster, the daughter of John of Gaunt. The accession of the House of Aviz marked the birth of Portugal as a modern nation. With external enemies at last neutralized, the new dynasty was able to commence a policy of expansion and development. The Portuguese shipyards flourished; from Portugal's harbors sailed flotillas of the squat, heavy, single-masted, square-rigged ships called *naos*, bringing cork, sardines, port wine, salt cod, and hides to England, and returning with wool, tin, and manufactured goods. The *naos* were awkward, stolid vessels that could take a great deal of punishment but whose usefulness was limited by their inability to tack—to move forward in a side wind or to sail into the wind. In favorable weather, a *nao* went forward; with the wind against it, it was helpless. But for the purpose of the trade with England, the *naos* served Portugal well.

João of Aviz looked to the south as well as to England. In 1411, when Portugal had arrived at an unaccustomed state of complete peace, he adopted Queen Philippa's suggestion to maintain the momentum of the national economy by sending an armed expedition to North Africa. João and Philippa envisioned a conquest of the Moorish kingdom of Fez, thereby reversing the Iberian calamity of 711 and opening the way for a Portuguese penetration, by land, of the supposed Christian kingdom of the fabled monarch Prester John somewhere in the heart of Africa. With Prester John's cooperation, perhaps, a new spice route could be established, with caravans crossing Africa and bringing pepper and cloves to Lisbon.

João's energies had failed him by then, and the queen herself organized the expedition, devoting three exhausting years to arranging the financing and assembling the arms, ships, and men. Her fierce determination to extend Portugal's power into Africa must have been a family trait, for her brother Henry, operating under the same inner imperatives, had usurped the English throne a decade earlier to rule as Henry IV of Lancaster, and Henry IV's son Prince Hal, destined for the throne himself in 1413, would in a few years launch his successful conquest of France. There was another Henry among Philippa's five sons, Prince Henrique of Portugal, later called Prince Henry the Navigator, and he, along with his elder brothers Duarte and Pedro, helped his mother plan her war against the Moors.

Prince Henry, born in 1394, was three years younger than Duarte, two years younger than Pedro. All three were coming to manhood almost at once and welcomed the opportunity to meet the test of war. It took until 1415 to ready the expedition; by the summer, 45,000 men aboard 200 ships waited in harbor at Lisbon for the moment of departure. Philippa's strength was nearly gone. She had spent herself entirely on the project, and her death weeks before the sailing of the armada turned the invasion into something of a sacred trust for her sons. The fleet sailed on July 25, with the old king and his three princes leading the campaign.

The inadequacies of the clumsy *naos* were revealed at once: as they headed south in the Atlantic, bound for the Moorish port of Ceuta, they were caught by a contrary wind and swept through the Straits of Gibraltar into the Mediterranean. This mishap had unexpectedly favorable consequences, for the defenders of Ceuta, seeing the Portuguese ships disappearing eastward, relaxed their vigilance and dismissed the reinforcements they had called up upon first learning of their danger. The Portuguese managed to swing a few of their heavy ships around by night when the wind changed, and, aided by oar-propelled galleys, descended in a surprise attack on Ceuta. The struggle was savage; at one point, Prince Henry was reported slain, though he was only wounded. But by nightfall the Portuguese flag flew over the citadel of Ceuta. Largely through Henry's valor, Portugal had taken the town known as "the key to the Mediterranean" and had begun the advance into Africa.

Queen Philippa's plan for reaching the Spice Islands through caravan routes across Africa came to nothing. Dislodging the Moors proved impossible, and even if it had not, beyond them lay the desert, and then the dark heart of the continent. Prince Henry swiftly grasped the truth: the way to the Indies lay *around* Africa, not across it. Though he made several more trips to fight in North Africa, he gradually withdrew from active campaigning to concentrate on geographical study that would lead toward attainment of that goal. In 1419 his father named him governor of the Algarve, Portugal's most southwesterly province, and the ascetic prince, who remained celibate and wore a hairshirt, established a center for research in that isolated region. On the promontory known as Cape Saint Vincent (at Sagres) he built a small town where he dwelled as a recluse, collecting information about the shape of the world and especially about the eastern Atlantic. He read the works of Arab geographers, he conferred with travelers and merchants, he purchased maps and astronomical instruments—and he sent out expeditions of discovery.

Within a year Portugal had occupied the island of Madeira at Henry's direction. From a map brought back from Venice by his brother Pedro he learned of the existence of the Azores and directed the rediscovery of those islands in the succeeding years. For these explorations, Henry scorned the lumbering *nao* in favor of lighter ships called *barcas*, which were nothing more than fishing boats with one big mast and a square sail, requiring a crew of about fourteen men. Later he used *barinels*, larger and longer vessels equipped with oars as well as sails, but even these did not give him the capabilities he sought. From 1440 on, Henry's expeditions were usually made in *caravels*, ships carefully designed to meet the needs of explorers. The early Portuguese caravels were vessels of fifty to a hundred tons, with two or three masts and lateen sails. They were capable of advancing in a side wind and, to some extent, of tacking into the wind, and so were not compelled to await fair winds at sea.

Prince Henry himself never sailed with his caravels. His task was to learn and to impart, not to explore, and he remained at his observatory at Cape Saint Vincent, directing his grand enterprise at a distance. In his person was focused all the accumulated navigational wisdom of the centuries. He surrounded himself with astronomers and geographers from abroad; he pumped his returning captains for details of latitudes, currents, winds, coastlines; he worked to perfect the astrolabe, the quadrant, the compass, and other navigational instruments; and he added each newly gathered bit of information to his charts. Systematically he sent his ships farther and farther, from Madeira to the Azores, from the Azores south along the bulging hump of Africa's western coast. His hardy little ships, with their mixed Arab and Mediterranean ancestry, underwent continual tinkering of design, and new combinations of sails, both lateen and square-rigged, came into use. The mariners grew more bold as they pierced deeper into the unknown. The dreaded burning tropics did not materialize even as they neared the equator, for the heat, while intense, was tolerable; but, discouragingly, there seemed to be no end to Africa. The interminable continent bulged farther to the west as Henry's explorers continued their southerly cruises. Looking shoreward, they saw only the desert wastes of the Sahara; but then the terrain improved, and in 1441 inhabited lands appeared. Two of the Portuguese captains celebrated the fact by inaugurating the European slave trade, coming home with a cargo of blacks and providing an economic basis for Henry's costly researches. Henceforth Portuguese caravels called frequently at the West African ports, where obliging native chiefs were ready to do business, offering elephant tusks, sacks of gold dust, hides, and slaves from villages in the interior. Prince Henry, a genuinely pious man, rejoiced at the opportunity thus gained to convert these enslaved Negroes to Christianity, while harder men in Lisbon agreed that the idealistic prince's investment in maritime exploration had begun to pay excellent dividends.

In 1444 a landmark was reached: the rounding of Cape Verde, Africa's westernmost point. Now the continent trended eastward, and the green and fertile lands south of Africa's bulging hump were open to the Portuguese. On past the mouth of the Senegal, on past Sierra Leone and the Ivory Coast, on to Guinea the caravels sailed—and still more of Africa lay ahead. In dark moments, the aging Prince Henry may well have felt that Ptolemy's guess had been correct, and that the land stretched to the South Pole, permitting no access by sea to the Indian Ocean.

Still the geographer-prince sought his goal. The east-ward trend of the land inspired hope. His researches produced a better southward route: instead of clinging to the North African shore, with its reefs and sandbars, the caravels now swung wide of the coast, far out into the Atlantic to catch favorable winds that sped them toward the slave ports. But the love of exploration for its own sake, never too strong in Henry's countrymen, seemed to be dying; most of the voyages now halted in known lands, and the southward impetus faltered.

Prince Henry had never forgotten his early vow to his dying mother to prosecute the war against the Moors. In 1458, when he was in his sixty-fourth year, he took part in another military campaign, fighting bravely and well in the capture of Alcacer, near Ceuta. But this adventure placed too great a strain on his resources, both physical and financial. In 1459, clearly a dying man, Henry was forced to send his nephew to Florence to arrange a loan for payment of his heavy debts. He offered as collateral, among other things, a patent of monopoly of the eastward sea trade to India, granted him a few years earlier by the pope. The Florentine bankers, skeptical of the worth of this asset, requested an opinion from a celebrated geographer, Paolo Toscanelli. He did not entirely rule out the possibility that India could be reached via Africa, but he felt that the fastest way to reach the Indies by sea was to sail westward across the Atlantic. Toscanelli cited the Viking voyages, and also the evidence of Marco Polo's book, which led him to think that the eastern limb of Asia extended far into the sea, terminating only a short distance west of Europe.

Much later, Toscanelli would express these ideas in a lengthy correspondence with a young Genoese named Columbus and would help to inspire a notable voyage. Now, though, he created confusion. Prince Henry still clung to the eastward route; but when he died in 1460, with the sea route to the Indies still unattained, younger men captivated by the Toscanelli theory tried to send caravels westward. The season and the wind were against them; the westward expeditions came to nothing, and for nearly a decade Portuguese exploration halted altogether. Only the slaving voyages to Africa's by now familiar western coast continued.

Prince Henry had supplied tremendous thrust, though, for continued discovery. The profits of West Africa were immense enough, but they were nothing compared with the yield to be had by reaching the Indies. In 1469 King Afonso V—the son of Henry's brother Duarte—awarded African trading rights to one Fernão Gomes of Lisbon in return for Gomes' promise to discover a hundred leagues of coast a year. The details of Gomes' voyages were kept secret, to discourage the ships of other nations, but their results were notable in both gold and geography. By 1472 the Portuguese were in the Cameroons; the following year they crossed the equator for the first time. A depressing factor had emerged, however: the coast of Africa, which had trended eastward for hundreds of miles from Cape Verde, was now clearly running southward again, putting what seemed to be an unending obstacle between the Portuguese and India.

When the Gomes concession expired in 1474, King Afonso awarded exploration rights to his own son, João, a man who had some of the questing spirit of his great-uncle, Henry the Navigator. The young prince's plans were curtailed between 1475 and 1479 by war between Portugal and Castile, arising once more out of dynastic conflicts. King Afonso had married the niece of the King of Castile and, through her, claimed the Castilian throne upon that king's death; but the crown went instead to the late king's sister, young Isabella. It was a family feud, for both Isabella and Afonso V were grandchildren of King João I of Portugal;

but it was also a bitter struggle between newly prosperous Portugal and her powerful Iberian neighbor, Castile, for the African trade route. Isabella encouraged her subjects to engage in the African trade and to intercept homeward-bound Portuguese ships. Portugal countered by destroying the Spanish vessels bound for Guinea. The war thus was fought on two fronts; at home, the Portuguese were badly beaten and had to renounce their claims to the throne of Castile, but overseas, they maintained their dominant position. By the Treaty of Alcaçovas, which ended the war in 1479, Castile conceded to Portugal a monopoly of fishing, trade, and navigation along the entire West African coast. It was the first stage in the staking of Spanish and Portuguese spheres of influence abroad.

Freed of the burden of this war, Prince João was able to pursue an energetic expansionist policy when he came to the Portuguese throne as João II in 1481. He built Portuguese fortresses on the Guinea coast, sent ambassadors to Ethiopia to confer with Prester John, and revived Prince Henry's practice of encouraging advances in the science and art of navigation. A pair of Jewish astronomers, Joseph Vizinho and Abraham Zacuto, calculated elaborate and extremely valuable tables for finding positions at sea; improvements were made in the design of caravels; new charts were drawn.

Once again, for the first time in more than twenty years, expeditions went forth in caravels equipped only for exploration, not for trade. João II, not a patient man, wanted the sea route to India found swiftly, and he urged his captains southward eagerly and aggressively, reacting with poor grace when they returned to tell him that still more of Africa kept them from turning east. In 1483 Diogo Cão reached the mouth of the Congo, explored the river to some extent, and continued along the coast to 13°S. before turning back. King João knighted him and gave him a pension, but almost immediately sent him on a second voyage. This time he got nearly to the Tropic of Capricorn, attaining 22°S. without finding the desired eastward route. The king was keenly disappointed when the Cão expedition returned to Lisbon in 1487 with no news of success. Cão, who had explored 1,450 miles of unknown coast, working against the current and the winds much of the time, disappeared from view, his career broken by his failure to find India. (One contemporary source says he died on the return voyage, another that he returned and was forced into retirement.)

Cão's successor, Bartholomeu Dias, brought the king happier tidings. Setting out in 1487, Dias traveled down the coast far beyond the most southerly point visited by Cão; after provisioning at Lüderitz in what is now South-West Africa, Dias' caravels were beset by storms and driven far into the Atlantic. On a great arc they swept around the Cape of Good Hope without sighting it, and by the time they could regain the coast, in the vicinity of Mossel Bay in the Union of South Africa, they had unwittingly crossed from the Atlantic to the Indian Ocean. This became only gradually apparent as the land trended eastward: Dias had amputated one great lobe of the vast supposed southern continent and had attained Africa's terminal point. The gateway to the Indies was open. But provisions were low and his men were exhausted by the rough weather; reluctantly Dias agreed to turn back. On the return voyage, the great southern cape came into view. He named it Cabo Tormentoso, "Cape of Storms"; but after Dias' arrival in Portugal at the end of 1488, King João rechristened it optimistically the Cape of Good Hope.

6

Much happened before that hope could be fulfilled. In March 1493 a battered little caravel called the *Niña* struggled into port at Lisbon. King João sent Bartholomeu Dias aboard to get an explanation of the ship's activities from her commander. That commander, a certain Italian named Columbus, readily admitted that he was in the employ of the Spaniards and that he had just completed a successful voyage to Asia by the westward route. Heavy seas and severe storms had assailed him on his way back, and so he had been compelled to stop first in the Azores, then at Lisbon. He asked leave to sail on now to Spain. Had he actually reached India or Cathay? No, Columbus replied, only the islands of the Indies. But he had no doubt that the Asian mainland lay nearby.

While Columbus continued on triumphantly to Spain, King João II contemplated the Genoese navigator's story with little pleasure. He knew, of course, of Columbus' theory, derived from Marco Polo and Toscanelli, that Asia could be reached by sailing westward. Columbus had explained all that to him in 1484 while he was in the Portuguese maritime service. The Italian had asked King João to finance a westward expedition. The king, though enthusiastic for exploration, was committed to the eastern route; he was at the moment tensely awaiting news of Diogo Cão's first voyage. Yet João submitted Columbus' plan to his councillors, who told him that the costs outweighed the possible benefits. After a careful hearing, Columbus' project was refused, and the Italian went off to sell his idea in Spain. In 1485 King João had a second thought and shrewdly, if none too honorably, mounted a Portuguese expedition to the west after all, under the command of Fernão Dulmo, a Portuguese from the Azores. Dulmo proposed to depart from the Azores, unaware that the prevailing winds in the North Atlantic blow from the west and would prevent such a voyage from being successful. Nothing came of it. Possibly Columbus, if he had sailed under Portuguese auspices, would have also tried the northern crossing and ended in failure. But after long delays he had won Spanish backing, had caught the steady trade wind that blows westward past Madeira and the Canary Islands to the Caribbean, and had made his crossing. King João's bitterness at being beaten to the Indies was compounded by the galling knowledge that he had let Columbus slip from his hands.

To make things worse, Columbus had found Asia for the Spaniards, with whom King João was having much trouble. After hundreds of years of fragmentation, the little Spanish kingdoms were suddenly united and posed a real menace for Portugal. The union had been taking shape since 1469, when Prince Ferdinand, heir to the throne of Aragon, married Princess Isabella, the heiress to the throne of Castile. Portugal's attempt to displace Isabella in Castile had been disastrous, and from 1479 on, Ferdinand and Isabella ruled undisputed in their jointly held kingdoms. Gradually they had extended their grip over the rest of Spain, the climax coming in that memorable year of 1492 when Granada, the last stronghold of the Spanish Moors, was conquered. João's Portugal now was neighbor to an uncomfortably strong nation undergoing a massive convulsion of reform and growth. Long landlocked, Spain was plainly envious of Portugal's lucrative empire on the West African coast; if Columbus had given Ferdinand and Isabella the sea route to the Indies, it would be Spain and not Portugal that emerged now as the wealthiest maritime power of Europe.

King João had family problems, too—which, since he was a monarch, were therefore national problems. In 1490 he had engineered a magnificent coup by affiancing his only son, fifteen-year-old Prince Afonso, to the daughter of Ferdinand and Isabella. Thus the boy, though weak and effeminate, stood next in succession to all the crowns of the Iberian

Peninsula, and Spain and Portugal would be united under his rule a generation hence. That bold dream was shattered within a year. In June 1491 Prince Afonso died under mysterious circumstances; the official story was that he was killed by a fall from his horse, but there were hints that he was slain by a disaffected branch of the royal family. King João's wife, who was also his cousin, belonged to that branch of the family, and so did her brother, Duke Manoel, who now became heir presumptive to the Portuguese throne.

Manoel, whose role in the death of Prince Afonso was never determined, feared King João's wrath. The duke placed himself under the protection of his sister, Queen Leonora, who had separated from the King after the death of their son. João's only hope of maintaining the succession for his own line lay in a young bastard son, George, on whom he now bestowed a dukedom, while seeking to have him legitimized by papal decree. But by 1493 it appeared inevitable that Manoel and not George would be Portugal's next king; with his dynasty destroyed and Spain in possession of Columbus' gift of Asia, João faced the future in bleak mood. In his desperation he resorted to a farfetched claim. Spain's patronage of Columbus, he said, was in violation of the Treaty of Alcaçovas and of various decrees of recent popes granting Portugal the exclusive right to explore the Indies. Columbus, said King João in the spring of 1493, had trespassed on Portuguese waters, for the isles of the Indies that he had found lay close to the Azores and might be considered part of that group. Therefore Portugal claimed ownership of whatever Columbus had discovered, citing as authority a bull, or decree, issued by Pope Martin V more than sixty years earlier, as well as bulls granted to Prince Henry the Navigator by Nicholas V in 1454 and Calixtus III in 1456, and most especially the bull *Aeterni Regis* issued by Pope Sixtus IV in 1481, confirming the terms of the Treaty of Alcaçovas. In a belligerent message João threatened war if Spain did not at once renounce her claims to Columbus' discoveries, and announced that he was about to send a fleet of his own to take possession of the newly found western islands.

Ferdinand and Isabella, having just concluded their expensive, decade-long war against the Spanish Moors, did not judge themselves ready for conflict with Portugal, but they were not about to give up the Indies, either. Therefore they made a mild, conciliatory reply to João, which nevertheless reasserted their right to Atlantic exploration. All the treaties and bulls cited by Portugal, they argued, applied only to waters to the south and east of the Azores, not to the west. When King João continued to raise loud objections, Ferdinand and Isabella played their trump card. João wished to cite papal bulls? Very well, said the Spanish monarchs: they suggested that the dispute be referred to the *current* pope for arbitration. Was he not the highest earthly authority? Was he not an austere and impartial potentate? Was he not also Don Rodrigo Borgia, a Spaniard, a native of Ferdinand's Aragon?

João was caught. He could not refuse the papal arbitration after his own reliance on the decrees of past popes. But the reigning Pope Alexander VI, who had been elevated to the throne of St. Peter on August 10, 1492, was that sinister and self-indulgent fantasy-figure of the Renaissance, the head of the House of Borgia, the father of Cesare and Lucrezia Borgia, the archetype of all corrupt popes, the owner of vast estates, the keeper of many mistresses, the friend of Spain. It was the Borgia pope who graciously consented to arbitrate the quarrel between Spain and Portugal.

The decree of Pope Alexander VI has been much misinterpreted as a document in which he bestowed all the undiscovered portions of the world on his two favorite chil-

dren, Spain and Portugal. So it was regarded by other nations, particularly by England, which within half a century
would come to reject the pope's authority altogether. The
English looked upon Pope Alexander's decree as an abomi-
nation devised for the special benefit of Spain and Portugal;
their attitude toward it is best seen in a fantastic and bom-
bastic essay written early in the seventeenth century by the
geographer Samuel Purchas, who said of Pope Alexander
that he was heir of all his predecessors' vices, "who having
procreated many Bastards, procured the Papacy by Simony
(some add, Diabolical Contracts) to advance them and himself, with unjust justice miserably plaguing those Simoniacal
Cardinals, which for Price and Promise had exalted this
Plague-sore into that Chair of Pestilence, where he acted
the Monster of Men, or was indeed rather and incarnate
Devil." But in fact Pope Alexander's decision was not so
much a gift to Spain and Portugal together as it was a
shameful stripping away of Portuguese privileges.

Ferdinand and Isabella had taken the precaution of
getting a ruling from Alexander before making their open
appeal to him. Spanish envoys went to the Spanish pope in
Rome, told him the wishes of the Spanish king and queen,
and came away with a series of bulls granted to Spain
without the knowledge or consent of Portugal. The first of
these, dated May 3, 1493, but issued in April, granted Spain
authority over lands and islands discovered or afterwards
to be discovered in the west toward the Indies in the Ocean
Sea, as the Atlantic was called. This conflicted with the
Treaty of Alcaçovas to some extent, for Columbus had
shown that it was necessary to go south to get the trade
winds before going west, and in the spring of 1493 he was
about to depart on a second expedition following just that
route. Obligingly, Pope Alexander gave Spain a second bull,
dated May 4 but not released until June, granting the Span-

ish sovereigns the islands and continents in the south as well as in the west.

Seemingly, this deprived Portugal even of the African route so laboriously pioneered all during the fifteenth century. The pope clarified his wishes with a third bull, the famous *Inter Caetera*, again dated May 4 but actually issued in July. This document, which praised the valor of "our well beloved son Christopher Columbus," repeated the assignment to Spain of all the lands and islands discovered or to be discovered to the west and south, but for the first time established a line of demarcation between the Spanish and Portuguese spheres of influence. The boundary, said the pope, would run from pole to pole along a line drawn one hundred leagues* west of the Azores and the Cape Verde Islands. What lay west of the line was open to Spanish exploitation; lands to the east were reserved to Portugal by implication, though there is no reference to Portugal in the text of the bull. "Let no person presume with rash boldness to contravene this our donation, decree, inhibition, and will," thundered the pope. "For if any person presumes to do so, be it known to him that he will incur the indignation of Almighty God, and of the blessed apostles Peter and Paul." A fourth bull, *Dudum Siquidem*, completed the series by revoking all previous papal grants to the Portuguese, again not mentioning Portugal but simply awarding Spain "all islands and mainlands whatever, found or to be found . . . in sailing or traveling towards the west and south, whether they be in regions occidental or meridional and oriental and of India."

Armed with these four bulls, Ferdinand and Isabella were cheerfully willing to submit to papal arbitration of the Indies question. King João, aghast at the trap into which

* One league equals three miles; but the length of the mile varied widely from country to country in the fifteenth century.

he had fallen, sent an anguished protest to Rome when he learned the contents of the bulls. The pope, who was heavily obligated to the Spanish monarchs in many ways, showed no interest in changing his decrees, high-handed and one-sided though they were. It was not a bashful age, and the Borgia pope could serenely bestow the Orient upon Spain without a tremor of conscience. João, risking excommunication, resolved once more on war with Spain. But it was a war that neither side really desired, and he was quick to accept diplomatic overtures from Spain. With the little comedy of papal arbitration out of the way, Spain and Portugal settled down to serious negotiation. João now knew that he could not enforce his brazen claim to Columbus' western discoveries, and Ferdinand and Isabella were aware that they could not make João peacefully swallow the pope's even more brazen rulings.

Both sides agreed to accept the third bull, *Inter Caetera*, as the starting point for a deal. Spanish and Portuguese diplomats met at Tordesillas in 1494 to arrive at some more realistic line of demarcation than the one the pope had proposed. The pope's line ran too close to Africa for João's comfort; at Portuguese insistence, the line was moved, after some haggling, to a point 370 leagues west of the Cape Verde Islands—that is, well out in the Atlantic. Spanish ships would be permitted to sail through Portuguese waters on their way west to the Indies, and so gain access to the vital westerly trade winds; but the eastward route remained exclusive to Portugal. Thus João protected his valuable African interests. With the signing of the Treaty of Tordesillas on June 7, 1494, the division of the world was confirmed, and the threat of war between Spain and Portugal subsided.

King João II could feel some satisfaction over the outcome. To his chagrin, he had let Columbus give the western route to Spain, but there was no way of undoing that; at least he still owned the eastern route. Bartholomeu Dias had proved in 1488 that Africa could be rounded. Meanwhile Pedro de Covilhão and Afonso de Paiva, João's emissaries to Prester John, had successfully carried out their reconnaissance of the eastern end of the route to India. They had left Portugal—forever, as it turned out—in May 1487. By way of the Mediterranean they reached Egypt, where, after suffering disease and the loss of the merchandise they carried, they joined a party of Moorish merchants and sailed down the Red Sea to Aden. There, in the spring of 1488, they parted. Paiva went westward into Ethiopia to seek the legendary Christian monarch whom Europeans called Prester John, while Covilhão boarded an Arab vessel and voyaged to India. In a month he landed at the port of Cannanore, the first Portuguese to set foot in the fabled land of India. Journeying down the Malabar Coast, the resourceful Covilhão studied the workings of the spice trade, observing the activities of the Arab and Hindu merchants who brought the goods from the isles of the Indies and sold them here. He learned of commodity prices, prevailing winds, sources of supply, and much else during a stay in the Indian port of Calicut. Among his discoveries was the information that there was open sea beyond the southern tip of Africa, a fact that Bartholomeu Dias was independently learning at first hand about the same time. To confirm this news of a sea route around Africa, Covilhão left Calicut for Ormuz, the great mart on the Persian Gulf, and in 1489 headed by ship along the coast of Arabia to East Africa. He ventured as far as Sofala at 21°S., some two-thirds of the way down Africa's eastern shore; Arab traders were busy there, and there could be no doubt of the existence of a seaway around Africa linking Europe to the Orient. He heard also of the large island of Madagascar and collected a wealth of data about harbors and sailing conditions in this part of Africa that would be of immense value later. Finally, in 1490, Covilhão returned to Cairo, where he learned of the death of his colleague, Paiva. He found two Portuguese Jews sent by King João to look for him, and turned a report of his travels over to them before setting out on further adventures. The astonishing Covilhão now disguised himself as a Moslem and made the pilgrimage to Mecca, apparently to satisfy his own curiosity; then he fulfilled his instructions by entering Ethiopia and reaching the court of Prester John to see about the possibility of arranging a land route across Africa from Ethiopia's Red Sea ports to Portugal's outposts on the Atlantic. There his wanderings ended, for the Ethiopian monarch did not believe in letting foreigners return to their native lands, and Covilhão was still in the land of Prester John 30 years later when another Portuguese ambassador arrived.

By 1494, with the trouble with Spain over, King João was at last free to capitalize on the knowledge won for him so strenuously by Dias and Covilhão. There *was* a sea route to India; the names of ports along the way were known; all that remained was to send out an expedition to the Orient and open trade relations. João felt a sense of urgency about the enterprise, now that the Spaniards had access to Asia from the west. He did not want his Iberian rivals to gain control of the spice trade before his own ships arrived.

João did not live long enough to comprehend the irony of recent events. The joke was on Spain, for Columbus had not reached Asia at all, merely some puzzling islands inhabited by naked savages. No one knew how much farther it might be to the true Indies. And a few years later it became apparent that Columbus' route could not get Spain to Asia at all, because two colossal continents amazingly blocked the ocean. Portugal alone had access to the Indies, via the east. But João died in 1495, only forty years old, perhaps a victim of poison, more likely carried off by dropsy or uremia. To Portugal's throne came Manoel the Fortunate, twenty-six years of age, handsome, ambitious, a good administrator, something of a miser, who would be the beneficiary of all the building the House of Aviz had done before him. In his reign the round world's imagined corners would be reached; Portugal would attain the empire in the Orient of which his ancestors had dreamed; and caravels laden with spices would stream toward Lisbon.

7

Manoel had none of Henry the Navigator's love of science, nor did he show João II's interest in exploration for its own sake. He was interested primarily in money and the power that could be derived from money. Though he did not treat his captains and courtiers generously—and ultimately his penuriousness would prove costly to him—Manoel spent huge sums to construct palaces, monasteries, churches, hospitals, and government buildings, and his extravagances in that respect nearly bankrupted his small country, which had a population of only about a million during its era of greatness. To meet his vaulting desires, Manoel needed an overseas empire. First India, then Egypt and Arabia, then all of Asia and Africa would have been incorporated into a Christian Portuguese domain if Manoel's dreams had been fulfilled.

First things first: India. When he came to power, he found an India-bound armada being constructed under the supervision of Bartholomeu Dias. Dias had earlier sailed in three-masted, lateen-rigged caravels, but these had given him trouble near Africa's windy tip, and to provide greater safety and comfort for the sailors on their long voyage to India, he was building two large old-fashioned, square-rigged *naos*. In 1496, after helping to finance the expedition by expelling the Jews and Moors from Portugal and confiscating their capital and businesses, Manoel ordered the purchase of two smaller lateen-rigged caravels. Thus the India armada made use of all the resources of late fifteenth-century ship design, just as it employed the accumulated knowledge of the sea and winds that had been collected since the time of Henry the Navigator. Supreme command of the expedition went not to the veteran Dias, who accompanied the armada only as far as Guinea, but to a twenty-eight-year-old nobleman and diplomat, Vasco da Gama. His prior naval experience is unknown, but evidently he had already won some reputation at sea. Manoel's faith was justified, for Gama successfully carried out the finest feat of navigation ever achieved up to that time, Columbus' voyage included.

The four Portuguese vessels left Lisbon on July 8, 1497. Many of Gama's men had served in the Dias voyage; some had even been to sea with Diogo Cão. Favorable winds took them through familiar waters as they sailed between the Canaries and the African coast, called at the Cape Verde Islands, rounded the bulge of Guinea, and headed for the Cape of Good Hope. Swinging far out into the South Atlantic as he had learned from Dias to do, Gama spent thirteen weeks in the open sea, the longest passage European seamen had ever made out of sight of land. (Columbus sailed five weeks between the Canaries and the Bahamas.) At last turning east—a little too soon—the Portuguese made land on November 8 at the Saint Helena Bay, about 130 miles north of the Cape of Good Hope. For eight days they remained, tending to their ships and collecting wood and water; Gama was wounded by the javelin of an unfriendly Hottentot in a skirmish before their departure. Six days later they rounded the Cape and halted in Mossel Bay. Despite storms, contrary currents, and an attempted mutiny. Gama pushed onward beyond Dias' farthest point, into the unknown. Now they turned north, up Africa's eastern coast, calling at various ports. All went well until they reached Mozambique, the southern limit of the Moslem coastal domain. The Arab traders had long regarded this section of Africa's Indian Ocean coast as their own property, and they were unenthusiastic about the arrival of Christian intruders; the Portuguese were driven out of Mozambique and the port of Mombasa, where Gama endured attack and sabotage for six days while trying to hire an experienced pilot to guide him to India.

Somehow the voyagers managed to obtain a warm greeting at the next port up the coast, Malindi, 2,500 miles north of Dias' stopping point of 1488. They reached it at Eastertime and enjoyed a pleasant visit; Gama was able to acquire the services of a famous Moslem pilot, Ahmed ibn-Majid, an authority on the Indian Ocean who had written several geographical texts in Arabic, and who astonished Gama by his familiarity with the astrolabe and the cross-staff. Ahmed ibn-Majid guided the armada safely through the atolls of the Laccadive Islands to India. On May 20, 1498, Portuguese ships at last appeared in the harbor of Calicut. The long quest was at an end; the sea route to the Indies had truly been found.

The Malabar Coast of southern India was then divided into tiny city-states, each ruled by a local prince whose chief occupation was squabbling with his neighbors. The princes and most of their subjects were Hindus, but the commercial life of the ports, particularly the export trade, was controlled by Arabs and Moslem Indians who had no wish to see Europeans cut into their profitable spice business. Gama, as wise a diplomat as he was a navigator, found his abilities fully tested as he negotiated to break the Moslem monopoly.

He approached the Zamorin of Calicut for permission to purchase spices, and that Hindu ruler was friendly at first; but he cooled toward the Portuguese when he saw how mean were the gifts that the thrifty King Manoel had sent to him. The Moslem merchants began to put pressure on the zamorin to refuse port facilities to the Portuguese, and, fearful of displeasing them, the zamorin yielded. Gama narrowly escaped assassination at the hands of the Moslems, and it was almost impossible for him to acquire spices. But he persisted, wheedling here and haggling there, and after three wearying months succeeded in obtaining a cargo of precious merchandise.

The return trip across the Indian Ocean was a dreadful one, taking another three months. Scurvy plagued the Portuguese so severely that, when they reached Malindi in January 1499, there were hardly enough crewmen to man the vessels. After a cheering respite at Malindi and an easy journey to the Cape of Good Hope, the explorers suffered again from the storms of the South Atlantic, and when Gama entered Lisbon the following September, he had only two of his four ships and had lost more than 100 of his 170 men. Yet the expedition was a triumph. In two years and two months he had covered 28,000 miles, he had found India, and he had returned with spices worth sixty times the cost of the voyage. King Manoel could not resist boasting of Gama's great achievement in a smug letter to Ferdinand and Isabella, whose daughter he had recently married:

". . . . We learn that they did reach and discover India and other kingdoms and lordships bordering upon it; that they entered and navigated its seas, finding large cities, large edifices and rivers, and great populations, among whom is carried on all the trade in spices and precious stones. . . . Of these they have brought a quantity, including cinnamon, cloves, ginger, nutmeg, and pepper, as well as other kinds, together with the boughs and leaves of the same; also many fine stones of sorts, such as rubies and others."

Manoel now began to style himself "Lord of Guinea and of the Conquests, Navigations, and Commerce of Ethiopia, Arabia, Persia, and India." To Manoel it was regrettable, though not really serious, that the merchants of Calicut had shown so little willingness to let Vasco da Gama do business there. Perhaps they could be persuaded to relent; if not, Portugal would simply have to conquer a few Indian ports and set up her own trade network to the Spice Islands. Certainly Manoel was not going to relinquish his great opportunity to establish Portugal as the premier seagoing nation of Europe. Within six months of Gama's return, King Manoel was ready to send out a second and far larger fleet, one that taxed little Portugal's resources to the utmost: 13 ships, 1,200 men.

Vasco da Gama stayed home this time, not because Manoel felt he deserved a rest so much as because it was Portuguese policy to keep the captains from growing too important. Diogo Cão had been cut down after his second great voyage; Bartholomeu Dias had played only a secondary role in Portuguese exploration since his grand accomplishment of 1488; and Gama now was quietly shunted aside for a while. The commander this time was another young aristocrat, Pedro Alvares Cabral. With him sailed old Bartholomeu Dias and many other veterans of earlier Portuguese expeditions. Leaving Lisbon on March 8, 1500, the great armada headed toward India by the traditional route, first south past the bulge of West Africa, then sweeping far west of Africa into the South Atlantic. Cabral swung a little too far to the west, or perhaps he was blown off course; in the latitude of 17°S. he unexpectedly impinged on the coast of Brazil before he could begin his eastward voyage around the Cape of Good Hope.

Europeans then were beginning only dimly to perceive the existence of the two American continents, and no one yet realized that they were continuous almost from the Arctic to the Antarctic. North America was known only by a bit of its northern coastline. In 1497 the Genoese seaman John Cabot, sponsored by Henry VII of England, had sailed northwest looking for a route to the Indies that did not fall into the Spanish sphere, and had encountered Newfoundland. Cabot thus became the first European since Viking days to reach North America and return to tell of it. King Manoel, always alert to opportunity, had allowed a Portuguese named Gaspar de Corte-Real to follow Cabot's track in 1500; Corte-Real rediscovered Greenland by sailing west from the Azores, reached Newfoundland, and deceived himself into thinking that the Gulf of St. Lawrence was a sea route clear to the Orient. He called it the Strait of Anian and thus helped to foster centuries of fruitless search for a northwest passage; both he and his brother Miguel were casualties of the quest for this passage within a few years.

Below Newfoundland, all was unknown for thousands of miles. Columbus had glimpsed the coast of Venezuela on his third voyage in 1498, though he was still convinced he was near India. In 1499 and 1500 several Spanish expeditions filled in the outline of the upper curve of the South American mainland; Vicente Yáñez Pinzón, a veteran of Columbus' first expedition, saw the coast of Brazil before Cabral, though he did not go ashore. Cabral, landing a few months later, demonstrated what Pinzón had quietly suspected: that South America bulged so far to the east that Brazil lay on the Portuguese side of the pope's line of demarcation. Though no one was quite certain where that line really ran, owing to the practical difficulties of determining longitudes, it seemed certain that Brazil was east of it and that Portugal would thus have a piece of the New World after all.

But there were no Portuguese settlements in Brazil until 1531. The New World—which nearly everyone but Columbus knew by 1500 was not Asia—had so far yielded only a modest return for Spain, and Cabral was not inclined to linger there for long. He sent a ship back to Portugal to announce his discovery of territory on the South American mainland, and continued on to the known and reliable source of wealth, India. The Atlantic crossing was a difficult one; he lost four ships with all hands, and among those who perished was Bartholomeu Dias. Despite the Brazilian detour and the stormy voyage, the surviving vessels reached the coast of East Africa remarkably quickly; Cabral hired a pilot in Malindi and his ships were in India by the end of August 1500, only six months out from Lisbon.

He obtained an interview with the Zamorin of Calicut and, despite renewed opposition from the Moslem merchants, won permission to set up a Portuguese trading depot, or factory, in the town. The Moslems were angered by this and even more furious when Cabral captured one of their ships in order to obtain an elephant as a gift for the zamorin. They retaliated for this piracy by destroying the newly built factory and slaying fifty Portuguese. Cabral's response was to burn ten Arab ships with their crews aboard, and to subject Calicut to a severe bombardment from sea—the beginning of Portugal's war against the Moslem traders of India. Hope of arriving at a peaceful accommodation with the zamorin was dead at that point, so Cabral sailed south to the port of Cochin, long a rival of Calicut's. The local ruler was cooperative, either out of a wish to get one up on the zamorin or simply out of fear of the Portuguese cannons;

[57]

he allowed Cabral to load spices at Cochin for two weeks. Then the Zamorin of Calicut, seeking revenge, appeared off Cochin with eight ships of his own. The Portuguese elected to withdraw, but they halted to buy more spices at the port of Cannanore north of Calicut before making their return voyage to Portugal. Cabral reached Lisbon in the summer of 1501. Only four caravels of his whole fleet came back, but they bore 2,000 hundredweight of pepper, 600 of cinnamon, and 400 of ginger, along with lesser quantities of cloves, lac, and benzoin.

Since Cabral had blundered into a war with Calicut, his voyage was hardly a diplomatic success, but as a commercial endeavor it gave King Manoel great delight. Lisbon's warehouses suddenly were rich with wondrous goods; bankers from Germany and Italy, sensing a new boom, were heading toward Portugal; and in Venice, Europe's spice emporium for more than a century, tremors of anxiety shook the countinghouses. Cabral's return, wrote a contemporary Venetian diarist, was a catastrophe, "the worst news the Venetian Republic could have had." A dramatic shift in the structure of the spice trade was about to occur.

The Portuguese could hardly have chosen a better time to reach India. Political confusions in the eastern Mediterranean had virtually cut off Venice's own spice importations, with a corresponding rise in commodity prices. In Egypt a governmental crisis beginning in 1496 had paralyzed trade and had compelled the spice bazaars of Cairo to suspend business. Venice and Turkey went to war in 1498 over control of the Dalmatian coast, and about the same time the French invaded Italy, creating more chaos. The links of the spice trade had snapped. Venice had, for the moment, lost access to Alexandria and Beirut, and by 1499 the price of pepper on the Rialto was 80 ducats per hundredweight, up from 42 ducats in 1496. Into this situation of strangled supply came the Portuguese, who found themselves able now to buy pepper in India for three ducats the hundred-weight. A Venetian envoy in Lisbon wrote his government after Cabral's return, "They took on a heavy cargo . . . at a price I fear to tell." Another Venetian observer estimated that the Portuguese could show a profit of a hundred ducats for every ducat invested, since their route to the Indies eliminated all the middlemen and tax collectors of the Near East, and he gloomily predicted, "There is no doubt that the Hungarians, Germans, Flemish, and French, and those beyond the mountains, who formerly came to Venice to buy spices with their money, will all turn towards Lisbon, for it is nearer to all the countries [of western Europe] and easier to reach."

Venice contemplated ruin; King Manoel contemplated wealth and grandeur. Of course, as spices continued to flood into Lisbon from India, the present scarcity-inflated prices would have to tumble; but when the economic dislocations were ended, Portugal was sure to displace Venice as the spice capital of Europe. Manoel himself would be the chief beneficiary of this prosperity, for most of the vessels that had gone to India thus far had been royal ships, the profit of whose cargoes would go to the king's private account. Manoel had proclaimed the spice trade a crown monopoly in 1500, although he was willing to let outsiders send licensed trading vessels to the Orient for a fee of one-fourth of the value of their cargo.

Simply bringing the spices to Lisbon was only part of the process of growing wealthy, though; Manoel had to be able to sell them, and that meant setting up distribution channels in Europe. There were many willing bankers eager to help him, most notably the German house of Fugger. The Fuggers, an Augsburg clan that had come to prominence late in the fourteenth century, had won their first wealth by selling German textiles to the Venetians. Fuggers imported wool, cotton, and dyes through Venice, shipped manufactured goods the other way, and gradually built powerful connections in the Italian city, Europe's center of commerce and finance. In time, the Fuggers were the chief outlet through which the pepper that entered Venice flowed on to the rest of Europe.

The attention of the Fuggers was diverted from Venice to Lisbon in 1485. The year before, Diogo Cão had returned from his first voyage to Africa, bringing a cargo of the spice known as malagueta pepper. More pungent than the pepper of the Indies, malagueta had never been available in commercial quantities in Europe before; now the Portuguese could bring it in far more cheaply than the regular Asian pepper. Jakob Fugger, twenty-six years old but already skilled in the family ways, persuaded King João II to let the Fuggers handle distribution of the African pepper. The Fuggers handled it so well that they were able to keep the price on a par with that of Asian pepper, producing immense profits for all concerned. When Jakob Fugger returned to Augsburg, he left as his lieutenant in Lisbon a Spanish banker, Christóbal de Haro, who was to become a key figure in the coming age of discovery.

The replacement of João II by Manoel in 1495 created problems for the Fuggers. They anticipated the attainment of India by sea and knew that it promised far greater profits than the relatively small trade in African pepper; but at first Manoel kept them at a distance, preferring to do business with Florentine bankers instead. Cristóbal de Haro tried to invest both in Gama's voyage and in Cabral's, but both times he was shut out in favor of the Florentines. However, Manoel needed loans to finance further voyages to India, and Haro made the boundless Fugger wealth available. As a result, the Fuggers were allowed to take part in the third Portuguese expedition to India, which left in the spring of 1501, even before Cabral's return. There were four ships under the command of João da Nova. En route, Nova heard of Cabral's troubles at Calicut, and so he went straight to Cochin to purchase spices; his next stop was Cannanore, where he took on more cargo and captured a ship of Calicut, taking possession of the pilot, three silver navigational instruments, and 1,500 pearls. He returned to Portugal in September 1502, laden with pepper. Thereafter, the Fuggers and Cristóbal de Haro were deeply involved in Portugal's spice trade. Through Fugger channels the spices went from Lisbon to Antwerp—where the Fuggers maintained warehouses—and thence through the British, Scandinavian, German, Flemish, and Bohemian markets, while the Florentines were distributors to Spain, Italy, and France.

As the European commercial picture thus changed, King Manoel took steps to assure the permanence of Portugal's new fortune. A logical beginning was retribution for the massacre of Cabral's men at Calicut. Late in 1501 a large fleet was assembled under Cabral's direction; but at the last minute Manoel performed a typical maneuver, abruptly sending Cabral into retirement and calling forth Vasco da Gama to command the armada. There were 25 ships, 12 belonging to Manoel, 13 to private merchants. With calculated savagery, Gama inflicted terrible revenge on the inhabitants of Calicut, intercepted and raided Arab ships wherever he found them, and otherwise achieved his purpose of intimidating the entire Moslem commercial community along the Indian Ocean. As a result, he was able to set up Portuguese factories, or warehouses, at Cochin and Cannanore, and arrived at treaties with the local rulers fixing weights, measures, and prices. When he set sail for Portugal in December 1502, he left a number of his ships behind to protect the factories and patrol Indian waters. Thus Portugal attained her first solid grasp on the Malabar Coast and guaranteed herself a steady supply of spices.

The arrival of seven of Gama's heavily laden ships at Lisbon in September 1503 sent new paroxysms through the Venetian spice market. The Venetians had ended their war with the Turks in 1503 and again were able to reach the ports of the Levant, but spices had become impossibly dear there and the Venetians could not compete with Lisbon. At Cairo, pepper was soaring toward its 1505 high of 192 ducats the hundredweight; meanwhile, at Lisbon, the price was falling to 40 ducats, to 30, in 1504 to 20, and still allowing a good profit. Envoys from Venice had told the Sultan of Egypt in 1502 that he must use his influence in the Moslem world to drive the Portuguese from the Indian Ocean. Unless he could guarantee to Venice a steady supply of spices at reasonable cost, they said, they would halt trade with Cairo altogether and get their pepper wholesale at Lisbon. The Egyptian ruler, though, had no way of blocking the Portuguese; the best he could do was tell the pope that he would attack the Christian shrines in the Holy Land unless the penetration of India by Portugal was ended at once. It was an idle threat; the Portuguese continued to sail to India, and by 1515 Venice was buying her spices in Lisbon, not in Alexandria, Beirut, or Cairo.

The Portuguese hand grew stronger. Gama's mission of conquest of 1502–03 was followed by another fleet in 1503, commanded by one of Portugal's grandest military heroes, Affonso de Albuquerque. This armada arrived at Cochin just in time to save that friendly Indian port from an invasion by Calicut. The grateful ruler of Cochin allowed the Portuguese to station a permanent garrison in his city. Soon after Albuquerque's return to Portugal, the Zamorin of Calicut attacked Cochin again; after a series of bitter battles, the zamorin was slain and the fleet of Calicut was dispersed by the Portuguese forces.

Once more a rich cargo of spices was unloaded at Lisbon. The successive and successful India voyages had so flooded the Portuguese market by the beginning of 1505 that there was real danger of undermining the spice trade completely. Accordingly, King Manoel began to rig the market. Working through the Casa da India—the arm of the Portuguese bureaucracy that regulated overseas trade— the king established fixed rates for the sale of spices by private merchant-venturers importing commodities from India for their own accounts. All spices brought in by the ships of these private merchants, such as Cristóbal de Haro or the Florentines, were deposited at once in the royal warehouses. The king collected his share first—25 to 30 percent of the cargo, depending on individual contracts—and the remainder was sold by officials of the Casa da India at the fixed prices on the merchants' behalf. Since the purchase prices in India were also fixed by contract, the only risk for the merchants or the king, in theory, lay in the loss of ships at sea. According to the 1505 regulations, pepper was bought in Cochin for three ducats the hundredweight and sold at Lisbon for 22; cinnamon, three and a half ducats the hundredweight to buy, 25 to sell; cloves, seven and a half to buy, 60 to sell; nutmeg, four ducats to buy, 300 to sell. It was a beautiful scheme, marred only by King Manoel's lack of control over the laws of supply and demand. As the caravels continued to return from India, Lisbon's warehouses began to overflow. By May 1506 some 40,000 hundredweight of spices lay in storage awaiting buyers. The merchants, eager to realize their profits, pressed the king to let them liquidate this backlog, even if it meant selling at lower prices. Manoel held firm for a while, but weakened when the merchants began to refuse him loans to finance his many expansionist ideas. By 1507 he was compelled to allow a freer trade in pepper and other spices. Luckily for Portugal, the dynamic growth of the distribution channels operating out of Antwerp prevented a collapse of the spice market after all, at least for several decades.

Manoel's other concern in 1505 was the possibility that the Sultan of Egypt would heed Venice's pleas and interfere with Portugal's access to India. The sultan's blackmail attempt involving the shrines of Palestine had come to nothing because, as Manoel had guessed, the sultan depended too heavily on the tourist revenue of Holy Land pilgrimages to make good his threat; but when word reached Manoel that the sultan had decided to build a fleet to attack Portuguese shipping, Manoel took action. The lesson of Albuquerque's voyage of 1503 was clear: only by building a chain of forts in the Orient could Portugal be certain of maintaining her trade route. The king conceived an ambitious program of military conquest and occupation in the spice lands. In 1505 he appointed Francisco de Almeida as his first Viceroy of India and assembled a fleet of twenty-two vessels. Almeida's assignment was to meet the Moslem threat by conquering and fortifying every important port on the Indian Ocean.

The armada sailed on March 25, 1505. Among the 1,500 sailors, soldiers, and laborers it carried was a young man making his first major voyage: Fernão de Magalhães, whom we call Ferdinand Magellan.

[2]

MAGELLAN

HE WORLD'S FIRST CIRCUMNAVIGATOR WAS born inland. Several Portuguese cities claim him, and the most persistent claim has been that of Sabrosa, in Portugal's northeastern province of Trais-os-Montes. Recent research appears to show that his birthplace actually was at Ponte da Barca in the province of Minho—west of Sabrosa, but still a long way from the sea. The Magalhães family, or the Magellans, as we may as well call them, following the French usage that has become universal outside the Iberian Peninsula, settled at Ponte da Barca about 1095, coming in the train of the Burgundian adventurers who founded the first modern dynasty of Portuguese rulers.

The Magellans established themselves as minor nobility under the Burgundians; when the Burgundian dynasty became extinct late in the fourteenth century, they took part in the agitation that brought the bastard João of Aviz to the throne. The circumnavigator's grandfather, Gil Annes Magellan, was a contemporary of Prince Henry the Navigator and very probably was in Henry's service, since the Magellan estate was a feudal fief of which Henry was liege

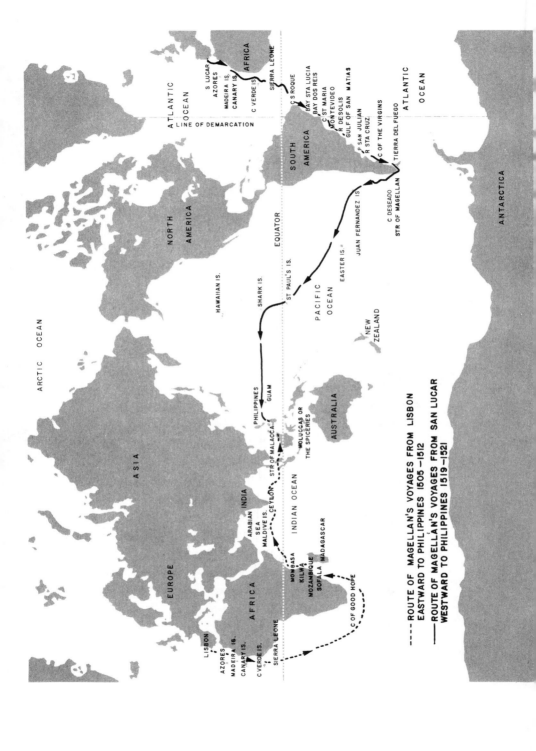

---- ROUTE OF MAGELLAN'S VOYAGES FROM LISBON
      EASTWARD TO PHILIPPINES 1505-1512

——— ROUTE OF MAGELLAN'S VOYAGES FROM SAN LUCAR
      WESTWARD TO PHILIPPINES 1519-1521

lord. The name of Magellan, however, does not appear in any record of Prince Henry's activities. Of Gil Annes' younger son, Ruy, we know only three significant facts: that his wife's name was Donha Alda de Mesquita, that he held the position of High Sheriff of the city of Aveiro, and that he was the father of three children: Isabel, Diogo, and Fernão, or Ferdinand.

Ferdinand was the lastborn, coming into the world about 1480. His brother, two years his senior, did not bear the Magellan name; he was known as Diogo de Sousa to emphasize his descent from the much more influential Sousa family. Both the wife and the mother of his grandfather, Gil Annes Magellan, had been Sousas, and Diogo bore the great name to qualify him for a share of his grandfather's estate. Ferdinand, as the younger son of a younger son, had no expectations of an estate to worry about and was reared as a Magellan.

Of Ferdinand's boyhood and even of his young manhood we know scarcely anything solid. The definitive modern biography of the circumnavigator bristles with qualifying phrases: "We may conjecture that—" and "It is extremely likely that—" and "Beyond much doubt—." But when we strip away the ingenious speculations, not much documented evidence remains. Ferdinand was reared on a hill-girded farm in a pleasant valley, lived as comfortably as any young aristocrat of a not too wealthy Portuguese family lived in the fifteenth century, grew up in the years when Diogo Cão and Bartholomeu Dias were exploring Africa's coast for King João II, and left home for the first time in the significant year of 1492, when he was twelve. His destination was the royal court at Lisbon, where his father had obtained for him an appointment as a page to Queen Leonora.

Every noble family had the privilege of sending its

heir to the court as a page, thereby to gain a free education and to seek the patronage of important courtiers. Diogo de Sousa had been named a page in 1490, and now, two years later, his younger brother, Ferdinand, joined him. It was unusual for a younger son to get such an appointment, so perhaps João II owed Ruy Magellan some favor, or maybe there was merely a shortage of pages that year. Conjectures again.

To plunge into the steamy environment of the Portuguese court at that time must have been a startling and dismaying experience for Ferdinand if he had the wit to comprehend the intricate conflicts swirling around the throne. The king was menaced by a rival branch of his own family, the House of Braganza, descended from an illegitimate son of João I. Queen Leonora herself was a Braganza; the Braganzas were said to have instigated the mysterious death of João II's only heir, Prince Afonso; the king had put several Braganzas to death, including one of the queen's brothers, and lived in dread of plots against his own life. King and queen dwelt apart much of the time, and Magellan, as the queen's page, saw little of João II and a great deal of the heir to the throne, Duke Manoel, the queen's brother.

Manoel, who was in his early twenties when Magellan came to the court, kept close watch over the pages, in particular supervising their studies of astronomy and navigation. Those subjects were a great concern to Manoel as a future Portuguese king, and he had a vested interest in encouraging the young nobles to master them. Magellan's other training in the pages' school was in such things as horsemanship, jousting, dancing, and hunting—the courtly skills. When not at their studies, the pages ran errands, carried messages, or performed menial tasks in the royal household.

We are told that Duke Manoel took a quick dislike to

Magellan: bad business for the boy's hope of a career. Why this hostility existed we do not know, and once more we must speculate. Was Magellan too slow in responding to one of Manoel's commands? Did he perpetrate some childish prank on the duke? Was it one of those inexplicable incompatibilities of temperament? Certainly Manoel could not have been displeased with Magellan's academic progress, for the young page showed special skills in mapmaking and maritime science. Like younger sons everywhere, Ferdinand had little hope of advancement at home and was already preparing himself for naval life and the chance to make his fortune overseas.

The years of his adolescence were eventful ones. First came Columbus' return from "Asia," the papal division of the world, and King João's command to get a fleet ready for the last stage of the discovery of the sea route to India. Then, late in 1495, João suddenly died and Manoel donned the crown. The proscribed Braganzas came into power; the older members of the family, conservative landowners, were more interested in agriculture than in overseas exploration, and under their influence King Manoel delayed at first to implement the sailing of the India fleet. Then, prodded from one side by the Florentine bankers and from the other by the Fugger agent Cristóbal de Haro, Manoel became more concerned with maritime expansion. The government agency that shortly would be known as the Casa da India took on a great many new employees, among them Ferdinand Magellan. Along with his brother, Diogo de Sousa, and his cousin, Francisco Serrão, another page, he became a clerk in the marine agency in mid-1496 and took part in the purchasing of supplies and instruments for the expedition of Vasco da Gama. Magellan was promoted, about that time, from page to the rank of squire in the royal household.

Vasco da Gama sailed, found India, and returned with

spices. Portugal became a major commercial center overnight. New armadas went to the Orient, and apparently Portugal made a few secret expeditions to the west about this time, sniffing at Spain's territories in the New World. Magellan, clerking at the Casa da India, had access to the reports of the Portuguese captains who made these furtive and illegal reconnaissances of South America, and took note of the theories they proposed—particularly the suggestion that there might be a strait leading through South America to the true Indies beyond. But his interest in such a westward route to Asia was, at that time, purely hypothetical; even if there were such a route, control of it would rest with Spain. Magellan, like any other young Portuguese at the beginning of the sixteenth century, hoped to reach India by the eastern route, the route the Holy Father had awarded to his country.

He tried and failed to enlist in the India expeditions. While other men came home wealthy from Cochin and Cannanore, he toiled on, obscure, impoverished, overworked. The Casa da India would not let him go, for all experienced clerical workers were needed to process the yield of the Orient that flowed so magnificently onto the quays of Lisbon. Finally, when the mighty Almeida expedition of 1505 was being organized, Magellan was able to secure a leave of absence from the court and enrolled in the armada. He was twenty-five years old, unmarried, unknown, short of stature, altogether a man of modest position and, so it seemed, of modest abilities.

Of the 22 ships in Almeida's fleet, 12 were vessels of war. The others were merchant ships owned by various German and Italian bankers. Magellan sailed aboard one of the king's caravels, though we do not know which one. With him were his fellow squires and Casa da India clerks, Diogo de Sousa and Francisco Serrão, and possibly they were aboard the ship commanded by João Serrão, Francisco's elder brother. (There is even some doubt that the two Serrãos were really brothers or that they were Magellan's cousins. Both played major roles in Magellan's later career.) As members of the nobility, Magellan and his companions were officially listed in the roster as supernumeraries, gentleman-adventurers serving without pay, rather than regular members of the crew. Their life aboard ship must have been as uncomfortable as that of any common crewman, though: a cramped, damp corner of the open deck on which to sleep and store their belongings, meals of salt pork, dried figs, raisins, and red wine, long hours of toil, and maximum exposure first to the chill of an Atlantic winter, then to the sticky humidity of tropical Africa.

Almeida's task was to break Moslem interference with Portuguese shipping by establishing naval bases and trading depots on the east coast of Africa and on the west coast of India. He led his fleet south by the usual way, rounding the Cape of Good Hope in June, when wintry blasts gripped that part of the southern hemisphere. Bypassing Mozambique, the first hostile port on the Indian Ocean side of Africa, Almeida went first to Kilwa, an important coastal city controlled by a Moslem sheikh. Vasco da Gama had forced the Sheikh of Kilwa to swear allegiance to King Manoel three years earlier, but the sheikh's annual tribute of gold had not been forthcoming. After ascertaining that the sheikh had repudiated his oath, Almeida stormed the town, drove the sheikh out, and built a sturdy fortress overlooking the harbor. This done, he established an obliging Arab puppet as the new sheikh, left a garrison of 550 men, and sailed north 500 miles to the great port of Mombasa. Among those assigned to garrison duty at Kilwa was Magellan.

In August 1505 Almeida captured and sacked Mombasa, collected a rich store of booty, and took his fleet across to India. He made Cochin his base while planning the conquest of the Malabar Coast. Meanwhile, the men who had been left behind were trying to rule a thousand-mile stretch of the African shore from the Kilwa fortress and from a second one at Sofala, far to the south. The commander of the Kilwa garrison, Pero Fogaza, had been given the task of gaining control for Portugal of the products of Central Africa: gold, ivory, copper, and slaves, mainly. Fogaza, who was somewhat less than an inspired leader—he had already been embarrassed on the outward journey by the sinking of his ship, the *Bela*, when it sprang a leak off Sierra Leone—was trying to channel this commerce toward selected ports of Persia and India, keeping African goods away from Egypt, whose sultan was making such threatening gestures at the Portuguese. But Arab smugglers bedeviled Fogaza by running the Portuguese blockade and shipping goods to Egypt anyway. In addition, he had to cope with harassment from the supporters of the deposed sheikh, which soon transformed itself into a full-scale civil war between the faction of the puppet sheikh and the faction of his predecessor.

To deal with the smugglers, Fogaza assigned a small, fast caravel to shore patrol, along with a flat-bottomed barge propelled by slave oarsmen. Late in 1505, Magellan was assigned to duty on this barge, or *bergantym*. Evidently he distinguished himself in this service, because the next time we hear of him (in a report sent by Almeida to King Manoel on December 25, 1506), he is listed as aide-de-camp to Nuno Vas Pereira, whom Almeida had sent to assist the beleaguered Fogaza. Pereira came hurrying back from India when Fogaza reported that the civil war in Kilwa was out of control. His arrival quelled the disturbance there, and apparently Magellan, seeing Pereira as a man worth following, attached himself to Pereira's service. When Pereira went to relieve the garrison at Sofala, Magellan went with him. The captain at Sofala had been killed, and Pereira replaced him, naming Magellan as his lieutenant. At the beginning of 1507 Pereira and Magellan moved on to Mozambique, midway between Kilwa and Sofala, which the Portuguese had occupied a short time previously. At Mozambique, Magellan met Affonso de Albuquerque, the leader of the 1503 expedition, who was on his way to India for the second time. King Manoel, rotating his heroes again, had decided to replace Almeida with Albuquerque as Viceroy of India, though the appointment was still secret.

For most of 1507 Magellan patrolled the East African coast, making the Kilwa-Mozambique-Sofala run many times, and no doubt wishing heartily he could get over to India. His chance came in September. Viceroy Almeida had learned that the long-threatened Egyptian naval attack on the Portuguese outposts in the Orient was about to materialize, with Venetian support. Almeida called Nuno Vas Pereira back from Africa to prepare for the conflict, and Magellan went with him.

2

Accompanied by Francisco Serrão, Magellan arrived in Cochin in October 1507. During the previous two years, Almeida had strengthened Portugal's hold on Cochin and Cannanore, her two bases on the Malabar Coast, and had been concentrating on breaking the power of the native sovereigns of the neighboring ports of Calicut, Goa, and Cambay. Those three Hindu rulers, as well as the Arab merchants who enjoyed trading monopolies in their city-states, were determined to drive the Europeans out. Almeida, knowing how precarious his position would become if the native monarchs were able to join forces with the approaching

Egyptian-Venetian fleet, hoped to wipe out Malabar naval strength before that fleet could arrive from the Red Sea. He placed his son, Lorenzo de Almeida, in charge of this project.

Pereira and Magellan, commanding the little caravel *Santo Espirito*, went to the assistance of Lorenzo. For several months they cruised the Indian coast, attacking native shipping. The newly arrived squadron under Affonso de Albuquerque was operating in the north at this time, attempting to secure the ports at the upper end of the Arabian Sea. Albuquerque and his lieutenant, Tristão da Cunha, captured the coastal towns of Somaliland, took the Oman Coast, and briefly occupied the key port of Ormuz. The plan was for Albuquerque to come south to Cochin when he had completed his work. Early in 1508 the fleet of Lorenzo de Almeida was off the hostile Indian port of Chaul when lookouts spied a squadron of European-rigged vessels advancing from the north. Lorenzo assumed that these were Albuquerque's ships, on their way from Ormuz; not until they were upon him did he discover that he was in the midst of the Egyptian fleet. Thirteen Egyptian ships, eight of them outfitted by Venice, were reinforced by more than a hundred Indian and Arabian vessels. Caught by surprise, the Portuguese were butchered. More than a hundred men died, including Lorenzo de Almeida and 13 other officers. Many men were wounded or captured. Magellan escaped this fiasco only because he and Pereira had had to take the *Santo Espirito* back to Cochin for repairs.

It was the first defeat the Portuguese had suffered in their conquest of the Orient. Momentarily their morale was broken; native allies, seeing that they were not invincible after all, reconsidered their alliances, and in Venice and Cairo there was renewed hope of recapturing the spice trade. But Viceroy Almeida took a terrible revenge for his son's death. Collecting every man who could be spared from the East African garrisons, Almeida sailed north along the Malabar Coast at the end of 1508, determined to demonstrate the dangers of angering Portugal. His wrath fell upon the city of Dabul, which until now had resisted all Portuguese approaches. Almeida stormed Dabul, slaughtered its defenders, blew up its walls and towers, and massacred every civilian who could be caught. Magellan took part in this pitiless attack. Taking to the sea again, the Portuguese came on February 2, 1509, to the port of Diu, where the navies of Goa, Calicut, and Cambay had made rendezvous with the Egyptian-Venetian fleet. Boldly Almeida led his ships into the midst of this much larger enemy armada and shattered it; the Egyptians fled, leaving many of their finest men dead, and the captured Venetian officers were inhumanly tortured before Almeida executed them.

It was the decisive battle of Portugal's war for India. Egypt was eliminated as an Indian Ocean power; Venice lost her last hope of maintaining the spice trade; the native princes of the Malabar Coast waited in terror for the mopping-up operation to begin. But it was a costly victory for Portugal. Among the many officers slain was Magellan's patron, Nuno Vas Pereira. Magellan himself was gravely wounded; it was six weeks before he could be transported from Diu to the hospital Almeida had built at Cochin, and then he remained at Cochin, recuperating, from March to July 1509.

During those months, the Portuguese at Cochin were given a taste of how King Manoel rewarded his great men. Almeida, the hero of Diu, returned in triumph to Cochin to find Affonso de Albuquerque waiting for him with the information that Almeida had been dismissed as Viceroy of India and was to yield his office to Albuquerque. At first

Almeida refused to accept this display of royal ingratitude and would not step aside; but, by November, Albuquerque forced him out, and Almeida bitterly left for home, to die at the hands of Hottentots near the Cape of Good Hope without seeing Portugal again.

Before that, though, Almeida set in motion one new attempt to extend Portuguese power. The Malabar Coast was virtually conquered; Almeida now wished to eliminate the next set of middlemen in the spice trade by taking possession of Malacca, the great port on the west coast of the Malay Peninsula. On August 18, 1509, he sent a fleet of five vessels eastward to Malacca under the command of Diogo Lopes de Sequeira. Among Sequeira's officers were Francisco Serrão and Ferdinand Magellan.

3

Malacca, founded about 1400 by refugees from a civil war in Sumatra, was a rapidly growing city of Malayan Moslems, cosmopolitan and prosperous. Though its climate was hot, damp, and unhealthy, its location, its natural resources, and its safe, easily accessible harbor had made it an ideal commercial depot for traders of all nations from Arabia to China. In its bustling harbor could be found Chinese junks, Arab dhows, Malay sampans; mariners from Japan, Bengal, the Malabar Coast, and the Indonesian isles jostled in its bazaars. To Malacca came cinnamon, cloves, and pepper, Chinese porcelains, Indian fabrics, the gleaming swords of Damascus, precious stones from Ceylon, fine woods, silks, medicines, ivories, jades—and slaves. All the luxury goods of the exotic Orient were bought and sold here, for Malacca controlled the strait through which traffic must pass from the Indian Ocean to the South China Sea. When Magellan and his comrades arrived before Malacca on September 11, 1509, they looked up at high ramparts bristling with cannon, at groves of palms, at busy wharves, at the domes and minarets of temples and mosques, at the mansions of the great merchants.

The Sultan of Malacca knew what had been taking place in the past few years along the Malabar Coast, and he realized that these Portuguese were unlikely to mean him well. Yet he welcomed the visitors with seeming cordiality, allowing them to go ashore, and expressing willingness to enter into a trade treaty with Portugal. Sequeira, delighted, gave his men shore leave at once. Magellan and Serrão were more suspicious. They observed that the trade in spices here was an Arab monopoly, and they had a proper Christian fear of Saracen treachery. Serrão, who could speak a Malabar dialect, picked up such information as he could overhear, and even went to the trouble of courting a Chinese prostitute to learn the true feeling toward the Portuguese newcomers. Serrão discovered that the Sultan of Malacca had been in correspondence with the Zamorin of Calicut, Portugal's chief enemy on the Malabar Coast, and that he had prepared a trap for his visitors: to lull them into false security, and then, when they were bemused by the odor of fragrant spices and the feel of fine silks, to strike. But Sequeira refused to heed Serrão's warning. When the Malayans piled up great sacks of pepper along the wharfs and invited the Portuguese to send men to pick up the cargo, Sequeira blandly despatched nearly all his crew, leaving the caravels virtually unguarded.

Magellan, who remained on his ship, watched the shore tensely. When he saw armed Malays quietly moving in, he hurried to his captain with the news; the captain sent him at once in a skiff to Sequeira's flagship nearby. Sequeira was enjoying a game of chess with a Malay official, with other Malays looking on. Showing no outward sign of alarm, Magellan calmly but urgently told Sequeira in Portuguese of the danger. Sequeira replied in a casual, offhanded way that would not indicate to the Malays that he was aware of the plot. He gave his orders—routine ones, as far as the Malays could tell—and a warning passed from ship to ship. Suddenly one of the native dignitaries drew his *kris*, or curved dagger. Sequeira, alert, stabbed the man, while his sailors drove the other Malays from the ship. The battle was joined. While the Portuguese on board the ships fired broadsides into the harbor, those on shore found themselves attacked and fighting for their lives. Serrão was among them. Magellan jumped into the skiff and rowed for shore to rescue his cousin. At the risk of his life, he got Serrão and several others free of the melee.

Thirty Portuguese died in the ambush, and 30 more were taken prisoner; but the disaster would have been total but for the vigilance of Magellan and Serrão. The guns of the Portuguese cut down the Malay sampans that had been poised to attack, and Sequeira was able to get his fleet out of the harbor. When an attempt to arrange the ransom of the prisoners failed, he put out to sea, dismal over the failure of his mission. In his anger and chagrin, Sequeira failed to keep his squadron together on the return voyage to Cochin; the ship on which Magellan sailed, the slowest of the fleet, was left behind and soon was overtaken by a Chinese pirate junk. The pirates grappled and came on board, only to be driven off by the Portuguese, who fought their way onto the deck of the junk. At this stage the Chinese cut the lashings and separated the vessels, leaving a small group of Portuguese—including Francisco Serrão—stranded on the junk. Magellan and four others entered the skiff, rowed through surging seas to the junk, and boarded it with such ferocity that not only were Serrão and his companions rescued, but the Chinese threw down their arms in surrender. The pirate ship proved to contain a fine booty in spices and silks; the Portuguese, abandoning their own wallowing ship, transferred themselves to the speedy junk and two days later caught up with the rest of Sequeira's fleet. Sequeira showed little pleasure at this remarkable exploit.

When the survivors of the ill-starred Malacca expedition straggled unhappily into Cochin in December 1509, they found Almeida fallen and Albuquerque the viceroy. Both Magellan and Serrão received commendations from Albuquerque for their valor; they were given the rank of captain, and each was placed in command of a caravel.

A month later, Magellan took part in a surprise attack on Calicut while the zamorin was away with most of his army on an inland campaign. The Portuguese breached the city's defenses and were looting the zamorin's palace when they were caught by an unexpected counterattack. The losses were severe. Magellan was badly wounded, and Albuquerque suffered near-fatal injuries.

This disaster, coming so soon after the Malacca fiasco, convinced Magellan that he had had enough of India. He had served overseas for five years, had acquired some honorable scars, and as his share of booty had collected a considerable capital in the form of pepper, which he could sell at high prices in Lisbon. No longer impoverished, he felt the time had come to seek some less dangerous profession. When he learned that three caravels were about to depart for home, he obtained his discharge and booked passage. But one of the caravels left a day before the others. To make up the time, the captains of the other two ships took a shortcut in the Indian Ocean and were shipwrecked by night on dangerous shoals. As the furious waves pounded the crumbling vessels, death for all seemed certain. But at dawn the sea grew calm; the crews of both caravels were transported by boat to a nearby uninhabited atoll, along with the provisions and water that had been intended to last them through the journey to Portugal. Magellan was alive, but he was a ruined man, for salt water had engulfed his sacks of pepper in the caravel's hold.

The officers conferred and, learning from the pilots that they were about a week's distance by rowing from Cochin, decided to send the ship's boats back for help. The *capitães e fidalgos*—the captains and noblemen—would go in the boats; the common-born sailors and soldiers would have to fry on the shadeless atoll until a rescue party arrived. This was quite in keeping with Portuguese naval tradition; officers were more important than seamen, aristocrats more important than commoners, and there was no question of an impartial drawing of lots to see who would be marooned, or of leaving captains behind to stay with their ships. However, the commoners objected and talked of seizing the boats from the *fidalgos*. They surrounded the water casks and would not let any be loaded aboard the boats. A mutiny threatened; the officers, though outnumbered, were better armed, and in any conflict the losses would have been heavy on both sides. But Magellan intervened. As an officer, he was entitled to a place aboard the boats, yet he volunteered to remain behind with the men, as a pledge that they would be rescued. It was a strangely noble gesture in the context of the era, illustrating with one stroke Magellan's courage, his compassion for the lowly, his faith in divine providence, and his ability to judge a situation—for his dramatic announcement ended the mutiny and the boatloads of officers departed unmolested. Just before they pushed off from the atoll, Magellan went forward to exchange a last word with one of his friends. Instantly the seamen, thinking he was deserting and betraying them, cried out, "Senhor, did you not promise to stay with us?" "I did," Magellan replied, "and here I am!" He came ashore and watched with the other stranded men as the boats rowed away.

For three weeks they suffered under the Indian Ocean sun before a rescue ship arrived. Nothing could be salvaged from the grounded caravels but ivory and porcelains; the sea had spoiled everything else, including Magellan's pepper, and there was no point now in returning to Lisbon. Despondently Magellan headed for Cochin to begin anew the task of winning his fortune.

4

Thus he was present during the epic years when Albuquerque was securing for Portugal her Oriental empire and turning the Indian Ocean into King Manoel's lake. The East African coast was already controlled from Sofala to Somaliland; Albuquerque had established command of the Arabian coast by reconquering Ormuz, at the mouth of the Persian Gulf, and by occupying the island of Socotra, at the entrance to the Gulf of Aden. (Aden itself would have been a better base, giving him control of the Red Sea, but it resisted Albuquerque's thrusts.) On the Malabar Coast, Almeida's stronghold of Cochin struck him as unsatisfactory, for its harbor was difficult of entry during the monsoon seasons. He chose instead as the capital of Portuguese India the island city of Goa, midway up the coast. In February 1510, while Magellan was still on his atoll, Albuquerque laid siege to Goa and captured it, only to be expelled within three months by a determined counterattack. Albuquerque at once began assembling a force to retake the city. Magellan had command of one of the 34 ships of war that arrived off Goa on November 24, 1510.

Against desperate resistance, the Portuguese fought their way into the city and took it again. Since the Arab population had led the defense, Albuquerque made a point of executing every man, woman, and child of the Moslem faith in Goa, some 8,000 in all. In that horrifying day of carnage,

Portugal acquired the keystone of her overseas domain; Goa replaced Cochin as the main colony of Portuguese India and soon was on its way to the brilliant, romantic flowering that made it a legendary metropolis of the Orient. (Goa was to remain Portuguese for more than four centuries, until the day in 1961 when a transformed India, weary of an alien enclave on her shore, took it in a single afternoon.)

Malacca was next. Albuquerque wished to avenge the treachery of 1509 and to gain for Portugal the gateway to the Spice Islands. To foil spies, he announced that he was launching another invasion of Aden; but the fleet of 19 warships and transports that left Goa on March 31, 1511, sailed north only a short distance before swinging about and making for the Bay of Bengal. Magellan, by now well entrenched as an important officer, again commanded a caravel. After a stormy crossing, the armada reached Malacca on July 1. Its fortifications had been strengthened considerably in the two years since Magellan had been there in Sequeira's fleet; 3,000 pieces of heavy artillery guarded the city, and 20,000 soldiers manned its garrison. Albuquerque had 800 Portuguese soldiers and 600 Malabar archers at his command.

He sent an ultimatum to the sultan, demanding release of the prisoners taken in the ambush of Sequeira's men. The sultan, who had hastily sent for reinforcements from other cities, tried to play for time, whereupon Albuquerque bombarded the city and destroyed the ships in the harbor. On July 24, the Portuguese entered the city after crippling the shore batteries; they were driven back, but a second thrust on August 10 was successful. The sultan fled on an elephant; the incredible riches of Malacca fell to Albuquerque's men. Magellan acquired a Malay slave, whom he named Henrique de Malacca, and his share of the spoils of the city would have given him the fortune of his dreams, if only the ship laden with Malacca's treasures had not gone to the bottom of the sea off the coast of Sumatra, en route to Goa. Albuquerque, who was aboard that ship, survived by clinging all night to a raft, but once again Magellan's capital was lost.

Magellan remained in Malacca during the latter half of 1511, helping to reorganize the captured city under Portuguese administration. The accounts of his activities in the succeeding months are contradictory, which is unfortunate, for on the details of what Magellan was doing in 1512 hangs the matter of whether he can technically be considered the first man to travel all the way around the world.

Magellan did not live to complete the great voyage of circumnavigation of 1519–22. He died in the Philippines in April 1521, some 1,500 miles east of Malacca. By that span of 1,500 miles, then, he fell short of being a true circumnavigator—unless, as some say, he had covered that span in 1512, and thus had encircled the globe in two voyages nine years apart.

There are three versions of his 1512 whereabouts. One depends on the fact that on June 12, 1512, Magellan's regular monthly salary at the court in Lisbon was paid, and that it was signed for by its recipient. If Magellan really did sign that June receipt himself, he could not have sailed east of Malacca, for there would not have been time to do that between December 1511 (when he was almost certainly still at Malacca) and June 1512 (when he was ostensibly back at Lisbon).

The second account places him in command of one of the three vessels of an expedition that Albuquerque sent out of Malacca at the end of 1511 to search for the Spice Islands. This enterprise was under the command of Antonio de Abreu; Francisco Serrão commanded one of the other ships, and the third, according to the early seventeenth-century historian Leonardo de Argensola, was commanded by Magellan. Argensola is the only authority for this statement; other chroniclers list one Simon Affonso as the captain of the third ship and give no indication that Magellan took part in the expedition at all. With or without Magellan, however, the caravels sailed along the eastern shore of Sumatra and the northern coast of Java, toured some of the lesser Indonesian islands, and entered the Banda Sea, where the true Spice Islands are to be found. At some point, the ships became separated. Abreu, cruising in the Amboina and Banda island groups, took on so heavy a cargo of cloves that he did not bother to go north to the Moluccas, where the cloves came from, but headed straight back to Malacca. If Magellan really went along, he returned to Malacca as well at this point. But Serrão, captivated by the fragrant isles, would not go back. He explored the Banda Sea until shipwrecked on a barren islet; capturing a Chinese junk that providentially appeared, he found his way to Amboina, and from there to Ternate in the Moluccas. What followed were adventures out of the *Thousand and One Nights:* Serrão offered advice and assistance to the Sultan of Ternate against his rival, the Sultan of Tidore, and helped the army of Ternate defeat the forces of the neighboring island. Thereby Serrão became a kind of grand vizier to the Sultan of Ternate, acquiring a harem which came to include the daughter of the Sultan of Tidore, and during the next eight years established himself as the white overlord of the whole Molucca group. By native messengers he sent word to the Portuguese in Malacca of his happy state and good fortune, inviting them to visit him and share in the wealth of the Spice Islands. But Portugal, already overextended by her conquests of Goa and Malacca, was hard put to maintain her hold there and could not yet reach out to the Moluccas; Serrão remained alone in his tropical paradise, though from time to time he wrote tempting letters to his cousin and dearest friend, Magellan, begging him to come to him.

Despite Argensola, the evidence seems slight that Magellan did accompany Abreu and Serrão to the Banda Sea, thus getting east of the longitude of the Philippines and covering in advance the final leg of his circumnavigation. But quite recently indications have emerged that Magellan went on a wholly unofficial and secret exploring mission that took him some 2,000 miles eastward from Malacca in 1512. By this account, John da Empoli, a Florentine merchant who had come to India in 1503 to supervise his firm's trading in spices, commissioned Magellan to undertake a private reconnaissance of the isles beyond Malacca. If we can accept the story, Magellan illicitly went off in his caravel on a tour of the South China Sea as far as the Philippines. This unauthorized exploit supposedly aroused the anger of the administrators in Goa, when they somehow learned of it, and led to Magellan's being relieved of his command at Malacca and recalled to India.

We may never know which of the conflicting stories to believe, although the third now carries the most weight. But it is certain that Magellan's career in Portuguese India was over by 1513. He was thirty-three years old; he was a veteran of many battles and bore marks on his hide to prove it; he was very little wealthier, except in experience, than he had been when he left Lisbon eight years before. Portugal took small notice of his return. He had been a leader of men in Goa and Malacca, but in Lisbon he was simply a junior squire of the court, and furthermore one whose long absence had left him out of touch with the sources of power. He reported to the royal palace to resume his duties and found that Manoel had built a new palace, incredibly grand, in which Magellan wandered unhappily for a long while before he could locate the official with whom he must register. When he called at the Casa da India, it was full of strange faces and new departments. After two days, Magellan left Lisbon for his brother Diogo's house at Ponte da Barca. Diogo, who had gone no farther east than Africa and had returned in 1507, had married, but not advantageously, and was living quietly on the family estate. The visit was not a success; Magellan, restless and even homesick for India, could not settle easily into the life of a modest country nobleman again.

The only faintly cheering aspect of his return was a promotion at court. His years of overseas service brought him an advancement of one notch, from junior squire to gentleman-in-waiting, or *fidalgo escudeiro*. That entitled Magellan to an increase in his monthly salary from 1,000 reis to 1,850, but even that larger sum was no huge amount, and Magellan felt that he was entitled to a still higher rank, that of *cavaleiro fidalgo*. He sought in vain for some influential courtier who would help him win his promotion, and when no one cared to become his advocate, he framed his own petition to King Manoel, citing his years in Africa, India, and Malaya, his accomplishments in battle, and his wounds, and requested advancement, or at least a private audience with Manoel in which to plead his case.

No reply came from the palace. Magellan, short of cash and feeling desperate, decided to gamble on winning fame by a military exploit that would bring him to Manoel's attention. The sheikh of a Moroccan state subject to Portugal had broken his allegiance and was withholding tribute; Manoel had named his nephew, the Duke of Braganza, to lead an expeditionary force to Morocco to punish the rebel. Although he knew nothing of combat on land, Magellan enlisted in the army and sailed for Morocco in August 1513.

The Moroccan expeditionary force was vast; it was a measure of King Manoel's displeasure with his North African vassal that he sent 18,000 men, or about ten times as many as he had given to Almeida for the conquest of India. The uprising quickly collapsed, and Azamor, the rebel

sheikh's capital, was taken. As a deterrent to other disgruntled Moorish sheikhs, the Portuguese army overran
the surrounding country, burning crops and raiding villages;
this enlarged the struggle and led to a concerted effort by the
Moors to retake Azamor in March 1514. During the bitter
hand-to-hand fighting of this campaign, Magellan was
wounded in the knee and left permanently lame.

The Portuguese army in Morocco now was led by
Count João de Meneses, who had replaced the Duke of
Braganza earlier in the year. General de Meneses found the
small, stubborn Magellan an attractive figure and began to
sponsor him as Nuno Vas Pereira had done earlier. He
awarded the crippled Magellan promotion to the rank of
quadrilheiro mor, a comfortable behind-the-lines post that
gave him responsibility for the safekeeping of prisoners of
war and the management of the cattle, horses, and other
booty taken from the Moors. There were great possibilities
for private profit in this office, since no records of the quantity of prisoners or horses on hand were kept, and it was quietly understood that the *quadrilheiro mor* had the privilege of
selling some for his own account. Since Magellan was essentially an upstart, lacking connections in the knightly orders
that dominated the army, it seemed astonishing to everyone
that he should receive such a lucrative appointment; and the
untimely death of Magellan's protector, General de Meneses,
gave the envious a chance to push him aside. Soon after the
general's death in May 1514, Magellan was confronted with
a charge of malfeasance in office. He had, it was said, been
secretly selling horses back to the Moors.

Everyone expected the *quadrilheiro mor* to do some
business on the side, but an accusation of trading with the
enemy was a serious matter. The new commanding officer at
once dismissed Magellan from his post and ordered him tried
by court martial. Magellan treated this development with

scorn. The war was over; he was lame and tired; he was not now going to let himself be crucified by greedy foes. His Moroccan venture had accomplished nothing, and the petty politics of the Portuguese aristocracy wearied him. He had received another letter from Francisco Serrão in the balmy Moluccas, telling him of the great hoard of spices Serrão had accumulated and begging Magellan to come quickly to the delightful islands. Impatiently, then, almost petulantly, Magellan left Morocco for Lisbon without waiting for the outcome of his trial and without requesting a discharge from his general.

Once in Portugal, Magellan renewed his request for an audience with the king, and this time he got it. Manoel had already received from Morocco an account of Magellan's astonishing desertion and assumed that Magellan wished to offer some explanation for his behavior; but when the swarthy little man limped into the throne room, he said nothing about Morocco at all. Instead, he spoke of his friend Serrão's happy life in the Moluccas and asked for a royal commission to lead a fleet eastward past Malacca to the Spice Islands, capture them for Portugal, and establish a colonial outpost there. The king, who for unknown reasons had disliked Magellan since the time, more than 20 years before, when Magellan had been a page at court, dismissed the project without consideration. He wanted the Moluccas, yes, but they would come to him in good time, and he would find someone other than Magellan to get them for him. Brushing the subject aside, the king berated Magellan for his absence from Morocco without leave and ordered him to return to his commanding officer there to stand trial on the double charge of malfeasance and desertion.

Magellan went back obediently and offered himself for trial. The trumped-up nature of the first charge now became evident: his enemies, having succeeded in ousting him from office, were willing to let the matter drop. Magellan insisted on vindication through trial, and proved, by his poverty, that he had scarcely profited from his office. And, though he was undoubtedly guilty of departure without leave, he managed to avoid punishment for that offense; he was let off on all counts with a vague "not proven," which served as an acquittal.

Again he journeyed to Lisbon. Again he worked his way through the bureaucratic maze, trying to win another audience with the king. Audiences were not so easily had; Magellan had to resort finally to presenting himself at court on a day set aside for the receiving of petitions from humble citizens. It was irregular procedure for a courtier like Magellan to insert himself into such a hearing, but he bribed his way on the list and, when his name was called, hobbled forward to the general surprise of Manoel and his officials.

What Magellan requested now was an increase in his monthly stipend by two hundred reis. This was a trifling amount—a few dollars, by modern reckoning—but, as both Manoel and Magellan were aware, the salaries of courtiers were precisely geared to the ranks they held. By asking for that small raise, Magellan by implication was requesting promotion to the rank of *cavaleiro fidalgo*, a signal honor. The king saw the ruse and angrily rejected the petition. Magellan remained kneeling, letting the words of royal abuse cascade down; and when Manoel had spent his wrath, Magellan again asked command of a caravel to the Moluccas. This too was refused, not unexpectedly, but Manoel added gratuitously that there was no room for Magellan anywhere in the royal navy. Badly shaken, Magellan fell back on his final hope: would the king, then, grant him leave to sail to the Indies on a private ship? No, said Manoel.

Magellan was unprepared for the cold brutality of the monarch's replies. In shock he blurted that he desired permission "to live with someone who would show him favor, where he might obtain more good fortune than with the king." Irritated, exasperated, Manoel this time gave assent. Yes, Magellan could go to another lord. Yes, Magellan was dismissed from royal service. Yes, Manoel did not care where Magellan went or what became of him.

The public humiliation was complete. Told that he was useless in Manoel's eyes, that his career was ended, that he might leave the country and do as he pleased, Magellan rose humbly, and with some reflex of loyalty bent to kiss the royal hand as a token of farewell. Manoel withdrew his hand and turned his back. Magellan stared in bewilderment for a moment; then, frozen-faced, he stumbled toward the door. A mocking courtier called out that Magellan was feigning his limp to win the king's sympathy. Too wounded even to show anger, Magellan simply flushed, and limped more hurriedly from the palace.

5

Shorn of all prospects, Magellan went now to the coastal city of Oporto. He could not remain at Lisbon, but he could not go far from the sea. There, late in 1514, he settled in obscurity at the waterfront, accompanied only by his Malayan slave, Henrique, and contemplated his disaster. His only capital—some money he had saved out of his Indian career—was tied up in litigation with a moneylender. His court salary had ended with his dismissal. He received a trickle of cash from lands he had inherited on the family estate, and perhaps he borrowed from his brother, Diogo, to see him through this difficult time. He remained at Oporto for more than a year before he had any clear idea of his next move. But an enigmatic letter that he wrote to Francisco Serrão during this dark period offers a clue to what was hatching in Magellan's mind. "I will come to you soon," Magellan declared, "if not by way of Portugal, then by way of Spain."

The phrase is ambiguous. On its simplest level, it means no more than that Magellan planned to transfer his allegiance to Spain. It was a logical step: the Portuguese navy and merchant marine both were closed to him by royal displeasure, Genoa and Venice were on the decline as maritime powers, France was too alien and too hostile to Portugal, and England, which was growing greatly interested in naval activities, was sending her ships to the northwest and northeast; Magellan knew nothing about northern waters. But even if he entered Spanish service, how could Magellan reach the Moluccas? Not by the eastward route around Africa and past India, for that belonged to Portugal, and the Spaniards had made no attempt to poach on it. So if Magellan were to come to Serrão "by way of Spain," he could do it only by sailing westward via Spanish waters—to the Americas and beyond, into the unknown ocean that lay between the New World and Asia.

Europe had only recently discovered that ocean—from both sides almost at once. Abreu and other Portuguese, sailing eastward from Malacca in 1512, had heard from the natives of the existence of a vast body of water beyond all the islands. This echoed what Marco Polo had learned more than 200 years earlier, and what Arab navigators operating in the South China Sea had found out before that. No one realized, of course, that this ocean was greater in area than all the land above sea level on the face of the globe, that it occupied one-third of the earth's surface, that it was at its widest 10,000 miles from east to west, and 10,000 from north to south, or that, although it contained 25,000 islands (more than in all the rest of the world's oceans combined) and those islands comprised more than 1,000,000 square miles of land, they were so widely scattered that one could sail for months and see only water.

While a few men were thus peering toward the Pacific from its western side, Vasco Núñez de Balboa was discovering it from the east. Spaniards had been nibbling at Central America since 1500, when gold was discovered near the Isthmus of Panamá. Columbus, on his fourth and last voyage in 1502, sailed southward along the eastern coast of Central America, acquiring a good deal of gold and looking for a strait that would give him passage to the west. The natives had assured him that he was "ten days' journey from the Ganges," but he found no break in the land. In 1509 attempts to colonize the north shore of Colombia and the eastern coast of Central America failed, but led to the conquest of Panamá by Balboa, one of the least despicable of the Spanish adventurers in the New World. After founding a village at a place the Indians called Darien and hearing grand tales of a golden land somewhere to the south, Balboa in 1513 launched an overland expedition through the jungles of the isthmus, hoping to find the sea that was said to be the gateway to that golden land. On September 25, 1513, he scrambled up a final hill and looked out over a boundless ocean. At that place, the Isthmus of Panamá runs east and west, so that Balboa's ocean lay to the south of his hill, and thus he gave it the name of "South Sea." Soon the Spaniards had made small settlements on the shore of the South Sea and were preparing to explore the western coast of the New World—an exploration that shortly brought them to Peru and an amazing treasure of gold and silver.

Very likely, Magellan had heard no later than 1515 of the South Sea's existence and had concluded that, if he could get to it and sail westward across it, he would reach his beloved Serrão in the Moluccas. But since Central America was clearly unbroken by a strait, what was the route from the Atlantic into the South Sea? Was Magellan planning to imitate the Spaniards and leave his ship on the Atlantic side of Panamá, trekking overland across the isthmus to build a new vessel on the Pacific side? No. Nor, evidently, did he consider a northerly sea passage, even though North America's existence then was unknown, and open water, broken only by islands, was thought to lie north of the Caribbean. The brothers Corte-Real had died early in the century trying to find a westward passage in the latitude of the Gulf of St. Lawrence, and so little had been learned in the decade since then that Leonardo da Vinci's map of 1515 showed South America as a great island stretching east and west from Africa to China, and North America merely as a chain of small islands. Ponce de León, sailing north from Cuba in 1513 to find the Fountain of Youth, found Florida instead, but did not suspect that he had reached the mainland of a great continent.

Magellan ignored the possibilities of a northern passage, and it was just as well for him that he did; otherwise he might have been the first to navigate the Atlantic shore of North America, but he would never have seen the Pacific. Instead, he looked southward for his strait to the South Sea.

He based this belief, apparently, on certain secret reports he had seen years before when he was a young clerk at the Casa da India. The discovery by Cabral, in 1500, that Brazil lay on the Portuguese side of Pope Alexander's line of demarcation had led to a good deal of surreptitious Portuguese investigation of the eastern coast of South America in the first decade of the century. On March 15, 1501, King Manoel had dispatched four ships under command of João da Nova to explore Brazil en route to India. One of these caravels was commanded by Diogo Barbosa, a member of an important Portuguese seafaring family. Barbosa had persuaded himself that a westward route to the Indies existed somewhere south of Brazil, and had filed a report to that effect. Magellan may also have heard this idea from Barbosa's son, Duarte,* whom he had met and become extremely friendly with in India.

Cristóbal de Haro, the shrewd Fugger agent in Lisbon, also became interested in a western passage to India and obtained permission from Manoel to send three caravels under Captain Cristóbal Jacques to Brazil on May 3, 1501. Jacques scouted the southern coast of Brazil without making important discoveries. King Manoel sent out a second expedition on May 13, 1501, to look for the westward passage in northern Brazil. One of the officers on this voyage was a Florentine businessman, Amerigo Vespucci, who in a letter to his employer, Lorenzo Piero Francesco de Medici, told of traveling as far south as the latitude of 52°. That was deep into the land later known as Patagonia; whether Vespucci got that far is uncertain and unlikely, but he did see enough of the coastline to convince himself that he was touring no island, but a gigantic continent. When the German geographer Martin Waldseemüller drew up a map of the world in 1507, he honored Vespucci by attaching the name of "America" to that continent.

Vespucci seemed to think that a westward passage through his continent existed, and in 1503 Cristóbal de Haro made another effort to discover it. By then, Portugal was sending regular fleets to India by way of the Cape of Good Hope, so King Manoel had no need of a westward route; but Haro, with his Fugger training, wished to cover all possible bets and wangled permission to send two more explorers to Brazil. Captain Gonzalo Coelho went first, in two caravels, and a little later Cristóbal Jacques made a second voyage with three. Jacques cruised around the bulge of Brazil and kept on going south, even though this was clearly a trespass

---

* It is not certain whether Duarte was Diogo's son or his nephew.

on Spain, since it took him west of the pope's line. Between 35° and 40°S. he came upon an immense gap in the coast. This was the enormous estuary of the river later to be called "Río de la Plata." Entering it, Jacques explored it for two days before storms drove him out, and apparently he thought it was a continuous waterway to the Indies. He continued down the South American coast for an unknown distance, quite likely to Patagonia and possibly even to the strait we call the "Strait of Magellan," at 52°S. When he returned to Portugal, Jacques told Cristóbal de Haro that he had found the westward sea route to the Orient, although we do not know if he meant by this the Plata estuary or the Strait of Magellan. Probably it was the former.

Haro reported the news to King Manoel, who was appalled, and ordered the story suppressed. The strait, if it existed, was clearly in Spain's half of the globe, and Manoel had no desire to hand his rivals a route to India. He much preferred to let the Spaniards think that an unbroken wall of land kept them from sailing west of the New World. And so the Jacques voyage was kept secret—though Magellan, filing papers in the Casa da India, seems to have heard of it prior to Manoel's order of November 15, 1504, imposing secrecy under pain of death on all maps, logs, and reports of Portuguese voyages.

There is one other possible source for Magellan's belief in a strait through South America. Antonio Pigafetta, an Italian gentleman who sailed on Magellan's voyage of circumnavigation and was its official historian, relates that Magellan was confident of finding the strait, for he had seen it "in the treasury of the King of Portugal, in a chart made by that most excellent man Martin de Boemia." The reference is to Martin Behaim of Nuremberg, a geographer who entered Portuguese service late in the fifteenth century. Behaim was the maker of the oldest known globe map, which he constructed in 1492; unfortunately it was instantly obsolete, since it showed only imaginary islands between Europe and Asia. Historians investigating Pigafetta's statement have suggested that Behaim may have made some later map or globe, prior to his death in 1507, which took account of Jacques' discoveries, but no such work has ever been discovered. What Pigafetta may have meant was the globe of Johannes Schöner of Nuremberg, fashioned in 1515 and still in existence, which does show a strait, though in too high a latitude; or, as one biographer has suggested, Magellan did see a map of Behaim's in the royal archives that showed the strait, and purloined it years later when he was planning his westward voyage.

However he came by his faith in a strait, it became an obsession with him after his fall from grace in 1514. The accepted geography of the time still spoke of a *Terra Australis Incognita* sprawling across the bottom of the world; Dias, in 1488, had lopped away the lobe of that imagined continent thought to join with Africa, but belief in a southern continent continuous with South America remained alive. Only via a strait, then, could sailors get west of the land mass that stretched to the south pole.

But if Magellan did succeed in finding his way westward through the hypothetical strait in a Spanish ship, what good would that be to him or to Spain? Did the Moluccas not lie in Portugal's half of the globe?

He was quite certain that they did not. For one thing, the pope's decree was hazy: no one had ever decided whether the line of demarcation extended through the poles and around the far side of the globe, or simply cut across the Atlantic at the stipulated 370 leagues west of the Azores. That line, it had finally been determined, lay along the meridian of 46° West, and if continued around the world would run along 134° East. Spanish and Portuguese diplomats had pondered the matter of continuation in a vague, harried way since 1494 without arriving at a definite conclusion. Perhaps it had been the pontiff's intention simply to compel Portugal to sail east to the Indies and Spain to sail west, without putting a specific boundary on their Asian spheres of dominion. It was a moot point just then, anyway, since with the primitive methods of calculating longitudes then in use nobody had been able to decide the precise location of the meridian of 134°E.

Magellan was then one of the very few Europeans who had been anywhere near that meridian. He had certainly been at Malacca, close to 100°E., and it appears quite probable that in 1512 he sailed as far east as the Moluccas or the Philippines, which lie between 120° and 130°E., roughly. Magellan had concluded that the Spice Islands lay right along the pope's continued line, and felt sure that most if not all of the valuable islands were east of 134°E., thus falling in Spain's half of the world. If so, the ironies of the Treaty of Tordesillas were multiplied; for by that treaty João II of Portugal had succeeded in having the papal line moved westward by 270 leagues. The same negotiation that had given Portugal Brazil, said Magellan, had also robbed her of the Spice Islands. (As it turned out, Magellan was wrong, and the 134th meridian passes to the east of the Spice Islands, but that remained to be proven in 1514.)

In arriving at his theories on the existence of an American strait and on the location of the Moluccas, Magellan had the aid and encouragement of a very odd individual, the astronomer Ruy Faleiro. They had known one another as pages to the court, years before; they had studied navigation together in the pages' school; and, while Magellan had chosen the active life of a mariner, Faleiro had become a scholar, mastering the intricacies of the movements of the planets, the higher realms of mathematics, the advanced theory of celestial navigation. It was Faleiro's ambition to become Portugal's Astronomer Royal, but Manoel could not bear to have him about the court, for he was something of a madman, with burning eyes and strange ways of speech, and was said to be in league with the powers of darkness. Frustrated, Faleiro retired to Oporto, where, supporting himself by casting horoscopes, he produced an elaborate system of formulas for computing longitudes.

Magellan encountered this brilliant but deranged man after his own disgrace at court, and examined with great care Faleiro's world globe, on which he had marked the longitudes according to his new system. From Magellan, Faleiro drew details of the islands east of Malacca, and, thus reassuring one another, they came to the conclusion that the Spice Islands lay on the Spanish side of the pope's line. By the summer of 1515 Magellan was seeking introductions to Spanish authorities, so that he could enroll in the service of Spain, impart his grand idea to King Ferdinand, and thwart Manoel by triumphantly annexing the Moluccas for Spain.

Then came a considerable blow: Magellan learned that the Spaniards had independently arrived at conclusions identical to his and were about to launch an expedition westward to the Moluccas. This enterprise had been entrusted to the Pilot Major of Spain, Juan Díaz de Solís, a disaffected Portuguese formerly known as João Dias de Solis. As early as 1512, Solís had won from King Ferdinand the commission to round the Cape of Good Hope, visit Ceylon, and take possession of the "Island of Maluco [the Moluccas] which lies within our demarcation," continuing on to Sumatra, Burma, and China. This voyage never took place, probably because the Spanish did not really dare to poach on the eastward route to Asia, but within a few years Spain was ready to get to "Maluco" by going west. Solís sailed at the head of three caravels on October 8, 1515. He touched the Brazilian coast at several points, and in February 1516 he came to the great mouth of the Plata, naming it "El Mar Dulce," "The Fresh-water Sea." It appeared to be the desired westward passage, but while exploring the "strait," the Spaniards were set upon by hostile Indians, who killed Solís and most of his men. Some of the survivors returned to Spain and made known what Cristóbal Jacques and others had observed more than a decade before: that south of Brazil the coast of South America trends westward, which put that part of the continent definitely on the Spanish side of the line. Some men drew from this fact the interesting possibility that, if the continent kept on trending westward, it might come to an end somewhere in the south, as Africa had, and permit navigation around its tip. But Solís had sailed farther south than the most southerly point of Africa, and still the mainland continued; Magellan went on believing that the only reliable way through the continent was via a strait, and that that strait had been found by one of Cristóbal de Haro's ships about 1503.

The failure of the Solís expedition created a new opportunity for Magellan. Powerful forces in Spain still were interested in reaching the Spice Islands by way of the Atlantic, and Magellan set about the slow, intricate process of bringing himself to the attention of those who might sponsor his project.

6

Juan Rodríguez de Fonseca, the Bishop of Burgos, was the most important of those who wished a westward voyage —indeed, one of the most important men in Spain. Fonseca came from one of the wealthy old feudal families of northern Spain, and had risen in the Church hierarchy as a matter of inherited position. His acquisition of religious authority was accompanied by a steady advance in political power, so that, by the last decade of the fifteenth century, he was one of the key figures in the administration of Ferdinand and Isabella. He helped bring Columbus to the notice of Queen Isabella and was involved in the preparations for Columbus' expedition; but he quarreled with Columbus, whose fame he envied, and was instrumental in causing the harassment that made the great explorer's last years so troublesome. As Spain extended her sway through the New World, Fonseca took charge of the bureaucracy that operated the new possessions; he organized the Casa de Antillas, Spain's counterpart to Portugal's Casa da India, and by 1511 had received from King Ferdinand the title of Chancellor of the Indies. Arrogant, avaricious, fond of power, the bishop was unable to tolerate challenges to his own ever-growing authority. He brought about the downfall of Balboa, the discoverer of the Pacific, in 1513; six years later, Fonseca would attempt to have Hernán Cortés, Mexico's conqueror, assassinated.

The deaths of Queen Isabella in 1503 and King Ferdinand in 1516 left Bishop Fonseca in a commanding situation. The thrones of Aragon and Castile—in effect, the throne of Spain—had passed to Ferdinand's adolescent grandson, Charles, with the elderly Cardinal Ximenes as regent. Fonseca, a far more vigorous man than the cardinal, outmaneuvered the regent in every way, and Ximenes' death in 1517 might well have been due to poison administered at Fonseca's suggestion. In any case, upon the death of Ximenes, Fonseca pocketed a few more official posts, made himself virtual dictator of Spain, and looted the royal treasury as he pleased while the young King Charles was kept in careful ignorance.

Fonseca had backed Juan de Solís in his disastrous expedition of 1515 in search of a westward route to the Moluccas. Upon news of Solís' death, the bishop had begun to look for another commander to make the attempt, for he believed that Spain would be shut out of the spice trade for all time unless access to the East Indies were attained before the Portuguese established a monopoly there. Pope Leo X, in 1514, had issued the bull *Praecelsae Devotionis*, giving papal blessing to the Portuguese conquests in the Orient, and in view of the changed picture at Rome, Fonseca felt the increased urgency of founding Spanish outposts in the East.

The bishop consulted in 1516 with Diogo Barbosa, one of the many Portuguese living in Spain. As we have seen, Barbosa had explored the coast of Brazil while still in King Manoel's service and had become convinced of the existence of a westward strait. After marrying a Spanish heiress, he had settled in Spain and had come into possession of the influential post of Director of the Arsenal of Seville; he enjoyed Fonseca's confidence and, in his 14 years of Spanish citizenship, had attained great power in the country. Barbosa proposed as commander of the bishop's new westward expedition one of his own countrymen, the veteran captain João Serrão. After a distinguished career in Portuguese India, Serrão had come back to Lisbon about the same time as Magellan and had received an equally discouraging welcome from King Manoel; renaming himself Juan Serrano, he had crossed the border into Spain and accepted a commission as pilot in the royal navy.

Juan Serrano, though, did not feel competent to undertake the quest of the Moluccas. He nominated instead his cousin, Ferdinand Magellan, who—next to his own brother Francisco Serrão—was the man most familiar with Moluccan waters. The nomination was seconded by Barbosa's son, Duarte, who had known Magellan well in India. The elder Barbosa proposed Magellan's name to Bishop Fonseca, who knew nothing at all of Magellan but who was willing to accept Barbosa's recommendation. It was time now to let Magellan know of all this: Duarte Barbosa, who, like his father, had been living in Spain, made a secret visit to Oporto to find out if Magellan would accept the assignment. Magellan, of course, accepted most readily, making only the stipulation that his friend, the wild-eyed astronomer Ruy Faleiro, be taken into the project as an equal partner. Duarte Barbosa, aware of Faleiro's high reputation as an astronomer and unaware of his personal eccentricities, agreed to this and told Magellan to come to Seville as soon as possible to consummate the arrangement. The expedition was not yet a certainty; Fonseca, powerful as he was, would have to win the backing of King Charles and certain Spanish officials before the ships could go to sea, and there was also the little matter of financing the venture. But the prospects were good. In the autumn of 1517, Magellan, accompanied by his Malayan slave Henrique, left Portugal behind forever and took ship for Spain.

Bishop Fonseca was not the only great man of his day interested in finding the western route to the true Indies, though. The wily Cristóbal de Haro, Portuguese agent for the vast Fugger interests, had independently been seeking the same thing since the turn of the century; and now, when all roads suddenly led to Spain, Haro's schemes and Magellan's destiny converged.

Haro, though a Spaniard, had been the Fugger man in Lisbon since 1486. He had not been able to win a place in the social life of King João II's court, probably because he came from a family of Christianized Jews, but his skill as a financier had given him access to the inner circles of the Portuguese administration. Haro had invested Fugger money in the early voyages to Africa and around the Cape of Good Hope and had been consolidating his position when João II died in 1495. Under King Manoel, Haro's situation had been more precarious; at first excluded from influence by Florentine rivals, he had regained his earlier importance by the sheer power of Fugger gold. Not only did Haro and the Fuggers underwrite the costs of the royal spice fleets, but they developed their own export-import organization, with fifteen swift square-rigged *naos* to fetch spices from India. The licensing agreement with the royal spice monopoly gave Manoel 40 percent of the gross value of the cargoes Haro's ships brought to Lisbon; but there still was ample room for profit on the remainder, since it was sold through the Fugger distribution network operating out of Antwerp at a high retail markup.

As the wealth of India flooded into Lisbon after Albuquerque's conquests, Manoel grew independent of the Fuggers and resented the resale profits that Haro and his employers were making. He wished to squeeze Haro out altogether and gain complete control over all imports from the Orient. From about 1510 onward, then, Manoel's attitude toward Haro grew steadily cooler; the great merchant found himself unwelcome at court, hedged about by new restrictive rules, and harried in his attempts to dispatch fleets to India. It was not difficult for him to see that his days in Lisbon were numbered, and so he revived his interest in a project that had first drawn his attention in 1501: finding a western route to the Indies. Anticipating the time when he would have to shift his allegiance to Spain, Haro now began to work toward the discovery of a route which would give him access to the Spice Islands through waters that were safely Spanish.

In the spring of 1514 he sent a mariner named João of Lisbon on a secret voyage to America. João, anticipating Solís by more than a year, found the mouth of the Plata (which another Haro captain, Cristóbal Jacques, had probably discovered in 1503) and sailed up the huge estuary a short way. It seemed to João, as it had to Jacques and would to Solís, that the Plata was the westward strait. But he could not linger, for he was on the Spanish side of the demarcation line, and Haro had expressly ordered him not to get caught trespassing. Hastily he took a latitude reading, charted the "strait" at 20°S., which was nearly 20° north of its true position, and made for the Portuguese waters off Brazil. When he returned to Lisbon, João told of his adventures not only to Cristóbal de Haro but to Magellan, whom he had met during the Moroccan campaign of 1513. João expressed the belief that the Moluccas could be reached through his supposed strait, or, failing that, that South America undoubtedly tapered off at the tip after the manner of Africa and could be bypassed by a voyage into high southerly latitudes.

Cristóbal de Haro was still pondering this information in 1516 when King Manoel commenced a series of overtly hostile actions designed to break his hold on the India trade. A fleet of Haro's ships, homeward bound laden with spices, was seized in one of the ports of southern India and relieved of all its cargo by the Portuguese governor of the port, who sent the ships empty to Portugal. Clearly this had been done at Manoel's orders; but when Haro protested the outrage to the king, he received such a silkily contemptuous response that he knew he would have no recourse there. A little recklessly, Haro outfitted a new fleet of seven *naos* and sent it eastward, only to learn that his ships had been attacked and destroyed by royal caravels off the coast of West Africa, exactly as though they had been intruders of some alien nationality. Now matters were beyond repair; fearing for his life, Haro put into operation a plan of escape devised some time before, and fled by horse through the mountainous back country to Spain, where Fugger power had been growing while it had been ebbing in Portugal. Charles, the new young Spanish king, was the grandson on his father's side of Maximilian of Habsburg, the Holy Roman Emperor, and Emperor Maximilian was deeply indebted to Jakob Fugger. The

Fuggers had extended their credit also to Maximilian's late son, who briefly had been King Philip I of Castile, and their coffers were at the service now of King Charles. Cristóbal de Haro could be certain of a friendly reception in Spain.

He went at once to Seville, to the magnificent palace of Juan de Fonseca, the Bishop of Burgos. Breathless, haggard, not even pausing to rest after his wild flight, Haro demanded an audience with the mighty bishop and informed a startled Fonseca that he was here to seek refuge from Manoel. He offered Fonseca his skills and his connections, and also the information concerning a South American strait that he had gathered, however hazily, from the explorations of Cristóbal Jacques and João of Lisbon. Haro knew, of course, of Fonseca's desire to attain that strait and reach the Moluccas for Spain; and now Haro himself, to recoup his fortunes, needed to reopen his spice trade from the Spanish side. Before long, the two men were in league for the same goal. Fonseca had Haro's assurance that a strait existed, and Haro had learned that Fonseca was already well along in planning a westward voyage.

Commanded by whom? Haro asked.

Why, by a certain Portuguese, was the reply: one Magellan, recommended by the Barbosas and Juan Serrano.

Haro knew of Magellan, at least by repute, and what he knew did not please him. The little man was said to be an excellent navigator and a forceful captain, but he was also supposed to be headstrong, quarrelsome, difficult. Haro knew that Magellan had had some difficulties with King Manoel, but that in itself was nothing unusual; everyone, Haro included, had been having difficulties with Manoel. Much more serious were the reports that Magellan had come into conflict with Albuquerque and other leaders of the Indian conquest, and that he had been involved in court-martial proceedings in

Morocco. Regarding the risks of employing Magellan as too severe, Haro put forth the name of yet another refugee from Portugal, Estevão Gomes, whom Fonseca had earlier considered and rejected for the assignment ultimately given to Solís. Fonseca mistrusted Gomes, for he had been told by Diogo Barbosa that Gomes was treacherously maintaining a secret correspondence with King Manoel; but upon Haro's earnest endorsement, the bishop agreed to hire him in place of Magellan. Fonseca insisted, though, that a young courtier named Juan de Cartagena be named co-commander with Gomes. Juan de Cartagena was Fonseca's protégé and heir; he was regarded euphemistically as Fonseca's nephew, but it was generally assumed, probably correctly, that the "nephew" was actually the bishop's illegitimate son.

By the early weeks of 1518, Fonseca and Haro had reached agreement: Magellan was to be discarded, and Fonseca would now seek royal approval for the Gomes-Cartagena expedition to the Moluccas.

This quiet arrangement casually torpedoed the elaborate project that Magellan and the Barbosas had been constructing for the past four months. Arriving at Seville from Portugal on October 20, 1517, Magellan had taken lodging with Diogo Barbosa. Very shortly, he was betrothed to Barbosa's daughter, Beatriz, and their marriage, celebrated in December of that year, made the thirty-seven-year-old Magellan a wealthy man at last, for Beatriz came to him with the impressive dowry of 600,000 maravedis.* (The swiftness with which the marriage took place argues that it had been arranged some time before Magellan's departure from Portugal.) With the aid of his new father-in-law, Magellan made formal application to the Casa de Antillas for permis-

---

* The maravedi was a copper coin valued at 375 to the gold ducat of 3.5 grams.

sion to lead a royal Spanish fleet westward to the Moluccas by a secret route. He would, he added, prove by this voyage that the Spice Islands lay on the Spanish side of the line of demarcation.

Neither Magellan nor Diogo Barbosa expected the permission to be granted, for their undisclosed patron, Bishop Fonseca, had not yet chosen to show his hand. Magellan received a routine interview before a board of examiners at the Casa de Antillas; the interviewers, though impressed by Magellan's credentials and by his connection with the Barbosa family, lost interest in his plan when he refused, upon interrogation, to disclose the nature of his secret route. Magellan had promised Ruy Faleiro—who was still in Portugal at this time—that he would mention to no one the existence of the westward strait. When Magellan insisted on keeping his proposed route to himself, the Casa de Antillas rejected the application.

However, one of the official examiners guessed what Magellan's secret must be and saw profit in it for himself. He was Juan de Aranda, a businessman who had enjoyed good relations both with the Barbosas and with Bishop Fonseca. Sending for Magellan, Aranda hinted that he knew Magellan's westward route and asked to be allowed to participate in the organizing of the voyage. Aranda offered to use his influence at court in persuading King Charles to overrule the Casa de Antillas and permit Magellan to undertake the Moluccas journey. There were two possible methods of financing such a venture. The king might choose to put up all the money for the expedition himself; the voyage then would be made for the royal account, and those who actually undertook the journey would receive a stated percentage of the royal profits as reward for their efforts. As an alternative possibility, the king might grant a license for private investors to equip the expedition; under this scheme, the investing syndicate would keep most of the profit, paying the king a share of the proceeds as the price of his permission.

Magellan had begun to lose faith in the patronage of Bishop Fonseca, a remote and inaccessible figure who had not, in any event, treated Columbus and other explorers very gently. Realizing how useful Aranda could be, Magellan transferred his hopes to him, took him into his confidence, and within a month, after checking of references on both sides, expanded the partnership to include Aranda. The extent of Aranda's participation in the expenses and in the profits of the enterprise would be determined later, when Ruy Faleiro had finished his business in Portugal and come to Spain.

Faleiro arrived at Seville late in 1517 and at once expressed his displeasure at the idea of taking in another partner. The dark-souled astronomer, whose sanity evidently was under heavy stress, saw no point in sharing the wealth of the Moluccas with even so helpful a man as Aranda promised to be. But he erupted in uncontrollable fury when he realized that Aranda was privy to the hypothesis of a South American strait. Disregarding the fact that rumors of such a strait had been circulating for more than a decade and that he himself had no more reliable knowledge of the strait's existence than anyone else, Faleiro berated Magellan as though he had given away the secret of transmuting lead into gold. Whether Magellan had told Aranda about the route, or whether Aranda had merely guessed it, we do not know; but Faleiro regarded himself as betrayed. The dispute was furious, and Aranda looked on in alarm as the wholly irrational Faleiro launched a noisy tirade.

It had been Aranda's plan for the three partners to proceed together to the city of Valladolid, where Bishop Fonseca was then in attendance upon the new King Charles, and obtain permission for their private venture to the Moluccas. Faleiro would not travel with Aranda, however, and so they journeyed separately to Valladolid, although the sulking Faleiro was willing to let Aranda pay his expenses. Late in January 1518 they met in an inn outside Valladolid. Here, disregarding Faleiro's belligerent outbursts, Aranda finally stated the terms of his participation. If he succeeded in helping Magellan win royal permission for a private venture to the Moluccas, Aranda wanted the right to invest in the voyage for his own risk and profit. If, on the other hand, King Charles became interested in financing the scheme himself, Aranda wanted one-fifth of the partnership's ultimate profits as a reward for his aid.

Faleiro exploded once more, refusing to discuss any arrangement that would cut Aranda in on the proceeds. Magellan, remaining calm, simply declared that a one-fifth interest was rather high, considering that Aranda would be staking no capital but merely providing political influence, and he offered a one-tenth share instead. They came to no bargain that day; Aranda rode on alone into Valladolid, leaving Magellan and Faleiro to talk things over together.

In Valladolid, Aranda discovered some distressing news: Cristóbal de Haro had already spoken to the king and his councillors about a voyage to the Moluccas under the command of Estevão Gomes, who had been one of his pilots in Portugal. Worse, the Casa de Antillas had given its approval to the Gomes expedition; worse yet, a royal commission had been drawn up for Gomes under date of February 10, 1518. Aranda suspected, although he did not have proof of it, that Bishop Fonseca had lost interest in the Magellan-Barbosa proposal and was somehow involved in the intrigues of Haro.

With their chances of any sort of profit rapidly evaporating, Faleiro and Magellan quickly came to terms with

Aranda, giving him a one-eighth share of their proceeds. A contract to this effect was signed on February 23; significantly, Magellan used the Spanish and not the Portuguese form of his name in signing. Now Aranda returned to Valladolid to learn if anything could be salvaged. He attempted to see Fonseca and failed, for the bishop and Haro were quite busy on behalf of their own project, involving Gomes and Fonseca's "nephew," Juan de Cartagena. Fonseca was preparing to approach King Charles about the voyage, and at the moment he was employed in winning the support of his three companions on the four-man junta that ruled Spain in the king's name.

Fonseca felt that he could handle his fellow regents, but he was uncertain about the king, who was unpredictable and given to asserting his royal prerogatives at awkward moments. The Spanish monarch was just eighteen years old that February and barely into his extraordinary, improbable career as ruler of most of western Europe and the Spanish possessions in the New World. His father, who had succeeded Isabella on the throne of Castile, had died, perhaps of poison, in 1506 when Charles was six years old, leaving him heir to Castile and a variety of properties in France and the Netherlands. His mother, Joanna of Castile, was insane, and so his grandfather Ferdinand acted as regent for his Spanish domains, and his grandfather Maximilian as regent for those elsewhere in Europe. Upon Ferdinand's death in 1516, Charles became King Charles I of Aragon and—technically sharing the throne with his demented mother—also King Charles I of Castile. Thus in effect he was King Charles I of Spain, and thereafter the thrones of Aragon and Castile would always be united in the same person. (By 1519, after the death of Maximilian, Charles would arrange to have himself elected Holy Roman Emperor, mortgaging himself heavily to the Fuggers in order to bribe the electors. Thus he would come by the title by which he is best known to posterity, Emperor Charles V. But it was as Charles I of Spain, not as Charles V of the Holy Roman Empire, that he heard proposals for a westward voyage to the Spice Islands.)

Charles had been reared in Burgundy and Flanders, and when he arrived in Spain in September 1517, he cut a strange figure: a solemn, ugly boy who could barely speak Spanish, knew nothing of the intricacies of the Spanish court, and seemed unlikely ever to be able to exert authority over the powerful nobles who had built little empires for themselves during King Ferdinand's last years. He was fortunate in the regent Ferdinand had chosen for him, though, the capable and devoted Cardinal Ximenes. But Ximenes was dead within two months of Charles' arrival in Spain, and power passed to a committee of four, three of them rascals and the fourth a simple, pious cleric.

Fonseca was the dominant member of the group, and the only Spaniard. He had collected so many high offices during the reign of Ferdinand and Isabella that he moved naturally into the regency upon the death of Ximenes; no one else had any clear idea how the government of Spain was run. His three colleagues were all imported from the Netherlands by Charles. One, the Flemish nobleman Guillaume de Croy, Lord of Chièvres, had been Charles' tutor; he became Lord Chancellor of Spain. Another, Jean le Sauvage, a follower of Chièvres, was named Spain's treasurer. The third, Adrian Cardinal Dedel, was a placid Dutch priest, later to become Pope Adrian VI. He alone remained virtuous while Fonseca, Chièvres, and Sauvage engaged in plundering Spain through the sale of privileges, the confiscation of land, and the taking of bribes. During his first twelve months in office, Chièvres was able to smuggle a million ducats—some 15,000,000 dollars in modern money—from Spain to Flanders, shipping it aboard Antwerp-bound Fugger ships hidden in bales of wood, bundles of hide, and casks of wine or olive oil. Since Chièvres and Sauvage, too, were thus dependent on Fugger complicity for their depredations, Fonseca had no difficulty in getting them to approve Cristóbal de Haro's project for a Gomes-Cartagena voyage. But Cardinal Adrian objected, citing the pope's bull of 1514 by which Portugal had won the exclusive right to exploit the East. His objections were overcome by the simple procedure of bringing the voyage to the king's attention while the cardinal was absent from court.

The three other junta members brought Cristóbal de Haro and Estevão Gomes before King Charles. Charles, who had borrowed heavily from the Fuggers in the past and was contemplating further loans, gave Haro a courteous reception but was strangely cool to the Moluccas project. Gomes was allowed to present the idea, and put it forward virtually as an act of piracy against Portugal. Despite some suave and hasty patching over by Haro, the king could not see the long-term benefits that would accrue to Spain by stealing the spice trade from Portugal, and regarded the whole enterprise as a distasteful raid on the legitimate property of his neighboring monarch. Relations between Spain and Portugal were then fairly friendly, and through a curious turn of events King Charles and King Manoel were about to become brothers-in-law. Charles' elder sister, Eleanor, who was twenty, had been betrothed to Manoel's son, Prince João. In 1517 Manoel's thirty-five-year-old queen had died in childbirth, and Manoel had announced his intention of abdicating in João's favor. But the crown prince had behaved boorishly, letting the courtiers know that he felt the abdication had come none too soon; and Manoel had taken an astounding revenge, first by deciding to remain on the throne after all, then by terminating João's engagement to Eleanor and, at the age of fifty-one, marrying his son's young fiancée himself. This grotesque and scandalous reversal caused dismay throughout the courts of Europe; but King Charles, who knew that empires were built through royal marriages, was as willing to give Eleanor to King Manoel as to Prince João, and wished to do nothing now that would jeopardize the forthcoming nuptials. Once the king's disapproval of the Molucca voyage was evident, Haro and Gomes abandoned their petition and withdrew.

Haro was too deep into the project to let it collapse now. The blunt-spoken, crude Gomes had failed to capture the royal imagination; but perhaps another man might. Bishop Fonseca, equally eager to retrieve the venture, thought once more of Magellan. Juan de Aranda was haunting Valladolid, trying to serve as Magellan's advocate before the court; Fonseca and Haro met with Aranda, let him know that there was still a chance for Magellan, and shortly Magellan and Faleiro found themselves in the presence of Fonseca himself. The bishop listened carefully, impressed more by the burning intensity of Magellan's personality than by the details of his proposals; Chancellor Chièvres likewise met the little navigator and was taken by him; Treasurer Sauvage added his approval. As for Cardinal Adrian, Magellan and Faleiro lectured him so glibly and persuasively on longitudes that he came to believe the Spice Islands must surely be on the Spanish side of the papal line, and so withdrew his opposition.

Artfully Chièvres coached Magellan for his audience with King Charles, telling him to stress his long service overseas, his experience as a mariner, the wounds he had suffered in righteous combat against the heathen, and especially the fact that he had come home poor after seven years in the East, a tribute to his selflessness. Magellan also was warned to make it clear that he was no renegade, but had received the formal permission of his sovereign, King Manoel, to seek employment in another country.

The interview went well. Magellan did not dread

Charles as he had dreaded Manoel, and he spoke powerfully and convincingly. Years of adversity had honed his spirit, laying bare the obsession at its core; it was clear to Charles that this lame little man was in some way extraordinary. After some preliminary conversation about Magellan's military experiences in Morocco, they began to speak of the Moluccas. Magellan did not make Gomes' mistake of gloating over the seizure of the spice trade from Portugal. Rather, he asserted that the Moluccas were rightfully Spanish and that the trespassers were the Portuguese. He quoted letters from Francisco Serrão, describing the beauties of the Moluccas, and cited the logs of voyagers to bolster his contentions. He introduced his slave Henrique, who staged a conversation in Malayan with a slave-girl from Sumatra—a pretty show which pleased the king. And—the most concrete demonstration—Magellan showed the king a globe of the world, fashioned by somber Faleiro. A few days earlier, Magellan had displayed the globe for Chancellor Chièvres; the Dominican friar Bartolomé de Las Casas—later famous for his defense of the human rights of American Indians—was in the chancellor's office when Magellan and Bishop Fonseca arrived, and wrote, "Magellan had a well painted globe on which the whole world was depicted, and on it he indicated the route he proposed to take, saying that the strait was left purposely blank so that no one should anticipate him. . . . Speaking with Magellan, I asked him what way he planned to take, and he answered that he intended to go by Cape Saint Mary, which we call the Río de la Plata, and from thence to follow up the coast until he hit upon the strait. But suppose you do not find any strait by which you can go into the other sea? I asked. He replied that, if he did not find any strait, he would go the way the Portuguese took. . . . This Fernando de Magalhanes must have been a man of courage, valiant in both his thoughts and in undertaking great things, although he was not of imposing presence, since he was small in stature and did not appear to be much."

This passage from Las Casas is revealing in several important ways: it shows that Magellan was aware of Solís' basic error and expected to find some strait other than the Plata, and it indicates that, if South America were impassable altogether, he was willing to go eastward to the Moluccas in violation of Portugal's rights. But when Magellan took the globe to King Charles, he said as little as possible about the strait, and nothing at all about turning eastward; he expressed his confidence that he would get past South America, either by a strait or by rounding its still unknown southern tip, and went quickly on to the more comfortable topic of the longitude of the Spice Islands. Maximilian of Transylvania, King Charles' secretary, wrote that Magellan and Haro "both showed Caesar that though it was not yet quite sure whether the city of Malacca was within the confines of the Spaniards or of the Portuguese, because, as yet, nothing of the longitude had been clearly proved, yet it was quite plain that the Great Gulf [the South China Sea] and the people of Sinae [China] lay within the Spanish boundary. This too was held to be most certain, that the islands which they call the Moluccas, in which all spices are produced, and are thence exported to the city of Malacca, lay within the Spanish western division, and that it was possible to sail there; and that spices could be brought thence to Spain more easily, at less expense, and cheaper, as they come direct from their native place."

King Charles was convinced. Fonseca, Chièvres, and Sauvage all had praised Magellan highly; Cardinal Adrian at least did not oppose him; Ruy Faleiro's geographical theories sounded valid; Cristóbal de Haro, whose judgment Charles admired and whose financial resources he needed, was now wholly in favor of Magellan, even though he had been an advocate of Estevão Gomes only a few weeks earlier.

Above all, Magellan himself radiated the unmistakable charisma of a heaven-blessed discoverer. The royal assent was given, and very quickly a contract for the voyage was being drawn—so quickly, in fact, that some of the prime movers behind Magellan found themselves shut out.

The king, suddenly enthusiastic about a Moluccas belonging to Spain, decided to finance the voyage himself in the hope of making maximum profit. Though he was, as usual, hard-pressed for cash, he preferred to be the sole investor in the voyage, giving Magellan a cut of the profits, rather than simply to license a venture to be made with other people's capital, taking a share himself. The one way, he bore all of the financial risk and stood to make 80 percent of the profit; the other, he put up no cash, but would take in 20 percent of the eventual yield. That Charles chose the more speculative but also far more profitable option is a measure of his confidence in Magellan's success. The king would be the heaviest loser if Magellan failed to attain the Spice Islands.

The contract was signed on March 22, 1518. Its carefully worded preamble specified that Magellan and Faleiro, both natives of Portugal, wished to render Charles "a great service in the limits which belong to Us in the ocean of Our demarcation." The following remarkable terms—devised by Magellan and Faleiro and agreed to by the king without much serious consideration—were outlined:

1. Magellan and Faleiro were granted the right to explore the Pacific in the area belonging to the King of Spain by papal decree. As a reward for their labors, they would have the exclusive use of their route and their discoveries for a period of ten years, and others wishing to exploit that territory would have first to give them the option of fitting out another expedition themselves.

2. Magellan and Faleiro undertook not to trespass on the territories belonging to the King of Portugal.

3. Magellan and Faleiro would receive from the king five percent of the net revenues, after all expenses, derived from lands discovered by them. They were also to have the title of *adelantado* (governor) of such lands. These titles would be hereditary and would remain in the families of Magellan and Faleiro so long as their heirs were Spanish citizens and married Spanish wives.

4. On subsequent voyages to the Spice Islands, Magellan and Faleiro would be permitted to carry trade goods of Spanish manufacture to the value of one thousand ducats a year. On the spices or other goods that they purchased with this merchandise they would pay a duty of no more than five percent upon importation into Spain.

5. If they should discover more than six islands, they could choose any two beyond those six, taking as their own one-fifteenth of the revenues therefrom.

6. The king granted to Magellan and Faleiro a twenty-percent share in the net profits of the cargo of this first voyage.

7. The king promised to equip five ships, two of 130 tons each, two of 90 tons, and one of 60 tons. He would provide crews, supplies, and armaments sufficient for a two-year voyage and for 234 persons, including captains and officers.

8. If either Magellan or Faleiro should die, the surviving partner was to carry out all the terms of the contract.

"You have my royal word that I protect you, as I hereby give the signature of my name," the agreement concluded. "Valladolid, on the 22nd of March, 1518.

I

the king"

7

Magellan and Faleiro had every reason to be delighted with this contract. If their voyage succeeded, they would become lords of the Pacific, proprietors of a vast new domain, owners of a five-percent interest in the revenues of the Spanish East Indies. True, they would by prior agreement have to give one-eighth of their take to Juan de Aranda and would also have to reward such early backers as Diogo and Duarte Barbosa, but what remained to them would still be immense. The only ones who appeared shut out of the spoils were the two men who had done the most to secure the king's approval: Bishop Fonseca and Cristóbal de Haro.

They had agreed to the hasty contract because they wanted to have the king's signature on some sort of formal document before his interest in the voyage waned, but they had no intention of letting Magellan and Faleiro reap such lordly rewards. Haro's backing of Magellan had been purely expedient from the start; he continued to feel that the Portuguese seaman was too independent-minded to be useful, especially now that King Charles had awarded him such magnificent terms, greater in potential value than anything bestowed on Vasco da Gama or Albuquerque. In Haro's eyes, such men as Magellan were employees, mere naval personnel, and not to be handed empires. As for Faleiro, he seemed to Haro a lunatic, dangerous and disreputable. Bishop Fonseca also feared and disliked Faleiro, and, while he had nothing against Magellan, he preferred to divert the proceeds of the voyage to his own reputed nephew, Juan de Cartagena. Therefore Fonseca and Haro conspired to eliminate the two partners, either in Spain or on the high seas, so that the profits of the venture would fall into other hands. The hereditary aspects of the grants were of no great concern, for Faleiro was a bachelor, and, though Magellan's wife was now pregnant, an infant heir would be no heir at all.

By a circuitous route, Haro and Fonseca moved their own men into positions of advantage. An attempt early in April to have Juan de Cartagena named co-commander, with rights equal to those of Magellan and Faleiro, failed to win the king's signature; but a week later Magellan agreed, at the urging of the bishop, to appoint Estevão Gomes as chief pilot of the fleet. Although Gomes was a distant relative of Magellan and was outwardly cordial toward him, he was privately disgruntled over losing command of the expedition and felt bitter jealousy on account of Magellan's sudden and unexpected rise to prominence. As a former employe of Cristóbal de Haro, Gomes was willing to listen to Haro's suggestions that Magellan be overthrown once the fleet was out to sea.

During the spring and summer of 1518, Magellan busied himself assembling his fleet, despite a notable lack of cooperation from the bureaucracy of the Casa de Antillas, which had been given the assignment of outfitting the ships. After a prodding from the king, the Casa de Antillas sent Juan de Aranda to Cádiz to purchase the vessels; he selected five elderly caravels that happened to be available, and sent them to the shipyards in Seville for repairs and overhauling. Duarte Barbosa journeyed to Bilbao, Spain's foundry city in the north, to acquire cannon, arms, and armor for the fleet. From there he went to Flanders to acquire rigging and other marine supplies. While these and other preparations were going forward, Fonseca and Haro were surreptitiously cutting away the liens on the voyage held by the various silent partners of Magellan and Faleiro. The first to fall was that of Diogo Barbosa, who had protested the appointment of Gomes, whom he disliked, as chief pilot. Fonseca outflanked the elder Barbosa by securing a royal letter warning sternly against any attempt to interfere with the selections of the Casa de Antillas. Recognizing a threat when he saw one, Barbosa withdrew from further involvement in the planning of the enterprise. Next, Fonseca dealt with Juan de Aranda, whose one-eighth interest in the profits of Magellan and Faleiro was an obstacle to the diversion of the venture's yield. When he discovered the existence of Aranda's contract with the two partners, Fonseca revealed it and denounced Aranda for making a clandestine agreement to his own profit while serving on the board that had control over the partners' petition. In October 1518 Aranda was suspended from his office and arraigned on a charge of using his position for his own gain. He came to trial before a hostile court the following June, described all his dealings with Magellan and Faleiro as well within the custom of the day—which they were—and asked for exoneration. At Bishop Fonseca's insistence, Aranda was strongly censured, and on July 2, 1519, a royal order was issued legally cancelling his contract with Magellan and Faleiro. Though he was neither fined nor imprisoned, Aranda's career was broken by this verdict, and he lost further influence at court. He was also out of pocket, as the hearings had revealed, the considerable sum of 1,500 ducats, which he had laid out for the expenses of his partners.

Shortly, Fonseca severed from the enterprise the touchy, quarrelsome, clearly deranged astronomer Ruy Faleiro. Faleiro had been nothing but trouble for everyone, including Magellan, since he had come to Spain, and it was quite obviously absurd to let such a man have the captaincy of a ship, let alone be allowed to serve as co-commander of the expedition. Faleiro's navigational skills were purely theoretical; he had never been aboard a ship except as a passenger. Practical seamanship was beyond him. With great guile, Fonseca incited Faleiro to demand sole custody of the royal banner to be carried by the captain-general of the armada. Magellan had no intention of relinquishing possession of this valuable symbol of authority, and soon the partners were quarreling tempestuously. The bishop now easily persuaded Magellan to petition the king for Faleiro's dismissal as co-commander, and for his replacement as captain of one ship by Juan de Cartagena. King Charles obligingly removed Faleiro from both posts; the astonomer was so far gone in madness at this point that he made no objections to remaining behind and even, coaxed by Fonseca, signed a paper giving up his share in the voyage, in return for the promised command of a non-existent second fleet supposedly going to follow Magellan's ships. Thus, to the surprise and relief of all, Faleiro dropped from the picture in the late summer of 1519.

Haro and Fonseca had been busy in other ways that year. The king had agreed to invest a stated sum, quite large, in outfitting the expedition. In his role as head of the Casa de Antillas, Bishop Fonseca requested that sum from Treasurer Sauvage. Sauvage replied that the treasury could not raise so much money, which was probably true, considering the extent of his and Chièvres' raids on it. Equipped with the deficiency certificate from Sauvage, the bishop told the king that he would have to admit outside investors, and Charles yielded. Cristóbal de Haro was given the assignment of underwriting a public subscription for one-fifth of the cost of the expedition. Haro put up most of the needed money himself; on behalf of the House of Fugger, he took an additional heavy share; Bishop Fonseca placed a large investment in the name of Juan de Cartagena; among the smaller investors, perhaps for the sake of keeping up appearances, was Duarte Barbosa. By this maneuver the conspirators got their wedge of potential profits, although the royal treasury still owned much the greater share of the venture.

To keep watch on the finances of the expedition, Fonseca inserted three of his own men as treasurer, accountant, and comptroller. Luis de Mendoza became treasurer, replacing one of Diogo Barbosa's friends. The comptrollership went to Antonio de Coca, who may have been the illegitimate son of the bishop's brother, or even of the bishop. Geronimo Guerra was chosen as accountant; he was termed the nephew and adopted son of the unmarried Cristóbal de Haro, but quite likely was Haro's illegitimate son. Luis de Mendoza, the treasurer, also received command of one vessel. Another captain selected at this time was Gaspar de Quesada, a friend of Juan de Cartagena. Three of the five ships, then, would be commanded by men secretly loyal to the bishop and Haro: Quesada, Cartagena, Mendoza. The fourth commander was to be Magellan's cousin, João Serrão, hispanicized as Juan Serrano; the fifth ship would, of course, be Magellan's.

Thus encircled by enemies, Magellan labored to ready his armada for departure. The conspirators did not plan to move against him until they were at sea, but another interested party was quite eager to keep the expedition from sailing at all. This was King Manoel, whose chagrin at seeing Magellan so suddenly important was immense. By the spring of 1518 it was open knowledge in Seville that two Portuguese were going to make a westward voyage to the Spice Islands, which they maintained were on the Spanish side of the demarcation. Portugal's ambassador in Spain, Alvaro da Costa, promptly communicated this to Manoel, whose first reaction was to scoff both at this tale of a western strait and at the thought that useless little Magellan might be the man to find it. Then he began to worry about the possibility that he had underestimated Magellan and that Spain might somehow snatch the Spice Islands from him. He asked Costa to speak to King Charles and to make strong representations against the voyage.

On September 28, 1518, Costa reported the results of

his conversation with the youthful monarch. Costa had declared that the proposed voyage would sorely mar the spirit of international amity that soon was to be solemnized by the marriage of King Manoel to Charles' sister. He spoke of Magellan and Faleiro as malcontents and renegades who meant only disservice to Charles, and begged the Spanish king to return them to Portugal. These blatant lies did not fool the king, who dismissed the ambassador by suggesting he talk to Cardinal Adrian. Adrian, though, was not available except in the presence of Bishop Fonseca, who vouched for the high character of the two Portuguese and advised Costa not to interfere with the voyage. In his letter to Manoel, Costa said that the only hope was to bribe Magellan to return to Portuguese service. Faleiro, he said, was unimportant: "I do not count him for much, for he is half crazy." The man who mattered was Magellan.

Manoel called an emergency meeting of his council. Yes, the royal advisers said: offer Magellan a bribe. If that failed, added the saintly Bishop of Lamego, then have him assassinated. The job of obstructing the expedition was given to Sebastian Alvares, the Portuguese consul at Seville.

Alvares did not think much of Magellan's chances. He visited the docks to see the five ships, and told Manoel, "They are very old and patched . . . and I would be sorry to sail even for the Canaries in them, for their ribs are as soft as butter." But Magellan, who had experienced both the discomforts of the tropics and the severity of the waves that rolled up out of the Antarctic toward the Cape of Good Hope, was rebuilding the vessels so they would withstand the extremes of climate, strengthening planks and ribs, caulking the seams with pitch, redesigning sails and rigging and decks, and adding heavy armaments in case Portuguese warships were encountered. Alvares therefore did his best to sabotage things. Late in October, while Magellan's flagship, the

Trinidad, was undergoing a refitting at Seville, Alvares came to the waterfront and observed that the only flags the ship was flying were four small banners bearing Magellan's coat of arms. As the ship's captain, he had the right to display his personal standard, though of course he intended to hoist the royal standard of Spain to its proper position of honor on the mainmast. The Spanish standard, though, had not yet come back from the flagmaker, who was repainting it, and so Magellan's flag flew alone. Alvares observed that the coat of arms of the Magellan family bore a certain well-known design emblematic of the King of Portugal. The presence of this emblem merely symbolized the status of the Magellans as members of the Portuguese nobility, but Alvares mischievously called together a crowd of loungers at the waterfront, showed them what he claimed was the Portuguese flag on the *Trinidad*, and worked them toward a riot. While the crowd tried to rip down the alien flags, a port official stupidly accused Magellan of treachery to Spain. Magellan, who had no time for fools, ordered the man off his deck; an attempt to arrest him followed, and a wild melee broke out. In touching off the absurd incident, Alvares hoped that someone would slay Magellan, and in fact Magellan was stabbed in the hand during the struggle; but when order was restored, Magellan took advantage of the episode to strengthen security precautions at the docks.

Alvares approached Magellan himself, trying to induce him to come back to Portugal, but neither promises of Manoel's royal favor nor grim warnings of the risks of the voyage produced any effect. A policy of bribing the four royal councillors of Spain to halt the expedition also failed. Chièvres and Sauvage both were in their final illnesses and beyond all concern with bribes and with Magellan; Cardinal Adrian was incorruptible; and Bishop Fonseca, though he would have been glad to take Portugal's money, was not about to stop an enterprise that meant riches for himself and fame for Juan de Cartagena. Alvares turned to minor harassment, bribing harbor police to look the other way while his agents pilfered the supplies being collected for the armada. His hope was to deceive Magellan into going to sea thinking his ships were well stocked, only to find himself short of essential stores at some critical time.

In September 1518 Beatriz Magellan produced an heir for the explorer, a boy named Rodrigo. In November, King Manoel consummated his controversial marriage to Eleanor of Habsburg, King Charles' sister; the following February, Charles sent a reassuring letter to his new brother-in-law, declaring that the Magellan fleet would remain wholly in the Spanish zone. This bland statement left Manoel enraged but helpless over the implied annexation of the Moluccas by Spain.

The lengthy preparations dragged on. Magellan paid fierce attention to detail, as though only by supervising every tiny aspect could he demonstrate that he was no longer a lame and obscure Portuguese mariner, but now captain-general of a Spanish fleet. He even helped to pack the boxes of dried provisions for the voyage, as Alvares found him doing one day when he came around for another attempt at bribery. In his planning, Magellan received the unwanted advice of King Charles, who sent him a voluminous document in which he naïvely outlined the conduct of the voyage as he imagined it should be. In 75 sections the king, who had never been a naval officer, instructed Magellan on the ways of manning boats, the proper techniques of dropping an anchor, the cleaning of pumps, the responsibilities of officers and men. The crew must neither swear nor gamble nor commit rapes when ashore; the captains of the ships must distribute rations fairly and pay kindly visits to the men on the sick list. Doubtless Magellan gave this tome the attention it deserved, and went on with his tasks.

He requisitioned a quantity of food so huge that it alarmed the officials of the Casa de Antillas and puzzled Sebastian Alvares. He asked rations for a two-year voyage: 21,383 pounds of ship's biscuit, or hardtack, 480 pounds of oil, 570 pounds of pickled meat, 1,120 pounds of cheese, 200 barrels of sardines, 238 dozen bundles of dried fish, and 1,700 pounds of dried fish in barrels. He took aboard stocks of lentils, peas, beans, honey, onions, garlic, rice, sugar, salt, marmalade, raisins, olives, and other goods. There were liberal supplies of wine. Fresh fruits and vegetables could be obtained in landfalls as they sailed; rain, it was hoped, would replenish the initial water supply; they could take fish and birds at sea. But why did Magellan want all this food? It took only a few weeks to sail to America; the journey through his supposed strait would surely require only a few weeks more; and, though no one had any idea of the size of the South Sea, it seemed reasonable to assume that it was no greater than the Atlantic. At worst, then, Magellan should need three or four months to reach the Moluccas, if that strait of his really existed. Some of the officials checking Magellan's accounts must have wondered whether he was bluffing about the strait, and therefore was overstocking his ships because he had no idea how he would reach the Indies, or how long it might take to find some navigable route.

Certainly the recruiting officers for Magellan's armada said nothing about the possibility of a two-year voyage. They held out the promise of a quick, easy journey to a warm land of cloves and pearls and rubies. Even so, getting men was difficult. Spain, like Portugal, had long suffered from chronic underpopulation. The discovery of the New World had already drained most of Spain's most adventurous mariners; an outbreak of the plague had recently thinned the ranks of those men who had stayed at home; and the risks of a voyage by an unknown route dampened the courage of the few available skilled seamen. The hardships of ocean life were well known: a diet of hardtack and pickled pork, exposure to chilling gales and tropical sun, cramped, wet quarters, the terrible isolation experienced on journeys that could last for years, above all the high mortality rates for men who entered surging seas in frail, clumsy vessels. The pay was poor, besides, and even one who collected a fat *quintalada*, or profit-sharing bonus, at journey's end would do no better than the man who had spent those years farming at home. Only 17 men of Seville cared to join the king's fleet, most of them young and inexperienced. To fill out his complement of more than 200 men, Magellan was forced to assemble an international crew.

In this he became involved in a political complication. Spain was full of veteran Portuguese sailors, many of whom Magellan had known in India, and quite naturally he turned to them now. Perhaps uneasy over the obvious hostility of some of his Spanish captains, Magellan wanted old friends and trusted companions about him, particularly as pilots and masters. (Aboard a typical Spanish ship of the early sixteenth century, the captain was usually an aristocrat with no specialized knowledge of seamanship, whose chief responsibility was to exert overall control over the direction of the voyage and to maintain discipline. Magellan and Juan Serrano, both experienced navigators, were exceptions to this rule; the three Spanish captains, Cartagena, Mendoza, and Quesada, were not. The second in command was the master, who understood navigation but whose main task was to hold executive control over the crew. The pilot, third in command, was in charge of navigation and took the daily observations by which the ship's course was plotted. The boatswain, fourth in a ship's hierarchy, supervised the crewmen working the sails and rigging.) Bishop Fonseca, unwilling to have Magellan go to sea with such a loyal cadre of compatriots, struck a cruel blow in June 1519: he induced King Charles to decree that no more than five men of Portuguese nationality could enroll in the fleet, and that these five could be only servants or pages. Magellan's protests must have been vigorous ones, for early in July the order was amended so that Magellan's five Portuguese could be of any rank. Thus such men as Duarte Barbosa, Magellan's brother-in-law, and Alvaro de Mesquita, a cousin of Magellan on his mother's side, were allowed to enroll, along with Estevão Gomes, whom Magellan falsely thought was his friend. The fourth and fifth permitted men were Juan Serrano and Magellan's own page. Most of the Portuguese pilots and masters, though, had to be dismissed.

The hiring went on slowly through the summer of 1519. About a dozen Basque seafarers signed up together, to Magellan's pleasure, for Basques were known as capable and industrious sailors. They arrived led by Juan Sebastian del Cano, or Elcano, a native of the Basque village of Guetaria. Cano, who was taken on as master of the ship to be commanded by Gaspar de Quesada, was only about thirty years old, but had already been captain of his own vessel, a merchant ship active in the slave trade with North Africa; he had lost his ship to creditors not long before, and was sailing with Magellan in the hope of recouping his fortunes. Technically he was in danger of imprisonment, for the men to whom he had been forced to sell his ship were foreigners, and it was against Spanish law to sell a ship to aliens. Cano's uncertain status with the law may have greatly influenced his decision to go to sea on so long a voyage as this promised to be.

Recruitment lagged after the arrival of the Basques, though, and Magellan tried once more to enlist Portuguese.

He announced to the Casa de Antillas that he interpreted the royal decree to mean he could hire only five Portuguese officers, but any number of ordinary seamen, and he proceeded to sign up more than 30. The Casa de Antillas, at Bishop Fonseca's orders, told him to discharge the Portuguese; Magellan's response was to seek an audience with King Charles, at which he won the right to enroll two dozen of his countrymen, 12 to be chosen by Magellan, 12 by the Casa de Antillas. With the tacit cooperation of the king, Magellan went beyond this and slipped 37 Portuguese into his crew—along with an unknown number of others who adopted Spanish names for the purpose of getting around the limitation. Thus this Spanish expedition was led by a Portuguese and had a solid phalanx of Portuguese among the crew.

Since the quality of Spanish and Portuguese artillerymen was not high, Magellan hired 15 gunners, who were mainly German, French, or Flemish. The master gunner, Andrew of Bristol, was the lone Englishman of the enterprise, though he was a naturalized Spanish citizen with a Spanish wife. Magellan picked up also 30 Italian seamen, 19 Frenchmen, and a scattering of Greeks, Negroes, Moors, and others.

Anticipating Portuguese attempts to attack his armada, Magellan obtained from the Casa de Antillas a hundred heavy steel suits of armor for his fighting men, and the same number of light breastplates for the sailors to wear as protection while they carried out their duties in the rigging during combat. The ships carried 60 crossbows, 50 matchlock arquebuses (then newly invented), and a good quantity of javelins, lances, pikes, and shields. From Bilbao had come 71 heavy artillery pieces. Aboard the flagship was a bergantym, an oar-propelled barge of the kind Magellan had found so useful in his service on the coast of East Africa in 1506; it was disassembled, with its parts numbered for swift reassembly. Then there were supplies: anvils, grindstones, forges, bellows, 89 lanterns, 50 spades and pickaxes, implements for masons and stonecutters to use for constructing a fortress in the Moluccas, extra rigging and canvas, nails, candles, fishing tackle, 13 anchors, drugs, medicines, salves. The records show that the navigators had six wooden quadrants, a wooden astrolabe made by Ruy Faleiro, 15 bronze-fitted wooden quadrants, six metal astrolabes, 37 compass needles, 18 hourglasses, six pairs of measuring compasses, and 23 charts, one by Faleiro.

For the account of the House of Fugger, the ships carried a cargo of flasks of quicksilver and copper bars for sale in the East, where such commodities were in strong demand; also in the hold were bales of textiles as trade goods and as gifts for Oriental monarchs: cotton, velvet, satin, fine laces and brocades. To barter for spices in the East Indies and to win the friendship of simple folk, Cristóbal de Haro added to the cargo some 20,000 small bells, 10,000 fishhooks, 900 cheap mirrors, 100 mirrors of a better grade, 5,000 German knives, and an assortment of beads, combs, brass and copper bracelets, and metal basins.

Despite the furtive interference of King Manoel's agents, the insolence and insubordination of the Spanish captains, and increasing harassment organized by Bishop Fonseca, Magellan brought the 18 months of preparation to their close in the late summer of 1519. King Charles, who in June had become the Emperor Charles V with the aid of Fugger money and who now seemed on his way toward turning the entire world into a Habsburg domain, had come to acquire a deep interest in the success of the venture and a corresponding admiration for Magellan, and had aided him invaluably in his battles with the bureaucracy and with those enemies of whose existence he was still unaware. Impatient to see the ships on their way, Charles arbitrarily set August 10,

1519, as the day of departure, whether the vessels were ready or not.

They were not ready, for the Portuguese malefactor Sebastian Alvares had intercepted much of the supplies before they reached the holds of Magellan's ships, and the shortages were discovered at the last minute, requiring a delay while replacements were loaded. Nevertheless, on August 10 the solemn High Mass of farewell was duly celebrated, elaborate ceremonies of blessing were enacted, and an official of Seville administered to Magellan an oath in which he swore allegiance to King Charles. Receiving the silken royal standard, Magellan stood by the altar while the four captains, the masters, and the pilots knelt before him to vow obedience to his orders. The king had delegated to Magellan the power of life and death over his men—"of the knife and the rope," as it was termed—which any naval commander held on the high seas. The officers acknowledged that power now, swearing "to follow the course ordered by him and to obey him in everything," although three of the four captains were secretly pledged to overthrow and slay him at sea. Don Antonio Pigafetta, the young Italian traveler who became the chief chronicler of the circumnavigation, noted in his journal at this time, "The captains hated him exceedingly, I do not know why unless because he was Portuguese and they Spanish."

When the festivities were concluded, the five ships hoisted anchor while drums and trumpets sounded and cannon roared; but they went downriver only 75 miles, to the port of San Lucar de Barrameda, where the Guadalquivir river empties into the Atlantic. There they remained another month while the supply shortages, so tardily discovered, were made up. During this time, Magellan executed his last will and testament. (An earlier will, dated 1504, is in existence, in which a then unmarried Magellan left his estate to his sister and her heirs. But a modern scholar has shown this to be an eighteenth-century forgery by claimants to Magellan's accrued legacy.) The genuine will of August 24, 1519, made no mention of Magellan's Portuguese property, which apparently he had forfeited by swearing allegiance to Spain. His present assets, including all benefits coming from his voyage, he left to his infant son, Rodrigo, and his legitimate heirs, with provision for the unborn child Beatriz Magellan was carrying. He also made bequests to his sister, Isabel, to his page, Cristóbal Rabelo, to his Malayan slave, Henrique, and to other friends and relatives. With great care he specified the place where he wished to be buried, the churches to which he wanted money left, and the number of Masses to be said over his body at his funeral. The will was a lengthy and elaborate document, wholly characteristic of Magellan's fondness for dwelling on details and contingencies. And it was a wholly futile document, too, for Magellan found burial in strange seas, his son, Rodrigo, did not live to the age of three, the child Beatriz carried was stillborn, and Beatriz herself died in 1522; none of the instructions concerning charitable bequests was carried out; Magellan's brother, Diogo de Sousa, who was supposed to inherit the estate in case of the extinction of Magellan's immediate family, got nothing, as did his sister, Isabel; and the litigation over Magellan's will continued until 1796, benefiting only the lawyers, before the matter was allowed to drop.

The true date of departure arrived: September 20, 1519. The grandest voyage in human history was about to begin, rotten with conspiracies before the ships left port. No one expected this to become a voyage around the world. It was a business venture, not a penetration of the unknown for the sake of adventure and discovery. From Magellan down to the lowliest deckhand, the primary motives for the enterprise were commercial, an extension for profit of the geographical achievements of the past century of exploration.

These were the ships that put to sea:

The *Trinidad*, the flagship, 110 tons,* crew of 62. Captain, Ferdinand Magellan.

The *San Antonio*, 120 tons, crew of 56. Captain, Juan de Cartagena.

The *Concepción*, 90 tons, crew of 43. Captain, Gaspar de Quesada.

The *Victoria*, 85 tons, crew of 44. Captain, Luis de Mendoza.

The *Santiago*, 75 tons, crew of 31. Captain, Juan Serrano.

"May God Almighty grant that they make a voyage like that of the Corte-Reals," wrote Sebastian Alvares, the Portuguese consul in Seville, to King Manoel upon the failure of his attempts to frustrate the departure of the expedition. He was referring to the two Portuguese brothers who had perished at the beginning of the century in their quest for a northwest passage to Asia.

---

* By comparison, Columbus' biggest vessel, the *Santa Maria*, was a ship of 100 tons, and the *Mayflower* a ship of 240 tons. Modern ocean liners reach tonnages of 50,000 and more.

THE LONGEST VOYAGE

HE SAILORS WERE IN HIGH SPIRITS AS THEY headed to sea, but it was a false jubilation, for they had no idea of the true extent of their task. Antonio Pigafetta tells us, "The Captain-General [Magellan] had omitted to disclose certain particulars of the voyage to the crew, to avoid their uneasiness in contemplation of the great impetuous reverses inherent in such an enterprise at sea."

We must depend on Pigafetta's lively, vivid journal for most of what we know of the first circumnavigation. Magellan's log, and any journal he may have kept, did not survive the voyage. Pigafetta, who was about thirty years old when he embarked, was a gentleman of good birth and education from the Italian city of Vicenza, who apparently had left his comfortable home to see the world, and particularly the wonders of the deep, or, as he calls them, "the very great and awful things of the ocean." He had served on the staff of the papal envoy to Charles V and had begged from Charles a letter of introduction to Magellan, who enrolled the young patrician as his private secretary. Pigafetta survived the voyage, not without some uneasy moments, and upon his return presented to Charles "a book written by my hand of all the things that had occurred day by day on our voyage." His journal circulated widely in manuscript and was published at Venice in 1536.

Aside from Pigafetta, we have only the brief narratives of two mariners, one a Genoese pilot named Baptista, the other an unknown Portuguese; and the logbook of one pilot, Francisco Alvo, also survives. Shortly after the return of the circumnavigators, the Milanese geographer Peter Martyr, then in the service of Charles V, interviewed many of the survivors and drew up a history of the voyage, which he sent to Pope Adrian VI in Rome, but the manuscript of this doubtlessly valuable work was destroyed when the French sacked Rome in 1527. A similar near-contemporary account derived from interviews was written by Charles' secretary, Maximilian of Transylvania, and has survived. The only other nearly contemporary source is the narrative of the Spanish historian Antonio Herrera, written late in the sixteenth century; Herrera had access to Spanish state papers which have since disappeared, and, though badly jumbled, his relation is strongest in the sections where Pigafetta's is the most skimpy.

From these sources, and mainly from Pigafetta, we can follow the grand armada as it made its way toward its first port of call, Tenerife in the Canary Islands. The *Trinidad*, as the flagship, sailed in the lead; the other captains were instructed to remain close behind and to set their sails after the manner of Magellan's vessel. At night the *Trinidad* would hoist lanterns at her stern to signal the rest of the fleet: two lanterns to reduce speed, three to warn of an approaching storm so that sails could be reefed, or taken in, and four lanterns to order sails lowered. Torches and gunshots from the flagship were the signals of shoals or reefs ahead. Each of these signals was to be acknowledged by every vessel; and Magellan insisted on strict observance of the etiquette by

which each captain was to salute him at evening. The ships
were to draw alongside the flagship, and the captains were to
hail Magellan with the formula, "God save you, Sir Captain-
General and Master and good ship's company!"

Through such methods, Magellan accomplished one of
the most difficult tasks of a fleet's commander: he kept his
ships together at sea. Thus there were no delays while waiting for some laggard to catch up, and thus the armada
remained prepared to defend itself against the possibility of
attack. There were rumors that King Manoel had hired a
fleet of Algerian pirates to attack the Spanish ships, and it
was known that a Portuguese fleet had lately collected at Lisbon, perhaps for the purpose of intercepting Magellan's vessels. But the six-day journey to Tenerife was uneventful; the
ships pulled into harbor on September 26 and the crewmen
began to load the supplies and provisions previously purchased for pickup there.

Pigafetta, whose interest in natural history was as broad
as his credulity was deep, made the acquaintance of the remarkable Raining Tree, sadly unknown to modern science.
The entire water supply of the island, he said, was derived
from this tree; each day at noon a cloud enveloped it, and the
tree's great branches absorbed a great quantity of moisture,
which traveled quickly downward to gush in great streams
from its roots into certain cisterns placed nearby. While Pigafetta was admiring this marvel, Magellan was contemplating more serious matters, for on September 27 a caravel from
Spain arrived bearing a secret message for him from Diogo
Barbosa. Barbosa had learned that the three Spanish captains were planning to kill Magellan at sea and replace him
with Juan de Cartagena. This confirmed a story that Magellan had heard earlier from Alvares, the Portuguese consul,
who had hoped to scare him out of making the voyage with
such tales of conspiracy. Magellan, unperturbed, sent word

back to his father-in-law that he would try to win the good will of the three Spaniards, and would keep close watch on his situation.

That night Magellan met with his captains and pilots to discuss the armada's course. The conspirators might well have struck there, for in Magellan's cabin on the *Trinidad* were the three treacherous captains, and two Portuguese pilots, Estevão Gomes and João Carvalho, against whom he had also been warned by Diogo Barbosa. The only man in the room whom Magellan knew he could trust was his cousin, Juan Serrano, who was aging and slow. Juan de Cartagena, Bishop Fonseca's proud and ambitious young nephew, called the meeting to order himself; through his insolence he seemed to be trying to provoke Magellan to some outburst that could lead to a scuffle and a quick dagger thrust. But Magellan, well schooled in patience by this time and aware of Cartagena's intentions, chose to be mild and even obsequious. He allowed Cartagena to run the meeting and gave polite assent to every decision the Spaniard made, leading Cartagena to think that he was an inept, easily dominated commander. Through his meekness, Magellan avoided any immediate confrontation with his enemies.

After three days in Tenerife, the fleet took to the sea again, with the *Trinidad* leading on the southwesterly course that Magellan, at Cartagena's insistence, had agreed to follow. The course was the usual one for sailing to Brazil, taking advantage of a steady wind. But at daybreak on October 5, the flagship abruptly changed her course to south-southwest, which would bring her much closer to the African coast. When the signal for changing course was posted, Cartagena brought his *San Antonio* alongside the *Trinidad* and asked the pilot, Estevão Gomes, what the course was supposed to be. "South by west," Gomes replied. Cartagena now demanded to know why the armada was deviating from the course that had been agreed upon at Tenerife. Magellan, who stood beside Gomes on the quarterdeck, broke in to say, "Follow the flagship and ask no questions." When the angry and astounded Cartagena objected to Magellan's unilateral reversal of the decision of the officers' council, the captain-general adopted a frosty expression, and to Cartagena's protest that it was bad navigation to take this coastward course, Magellan replied sharply that the Spaniard was "to follow my flag by day and my lantern by night."

Cartagena was enraged; but he had missed his chance to kill Magellan at Tenerife, and now he impotently followed the *Trinidad* on its incomprehensible southerly course. For two weeks the armada made its way between the Cape Verde Islands and the African mainland. This was not the way to get to Brazil; this was not even the customary route of Portuguese ships bound for India; this was no route at all. Then the weather changed. There came baffling headwinds that halted the ships entirely. The winds built in force, until on October 18, when the armada was off the coast of Sierra Leone, terrible gales buffeted the struggling vessels, which dipped so far to their sides that the yardarms touched the waves. On the masts danced the terrifying glow of St. Elmo's fire, which both frightened and reassured; for this blinding brilliance, an electrical manifestation, told the seamen that the saint protected them. As the blessed light left the rigging, the wind died, the sea grew calm, the sailors gave thanks.

And the sea remained calm, for the fleet now wallowed in the horse latitudes, where no breezes blew, and the ships were stilled and idle. Toothy sharks surrounded the motionless vessels. The sailors caught some and cooked them, and Pigafetta discovered that he had no fondness for the taste of shark. The Italian observed more wonders: seabirds that had no feet, spent all their lives skimming the waves, and laid their eggs on the backs of the males. The ships continued to

make no headway, and the men began to mutter that Captain-
General Magellan had foolishly led them into the doldrums
against the will of Captain Cartagena. The tropical sun
roasted them daily, melting the tar in the seams and turning
the deck into an oven. The heat was unbearable, the humidity
worse. Among the men circulated a certain bawdy priest,
Padre Pedro Sanchez de Reina, who stirred their discontents.
Padre Reina, one of three priests on the expedition (there
was also an astrologer, but only one surgeon), was an associate of Juan de Cartagena; as he moved about, singing scandalous songs, downing vast quantities of wine, and offering
easy absolution for all sins, he deprecated Magellan's judgment and praised that of Cartagena.

Magellan, a remote, lonely figure, kept to himself during the 20 terrible days of the doldrums. The other captains
rowed back and forth from ship to ship, but he saw no one,
and waited for the calm to lift. On the twenty-first day came a
puff of wind, which grew stronger, and the sails bellied, and
the fleet broke from its stasis and moved out into the belt of
the trade winds that blew from the southeast. It had been a
brutal three weeks, during which the ships had advanced
only three leagues all told, and the rations of wine, bread, and
water had had to be reduced; but now they were on their way.
And Magellan's deliberate plunge into the horse latitudes
had served its purpose: King Manoel's squadron of caravels,
sent out from Lisbon to intercept his armada, had failed to
find it and had turned back. Now the route to America was
clear.

2

Juan de Cartagena had learned from this that the meek
Magellan of Tenerife was not the true Magellan, and he was
ready to take more direct action against the captain-general.
On November 20 the armada crossed the equator; now the

polestar could no longer be seen, and the navigators would have to reckon latitudes at night by measuring the elevation of the Southern Cross. During this stretch of the voyage Cartagena made his move. Shortly after the crossing of the equator, the ships were making the required nightly salute to Magellan; as the *San Antonio* drew near the flagship, Cartagena said nothing, but instructed his boatswain to call out discourteously a salute that hailed Magellan merely as captain, not as captain-general. When Magellan rebuked the man, Cartagena appeared and shouted, "I sent the best man on this ship to salute you, but next time, if I wish, I'll have one of my cabin boys do it." Then the *San Antonio* swung away.

It was calculated insolence, and all hands wondered how Magellan would respond to it—or whether he would respond at all. He was regarded contemptuously by most of the seamen at this time because, as they saw it, he had wasted nearly two months by his bungling choice of a course to Brazil. For three nights running, Cartagena omitted the salute altogether, though the other three captains continued to fulfill their duties. Magellan remained aloof, seemingly accepting the grievous insult without comment. On the third evening, as he drew by to salute, Captain Luis de Mendoza of the *Victoria* reported that his boatswain had been apprehended in an act of sodomy—a crime punishable by death in Spanish maritime law, though the usual sentence was a flogging. Magellan called a meeting of all the captains aboard the *Trinidad* the next day to hold a court martial.

The ships gathered; the four captains came to the flagship; the boatswain and his paramour were tried and swiftly sentenced to death, the executions to be deferred until Brazil had been reached. The prisoners were removed. Magellan and Juan Serrano again faced the three Spanish captains. Here was Cartagena's opportunity to make up for his misjudgment in a similar situation on Tenerife: he lectured Magellan arrogantly on his change of course, taunted him as an incompetent navigator, strutted mockingly about the cabin. Magellan, as at Tenerife, seemed to be in awe of Cartagena and made only a feeble, vacillating response. As though impressed by his own ringing words, Cartagena now cried that he would no longer obey the orders of a fool like Magellan— whereupon Magellan struck. Cartagena's defiance constituted an act of mutiny, committed in the presence of the captains of a royal armada. Magellan gave a signal, and a group of armed guards burst into the room. While Juan Serrano drew his dagger and Duarte Barbosa and the page Cristóbal Rabelo flanked Magellan with naked swords, the captain-general seized Cartagena by the shirt, accused him of insubordination, and ordered him imprisoned.

Cartagena cried out to Mendoza and Quesada to aid him, thereby revealing the conspiracy, but they did not dare move. The men at arms dragged the elegantly garbed captain from the room, pulled him out on deck, and thrust his legs into the stocks used for the imprisonment of common seamen. Aboard all five ships there was wholesale astonishment at this spectacularly visible demonstration of how Magellan had met the challenge of Cartagena's goading jeers.

The point was made; Magellan did not wish to overplay his hand. Cartagena could not be kept in the stocks indefinitely, and so the captain-general sent him to the *Victoria* as a prisoner in care of Luis de Mendoza. Magellan knew that Mendoza was his enemy, but hoped in this way to neutralize him. As another mollifying step, he replaced Cartagena as captain of the *San Antonio* with Antonio de Coca, who, like Cartagena, was an illegitimate scion of the Fonsecas. The incident was closed; with Cartagena in irons, no one need doubt further who the master of the armada was and would be.

On December 8 the coast of Brazil came into view.

This was Portuguese territory, and Magellan, though he planned to trespass on it, did not intend to stay long. After 11 weeks at sea the armada needed fresh fruit and vegetables, and he would get these from the natives, then move southward in quest of his strait. They landed on December 13, after checking carefully for the presence of a Portuguese fleet. The *Trinidad* led the way past a mountainous island into a superb harbor. It was the feast day of St. Lucy, and Magellan named the lovely harbor the Bay of Santa Lucia; we know it as Rio de Janeiro Bay.

It was midsummer in Rio, and there had been no rain for two months. But it rained the day the Spanish fleet arrived, and the natives, thinking the strangers had brought heaven's bounty with them, came out happily to give welcome. They were cheerful, innocently naked people; Pigafetta relates that "They are without religion. Natural instinct is their only law. It is not uncommon to see men 125 years of age, and some of 140. They live in long houses or cabins that they call *boc*, one of which sometimes contains a hundred families. They are cannibals, but eat only their enemies. They are olive-colored, well made, their hair short and woolly. They paint themselves both in the body and in the face, but principally the latter. Most of the men had the lower lip perforated in three places, in which they wore ornaments, generally made of stone, of a cylindrical form, about two inches in length. Their chief had the title of Cacique. They are of a good disposition, and extremely credulous. When they first saw us put out our boats, and that they remained close to the sides of the ships, or followed, they imagined them to be the children of the ships."

These natives, Guaraní Indians, had had some sketchy contact with Europeans before when Portuguese ships had called at Brazil, but they had not yet learned that white men were to be feared; and, guileless, childlike, they hurried out in their large canoes to welcome the visitors and do business with them. Trade was brisk. The pilot João Lopes Carvalho, who had been to Brazil while in Portuguese service, spoke their language and served as interpreter. In exchange for sleazy European trinkets and such modest souvenirs as playing cards, the Guaranís offered pineapples, sweet potatoes, sugar cane, and fowls. "For a king of clubs I bought six chickens," declared Pigafetta, "and yet the Brazilian thought he had made the best bargain." A comb brought two geese, a pair of scissors enough fish to feed ten men. The Indians had no metal tools, and offered their daughters in exchange for hatchets at an exchange rate of one hatchet for one virgin, or sometimes two or three. Magellan's seamen began to acquire Brazilian girls at a great rate, which temporarily solved the sodomy problem; but the captain-general sternly announced that the girls were to be left behind when the fleet left port, for he did not wish to be accused of having conducted a slave raid on Portuguese territory. For the time being, though, pretty young women, completely naked, swarmed through the ships, to Magellan's annoyance and uneasiness. Austere in his own personal life, he disliked the licentious scenes now being enacted, and was eager to finish loading provisions and water and get the armada going onward before Portuguese ships appeared. "These daughters of Eve," said Pigafetta, "were perfect and well-shaped in every possible way." They found the sailors fascinatingly alien, and examined every part of the ship with care. Pigafetta describes how one girl, finding a large iron nail lying on the deck, seized it as a trophy, and, thinking she was unobserved, slipped it into "her private parts," her only available hiding place, and went shuffling uncomfortably into a canoe to escape with the prize. (Bowdlerizing historians of the nineteenth century would have us believe that the girl hid the nail in her hair.)

Pigafetta collected about a dozen Indian words, some of

which found their way into European languages. The suspended beds of the natives were called *amache* or *hamac*, he said, giving us "hammock." Their boats were *canot*, which became "canoe." The root they ate, which "has almost the form of our turnip, and its taste resembles that of chestnuts," was the *patata*, our "potato."

During the 13 days of this Brazilian idyll, some of Magellan's key officers were seduced into going ashore for revelry in the native village. Duarte Barbosa, rebuked by Magellan for such carousing, responded by spending three days and three nights on shore without leave, giving Magellan no option but to have his brother-in-law arrested and put in irons. While this unhappy episode was taking place, Antonio de Coca, whom Magellan had made captain of the *San Antonio* in place of Juan de Cartagena, suddenly released Cartagena from his captivity aboard the *Victoria*, and the two illegitimate Fonsecas attempted to lead a mutiny. Magellan quickly crushed the uprising and seized Coca and Cartagena; but he hesitated to put the kin of the powerful bishop to death, even though execution was deserved, and when Captains Mendoza and Quesada begged for clemency for them, Magellan yielded. Once more Cartagena was imprisoned in custody of Mendoza on the *Victoria*. Coca was merely demoted from his captaincy. The *San Antonio* received her third commander of the voyage. The man entitled by rank and ability to the post was Duarte Barbosa, but he was currently in disfavor for his shoreside orgy, and so Magellan unwisely named his own cousin, Alvaro de Mesquita, a man of experience but little force, as the *San Antonio*'s new captain.

An important astronomical event—a conjunction of the moon and the planet Jupiter—occurred about this time. Magellan felt that this might yield valuable data on "the height of east and west," which is to say the puzzle of longitude. Accordingly he called his pilots together to assist while Andres de San Martín, the fleet's astrologer and astronomer (the two professions then were one), attempted on the basis of the celestial movements to calculate the longitude of the Brazilian coast. Possibly Magellan hoped to demonstrate that Brazil really lay on the Spanish side of the pope's line, which would vex King Manoel enormously. But San Martín's findings were unclear, and Ruy Faleiro's system for obtaining longitudes did not seem to work properly here, although Pigafetta's lay attempts to explain the proceedings indicate only his total bewilderment over the navigational arts. The problem of longitude remained unsolved. Astronomical calculations of longitude could not be made accurately without a reliable chronometer suitable for shipboard use, and such a chronometer was still two centuries away from development. The difficulties were compounded by the fact that the value in miles of a degree of longitude at the equator is much greater than in higher latitudes, owing to the convergence of the meridians at the poles, and no one yet knew how to compute the intermediate values. Magellan—who had much more than a theoretical concern with knowing the longitude of the Moluccas—resigned himself to continued use of the archaic method of log-line measurement: throwing overboard a piece of wood attached to a long cord, while the ship is in motion, and timing the interval required for the ship to sail past the floating wood. That gave a rough estimate of the speed of the vessel, and the approximate distance covered could be figured; but, as is obvious, the multitude of variable factors in these measurements introduced a cumulative error that would become immense on a voyage as lengthy as Magellan's. (The daily record of observations with the log line became known as the "book of the log," and the name remained long after its original meaning was forgotten.)

On Christmas Eve Magellan told his men to send their native women ashore and prepare for departure, and on December 27, 1519, the reprovisioned armada paid a fond fare-well to Rio and headed south. It relieved Magellan's fears to get out of Portuguese waters, but he was far from tranquil now; the burden was upon him to find the westward strait, and he knew he would be at the mercy of his enemies if he did not produce the promised waterway. Mutiny was a continued threat. He had learned that he could not rely on the voluptu-ary Duarte Barbosa, and neither of his two cousins, Juan Ser-rano and Alváro de Mesquita, was a man of much dynamism. His only confidants at this point seem to have been his page, Cristobal Rabelo, his slave, Henrique de Malacca, and the coarse but trustworthy master at arms, or fifth ranking offi-cer, of the *Trinidad*, Gonzalo Gómez de Espinosa. With God's aid and the comfort of these men, he would find the strait or perish trying.

3

The armada followed the coast southward, probing at every inlet. Magellan had calculated the latitude of his Bra-zilian bay at about 24°S., and he believed he would find the strait at 40°S. or even a lower latitude. On January 11, 1520, the ships came in view of Cape Santa Maria, the landmark Magellan had awaited: for the pilot João Lopes Carvalho, who had been here in 1514 on the secret expedition of João of Lisbon, said that the inland waterway began just south of that cape. Carvalho was right; as they rounded the cape, in 35°S., a vast westward-stretching passage came into view.

This was the estuary of the Río de la Plata, which had been seen by several *sub rosa* voyagers between 1503 and 1514, and officially "discovered" by Juan de Solís in 1516. Although Magellan seems to have embraced several contra-dictory theories of the strait—that it was here, that it was much farther to the south, that South America terminated like Africa, that South America was continuous with the

Terra Australis—he seized on the Plata as his route to the Indies. On January 13 he sent the *Santiago*, his smallest and most maneuverable ship, into the passage on an exploratory mission. Mindful of the fate of Solís, devoured by cannibals on what is now the Uruguayan side of the estuary, Magellan warned Captain Juan Serrano to keep away from shore.

While Serrano sailed westward, Magellan boarded the *San Antonio* and went to search for the north shore of *Terra Australis*, which he imagined lay south of the "strait." He chose to leave the *Trinidad* behind because she was better armed, and he wanted Gonzalo de Espinosa and Duarte Barbosa to have the use of her guns if a mutiny broke out in his absence. Magellan crossed the estuary and found what he took to be the new southern continent, though shortly he would realize that it was merely more of South America; following the coast westward, he went perhaps as far as the present site of Buenos Aires. There he saw the "strait" narrow and turn northwestward, and, satisfied, he returned to the fleet. On the way back, he sighted high land on the Uruguayan shore and called out, "I see a mountain," thereby giving the future city of Montevideo its name.

He found that Serrano and the *Santiago* were back, bearing bad news. The supposed strait was shallow inland, and its water was not salty, and there was a distinct eastward current. So it was no strait at all, but just some immense river. Years of false geography had persuaded Magellan that the Plata ran from sea to sea, and now he was slow to accept the shattering blow; he carried out a methodical reconnaissance of the estuary, convincing himself with effort that he must look elsewhere for his strait, and finally, feigning a serene confidence that he could not have felt within, Magellan announced that the strait lay to the south and they would now continue the quest. Had he not said all along that the strait was somewhere about 40°S.? Was not this gigantic bay merely at 35°S.? The armada sailed at the beginning of February.

Doggedly Magellan investigated every break in the shoreline, with no luck. The only significant event was the discovery of a population of giant cannibals; Pigafetta describes a man of immense size who appeared alone in a canoe, showing no fear, and asked "with a voice like a bull" if he could come aboard the *Trinidad*. Magellan gave the giant a linen shirt and a red cloth waistcoat, and the next day sent a shore party out to learn more about these monsters; but a group of the giants, panicking, ran away, and "did more with one step than we could cover with a leap." There would be more contact with giants later.

The shore of this unknown coast began to look bleak and inhospitable; the weather turned bad, with dark skies and icy winds; strange creatures appeared, peculiar "geese" and "sea wolves," occupying in great numbers two islands. The "geese" were black and could not fly, had beaks like crows, and were extraordinarily plump: Europe had, in fact, discovered the penguin, and Magellan's men collected a goodly number of these fat "geese" to eat. The "sea wolves" had no legs, said Pigafetta, but their teeth were formidable, and if only they could run, they would doubtless be "very bad and cruel." They were seals or sea lions; the armada was nearing the sub-Antarctic world. The topsy-turvy nature of the southern hemisphere's seasons was not then clearly understood, and the men concluded from the increasingly colder weather that they had simply caught up with winter, since they were accustomed to cold Februaries. Those who had least faith in Magellan and least enthusiasm for the voyage suggested that they return to the Bay of Santa Lucia for a month or two and try this southern coast again in April, when it would be warmer. What they did not know was that it was still late summer here, and that even summer is wintry in the high southern latitudes they had begun to enter. The season approaching now was not spring but autumn, and if they returned in April, they would find the climate greatly worsened. Magellan probably did not realize this, but refused to go back to Brazil, simply because he expected to find the strait just ahead. A little farther, he said, and they would turn west and make for the warm Moluccas. A little farther.

The men who went to the islands to kill seals and penguins were caught by a storm and had to huddle under the carcasses of their prey to keep from freezing to death. Sudden furious squalls whipped up at them from the pole. And onward into the gathering winter they sailed. On February 24 they found another large bay, but the pilot's terse log entry tells the story: "Feb 24–25, 1520, Latitude 42°54′S., entered gulf which we named St. Matthias because it was his day. We searched for an outlet to Maluco [the Moluccas], and, there being no anchorage, sailed out again."

For a few hours the crewmen had begun to believe in Magellan's strait once again; but the disappointment of St. Matthias' Day brought a collapse of hopes. The other officers begged Magellan to turn back for the winter, or to give up the search for a strait altogether and head to the Spice Islands by the eastward route. A more flexible man, knowing that he lived every day with incipient mutiny and having no real assurance of a strait's existence, would have yielded. Magellan stubbornly went on, perhaps because he clung to the delusion that the secret maps he had seen in Lisbon told the truth, possibly because he was in the grip of an obsession so powerful that no retreat was possible for him. It was an irrational decision, even the act of a madman, and we will never know to what degree Magellan's magnificent and imperishable achievement was spurred by a divine lunacy. They sailed on.

Just a little farther, and yet a little farther, and they

found no strait, and the world became more terrible. The days grew shorter, a strange thing to be happening as February gave way to March, and icy fogs covered the land, and cutting gales shrieked through the rigging. Hail and sleet bedeviled them; mountains of ice floated in the choppy sea; beards and ropes and fingers froze on deck; the cold rain doused all fires; sailors moved about in drenched, ice-stiffened clothing; the tiny ships were tossed mercilessly about. Men had never been this close to the south pole before, except perhaps for Amerigo Vespucci when he wrote of sailing to 52°S. in 1502, yet the hardships Vespucci had described were nothing like these.

Magellan worked beside his men, submitting to all privations to win their support. He froze with them, but they loved him none the more for it. He was a harsh man, solemn and taciturn, with few intimates; as he limped about the deck he seemed superhuman, and therefore forbidding. Half a year had gone by since leaving Seville, and he seemed to be driving everyone on to a frigid death. They were two months and a thousand miles south of the Plata estuary; where was the strait? The coast was endless and ever more barren. This was even worse than Bartholomeu Dias' voyage toward the Cape of Good Hope more than 30 years before, for they were already far south of Africa's southernmost point, and so that much deeper into the fringes of the Antarctic, and still there was no place where they could turn toward a happier clime. By mid-March, Magellan knew that the endurance of his men and, much more important, their patience had come to an end. Rather than turn back, he chose to find some sheltered harbor where they could wait out the winter before continuing the search for the strait.

They entered a bay, only to suffer six days of the worst storms they had yet endured. Naming it the Bay of Toil, they put out to sea again, tested other anchorages and found them unsuitable and, on March 31, came to an adequate winter harbor which they named Port San Julian. Magellan reckoned its position at 49°18′S. The bay had a narrow entrance, through which a tide as high as 37 feet rushed with great force; but once past that turbulent opening, the ships came to rest in a quiet enclosure with good beaches, plenty of fish, fowl, and edible shellfish, and an ample supply of fresh water. Realizing that they might be held here by the weather for many months, Magellan commanded that the daily ration of wine and ship's biscuit be cut in half; they would depend instead on the bounty of Port San Julian. The men, seeing the barren land beyond the beaches and staring glumly at the gray skies, began to grumble despite Magellan's assurance that they would have little work to do during the stay here, nothing but patching the rigging and scraping the hulls, and could spend most of their time hunting and fishing. How long, they wondered, would it be before they saw the Moluccas? That strait of which the captain-general talked had not yet been found; would they spend the rest of their lives at sea? Would they sail to the pole itself, looking for a westward route? Tensions rose, and there were mutinous whispers. Pigafetta offers this concise account of the events of Port San Julian:

"Here much dissatisfaction and distrust rose up against Magellan. Immediately after we had dropped anchor in this harbor, Magellan gave orders for dwellings to be erected on land. He also ordered the daily rations to be cut so that they would last for a longer period of time. The crews and also the captains objected to both these commands. The dissatisfied demanded to return home. Magellan refused even to discuss the matter and, when his crew persisted, he had some of the worst offenders arrested and punished. On the 1st April, 1520, when Magellan had ordered us all to go ashore and to attend Mass, the captains Juan de Cartagena, Luis de Mendoza, and Gaspar de Quesada did not appear. Open mutiny broke out not long after."

It was an Easter uprising. April 1 was Palm Sunday; Magellan had invited all the captains to breakfast with him after Mass, but the three Spaniards stayed away, and only his cousin, Alvaro de Mesquita, the newly appointed captain of the *San Antonio*, came to his cabin. (We do not know why the loyal Juan Serrano was not there; perhaps he was out in the *Santiago* on a scouting trip.) Though the absence of the Spaniards foretold trouble, Magellan took no action. He was aware of the gathering mutiny, for he had already told his captains and delegates from the crew that he was determined to see the enterprise through to its finish, appealing to their pride as Spaniards to follow him, and they had stalked off coldly.

At midnight a boatload of some 30 men left the *Concepción*, Gaspar de Quesada's ship, and rowed silently to the *San Antonio*. Captain Quesada was aboard ship, as was his pilot, the Basque Sebastian del Cano, and also Juan de Cartagena, who had been released that evening from imprisonment on Mendoza's *Victoria*. They were met by Geronimo Guerra, the nephew or possibly the son of Cristóbal de Haro, who guided them aboard; Guerra had hoped to be made captain of the *San Antonio* upon Coca's demotion, and hated Magellan for picking Alvaro de Mesquita instead. With Guerra's help, the boarding party seized the sleeping Mesquita, chaining him in Guerra's cabin, and went after the other officers. The *San Antonio*'s master, a Basque named Juan de Lloriaga, awoke and ordered the intruders to leave; Quesada fell upon the unarmed man and stabbed him six times, so that he dropped unconscious to the deck. Swiftly the takeover was completed. Everyone loyal to Magellan was placed in irons; Quesada, with Sebastian del Cano to assist him, appointed himself captain of the *San Antonio*, and Juan de Cartagena rowed over to the *Concepción* to take charge of Quesada's former vessel.

The balance of power had been restored to its original position: three Spanish captains, two Portuguese. On the morning of April 2 Magellan awoke to learn of the coup; he planned to send a party of men ashore to fetch water, drawing from the crews of the *Trinidad* and the *San Antonio*, but when the men of the flagship took their boat across to pick up the men of the other vessel, they were told that the *San Antonio* was now under command of Gaspar de Quesada. Soon a boat came from the *San Antonio* bearing a message from Quesada: the three rebels would recognize Magellan once more as their captain-general if he agreed to make certain concessions, having to do with rations, the duration and purpose of the voyage, and so forth. Quesada invited Magellan to come to the *San Antonio* to discuss terms.

Magellan did not intend to place himself in the hands of the mutineers. He considered his position. He had only the *Trinidad* and Serrano's little *Santiago;* if Quesada, Mendoza, and Cartagena chose to attack, he could not stand them off for long. Yet he doubted that the rebels would open fire, for it would be bad tactics for them to destroy ships when all they needed to do was gain possession of Magellan and put him to death; after that, the expedition would be theirs. He gambled that they would wait a few hours, hoping to get a peaceful capitulation from him, before they resorted to force. That would give him time to save himself by the only means possible against such odds: trickery.

Magellan resolved swiftly on an audacious and ruthless scheme which would require careful coordination and a great deal of luck to bring off. He explained what he had in mind to Duarte Barbosa and the faithful master at arms, Gonzalo Gómez de Espinosa, outlining the parts they would have to play. Then he seized the men who had rowed over from the

San Antonio bearing the invitation to come and be killed; that left Quesada temporarily uncertain of the situation while he awaited a reply from Magellan that would not come.

Next, the captain-general wrote a letter to Luiz de Mendoza of the *Victoria*, setting forth the same disingenuous suggestion Quesada had made to him: come to my ship, and let us parley. Espinosa, accompanied by five men, went by boat to the *Victoria* to deliver the message. Beneath their cloaks they carried weapons. The short day was over; the night was dark and misty. As Espinosa's boat vanished into the fog, 15 armed marines led by Duarte Barbosa entered a second boat. They too, more silently, rowed toward the *Victoria*.

Espinosa was allowed to board the *Victoria* when he called that he bore a message for Mendoza from Magellan. The master at arms and his five men stood close together, huddled in their cloaks. Espinosa presented the letter; Mendoza took it, scanned it quickly, laughed at the transparency of the ruse. "I am not to be caught like that," he said scornfully, crumpling the letter. Espinosa bowed, reached out a hand as if to take the rejected letter, and instead grasped Captain Mendoza by the beard; up from the cloak came Espinosa's other hand, gripping a knife that he drove into Mendoza's exposed throat. In that moment Duarte Barbosa and his 15 men, who had come alongside, rushed onto the *Victoria*'s deck and took control of the ship before her crew even realized that her captain had been assassinated. Under Barbosa's command, the *Victoria* hoisted anchor and moved toward the *Trinidad*.

Captain Quesada, studying the bay from the *San Antonio*, could not understand where Mendoza was going, and tried to hail the *Victoria* as she passed him. When Mendoza did not appear, Quesada asked for an explanation, and was told that the captain was in his cabin, writing a letter to Magellan. But the true situation was clear moments later, for now Magellan's ship was flanked by the *Victoria* and the *Santiago*, so that the mouth of the harbor was blocked, and all three ships flew the banner of the captain-general!

In the dark, starless, wintry night, the captains of the remaining rebel ships realized that they were trapped. Quesada, panicking at this mysterious change of fortune, decided that his only safety lay in getting past the blockade into the open sea. He had two of the *San Antonio*'s anchor cables cut, planning to lift the remaining one and slip away without waiting for Cartagena and the *Concepción*. But the wind from land strengthened, and the *San Antonio* started to drag her anchor; she swung around and drifted stern-foremost toward the *Trinidad*, as though fate were delivering her to Magellan. The guns of the flagship boomed out a broadside, and the mutineers scurried belowdecks. Quesada, emerging from his cabin to find that his ship was adrift, stood alone on the quarterdeck, trying to rally his men while the archers of the *Trinidad* filled his shield with arrows. Boarding parties now set out from the *Trinidad* and the *Victoria;* Magellan himself was among the men who clambered without meeting resistance onto the *San Antonio;* Quesada surrendered, and his ship was taken without the loss of a man.

Now only the *Concepción* remained mutinous, but not for long. Juan de Cartagena could see the other four ships side by side, arrayed against him, and he watched dispiritedly as Espinosa and a party of marines approached him. The master at arms hailed the ship and asked where her allegiance lay. Bitterly Cartagena replied, "We stand for King Charles and for Don Ferdinand Magellan as his captain-general."

The mutiny was over. Through iron will, through charisma, through cool defiance of probability, Magellan had smashed the insurrection before it had fairly begun. The ringleaders were in irons; only one man, Mendoza, had died, although the *San Antonio*'s gallant master, Lloriaba, had been gravely wounded and would succumb after lingering for three months. Once again, by swift, bold strokes, Magellan had mastered a situation that had seemed hopeless.

On April 4 Magellan convened a court martial to decide the fate of the mutineers. All formalities of naval law were to be observed; and the trial began grotesquely, for the first defendant was the slain Luis de Mendoza. His corpse, still in its bloody armor, was brought ashore from the *Victoria* and thrown before Magellan, who addressed it as traitor, found it guilty of treason, and condemned it to be hanged, drawn and quartered just as if Espinosa's sly thrust had not already sent the Spaniard's soul from the world. So it was done. While his fellow conspirators looked on cheerlessly, Mendoza's body was mutilated and hacked into quarters, and the quarters impaled on stakes as an example to others.

Gaspar de Quesada followed Mendoza into the place of judgment. Quesada had defied the authority of the captain-general, had proclaimed himself chief officer of the *San Antonio*, and had inflicted what would prove to be a fatal wound upon Juan de Lloriaba. Clemency was impossible. Magellan sentenced him to the same penalty as Mendoza. It was a terrible death, for hanging, in the Spanish style, did not break the neck, but merely inflicted a partial strangling, after which the gasping Quesada would watch his entrails drawn forth and his limbs severed. Surprisingly, considering the reputation for cruelty that the Spaniards were winning elsewhere in the Americas at this time, no one cared to serve as Quesada's executioner, and Magellan turned to Quesada's private secretary, Luis de Molina. Molina, too, had been found guilty and sentenced to death, but Magellan promised to pardon him if he would take his master's life. Molina would not have to strangle Quesada, merely to behead him, a far more merciful fate. Quesada urged the horrified Molina to agree, out of fear that he might otherwise yet be hanged, and on April 7 Molina grasped a sword in trembling hands and parted Quesada's head from his shoulders.

The court martial also found Juan de Cartagena, Antonio de Coca, Juan Sebastian del Cano, and Geronimo Guerra guilty of treason, along with the worldly priest, Padre Pedro Sanchez de Reina, and some 40 of the crewmen. Magellan drew back from executing Cartagena and Coca, those heirs of the Fonseca family, nor did he wish to put Cristóbal de Haro's heir, Guerra, to death, and Sebastian del Cano, though faithless, was too valuable a pilot to kill. The captain-general hesitated, too, to take the life of a priest. As for the 40 crewmen, they could not be spared at all for the voyage ahead, and Magellan believed that he had made sufficient show of his vengeance to discourage them from rebelling again. Therefore he commuted all the death sentences that remained. The aristocrat Juan de Cartagena was confined to his cabin; the rest were condemned to hard labor in a chain gang, with the tacit understanding that they might be pardoned if they worked well in the months before the fleet was to leave Port San Julian. Magellan put his cousin, Mesquita, in charge of the chain gang, and Mesquita kept his prisoners busy at the pumps, scraping hulls, and hewing wood. But Juan de Cartagena, who alone escaped even this punishment, could not be deterred from conspiracy. Soon he and Padre Reina were plotting against Magellan again, but their new rebellion was feeble and quickly suppressed. A second trial was held, and this time Magellan chose to spare himself further trouble from Bishop Fonseca's arrogant scion. He imposed upon Cartagena and the priest a doom that seemed kind only at first glance: when the armada sailed, they would be left behind, marooned in this bitter land where no European ship had ever called before. And so it was done; and their fates are unknown.

[*157*]

4

The dreary darkness of the sub-Antarctic winter descended. Storms swept the desolate coast; the sun was rarely seen; bitter gales cut across the flat pampas. Though he had promised his men leisure, Magellan found it was best to keep them busy, so that they would not give way to the depression such an environment could induce. They built barracks on shore, clothed themselves in seal pelts and the skins of seabirds, and set to work refitting the ships, replacing battered timbers, repairing and greasing worn parts. Everyone was occupied felling trees, hammering, drilling, caulking, scrubbing, painting. The main project, as on any long voyage of the time, was careening the ships, which meant floating them onto the beach at high tide and anchoring them at bow and stern. Cargoes were unloaded and all guns shifted to one side; as the tide dropped, the ships tilted to expose the hull on the other side, so that worm-eaten planks could be removed, seaweed and barnacles scraped away, seams patched, the keel strengthened, the bilges pumped. Then the heavy guns were shifted to the other side and, as the ships heeled over, the rest of their hulls could be dealt with.

Though the winter was clearly deepening and not receding, Magellan in his impatience wished to get on toward the strait—especially when he came to see that, through Portuguese perfidy, his stores of ship's biscuit and wine were much lower than they should be. Since, for all its abundance of fish and fowl, Port San Julian had no fresh fruits or vegetables, the health of the mariners was impaired, and the captain-general thought of moving on. At the beginning of May, after only a month in Port San Julian, Magellan sent Juan Serrano in the *Santiago* on a scouting voyage along the coast to the south. The little ship, best suited of all the fleet for such work, disappeared into the stormy darkness and prowled the coast. Twenty leagues below Port San Julian, Serrano discovered the wide mouth of a river that he named the Santa Cruz, for he found it on May 3, the day of the feast of the Holy Cross. When trying to proceed south of the Santa Cruz, Serrano encountered heavy weather; an easterly gale drove against the *Santiago* and fearful waves ripped away her rudder. He managed to guide the helpless ship safely to shore, where she was hurled onto the beach, and her crew of 37 men dropped to the sand "without even getting wet," as Pigafetta says. Only one man was lost, Serrano's Negro slave, who jumped badly and was carried away by a wave. While the mariners scrambled to higher ground, the ship broke up under the pounding of the sea and vanished with all its cargo and gear. Without food, with no weapons but their knives, the castaways shivered miserably on the exposed beach until Serrano, who had a flint and steel, managed to build a fire. Finding some planks on the shore, they constructed a small raft on which two men were able to cross the Santa Cruz and continue back to Port San Julian by land to obtain help. The others, living on shellfish and weeds, remained on the far shore.

It took 11 days for Serrano's two men to reach the main camp. Gaunt and haggard, they stumbled in by night to bring the news of the disaster. Magellan, grieving for the loss of the useful little *Santiago*, his most versatile vessel, sent a 20-man rescue party via the land route, not wishing to risk a second ship in this season of storms. By June, Serrano and his men were back at Port San Julian; but Magellan left a small party camped at the Santa Cruz in the hope that some of the goods from the *Santiago* might wash up on the beach.

Early in June came a diversion from these hardships and misfortunes. They had seen no natives at Port San Julian, nor any since the giants so briefly glimpsed up the coast in February. But one day about two months after their arrival at the bay, said Pigafetta, a strange figure of colossal size appeared, "singing and dancing on the sand, and throwing dust upon his head, almost naked. The captain sent one of our sailors on shore, with orders to make the same gestures as tokens of peace. This the man did; he was understood, and the giant permitted himself to be led to a little island, where the captain had landed. I was there also, with many others. The giant expressed much astonishment at seeing us. He pointed to heaven, and undoubtedly meant to say that he thought we descended from heaven.

"This man," Pigafetta goes on, "was so tall that our heads hardly came up to his belt. He was well formed; his face was broad and colored with red, excepting that his eyes were surrounded with yellow, and he had two heart-shaped spots upon his cheeks. He had but little hair, and this was whitened with a sort of powder. His dress, or rather cloak, was made of furs well sewed—taken from an animal well known in this region, as we afterwards found. This beast, it seemed to us, had a large head, and great ears like unto a mule, with the body of a camel, and tail of a horse.* The feet of the giant were folded in this skin, after the manner of shoes. He had in his hand a short, broad bow, the string of which was made of a sinew of that beast. He also had a bundle of long arrows, made of reeds, feathered after the manner of ours, but tipped with sharp stones instead of iron heads."

The colossus seemed about eight feet tall to the small-statured Mediterraneans in Magellan's crews. Magellan gave him food and drink and presented him with a mirror. "When the giant saw himself in it," says Pigafetta, "he was so frightened that he stumbled backwards suddenly, knocking down four of our sailors, who by chance were standing close behind him." But he recovered from his alarm and accepted from Magellan the gift of some bells, a comb, and a pair of

* It was the guanaco, a South American camel related to the llama.

glass beads. This encouraged other giants to appear, although the various accounts of the voyage differ in exact details. Pigafetta says that a second giant came, and then none for 15 days, followed by four more; Herrera, the official Spanish historian, talks of six giants coming the first day, and as many as 18 arriving at once, including some females.

Another sixteenth-century historian, Lopez de Gomara, says that a group of the great ones signaled that they wished to come aboard the vessels, "greatly marveling to see such large ships, and such little men." Herrera declares that six natives did come aboard, the smallest of them larger and taller than the stoutest man of Castile. They were offered a kettle of soup and biscuit, sufficient to feed 20 ordinary men, and the six of them devoured it all without difficulty. The next day, two giants brought some guanaco meat, and received red jackets in return, which greatly pleased them. One of these titans made several subsequent visits. This friendly behemoth, who apparently was the biggest of all, was "very tractable and pleasant," according to Pigafetta, and so huge that when he danced he left prints four inches deep in the earth. He frequently pointed to heaven, as if to indicate his spiritual kinship with his little Christian visitors, and the men taught him to say the Lord's Prayer and the names of Jesus and Mary, which he bellowed in a mighty voice. At length he was christened Juan Gigante, "John the Giant," and Magellan gave him a white linen shirt, a woolen coat, a cap, a comb, a looking glass, and other fine things, for which he brought a whole guanaco. But after six days, Juan Gigante ceased to return, and the Spaniards suspected he had been slain by his own people for becoming too intimate with the strangers.

The women, too, were huge, although not so massive as the men—the account of the Genoese pilot says they were rather small—and went all but naked; their husbands seemed to use them as pack animals, but, says Pigafetta, guarded them jealously when they were with the Spaniards. Pigafetta learned a good deal about the anthropology of the giants. "They say, that when any of them die, there appear ten or twelve devils, leaping and dancing about the body of the dead, and seem to have their bodies painted with diverse colors, and that among the others there is one seen bigger than the rest, who makes great mirth and rejoicing. This great devil they call Setebos, and they call the small ones Cheleule. One of the giants declared by signs that he had seen devils with two horns above their heads, with long hair down to their feet; and that they cast forth fire at their throats both before and behind." (Setebos found his way into Shakespeare's *The Tempest*, in which the bestial Caliban owns him as his mother's god.) Pigafetta also informs us that the giants "live on raw flesh and a certain sweet root, which they call capar. . . . When they are sick at the stomach, they put an arrow half a yard or more down the throat, which makes them vomit green choler and blood. For headache, they make a cut over the forehead, and let themselves bleed, doing the same on the arm or leg, in any aches." The Italian voyager provides a lengthy vocabulary of the giants' language, which does not, unfortunately, correspond in a single word with any language known to have been spoken in that part of South America. (The vocabulary he compiled in Brazil was much more reliable.)

To gratify the curiosity of King Charles, Magellan committed a grave breach of hospitality upon the colossi. He had hoped to bring the amiable Juan Gigante back to show the king, but after Juan's disappearance Magellan resorted to one of his characteristic ruses in capturing two young, strapping natives. "Giving them knives, mirrors, bells, crystal beads, and such other trifles," Pigafetta writes, "he so filled their hands, that they could hold no more. Then he caused two pairs of iron shackles to be put on their legs, telling them by signs that he was also giving them those chains, which they liked very much, because they were made of bright and shining metal. When they felt the shackles fast about their legs, they began to doubt: but the captain comforted them, and bade them stand still. In fine, when they saw how they were deceived, they roared like bulls, and cried out to their great devil Setebos, to help them. Being thus taken, they were immediately separated and put in different ships."

Hoping to breed the race of giants in Europe, Magellan tried to seize two other male giants, planning to exchange them for females, but this failed; nine Spaniards succeeded in throwing the two giants down, yet in a moment they broke loose and fled, and in the pursuit one Spaniard was killed. (In another account, the casualty occurred when nine armed giants attacked a Spanish scouting party soon after the kidnapping of the two tricked giants.) The fate of Magellan's captive colossi is equally unclear. Pigafetta says that one died in a few days, because he would not eat anything, but that the other was more peaceful, and exchanged words in his language for Spanish words. "One time, as one made the sign of the Cross before him, he suddenly cried Setebos, and declared by signs, that if they made any more Crosses, Setebos would enter into his body, and make him burst. But when he saw no hurt come of it, he took the Cross, and embraced and kissed it often, desiring that he might be a Christian before his death. He therefore was baptized and named Paul." But Pigafetta adds that Paul perished some months later when famine struck the fleet while it was crossing the Pacific. The account of the Genoese pilot, though, claims, probably without foundation, that one giant reached Spain alive. What is certain is that Pigafetta's pages on the giant men of lower South America caused a great sensation in Europe and created far more commotion than the successful circumnavigation itself. Magellan gave the giants the names of *patagones*, "big feet," and thereafter every expedition to that part of the world made a point of looking for the Patagonian giants—with, as we will see, highly variable results.

The interlude of the giants lightened the dark months at Port San Julian, but, although the winter had not yet ended, Magellan was eager to quit the place, with its memories of mutiny and murders. At Juan Serrano's suggestion, he decided to shift the winter camps to the estuary of the Santa Cruz. The ships were ready, and the men of the lost *Santiago* were distributed among the other four vessels. Magellan gave command of Mendoza's ship, the *Victoria*, to Duarte Barbosa, and made Juan Serrano captain of Quesada's *Concepción*. Mesquita, who had been captain of the *San Antonio* at the time of the mutiny, was restored to that post. After taking possession of Patagonia in the name of King Charles and erecting a cross at the top of a hill, the voyagers departed from ill-omened Port San Julian on August 24, 1520, leaving behind the quartered remnants of Luis de Mendoza and Gaspar de Quesada, and leaving behind also two living men, Juan de Cartagena and Padre Pedro Sanchez de Reina, freed of their chains, amply supplied with bread and wine, and destined never to be seen again by Christian men.

Through storms and wintry darkness the fleet made its way to the mouth of the Santa Cruz in a grim two-day voyage and set up winter quarters once more. Here the explorers remained for two more months. Fate sprang a raw trick on Magellan now, for only 250 miles to the south—three days' sailing away—lay the strait on whose existence he had staked so much. He did not even send out a boat to search for it in those long two months. As though sapped by his fearful strains and chastened by the loss of the *Santiago*, Magellan stayed tight to his camp, waiting for the sun to return. By mid-October the weather had improved, though it was hardly pleasant, and the orders to make ready for sailing were issued.

The destruction of the mutinous captains had not put an end to discontent, however. The main force of opposition at this time was Estevão Gomes, the chief pilot of the armada and Cristóbal de Haro's original choice for captain-general. Gomes, calling a meeting of the officers, pointed out that the strait had not yet been found and might well not exist. Provisions were running low and the men were enfeebled by their bout with the Patagonian winter. The chief pilot proposed turning eastward, crossing the Atlantic far below the Cape of Good Hope (which would avoid the problem of a collision with the Portuguese), and sailing that way to the Moluccas, where Francisco Serrão would greet them warmly and sell them spices from his rich hoard in return for the copper, iron, and trade goods that they carried. Even the officers most loyal to Magellan thought this was a reasonable idea, and the proposal was carried to Magellan. Though inflexibly bound on his westward course, Magellan adopted a conciliatory pose; he admitted for the first time that he had no clear knowledge of the strait's exact location and agreed that, if it did not turn up by the time they reached 75°S., he would adopt the eastward route to the Moluccas.

This apparent compromise did not please Gomes. It involved sailing several months more, deep into the Antarctic, into a region surely far more inhospitable than anything they had yet seen. (In fact, no ships would get as far as 75°S. until the expedition of James Clark Ross reached 78°4' in 1842.) Moreover, Magellan's casual confession that he had been bluffing all along about his knowledge of the strait infuriated Gomes into suggesting a new mutiny: he urged that Magellan be put in irons and that the armada go back to Port

San Julian, find Juan de Cartagena and make him captain-general. It was only that rash suggestion that saved Magellan's westward scheme; for although even such men as Duarte Barbosa and Juan Serrano were greatly tempted to give up looking for the strait and head eastward at once, Gomes' wild talk of rescuing Cartagena called them to their senses and they resolved once more to follow Magellan, at least to the stipulated turning point of 75°S.

5

On October 18, 1520, the four ships left the Santa Cruz estuary and, after some hard sailing through a fierce polar storm, came to another large bay several hundred miles to the south, at about 52°S. It was St. Ursula's Day, and in her honor Magellan named the great cape just north of this bay the Cape of the Eleven Thousand Virgins. Great mountains rimmed the inlet, and the bay appeared shallow, leading Magellan's officers to think this was merely the outlet of another river; the wind was blowing well from the north, and they besought him to take advantage of it and continue along the coast without pausing to investigate this barren-looking place. Magellan, though he was determined to explore any waterway that might prove to be the strait, went to the trouble of calling another council of his officers and listening to their views. He was distressed to find that Captains Barbosa, Serrano, and Mesquita, and their three pilots, Carvalho, Gomes, and Cano, all opposed searching the bay. He heard them out and issued his orders: Mesquita and Serrano would take the *San Antonio* and the *Concepción* and sail westward into the bay to see how far it extended, while he and Barbosa would examine the northern and southern shores of the bay in the *Trinidad* and the *Victoria*. All four vessels were to meet five days hence within the shelter of the Cape of the Eleven Thousand Virgins.

Though clearly disgruntled, Mesquita and Serrano set out. Almost at once a tempest assailed the fleet. The *Trinidad* and the *Victoria* were able to get behind the cape and cast anchor, but the other two vessels were blown helplessly into the bay Magellan had ordered them to explore. The captain-general dismally watched the *San Antonio* and the *Concepción* run before the gale until they were lost to sight, and realized that they would surely be driven onto the rocks that lined the shore of the bay, to be destroyed with all their provisions. He had little time to bemoan this halving of his armada, though, for his own ship and the *Trinidad* were hard-pressed and dragging anchor. It was too dangerous to remain this close to the rocky coast within their harbor; under storm sails, the *Trinidad* and the *Victoria* fought their way past the headland and into the open sea, where they were separated for two days of torrential rain and intense winds. The *Trinidad*'s deck was awash, her hold filled with water; believing that his vessel alone remained, Magellan wondered whether to return to Spain if the tempest spared him, or to continue the quest alone. But when the storm abated he found the *Victoria* nearby, and the two ships returned to the Cape of the Virgins at nightfall.

In the morning a column of smoke was seen rising deep in the bay, as though survivors of the *San Antonio* and the *Concepción* were signaling for rescue. Magellan ordered the *Trinidad* and the *Victoria* to head into the bay to pick up the castaways from the ships of Serrano and Mesquita. As they rounded the cape, though, lookouts reported seeing a sail in the bay, and then another. The *San Antonio* and the *Concepción* were safe! Pigafetta reports, "The two ships had been driven far into the bay by the sudden storms. Those on board feared certain shipwreck on the rocky shores, when suddenly they noticed that the bay opened up on the other side also. They followed this new passage and came to a further bay and thence into yet a third one. They then turned back to carry this promising news to Magellan as speedily as possible. They were under way for two days. We had taken it for granted, since we could not see them, that they had foundered in the storm. When we saw smoke rising from the shores we thought that this was a signal lit by the survivors to attract our attention. Then both ships came towards us from the bay with billowing sails and flying flags. Cannons roared and shouts of joy could be heard."

The *paso*, the westward waterway, had been found.

The *San Antonio* came alongside the *Trinidad*, and Captain Alvaro de Mesquita, his face aglow, boarded the flagship to declare, "I have the honor to report the discovery of the *paso*. It is a narrow, deep strait, with a heavy tidal flow, and we penetrated over a hundred miles before turning back!" He told of the sequence of bays, of the saltiness of the water throughout, of the absence of any sign of a river current. The strait! The strait! Men danced and cheered, knelt in prayer, hugged one another in delight; Magellan crossed himself and bowed his head in thanksgiving.

He tried to take tactical advantage of the discovery, claiming that he had known all along the strait would be here, and, if we can believe Pigafetta, the captains and pilots forgot all about his troubled probing of a thousand miles of coastline, and hailed him for his wisdom and knowledge. Jubilantly Magellan called one more council of his officers, wishing quick ratification of his plan to enter the strait and sail quickly to the South Sea. But he met unexpected opposition. Serrano and Mesquita had described the strait in detail to their fellow officers, pointing out that it was an intricate maze of bays and channels, many of which no doubt led to dead ends. They had no idea of the extent of the strait; it might take months or even years to traverse it from end to end, if they got lost in its complexities. The fleet was short of food, and much of what it still carried was decaying; the world here looked cold and bleak; this strait was no place for tired men. Estevão Gomes recommended that they note the strait on their charts and leave it for now, making a quick eastward voyage to the Moluccas to buy spices and to reprovision. Then, after carrying a rich cargo to Spain, they could outfit a new fleet, go directly to the strait, solve its mysteries, and proceed to the Moluccas by the new westward route.

The other officers agreed. Magellan bluntly declared them outvoted. According to Pigafetta, he said that "even if they were reduced to having to eat the leather on the ship's yards, he was determined to proceed, and keep his promises to the Emperor, and he trusted that God would assist and conduct them to a happy conclusion." All but Gomes were cowed by the force with which this formidable man made his declaration; when Gomes continued to grumble and mutter, Magellan announced that the meeting was adjourned. At dawn the next day, the armada entered the strait.

The ships passed through the first bay and into the narrows beyond. A shore party sent to investigate a cluster of huts on an inland hill paused to stare in awe at the rotting body of a stranded whale, then reached the huts and found that they were the thatched burial mounds of partly mummified natives, all of them over six feet in height. Beyond this eerie cemetery stretched a broad prairie that bore no sign of life.

The narrows admitted them to a second bay, and after that came a second narrows and a third bay. Towering granite walls, sometimes a mile high, flanked them as they traversed these narrows. By October 29 they were in the wide section of the strait now known as Broad Reach, which trends due south, and here, for the first time, Magellan was confronted with a choice of passages. One opening led to the southwest, and seemed to be the most likely one; but Magellan could not be certain, and he split his fleet into two groups; the *Trinidad* and the *Victoria* would go to the southwest, the *San Antonio* and the *Concepción* would enter the southeastern channel, and they would meet again in five days at the place where the strait divided.

Magellan continued to the southwest, past needle-sharp rocks, through impenetrable mists, over water that surged and boiled from one wall of the channel to the other. But the strait grew more attractive: green trees covered its mountainous slopes now, and waterfalls leaped spectacularly through pine groves to the shore, so that Pigafetta was moved to write, "I believe that there is not a more beautiful or better strait in the world than that one." The channel had bent round to take them on a northwestern course. To the left, on the southern shore, which they believed was the northern coast of *Terra Australis*, they saw lights burning at night, the glow of Indian campfires, and Magellan gave that coast the name of Tierra del Fuego, "the land of fire," which it still keeps. There were many good anchorages; Magellan chose one at which to halt, where a little river full of silvery fish emptied into the strait. He called it the River of Sardines, and some of his men set to work with nets, catching the tiny fish by the thousands and loading them into barrels.

Here Magellan sent Gonzalo de Espinosa in the *Trinidad*'s longboat ahead to explore the next stretch of the strait. The boat was gone three days; when it returned, the oarsmen were pulling with all their might and Espinosa, standing in the bow, fired off gleeful gunshots and waved as a banner a scrap of cloth fastened to a lance. They had found the South Sea, he announced. Though it had been a tempestuous passage past whirlpools and eddies, and though they had been caught in the wild tides created by the rushing of water from sea to sea, they had come to a long promontory jutting sharply outward, and beyond that cape was open water, a vast blue domain that could be only the South Sea. At this, Magellan's iron soul melted, and he shed tears before his men, says Pigafetta, for joy at this discovery. The ultimate cape he named Cape Deseado, "the desired cape." The door to the Pacific lay open. As soon as the *San Antonio* and the *Concepción* returned from their reconnaissance of what Magellan now knew must be a false route, they would proceed to the Spice Islands.

Five days had passed since the dividing of the fleet, and the other two ships had not appeared. Magellan put back from the River of Sardines to look for them. Soon he met with the *Concepción* alone; and Juan Serrano, her captain, had no more idea of what had become of the *San Antonio* than Magellan himself. They had entered the southeastern channel together, said Serrano—going into what now is called Admiralty Sound—but on the first day, the speedy *San Antonio* had left the *Concepción* behind, and Serrano never saw her again. He had searched Admiralty Sound for a few days, determining that it trended eastward and was of no use to them; then, turning the *Concepción* around, he returned to the rendezvous points in the western passage. Magellan, fearing that the *San Antonio* had been wrecked, looked for her right up to the head of Admiralty Sound, firing signal guns constantly, posting banners and messages at several capes and islets, and prowling every possible anchorage. There was no sign of her. Mystified, and thinking there might have been some confusion over the rendezvous point, he sent the *Victoria* back up Broad Reach. Though she threaded the narrows from bay to bay and went even to the mouth of the strait and into the Atlantic, the *Victoria* found no trace of the *San Antonio*, and returned to Magellan.

The captain-general turned to his astrologer, Andres de San Martín, for an explanation. San Martín studied the heavens, cast a horoscope, and offered his findings: there had been a mutiny, he said; Captain Alvaro de Mesquita was a prisoner on his own ship; Geronimo Guerra and Estevão Gomes were in command, and were taking the *San Antonio* back to Spain. Magellan realized that the soothsayer had given him the most probable solution to the mystery, and so it turned out, for Mesquita had indeed been deposed by Gomes, who had circled round in Admiralty Sound and headed up the strait for home. The *San Antonio* arrived in Seville in May 1521, carrying a cargo of lies about Magellan's conduct of the expedition; the fact that the homeward voyage lasted six months suggests that Gomes and Guerra stopped in Port San Julian to look for Juan de Cartagena, but whether they did is not certain, and in any event the marooned men were never rescued.

The loss of the *San Antonio* was the most severe blow yet. Though Magellan was rid at one stroke of Gomes and that other troublemaker, Geronimo Guerra, he had also lost his largest ship, which had carried more than a third of his remaining and already inadequate provisions. Conferring frankly with Barbosa and Serrano, Magellan admitted that it was hazardous to continue the expedition, but pointed out that it could be far more dangerous to return empty-handed to Spain, where Gomes would have had ample chance to spread his calumnies. At a council of his captains on November 21 or 22, Magellan called once more for a vote of confidence, asking Barbosa and Serrano to give him in writing their opinion on whether to go on. Probably seeing a court martial in his future when he returned to Spain, he wished now to carry documentary proof that he had consulted with his officers, and not, as Gomes was certainly claiming, acted highhandedly and unilaterally throughout. Barbosa and Serrano gave ambiguous but generally favorable replies, and anchors were lifted on November 24. The fleet went forward.

On November 28, they reached the cape Magellan had already named Deseado, and, after occupying themselves for a full month in the 375 miles of the strait, the explorers embarked on the limitless waters of the Pacific Ocean. Magellan bestowed on the waterway the name of the Strait of All Saints; posterity has replaced that name with Magellan's own.

6

The sea was calm on the day that European ships entered it for the first time. The sky was wondrously blue, the clouds were fleecy, the waves were no more than rippling wavelets, burnished by the brilliant sun. The scene was so tranquil that Magellan gave Balboa's South Sea a new and hopeful name: El Mar Pacifico, "the peaceful ocean." Surely it seemed to him and his men that the worst was behind them. Through skill, deviousness, and perseverance he had survived mutiny and storm, and had dramatically extended man's horizon by finding the link between ocean and ocean. All that remained for the voyagers was to cross the bosom of the Pacific and quickly come to rest in the happy isles of the Moluccas. But they were wrong, for they were setting out on a sea so vast it was beyond all imagining, and worse, very much the worst, yet awaited them.

Magellan did not immediately turn west to keep his promise to Francisco Serrão and come to him "by way of Spain." The sea was calm, but the air was biting cold, and the captain-general held to a northerly course to get into a milder latitude. With provisions running short, this was something of a calculated gamble, but Magellan had little choice: the winds in the vicinity of South America's tip blew out of the west, and the currents likewise swept eastward, so that he never could have made headway against them going due west. At the beginning of December, the three ships began to move northward, keeping away from the coast most of the time but sighting it often enough to give Magellan credit for the discovery of Chile. Soon they picked up a favorable current that sped them past 40°S., and Magellan began to look for the eastern shore of Asia, which he believed jutted close to the New World at about 35°S. This was an idea that had been handed down since Marco Polo's time, but Magellan soon found out that there was nothing to it. (The continents do meet, but only at the Arctic Circle.) By December 18, when he had gone as far as 32°S. without seeing the Asian coast appear on his left, Magellan decided to turn west. Perhaps he had already come to some suspicion about the true size of the ocean that lay between him and the Moluccas; certainly he was aware by this time that it must be at least as big as the Atlantic, which no one had suspected before.

By going so far north before turning west, Magellan brought himself into the belt of the trade winds that blow westward across the Pacific, and so he shortened his voyage. But he was unlucky in his choice of a course. From the Tropic of Capricorn north to a point well above the equator the Pacific is strewn with lovely archipelagoes: flat, palmy coral atolls, white against the green water of shallow lagoons. Had he caught sight of the eastern end of these groups his mariners could have sailed happily from one cluster of atolls to the next, refreshing themselves as the need arose. But Magellan, following the trade winds and knowing that the Spice Islands lay above the equator, sailed on a sharp diagonal to the northwest, missing the islands of Juan Fernández near the Chilean coast and bypassing also isolated Easter Island in the eastern Pacific, which could have led him into Polynesia. He continued on this great diagonal so long that it took him far to the north of the Polynesian isles, into the only part of the ocean that is devoid of land. This prank of fate condemned the explorers to endure the terrible monotony of an empty sea for 98 days, three times the length of Columbus' journey on the Atlantic.

The enemies were tedium, thirst, hunger, and scurvy. By day, the sun was harshly bright in a cloudless sky, and there was no rain. By night, strange stars appeared. Pigafetta noticed "five brilliant stars arranged like a cross in the western sky"—the Southern Cross. And the men stared at two mysterious glowing patches in the heavens; we know them to be our neighboring galaxies, which we call the Magellanic Clouds.

In the mocking calm of the Pacific, the suffering increased daily. The biscuit crumbled into powder, and worms and rats reveled in it; the water turned yellow and evil in the casks; the penguin meat that had been collected in the strait, improperly smoked, rotted and putrified. The wine was long gone. The pickled meat was so bad that it glowed in the dark. Men ate chips of wood and mounds of sawdust, and went down into the foul-smelling holds to hunt the rats that scurried through the ruined stores. The market value of rats rose as the nightmare continued; at first they traded for a few copper maravedis, but by early January, men would pay a golden ducat for one. At least it was fresh meat.

There were fierce quarrels over the division of shares in the cargo they would one day load in the Moluccas. Nerves were raw, and men fought under any provocation. As the famine deepened, the oath that Magellan had made to Estevão Gomes was fulfilled, for they went onward even though they ate the leather of the ship's yards. Pigafetta says, "They were very hard on account of the sun, rain, and wind, and we left them for four or five days in the sea, and then we put them a little on the embers to broil and so ate them."

The sailors could fight off hunger by chewing pieces of

leather, but they could not resist scurvy, the dreaded vitamin-deficiency disease whose causes were so long unknown. "Our greatest misfortune," writes Pigafetta, "was being attacked by a malady in which the gums swelled so as to hide the teeth as well in the upper as the lower jaw, whence those affected thus were incapable of chewing their food." Nineteen men died, including Paul, the Patagonian giant; 30 other men were helpless with pain. Even the compasses went awry, and lodestones had to be applied to them to reawaken their magnetism. The insides of the casks that had held honey or raisins were scraped, and the scrapings boiled into a broth. The sailors stalked the decks like living skeletons, experiencing torments never known to mariners before, because this was the longest voyage ever undertaken. With weary eyes they scanned the horizon for land, and there was no land; and still the obliging wind carried them westward. At one point, Pigafetta notes, Magellan ordered the course changed to west by south, so that they might search for a point marked on their charts as Cape Gaticara. But, he comments bitterly, "That cape, with the pardon of cosmographers, for they have not seen it, is not found where it is imagined to be."

The three little ships, like toy crafts on the mighty bosom of the Pacific, advanced at 50 or 60 leagues a day, but yet there seemed no end to the emptiness. Shambling through their nautical duties, the men endured the blazing eye of the sun, the grip of thirst at their throats, the taste of leather and sawdust on their tongues, the pangs of scurvy in their limbs, the stink of the rotting things in the hold, the silent laughter of death, waiting patiently for his chance to come. "If our Lord and his Mother had not aided us in giving us good weather," wrote Pigafetta, "we should all have died of hunger in this very vast sea, and I think that never man will undertake to perform such a voyage."

On January 24, 1521, nearly two months out of the

strait, the spell broke: an island appeared. It was a barren place that they named San Pablo Island in honor of the saint of that day; perhaps it was Pukapuka, chief island of the Danger Islands. Finding an anchorage was difficult, and at first it seemed that they would have to pass by without landing, for Magellan did not dare send a boat ashore unless he could anchor his ships; otherwise, the unending wind might sweep the ships away and leave the shore party marooned. But shallows appeared, finally; the *Trinidad* anchored and put out her longboat, and shortly men from the *Concepción* and the *Victoria* were joining them on shore.

They did not leave San Pablo empty-handed, but it was not the tropical paradise they expected. It was hot, dry, and uninhabited by man. It did not provide the fresh fruit they needed so badly, nor was there any supply of water other than pockets of brackish rainwater stored in the sand. They needed firewood, but no trees grew here, only stunted, twisted shrubs. Still, they made the most of what they found. Edible crabs scuttled over the coral rocks at the beach; an abundance of sharks and fish waited to be taken along the reef; smaller fish were available in the island's shallow central lagoon. Seabirds were numerous and, since they had never seen enemies before, were easily slaughtered on their nests. Magellan's men dined on terns, rails, goonies, and sea eagles, stored the surplus on the ships, and gathered great numbers of eggs. Duarte Barbosa, skilled in such things, showed how to find turtle eggs buried in the sand and where to look in the glistening waters of the lagoon for the thick, sluglike sea cucumbers, animals related to the starfish and favored by Orientals as a delicacy. A lucky squall brought fresh water, too, which they caught in their sails and funneled into newly cleansed casks. Then they moved on, after four days.

A second island appeared on February 4. It seemed as

lonely and as desolate as San Pablo, but Magellan spied palm trees ashore heavy with coconuts. There was no way to land, however; the atoll was a coral fringe at the summit of a steep-sided undersea mountain, and no bottom could be reached. Sharks snapped malevolently at the men who were sounding the depths for a place to anchor. Soon the winds carried them past the island and its coconuts and its *tiburones*, its sharks. Isla de Tiburones was what Magellan named it: "isle of sharks." He grouped it with San Pablo as the Desaventura-das, "the unfortunate islands." Leaving them behind, he maintained his west-northwest course, crossing the equator on February 13 at a longitude of about 160°W., skimming past the Gilbert Islands and the Marshalls without sighting land. Now, under the equatorial sun, the anguish of the crew doubled and redoubled; the hellish journey was into its fourth month, and men were dying each day, and westward yet they sailed, searching as desperately for the solace of a friendly shore as once they had for the strait that had admitted them to this incredible ocean.

Respite came at the moment of total despair. By March 5 the last food was gone, water was rationed to a single sip a day, and the crewmen were so plagued with disease and fatigue that they could scarcely move about. But at dusk that night, a seaman saw land on the horizon, and in the morning there appeared three islands, mountainous, fertile-looking, lush. All day long the haggard voyagers guided their ships toward land, licking their cracked lips when they drew near enough to see waterfalls tumbling down lofty cliffs. They made for a bay; Magellan, doubting that his men had strength enough to lower the sails the proper way, had his master and the boatswain do it by cutting the halyards with axes. The canvas fell and the anchors were thrown overside, and with enormous effort the men launched a boat, nearly capsizing it in their weakness as they pushed it into the water. Before a shore party could set out, though, natives came up by the dozens in outrigger canoes—hollowed tree trunks with stabilizing beams lashed to their sides. Handsome olive-brown people, naked, with long black hair and black beards, and teeth stained from chewing betel, thronged about the Spanish ships, fascinated by the white-skinned strangers. Showing no fear whatever, the islanders swarmed onto the vessels and proceeded, "with much address and diligence," according to Pigafetta, to loot them of everything that could be removed. They showed no malice in this; it was simple curiosity that led them to collect hatchets, knives, ladles, stools, and anything else that was portable. The island was Guam, never before visited by Europeans, and the natives were making the discovery of metal as they fondled and licked and tapped the tools they seized from the astonished Spaniards.

Magellan attempted to take a firm but friendly attitude, ordering his men into their armor but avoiding any show of force. He directed Gonzalo de Espinosa to clear the deck of islanders and to retrieve from them the objects they had appropriated. The natives, seeming greatly amused, headed for their canoes still clutching their prizes. When Magellan's enfeebled men tried to stop them, the islanders thrust them aside, knocking one sailor down and kicking him senseless. It was no longer a joke; at a signal from Magellan, Espinosa felled a powerful-looking chief with a bolt from his crossbow. Other bolts followed, and half a dozen islanders fell to the deck. The others fled, but they did not neglect to make off with the *Trinidad*'s boat as they headed for land. Magellan, his temper badly frayed by the hardships of the ocean voyage, retaliated grimly for this brazen theft, sending 40 armed men ashore to raid the village. The natives did not even have the use of the bow and arrow, and, armed only with stone knives and bone-tipped spears, were no match for the crossbows and muskets of the Spaniards. Seven villagers were slain and the rest escaped to the interior of the island, while Magellan's men burned 50 houses and many canoes, and collected pigs, chickens, yams, bananas, coconuts, and rice, as well as retrieving the stolen boat and filling the ships' casks with fresh water from a river. It was a sad beginning for the intercourse of white man and native in the Pacific. But the Spaniards ate well that night for the first time in too many months. Even so, the feast came too late for some, including the English master gunner, Andrew of Bristol, who died during the stay at Guam.

The slaughter of the islanders had saddened Magellan, and he tried to make amends at the neighboring island of Rota, where the fleet called a few days later to add to its provisions. The Rotans, forewarned, did not attempt to invade the ships of the white men; three priests in bizarre masks did come aboard, and Magellan loaded them with gifts, opening the way for friendly commerce. Thus the Spaniards were able to obtain through trade a further supply of yams, bananas, rice, water, and, above all else, coconuts, which an awed Pigafetta described in detail, as befitted such a miracle of nature. It was, he said, "the fruit of certain date-trees, whereof they make bread, wine, oil, and vinegar. They make wine in this manner: they cut a big branch of the tree, and hang thereat a reed as big as a man's leg, into which drops a sweet liquor from the tree, like white wine, somewhat tart; and they let the reed continue there from morning till evening, and from evening to morning. The fruit of this tree is as big as the head of a man, or more. The first rind of this is green, and of the thickness of two fingers, having in it certain threads, whereof they make the cords with which they tie their boats. Under this rind there is a thick shell, which they burn and make powder thereof, and use as a remedie for certain diseases. Under this shell is a white substance, like the kernel of a nut, being a finger in thickness, which they eat with meat and fish, as we do bread. It has the taste of an almond. In the midst of this kernel is a clear and sweet water, being very wholesome and cordial. . . . With the juice of two of these date-trees, a whole family of ten persons may be maintained with wine, using one tree eight days and the other the next eight days. . . . These trees live for the space of a hundred years."

The Spaniards left Rota on March 9, much buoyed by a few days of rest and good food. Magellan gave to the islands the name of Ladrones, "the isles of thieves"; but today they generally are known as the Marianas. The explorers were now about 13° north of the equator, and Magellan was aware that the Moluccas lay only three or four degrees above the line, and therefore considerably to the southwest of his present position. Yet the course he chose was due west from the Ladrones. Several explanations for this have been offered. One is that he had erred in his calculations of the latitude of the Ladrones, and thought he was much closer to the equator, so that he could reach the Moluccas by sailing due west. Another is that he feared going immediately to the Moluccas, since they might well be held by a strong Portuguese garrison, and wished to spend more time among the islands to the north until his men had returned to full health. One of Magellan's nineteenth-century biographers even suggested that he might have been trying to sail to China.

But it seems unlikely that, after crossing thousands of miles of emptiness broken only by five islands, two of them barren, he would deliberately go in search of other unknown islands instead of making straight for the Moluccas. Nor did his orders say anything about China, which the Portuguese had reached from Malacca in 1513 but which thus far had shown little interest in welcoming foreigners. The first theory is the most probable: that Magellan had miscalculated his latitudes as well as his longitudes, and believed that the Moluccas lay but a short distance west of the Ladrones.

On March 16, 1521, after covering 300 leagues in a week without sighting land, the Spaniards glimpsed a mountain ahead, and shortly came upon two islands, a large one and a small. It was the day of St. Lazarus, and Magellan gave the saint's name to the large island. When he realized that he had come upon a group of many islands, he christened the archipelago after St. Lazarus too, but the name did not last, for within a generation it would be renamed in honor of King Philip II of Spain. Magellan had in fact discovered the Philippines, some 7,000 islands stretching in a great arc for more than a thousand miles across the Pacific. Or, if we can credit him with the secret voyage of 1512, he had *re*discovered the Philippines. If indeed he had sailed to this longitude in 1512, he now became the first man to circle the globe completely; and here, in the Philippines, the great captain's voyage came to its end.

7

The large island was called Samar; its small companion, which was uninhabited, was known as Homonhon. Magellan learned these names from nine friendly natives who came to him in a canoe on March 18 while the Spaniards were resting, careening their ships, and collecting water on the small island. These nine came from still another island in the vicinity, Suluan, and were gentle and amiable, strong, stocky men who wore little clothing, rubbed their bodies with scented oil of coconut, and—most interestingly—adorned themselves with bracelets and earrings of gold. Magellan's slave, Henrique, tried to speak to them, but reported that he could not understand their tongue, though by sign language he struck up a warm relationship and received from them the gift of some coconut wine and a large fish. The fact that they spoke a language strange to Henrique gave the captain-general a good indication that he had not, after all, reached the Moluccas; and some careful work with the quadrant confirmed the fact that he was still a full 10° too far to the north.

That was not at all disappointing, for these Islands of St. Lazarus seemed highly promising in themselves. One of the objects of the voyage had been to gain new territory for Spain, and these uncharted islands, which certainly lay on the Spanish side of the pope's line, would make an admirable addition to the growing empire of Charles V. (By the reckoning of Magellan's pilots, even India might have been said to lie on the Spanish side of the line, for the accumulated error in the figuring of longitudes had reached 52°55′ at that point in the voyage, or one-seventh of the circumference of the globe.) Under the terms of his own contract with Charles, Magellan and his heirs were entitled to the title of governor of all newly discovered islands, as well as a share of the revenues of any two islands after the first six to be discovered. The lonely Unfortunate Islands were no prizes, and the Ladrones produced nothing but pigs, yams, bananas, coconuts, and other such humble goods. But there were islands all about in this new archipelago, and with golden bracelets glittering on the arms of fishermen, who was to say what treasures these islands might not hold? Even if he failed to secure the Moluccas for Spain, Magellan was certain now to be a rich man.

The nine islanders from Suluan promised in sign language to return in a few days with their chief, and they kept the promise. The chief was a majestic figure with a tattooed face and a skirt of cotton fringed with silk; he carried a javelin and a dagger of bronze encrusted with gold, a shield that also sparkled with the yellow metal, and wore earrings, armlets, and bracelets of gold. Magellan warned his men to show no sign of interest in such things, for fear of raising the price of gold in terms of bells, mirrors, and beads. The Sulu-ans brought oranges, coconuts, a rooster, more palm wine, and also, unbidden, such commodities as cloves, cinnamon, ginger, pepper, nutmegs, and mace. At last the wonders of the Indies were within grasp.

For more than a week the ships remained at anchor off Homonhon while Magellan tended the sick, supervised the overhauling of the ships, and contemplated his good fortune. The fragrance of spices was in his nostrils; he could not now be far from his dear friend Serrão; his son, Rodrigo, would be the richest lord in Spain. Each day there were callers from Suluan who told of the far wealthier islands to the south.

On March 25, as the Spaniards were preparing to seek those islands, history nearly suffered an immeasurable loss: for Antonio Pigafetta, fishing over the side of the *Trinidad*, slipped on a spar wet from recent rain and toppled into the sea. Swimming was an art unknown to him, and he was close to drowning when he found a rope dangling from the main-sail. Clutching it, he shouted for help and a boat picked him up. "I was saved," he wrote, "not, I believe, through my own merits, but through the mercy and grace of that fountain of charity, the Blessed Virgin Mary." Later that day the fleet left Homonhon.

Refreshed, their sores healing, their swollen limbs re-turning to normal size, the now-buoyant voyagers made their way through a channel with islands on every side, and halted on March 28 at the small isle of Limasawa, south of Leyte. A canoe bearing eight men approached, and Henrique was able to make himself understood in Malay. They were wary of coming aboard the ships despite Henrique's assurance of his master's peaceful intentions, and presents had to be floated to them aboard a plank. But soon the island's *datu*, or para-mount chief, whose name was Colambu, came out aboard his royal barge to investigate the strangers. He, too, was cautious; he reclined comfortably on mats, keeping the barge a little more than a spear's throw from the *Trinidad* without realizing that his visitors had weapons more powerful than spears, and chatted in Malay with Henrique. The Limasa-wans repaid the Spaniards for their gifts by putting fruit, nuts, vegetables, and a pot of palm wine on a raft and sending it on the current to the *Trinidad*. The offering included some cooked dishes, too, and these were contained in vessels of Chinese porcelain, providing the encouraging information that China must lie within easy trading distance. Through Henrique, Magellan delivered a long discourse on the grandeur of the King of Castile and on his own wish to establish friendly commerce. Finally, two native emissaries came on board and enjoyed a pleasant visit. Satisfied that the Spaniards meant no harm, the datu himself consented to board the Spanish ships.

Magellan received him in velvet cloak and plumed hat, showed him globes, compasses, and hourglasses, and terrified all the natives by having the ship's guns fired. Then he cunningly staged a mock battle in which three men with spears and swords fought one in full armor. The chief, watching the weapons clang in vain off the armor, commented that one such man was worth a hundred of his own soldiers. After this display of science, pomp, and might, Magellan provided a banquet for his guests, and during a long and amiable conference he and the datu performed a Malay rite of blood-brotherhood. The meeting ended with a ceremonial exchange of gifts; Colambu offered a basket of ginger, which Magellan accepted, and a large bar of solid gold, which despite all temptations Magellan refused, pretending that he had no interest in it.

When the chief went ashore, Pigafetta and another man were ordered to accompany him. The two Europeans were taken to a shelter of bamboo, where they were given a dish of pork and rice, and, though it was Good Friday, they decided it was wisest to accept the offering. They drowned their consciences in palm wine, and Pigafetta's companion became quite drunk. Pigafetta, clearly a man of great sobriety, retained enough presence of mind to produce his notebook and jot down a list of native words and their equivalents. The datu was so astonished when Pigafetta read this list back to him that he cried out that the visitors must surely have come from heaven.

The feasting went on far into the night, with poor Pigafetta doing his best, as a diplomat must, to eat all that was set before him. The datu, he said, "was the handsomest man I saw among these people. . . . On each of his teeth were three golden dots, so placed one would have thought his teeth had been fastened to his head with this metal." When the chief retired he left his son to entertain the two men; they got a few hours of sleep at length, and in the morning the datu awakened them and sent them back to their ship accompanied by his brother, the ruler of a district on another island, who then was staying with him. Pigafetta discovered that during the night Antonio de Coca, the last mutineer still with the fleet, had died and was buried at sea.

Easter had come again, and that other Easter of conspiracy and executions in Port San Julian seemed only to be a dream. On March 31, Easter Sunday, Magellan and fifty of his men came ashore to celebrate a solemn High Mass; they wore no arms but their dress swords, and had donned their finest clothes, sea-stained though those might be. Colambu, having been told that a religious ceremony would be held, came with his brother to attend and brought gifts of pigs. The two monarchs stood beside Magellan at the improvised altar of boughs and sailcloth and knelt while the Host was elevated to the sound of six guns firing from the ships; they kissed the Cross and took communion. Afterward, Magellan explained some of the tenets of Christianity and questioned them about their own religion, learning that they worshipped a god whom they called Abba. This relieved him, for he had feared they might be Moslems. He instructed them to erect the Cross on their highest mountain and make obeisance to it every morning; "if they did this," he said, "neither thunder nor lightning nor storm would do them hurt."

From the Datu of Limasawa, Magellan heard a good deal about the surrounding islands, in particular about Cebu, the most populous and wealthiest of all, which lay a week's sail away. When Magellan requested a native pilot to guide them to Cebu, Duarte Barbosa and Juan Serrano protested, saying that it was time to get on to the Moluccas; but the captain-general made it clear that the Moluccas could wait and that he planned to conduct an extensive reconnaissance of this archipelago, visiting the important islands, converting the natives to Christianity, and annexing their territory to Spain. Barbosa and Serrano, seeing the familiar glint of determination in their leader's eye, subsided.

The datu himself offered to lead the Spaniards to Cebu, if they would wait a few more days while he completed the rice harvest. To speed matters up, Magellan sent some of his own men to help with the harvest, which was quickly handled. There followed a wild, orgiastic harvest festival in which the Spaniards took part, somewhat to Magellan's displeasure, and when everyone was sober the fleet departed, on April 5, 1521, with Colambu's ship showing the way.

The route was northwest, past Leyte, Bohol, and other islands where they did not stop. West of Leyte, the Spaniards had to wait for the datu's much slower vessel to catch up with them, and to avoid further delay they took him aboard the *Trinidad* with several of his chieftains. On Sunday, April 7, the ships approached the eastern coast of the great island of Cebu. As they neared port, Magellan had his men fire a booming salute with the heavy guns, which so terrified the people on shore that they sped away in panic, leaving the docks deserted.

But this was no primitive island of simple folk. Cebu was a wealthy island, and its ruler, Rajah Humabon, was a man of might and substance who was accustomed to extracting tribute from all trading vessels that stopped in his harbors. At the moment, Magellan could see, a large Chinese junk was at port here, an indication that Cebu must be close to the western end of the Pacific. The captain-general sent Pigafetta and Henrique ashore to seek an audience with the rajah. They crossed the now empty piers and entered the city, a handsome one with wide streets. The royal palace lay nearby, and soon they came before Rajah Humabon, a plump brown-skinned man wearing a loincloth and a yellow turban. He had a broad face, high cheekbones, a flat nose; purple and red geometric tattoos covered his bare torso. Gold earrings and a necklace of pearls testified to his affluence. He sipped palm wine quietly through a reed from a porcelain jar as the emissaries from Magellan entered; behind him stood two rows of chiefs, richly garbed, formidably armed with curving copper daggers thrust into beaded cloth belts.

Henrique offered apologies for the fusillade of cannon fire, explaining that the great noise had merely been a signal of peace and friendship and a token of honor to the Rajah of Cebu. He added that Magellan was the captain of the ships of the greatest prince in the world, and that they were now en route to the Moluccas, but had called at Cebu to engage in trade and to pay their respects to the puissant Humabon. They had learned of the rajah, said Henrique thoughtfully, from his colleague, the Datu of Limasawa, who happened just then to be a guest aboard the Spanish vessels in the harbor.

The rajah accepted this information without much

show of excitement and gave a cool glance to the gilded beakers of Venetian glass that Pigafetta presented to him. After chewing languidly on betel for a moment, he replied that the visitors were welcome to do business here, but that first there was the little matter of the tribute payable on arrival by foreign ships. He indicated an Arab merchant by his side and said that the Moor had come just four days previously aboard the junk in the harbor, which had sailed from Siam laden with gold and slaves; the traders on the junk had paid the customary tribute, and the rajah expected Magellan to do the same.

Henrique, who had been coached on this point, observed that a captain in the service of the King of Castile had never paid tribute to anyone and was not about to begin now. "Take this for our answer," said Magellan's slave: "If you accept the peace we offer you, you shall enjoy it; if you desire war, though, you shall have your hands full."

As Humabon frowned over this poorly veiled threat, the Arab merchant bent close to him and said, "Take heed, sir, for these are the same men that have conquered Calicut, Malacca, and all greater India; if you treat them other than well, it will be so much the worse for you, for they are terrible in their wrath." Henrique broke in to say that the merchant was mistaken, for Malacca and India had been conquered by the Portuguese, a people much inferior to the Spaniards who now sought admission to Cebu. East and west had met; the spheres of influence of Portugal and Spain were touching at the borders; and the news that a second and apparently mightier European power was about to burst into the island world of the Pacific produced immediate distress in the rajah's throne room. Once more Henrique offered the choice between friendly trade and a devastating war, and Humabon, attempting to look as composed as before but clearly agitated and disturbed, asked for two days' grace to arrive at a deci-

sion. Meanwhile, he begged the envoys to accept his hospitality and caused a dinner of meat and palm wine to be served
on sumptuous porcelain dishes.

The outcome was inevitable. There was an exchange of
gifts; the next day Colambu of Limasawa went ashore to tell
his fellow potentate that the Spaniards were peaceful and
brought useful goods for barter; Humabon, listening to the
words of the datu and also to the words not spoken, capitu-
lated gracefully and made no more talk of tribute. In the days
that followed, messengers scurried back and forth between
Magellan's flagship and the palace, weaving an intricate web
of diplomacy. During these busy days Magellan remained
secluded aboard the *Trinidad*, neither inviting Humabon
aboard nor accepting invitations to go ashore, and this en-
hanced his impressiveness considerably. Humabon sought
reassurance that he was not going to become a vassal of the
King of Castile, and Henrique affirmed that Magellan merely
sought trading rights. This so eased the rajah's fears that he
drew a few drops of blood from his right arm and sent them
to Magellan, urging that the captain-general respond in kind
to seal their alliance; and so it was done.

Now Magellan departed from his policy of remaining
invisible and asked Humabon to the *Trinidad* for a feast of
friendship. But the rajah, remembering his own regal rank,
coyly replied that he was too busy preparing his gift for Magellan just now, and would send two of his nephews, some
officials of his court, and the Arab merchant from the junk, in
his place. When they came, Magellan again had a display of
Spanish armor staged, with the same effect here as at Limasawa. In any battle, Magellan casually told the Moor, all his
men fought in such impervious garments. Knowing that the
merchant was a practical politician who would convey a good
view of the realities to Humabon, Magellan told him to fear
nothing from Spanish power, "for our arms are soft to our

friends, and rough to our enemies; and as a cloth wipes away the sweat from a man, so our arms destroy the enemies of our faith."

Magellan's faith had now become as much of an obsession with him as his geographical theories once had been. He had always been a devout man, unusually so even for an age when warriors went into battle transfigured by the joy of slaying in Christ's name. His will, with its long list of charitable bequests (one real of silver to the Holy Crusade, another for the ransoming of Christians captive to the Moors, gifts to paupers on condition that they remember his soul in their prayers), testifies to his concern with matters of the spirit. Here in the Philippines, with all his dreams of wealth fulfilled, he addressed himself with burning and ultimately fatal zeal to the task of the conversion of the pagans.

Pigafetta relates that, as soon as the trade alliance was concluded, Magellan began to harangue the Cebuan emissaries on the advantages of becoming Christians, telling them "how God had made heaven and earth and all other things in the world, and that He had commanded that everyone should render honor and obedience to his father and mother, and that whoever did otherwise was condemned to eternal fire." The Cebuans, like the Limasawans, displayed an intense interest in the details of Christian dogma; their own religious feelings seem to have been malleable, and probably they deemed it wise policy to show enthusiasm for the creed of their well-armed callers. Pigafetta says that they "besought the Captain to leave them two men to teach and show them the Christian faith, and they would entertain them well with great honor. To this the Captain answered that for the moment he could not leave them any of his people, but that if they wished to be Christians his priest would baptize them, and that at another time he would bring priests and preachers to teach them the faith. They

[*191*]

then answered that they wished first to speak to their king, and then would become Christians."

Pigafetta goes on, "Each of us wept for the joy which we felt at the goodwill of these people, and the Captain told them not to become Christians from fear of us, or to please us, but that if they wished to become Christians they must do it willingly, and for the love of God, for even though they should not become Christians, no displeasure would be done them, but those who became Christians would be more loved and better treated than the others. Then they all cried out with one voice, that they did not wish to become Christians from fear, nor out of servility, but of their free will. The Captain then said that if they became Christians he would leave them the weapons which the Christians use, and that his king had commanded him to do so. At last they said they did not know what more to answer to so many good and beautiful words which he spoke to them, but that they placed themselves in his hands, and that he should do with them as with his own servants."

The meeting ended in a warm embrace. Magellan, weeping with delight, thanked his guests for this profession of faith, and gave them red caps, glass vessels, and a Turkish robe of red and violet silk to take to Humabon. Pigafetta was once more dispatched to accompany the islanders as they returned to the rajah. "When we came to the town," he writes, "we found the King of Cebu at his palace, sitting on the ground on a mat made of palm with many people about him. He was quite naked, except that he had a cloth round his middle and a loose wrapper round his head, worked with silk by the needle. He had a very heavy chain round his neck, and two gold rings hung in his ears with precious stones. He was a small and fat man, and his face was painted with fire [tattooed] in various ways. He was eating on the ground on another palm-mat, and was then eating tortoise-eggs in two china dishes, and he had four vessels full of palm wine, which he drank with a cane pipe. We made our obeisance, and presented to him what the Captain had sent him, and told him through the interpreter that it was not as a return for the present he had sent the Captain, but for the affection which he bore him. That done, his people told him all the good words and explanations of peace and religion which he had spoken to them. The king wished to detain us to supper, but we made our excuses and took leave of him. The prince, nephew of the king, conducted us to his house, and showed us four girls who played on four instruments, which were strange and very soft, and their manner of playing is rather musical. Afterwards he made us dance with them. These girls were naked, except from the waist to the knees, where they wore a wrap made from the palm-tree cloth, which covered their middles, and some were quite naked. There we made a repast, and then returned to the ships."

That night a sailor died aboard one of Magellan's ships, and in the morning Pigafetta and Henrique went ashore again, this time to ask for permission to bury the man on Cebu. Permission was quickly given to inter the sailor—and another who died the same day—in the marketplace at the center of town. The Cebuans attended the ceremony in great numbers, showing enormous fascination for the ritual of burial, and afterward paid homage to the crosses erected at the graves. While they studied Christian customs, Pigafetta was studying theirs. He saw them as people who "live with justice, and use weights and measures." Lovers of "peace, ease, and quiet," they were fond of the fleshly pleasures, spending four or five hours a day at their meals, and keeping as many wives as they desired. "Their houses are made of logs and sawed boards, and are so built above the ground upon props and piles that they ascend to them by stairs. Under their houses they keep their hogs, goats, and hens."

Always ready to believe a tall tale, Pigafetta listened to stories of "certain goodly waterfowl as big as crows, called *laghan*, which the whales of those parts sometimes swallow down, but so are themselves devoured, the fowl gnawing the heart of the whale, and killing him; the dead body floats to land and the fowl is found living within. The flesh of this fowl is delicate, but the skin is black."

The anthropologist in him took note of the fact that males of all ages have their sexual organs "pierced from one side to the other, with a gold or tin bolt as large as a goose quill." He described with care a religious ritual in which pigs are sacrificed by elderly women who caper about blowing reed trumpets and smear the blood of the sacrifice upon the foreheads of the men. When a chief dies, reported Pigafetta, "the women of the town go to his house, and set boughs about the corpse, in every bough a piece of cotton, so that the place is like a tent. Herein they sit, arrayed in white cotton, each having a palm-leaf fan. A woman comes with a knife and cuts off little by little the dead man's hair, after which his principal wife lies upon him, applying her lips to his, her hands to his hands, and her feet to his. When the one cuts, this other laments; when she ceases to cut, this one sings. About the chamber are porcelain dishes in which they burn myrrh, storax, and other incenses. This ceremony lasts five days. During this time, they say, a raven lights on the house at midnight and cries; the dogs howl five hours each night. After all this they enclose the corpse in a coffin and bury it."

A lively trade sprang up between the Spaniards and the Cebuans. Such commodities as iron and brass, being unobtainable in the islands and obviously useful for tools and weapons, were far more desirable to the Cebuans than so soft and trifling a metal as gold, which they had in abundance, and so they gladly gave gold for iron despite the feigned reluctance of the Spaniards to accept the yellow metal. Pigafetta says that the exchange rate was ten pieces of gold, worth 15 ducats, for 14 pounds of iron; at the modern price of gold, that works out to 16 dollars in gold for a pound of iron. The Spaniards also accepted ginger, sugar cane, fruit, palm wine, coconuts, goats, and fowl; they were less interested in the only native manufactured goods—utensils and ornaments cast in bronze by the "lost wax" method—but they acquired some samples of Cebuan gongs, betel boxes, flagons, bowls, and mortars to take to Spain. Gold and pearls, pearls and gold—those were their main concerns here, where no spices grew.

Magellan's main concern was the souls of the islanders. While his men, including even Juan Serrano and Duarte Barbosa, engaged in furtive private trade with the Cebuans against official orders, piling up individual stores of gold and pearls, Magellan took no notice, for he was intoxicated with holy fervor. Rajah Humabon had signified his willingness to be baptized, and on Sunday, April 14, Magellan came ashore for the first time to participate in this historic event. Preceded by 40 unarmed men, he marched to the improvised chapel that had been set up the day before; the ship's guns boomed a salute, frightening the people once more, although Humabon had been warned of it and stood his ground. Through Henrique, Magellan delivered a fiery sermon, imploring the islanders to burn their idols and accept the Cross; and the captain-general served as godfather while Humabon was baptized and christened Carlos, after the Emperor Charles. Humabon's brother followed and was renamed Hernando, for Charles' brother Ferdinand; the Datu of Limasawa was awarded the baptismal name of Juan; the Arab trader lately of Siam knelt to become Cristóbal. Fifty chieftains of Cebu took their turns before the font, and then, greatly pleased with his morning's work, Magellan returned to the *Trinidad*.

"After dinner," Pigafetta declares, "our chaplain and

some of us went on shore to baptize the queen. She came with forty of her ladies, and we conducted them on to the dais, then made her sit down on a cushion, and her women around her, until the priest was ready. During that time they showed her an image of Our Lady, of wood, holding her little child, which was very well made, and a Cross. When she saw it, she had a greater desire to be a Christian, and, asking for baptism, she was baptized and named Jehanne, like the mother of the Emperor. The wife of the prince, daughter of this queen, had the name of Catherine; the queen of Lima-sawa, Isabella; and the others each had their name. . . . The Queen of Cebu was young and handsome, and went appareled in white and black, with a great veil of silk upon her head, fringed about with gold, which covered her hat and hung down to her shoulders; she also had a great train of women following her, being all barefoot and naked, except that upon their heads and privy parts they wore veils of silk. After we baptized the queen she begged us to give her the little wooden boy to put in the place of the idols. This we did and she went away." That figure of the Christ child remained an object of worship on Cebu long after the natives had lapsed from their Christianity; it was discovered among heathen idols by the next Spaniard to visit Cebu, in 1565, and was rediscovered in 1598 by Spanish missionaries when they converted the islanders once more, this time permanently, re-storing the figure to its place of honor in their church.

Within eight days, Magellan could credit himself with 2,000 converts; he came ashore daily to hear the Mass and expound on the dogmas of the faith. How much of this the Cebuans understood is doubtful, for everything was funneled through the mind of Henrique, whose translations of the doctrines of the Trinity and the Immaculate Conception may have acquired a certain exotic coloration. On Henrique, too, the visitors depended for their comprehension of what the islanders were saying, and it is reasonable to suspect that the slender Malay often told his master what was likely to be pleasing to him, rather than what was in fact the case. Thus, in the course of one of his religious discourses, Magellan asked Humabon-Carlos to swear on the image of the Virgin that he would be the faithful servant of the Emperor Charles V. What Henrique actually relayed to the rajah is unknown, but the rajah duly knelt before the Virgin and vowed something, and Magellan was content that he had sworn allegiance to Spain. It was glorious to reflect on the splendor of this peaceful annexation of a great island; but one wonders what Humabon actually believed he was doing.

At any rate, the islanders did burn their idols, but they retained a few and continued to pray to them. When Magellan rebuked them for this, he was informed that they did not pray on their own behalf, but for the sake of a certain sick man, a brother of Prince Hernando, said to be the wisest man of Cebu, though he had not become a Christian. This man lay close to death, and for four days had been unable to speak. Magellan replied that the cause of his illness was his failure to accept the new faith. Pigafetta says that the captain-general "was seized with zeal for religion, and said that if they had a true faith in Jesus Christ, they should burn all the idols, and the sick man should be baptized, and he would be immediately cured, of which he was so certain that he gave them leave to strike off his head if the miracle did not take place. The rajah promised that all this should be done, because he truly believed in Jesus Christ. Then we arranged, with all the pomp that was possible, a procession to the house of the sick man. We went there and found him unable to speak or to move. We baptized him with two of his wives and ten girls. The Captain then asked him how he felt, and he at once spoke, and said that by the grace of Our Lord he was well enough. This great miracle was done under our eyes.

. . . On the fifth day the convalescent rose from his bed, and as soon as he could walk, he burned in the presence of the king and of all the people an idol which some old women had concealed in his house. He also caused to be destroyed several temples constructed on the seashore, in which people were accustomed to eat the meat offered to idols. The inhabitants applauded this, and, shouting, 'Castile, Castile,' helped to throw them down, and declared that if God gave them life they would burn all the idols they could find, even if they were in the king's own house."

Still several chiefs in remote parts of the island remained faithful to the old ways. Magellan here practiced a technique of conversion that was more common among those Spaniards then raping the Americas: with 40 men he appeared at midnight in a pagan village, set the place afire, and erected a cross. Thus he demonstrated the dangers of failing to accept the creed of the new god of love and sweet charity, and the Cebuan backwoodsmen hastened to their baptisms.

It was necessary at this time for Magellan to give some attention to the souls of his own men as well, for after a celibate 16 months since their idyll in Brazil they were gleefully accepting the willing favors of the scantily clad girls of Cebu. Duarte Barbosa's sprees in particular were becoming notorious; as in Brazil, Magellan's brother-in-law had to be fetched back in irons from one lengthy debauch, and Magellan stripped him of the captaincy of the *Victoria*, awarding the post to his loyal but youthful page, Cristóbal Rabelo. The expedition's chaplain delivered a thunderous sermon, calling it a mortal sin for any Christian man to have carnal knowledge of a pagan woman; thereafter the crewmen took the trouble to baptize any girls they were about to sleep with. But, though the polygamous Cebuans were untroubled by European sexual morality and generously made their women available to the voyagers, their jealousies were aroused by the

[*198*]

open enthusiasm the women displayed for the rough and virile seamen, whose coarse style of lovemaking evidently pleased them greatly. Magellan, lost in his transports of religious ecstasy, took no notice of the rising tensions.

He wished now to establish a protectorate of Christian islands, with the Christian rajah, Humabon, ruling over them in Charles V's name. With Humabon's blessing, Magellan sent envoys to all the surrounding islands, inviting them to swear allegiance to the Rajah of Cebu and to accept Christianity. Nearly all the neighboring chiefs speedily consented, having heard by this time of the might of the Spaniards; but a certain datu named Cilapulapu, who ruled a district of the island of Mactan directly across the strait from Cebu, defied the request. Magellan learned from Humabon that this Cilapulapu had been troublesome for a long while, refusing to recognize his sovereignty in the past. One night the captain-general sent a boatload of marines commanded by Gonzalo de Espinosa to burn and sack Cilapulapu's capital, the town of Bulaia. The surprise attack was effective; Bulaia was put to the torch, many of its women were violated, and a cross was erected. Yet Cilapulapu refused to submit. He sent word that he desired to be on good terms with the Spaniards, but he owed no obedience to strangers of whom he had never before heard, and certainly would not do reverence to the Rajah of Cebu, whom he despised. Although he sent some hogs, goats, and coconuts as a token of friendship, he refused to pay tribute or to adopt the religion of the strangers.

Magellan, infuriated, chose now to make a demonstration of the invulnerability of good Christian warriors. He announced that he would invade Mactan, bring the impudent Cilapulapu to his knees, and establish the rule of Christ on the refractory island. Magellan's officers were aghast at this proposal. Juan Serrano argued that they had no business risking Christian lives in a dispute between two half-naked chieftains; let Humabon himself deal with Cilapulapu. He reminded Magellan that they were not here as missionaries, or as founders of colonies, but merely to find the western route to the Moluccas and acquire spices for Spain. They now had spent three weeks at Cebu; it was time to go on to the Moluccas, which, according to Cristóbal the Moor, lay only a fortnight's easy sail to the south. Magellan retorted that they would not leave Cebu until he had fulfilled his commitment to Humabon, for loyalties must operate in both directions. Not only had he come to regard it as his duty to defeat Cilapulapu, but he now told his dumbfounded officers that he would lead the attack in person. This transgressed against the elementary principles of any expedition; in anguish, Duarte Barbosa reminded the captain-general of the needless deaths of such famed commanders as Francisco de Almeida and Juan de Solís, who had foolishly exposed themselves in battle. Magellan wavered; but when Sebastian del Cano slyly hinted that he might be too old, at forty-one, to take part in hand-to-hand combat, his resolve deepened.

Pride in his own piety dictated Magellan's actions now: the overweening pride that the old Greeks knew led great men to destruction. Blind with zeal, inflamed with confidence that the Virgin would lead him to glorious victory, Magellan told his officers that he would permit none of them to take part in the attack on Mactan. Nor would he accept even the aid of his bravest soldier, Espinosa, the slayer of the mutinous Mendoza. He would go to Mactan with just 60 men, all volunteers from among the crew, and with his cross and his sword he would prevail. The Rajah of Cebu offered him a thousand tried warriors; Magellan refused them, and forbade Humabon to meddle in the conflict. The crown prince suggested leading a diversionary attack on another part of Mactan; Magellan rejected the proposal. The son of another datu

of Mactan, who ruled half the island and was hostile to Cilapulapu, brought word that his father would strike at Cilapulapu by land when Magellan came ashore; the captain-
general declared that he would need only his own handful of
men to deal with the rebel. A divine madness was upon him.
In his own mind he partook of God's omnipotence. Hearing
nothing but the thunder of his own thoughts, Magellan prepared to celebrate this further triumph.

8

At midnight on Friday, April 26, 1521, three Spanish
longboats pushed off from Cebu for Mactan, a few miles
away. With Magellan went 60 volunteers—stewards, cabin
boys, common seamen—decked in unaccustomed armor and
gripping swords, lances, arquebuses, and crossbows in the
awkward manner of those with little experience in battle. On
Cebu, a black bird like a crow was croaking a sound of ill
omen, and the dogs were howling, and Juan Serrano and
Duarte Barbosa and the other officers quietly prayed that
their leader would return to his senses and draw back from
this suicidal mission.

Well before dawn the three boats arrived off Mactan.
Behind them in the strait were 20 or 30 large Cebuan war
canoes aboard which were Humabon, his son, a number of
island chiefs, and Humabon's thousand warriors. Magellan
had invited them all as spectators so that they might behold
his glorious victory, but they were under strict orders not to
intervene in the battle.

Magellan sent an envoy wading ashore: the Arab,
Cristóbal, who carried a message to Cilapulapu. Swear fealty
to the Emperor Charles, pay homage to Christ, and send tribute to Humabon, Cilapulapu was told, and all would go well;
otherwise, he would feel the sting of Spanish lances. Cilapu-
lalu replied that his men had lances also, and though they

were only of fire-hardened bamboo, they could sting as pain-fully as Spanish metal. The defiant chief added a comical re-quest: please do not attack before daylight, for I am expect-ing reinforcements in the morning.

Magellan assumed that this was some ruse designed to trick him into attacking in the dark, for obviously Cilapulapu did not expect him to heed the silly message and hold back till dawn. He concluded that the defenders must have con-structed a line of pitfalls in the underbrush back of the beach, and decided not to risk an invasion until his men could see where they were going. It is hard to comprehend whether Cilapulapu was being naïve or formidably devious, but in either case he achieved his purpose; for his message induced Magellan to wait until morning, and by then Cilapulapu's reinforcements had arrived.

By morning, too, the tide had ebbed, and coral fangs now jutted above the surface of the water. It was impossible to bring the boats close to shore; Magellan's men had to wade, armor and all, through thigh-deep water and a maze of sharp coral. Once more the Rajah of Cebu begged to be al-lowed to add his thousand men to the struggle, and once more Magellan refused. Musketry, armor, and faith would make him invincible.

He left 11 men in the boats to provide an artillery cover and, with the rest, went stumbling and tripping toward the beach. The boats were so far from shore, though, that their guns were useless, and as the invaders lurched over the half-concealed coral that fringed the shore, Cilapulapu drew up his troops in battle array undisturbed by the distant popping sounds of the Spanish guns. He had some 1,500 men; but what were odds of 30 to one against the aid of Christ and the Virgin? Breathless, soaked, already weary, Magellan and his 49 followers staggered onto the beach. Three parallel trenches lay before them; back of the trenches waited the

enemy, drawn up in a long crescent that outflanked the Spaniards on both sides.

Magellan's men at once set up a ragged, irregular fire,
but their arrows, crossbow bolts, and bullets could barely
reach across the ditches. Easily the defenders deflected the
missiles with their light wooden shields. Magellan cried out,
trying to get his men to hold their fire until the enemy was at
point-blank range, but the untried Spaniards were too terrified of the great army confronting them to listen, and the
waste of ammunition continued.

Still in the grip of his mystic self-assurance, Magellan
led the way forward over the triple row of deep, slippery
ditches. Cilapulapu let them advance unchecked, knowing
that the Spaniards would be in serious trouble if they had to
make a retreat over those same trenches. Now the two armies
faced one another across a few dozen yards of open sand. For
a moment the islanders actually seemed cowed by the incomprehensible confidence of the fiery little lame man in the steel
armor, and they faltered. But the moment passed, and the
invaders were subjected to a hail of javelins, bamboo lances,
stones, even handfuls of mud. The Spanish armor withstood
the onslaught, but Magellan sensed that his men were near
panic in the face of this howling army of natives, and he attempted a diversionary tactic, splitting his slim force to send
a few men under Cristóbal Rabelo inland to set fire to Cilapulapu's village. Rabelo started to move around the islanders'
flank; swiftly he and his men were surrounded, engulfed,
pulled down. Magellan saw Rabelo die, and a moment later
Juan de la Torre, the son-in-law of Juan Serrano, perished.
Abruptly his religious ecstasy left him. It no longer mattered
that the Savior had guided him infallibly through the strait,
had spared him from the schemes of evil men, had brought
him through the ordeal of the Pacific crossing, and had given
him the privilege of illuminating the lives of countless pa-

gans with the teachings of the Lord. Even the chosen ones of Heaven might meet martyrdom, Magellan suddenly realized, and he gave the order to retreat to the boats.

The demoralized Spaniards fled toward the ditches across which they had so recently struggled, and the islanders, sensing victory, followed in a great rush. By now, Cilapulapu's men had solved the secret of Spanish armor: instead of aiming at the heads and trunks of their foes, which were protected, they began to thrust their spears at the legs of the Spaniards, which were not. Fiercely Magellan shouted to his men, whipping them into two groups, each in turn to hold the enemy at bay while the other crossed a ditch. This tactic worked brilliantly so long as Magellan could direct it, and virtually all the Spaniards survived the three trenches and began to run toward the water; but a poisoned arrow struck the captain-general in his one good leg, as he was covering the last group of retreating men. He remained upright, somehow, and continued to fight. Only eight men stayed beside him, among them Pigafetta and Henrique.

These valiant nine stood off Cilapulapu's entire force until all the others were safe in the boats; Pigafetta says that Magellan turned his head many times to see if his men had carried out their retreat. When the rest had escaped, he began his own withdrawal. Slowly, in great pain, he hobbled to the water, his last few staunch men about him and protecting him with their shields. The islanders seemed to realize that he was the captain, and concentrated their fury on him. Twice his helmet was knocked off by stones; twice his men replaced it. Now they stood in shallow water, with hundreds of islanders about them, and for an hour the battle raged. Just beyond the reef, 40 armored Spaniards sat in their boats, not one going to the aid of the captain-general. A little farther away were the canoes of Humabon and his thousand men, here to witness the miraculous victory; they remained still.

When only four men still fought at Magellan's side, Humabon could hold back no longer and sent a rescue party toward shore. At the same moment, though, the Spaniards in one boat broke from their trance and fired an artillery piece that discharged a shrapnel of stones and bullets; by mischance, it ripped through the Cebuan rescuers, killing four of them, and the rest scattered.

While this was taking place, Magellan suffered a spear wound in the face. He drove his lance into his assailant's breast, but could not withdraw it, and it was wrenched from his hand. As he struggled to draw his sword, he was struck in the right arm by another spearsman, and his muscles failed him with the sword still half in its scabbard. Defenseless, Magellan depended now on his shield and those of Pigafetta, Henrique, and two other men. Clustered tightly, they tried to move in a phalanx out to the deeper water, but the islanders slashed below the shields and Magellan took a scimitar blow on his left leg that crumpled his face down into the surf. The attackers crowded around; he was seen to look up, as if trying to see if his companions were safe; and then he disappeared beneath the spears and cutlasses of the men of Mactan. "Thus," says Pigafetta, "they killed our mirror, our light and comfort, and our true guide. Thereupon, beholding him dead, we, being wounded, retreated as best we could to the boats, which were already pulling off."

9

Certain men seem so beyond the reach of mortality that their death comes with an impact that strikes at the fabric of the universe. So it was with Magellan. During the long months of the voyage, his prestige had risen so that the small lame man mocked by Juan de Cartagena off the African coast had come to stand like some Patagonian giant above all his men. Somehow, they had shared his strange and burning

faith in his own invulnerability and had expected him to prevail even when he went with 50 men against a host of enemies, and his senseless death on a Philippine beach opened a
terrible vacuum in the armada. Back to Cebu went the blood-
ied survivors to tell the tale, or as much of the tale as they
dared to tell. Only Pigafetta, whose part had been wholly
honorable, set down the real story of how Magellan's men
had panicked in combat, had blundered in retreat, and finally
had merely run away, leaving their captain-general to be
slaughtered while they looked on in safety. The men of the
fleet were stunned; the new Christians of Cebu, who had seen
a god fail his prophet, were shaken beyond measure. Rajah
Humabon wept openly as he saw Magellan die, and attempted in vain to ransom the captain-general's corpse from
Cilapulapu; but with Magellan no longer there to inspire
with his fanaticism, the rajah began to entertain some second
thoughts about the merits of the god whose faith he had
adopted.

Aside from Magellan, only seven men had been killed at
Mactan, but the collapse of Spanish prestige and confidence
was so great that it seemed as if the expedition had been deci-
mated. Duarte Barbosa and Juan Serrano, who were elected
joint holders of the post of captain-general at once, found
themselves paralyzed by indecision; they could not bring
themselves to launch a punitive attack on Mactan to recover
Magellan's body, and one of their first acts was a timid, petu-
lant one: they had all the Spanish trade goods withdrawn
from the marketplace of Cebu to the ships, as though they
could no longer trust their own Christian allies on this island.
This created great dismay among the Cebuans, who began to
see that the companions of Magellan were lesser men than
their fallen leader.

The Spaniards were low on provisions, and Duarte Barbosa told Henrique to go ashore, as before, to barter for food.

But the Malayan interpreter had been wounded at Mactan, and his spirit had been crushed by the loss of his master; furthermore, he was a slave no longer, for he knew that by the terms of Magellan's will he became free upon the captain-general's death. Henrique's only response to Barbosa's orders was to wrap himself in his sleeping-mat and turn his face to the wall. Angrily Barbosa ordered him to rise and go ashore, telling him that he was still bound to obey. If he refused, said Barbosa, it would be arranged that Doña Beatriz Magellan would keep him in slavery forever. Still Henrique huddled in silence and Barbosa fell upon him savagely, kicking and pummeling him, until at last the Malayan rose and dressed and went ashore.

He did his business in the marketplace, and then he took his revenge upon Barbosa. Henrique's loyalty was only to Magellan, not to those who now led the voyage. On his own inspiration, therefore, he sought an audience with Rajah Humabon and pointed out how useful the ships of the Spaniards would be in the fleet of Cebu, how valuable the Spanish armor was, how desirable the merchandise carried in the holds. Take no notice of the god of the Spaniards, Henrique advised. That god had shown himself to be worthless at Mactan. Seize the ships! Slay the white men! Humabon listened, and his Christianity faded, and he and Henrique devised a treacherous plan.

On Wednesday, May 1, Henrique returned from his marketing, bearing a message from Humabon to Barbosa and Serrano. The gift of jewels that the rajah had promised Magellan was now ready: rubies, diamonds, pearls, and some gold nuggets. The commanders and officers of the expedition were invited ashore for a farewell banquet at which the royal gift would be handed over.

Juan Serrano, always cautious, suspected some trap and expressed misgivings. For this he was mocked by the rash

Barbosa, and, stung, Serrano retorted that to prove he was no coward he would be the first man into the boats. Barbosa followed; in all, 29 of the ships' captains, pilots, and officers went ashore, among them the astrologer and the chaplain, but fortunately not including Antonio Pigafetta, who lay abed suffering from the venom of an arrow that had struck him in the forehead on Mactan.

Smiling Cebuans escorted the voyagers to the hut in which the banquet was to be held. As they walked through the town, the Portuguese pilot, João Lopes Carvalho, noticed a curious thing: the native prince who had been miraculously healed through baptism came up to the chaplain, Padre Valderrama, spoke a few words with him, and detached him from the procession, taking him to his own house. Carvalho, who already had grave doubts about the wisdom of going ashore, interpreted this to mean that the grateful prince was trying to spare the priest from some doom in store for the others. He mentioned his fears to Gonzalo de Espinosa, who agreed that it was best to turn back; quietly the two men left the group, returned to the docks, and rowed to their ships, Espinosa to the *Trinidad*, Carvalho to the *Victoria*.

Pigafetta appeared and asked Espinosa why he had left the banquet so soon. Espinosa explained, and just as he finished his tale they heard shouts and cries of anguish from the town. The islanders had attacked the unarmed officers and were slaughtering them. Humabon's men appeared, dragging the dead bodies to the waterfront and casting them into the sea. Immediately the three ships went into action; anchor cables were cut to save the time of pulling them in, and the vessels moved toward shore and commenced a bombardment of the town. Moments later a mob of natives brought Juan Serrano, bound, stripped, and bleeding, into view. Serrano called out to Carvalho to still the guns or the islanders would butcher him at once. All the others, he said, were dead except

Henrique and Padre Valderrama. The Cebuans were offering Serrano for ransom, and he implored his friend Carvalho to send some copper bars and two small cannons to shore as the price of his freedom.

Carvalho began to order out a boat with the ransom; but then, it seems, he reflected that, with Barbosa and Serrano both dead, he would become captain-general. Pigafetta declares that Seranno "begged us earnestly to redeem him with some of the merchandise; but João Carvalho, his boon companion, and others would not let the boat go ashore, so they might remain masters of the ships. But although Juan Serrano wept and asked us not to set sail so quickly, for they would kill him, and said he prayed God to ask his soul of João Carvalho his comrade, in the day of judgment, we immediately departed."

Sails were hoisted; Espinosa took command of the *Trinidad*, Carvalho the *Victoria*, and Juan Sebastian del Cano, who somehow had not been invited ashore, the *Concepción*. As Juan Serrano watched in disbelief, the armada hurried out to sea. "I do not know if he is dead or alive," Pigafetta concluded. The fates of Humabon's victims were never known; presumably all perished, but two Portuguese writers declared that eight of Magellan's men were sold into slavery in China, and rumors of the survival of Juan Serrano and Duarte Barbosa circulated for a number of years. Indeed, a few years after the Cebu massacre, a Duarte Barbosa turned up on the Malabar Coast, but it was a common Portuguese name and may not have been the same man.

The Cebu adventure, which had for so many weeks been a stirring hymn of faith, thus ended with the death of the greatest of captains, the perfidy of the island's rajah, and the cowardice of those who would not rescue Juan Serrano. The cross in the marketplace was torn down; the dream of Spanish empire in the Philippines came to nothing; the failure of the fiery little commander to produce his guaranteed miracle at Mactan sent the Cebuans back to their idolatry. And, shorn of their leaders and their purpose, the remnants of the grand Spanish fleet went spinning wildly off into a career of dismal piracy.

Only 115 men, less than half the original complement, now remained, not enough to operate all three ships; nor were there enough officers to lead the way. Carvalho, the new captain-general, brought the fleet to the nearby island of Bohol, where the *Concepción* was beached, unloaded, and burned, her men and cargo divided between the *Trinidad* and the *Victoria*. Carvalho proved wholly incapable as a commander, though, and his skills as a pilot were useless in seas for which he had no charts. Magellan evidently had not shared with his officers much knowledge of the location of the Moluccas, for, instead of making the short journey to the southeast that would have brought the ships to the Spice Islands, Carvalho embarked on an aimless, blundering cruise in the Sulu Sea.

He began poorly, sailing southwest to the large island of Mindanao, where a friendly datu greeted them and came on board. In the absence of Henrique, Pigafetta acted as interpreter, and apparently he had picked up enough of the islands' *lingua franca* to get along satisfactorily; the datu invited him ashore, and he went—alone—to accept the chieftain's hospitality. The natives rowed him two leagues upriver to the datu's house, where some chiefs and two "rather handsome ladies" were imbibing freely of palm wine. Prudently he took only one drink himself, and so in the morning was capable of conducting an anthropological survey of the village. Its customs were much like those he had recorded on Limasawa and Cebu; he noted details of how the natives cook their rice so that it "becames as hard as bread," and observed that, while golden utensils were abundant here, food was not. He visited the queen, who performed for him on four metal drums, and on his return journey to the sea he noticed three lawbreakers who had been hanged on a tree. Gold in this region was "more abundant than hairs on the head," he declared, but the natives, lacking iron tools with which to dig, were too lazy to do much mining.

The Spaniards' departure from Cebu had been so hasty that they came away with little food, and their visit to Mindanao did not aid them in that respect. Nor was there anything to eat at their next port of call, Cagayan Sulu, which was inhabited by a few Moslem outcasts from Borneo who lived in nudity and poverty. Borneo, of which Europe then had never heard, sounded like a good place to obtain provisions, but Carvalho had no idea how to find it and proceeded to go even farther astray by steering northwest, precisely the opposite direction from where the Spice Islands lay. This took them to the large island of Palawan, which, as Pigafetta says, they "found to be a promised land." The leaders of the expedition became blood-brothers to Palawan's ruler; the natives supplied them with water and food, and let them sample a distilled wine made from rice, which proved to be more potent than the palm wine of the Philippines. Pigafetta took particular note of the national sport of cockfighting— large bets were placed on champion cocks—and set down a detailed description of the blowpipes and poisoned arrows used by the Palawanese. It was a cheering visit, and afterward the Spaniards, still going away from the Moluccas, found their way to Borneo and went down its northwestern shore to the great port city of Brunei.

St. Elmo's fire danced on the masts as they entered Brunei, foretelling good things. The island's ruler sent a *prau*, or large canoe, out to greet them; it was ornamented with gold and peacock feathers and bore eight chiefs, who ceremoniously presented Carvalho, Espinosa, and Cano with betel, rice wine, sugar cane, and caged fowls. Pigafetta, Cano, and six others went ashore bearing offerings for the rajah and his lady: "A Turkish coat of green velvet, a chair of violet-colored velvet, five ells of red cloth, and other gifts" for him, and for the queen "three ells of yellow cloth, a pair of slippers decorated with silver, and a silver case full of pins." Elephants carried the wondering voyagers to the palace, where they slept that night on silken sheets and the next day had audience with the rajah. He remained inaccessible at the far end of a great hall; contact with him was made through a relay of officials who whispered all messages from one to the other until the last, who stood beside the rajah, transmitted it to him through a speaking-tube in the wall. Though restraining with difficulty their laughter over such absurdities of pomp, Pigafetta and Cano managed to communicate the wish of the King of Castile to enter into friendly relations with the Rajah of Borneo. The rajah received their gifts with an indifferent nod, but granted the Spaniards trading rights, and a curtain was drawn to signify the end of the audience.

A snack of cloves and cinnamon was served at the palace, but at the house of the chief minister a sumptuous banquet was offered. Pigafetta says: "We partook of the flesh of various animals such as veal, capons, fowls, peacocks, and others, with different sorts of fish, so that of flesh alone there were thirty or thirty-two different viands. We supped on the ground on a palm mat; at each mouthful we drank rice-wine from a little china cup the size of an egg. We used spoons like our own, but these were made of gold."

For a month the Spaniards remained at harbor in this magnificent city of 25,000 families, caulking their ships and conducting trade. All seemed well; but all had seemed well at Cebu, too, and toward the end of July Carvalho began to grow suspicious. Nevertheless, he let himself fall into a trap set for him by the rajah, who had come to covet the Spanish ships and the goods they carried. Carvalho had brought with him on the voyage his young son, born of a Brazilian Indian mother on one of his earlier expeditions; the rajah attempted to entice this boy ashore, kidnap him, and ambush the rescue party that would certainly follow. He sent word that his own young son wished to play with Carvalho's boy. Carvalho, who needed wax and other commodities from the rajah, could not refuse, but he sent an escort of five men, including Espinosa and Cano. For three days they were gone; then Espinosa and Cano returned with news that the child and the other two had been captured, and that they themselves had escaped after failing to free them.

Carvalho, remembering Mactan, was too shrewd to send a rescue party ashore to certain destruction, and in any case the rajah gave him no chance to do so, for suddenly some 150 small canoes and junks began to move toward the *Trinidad* and the *Victoria* in a quite menacing way. Afraid of being attacked from all sides, Carvalho ordered sails lifted, and the Spaniards quit the harbor with such haste that they left an anchor behind. Their heavy guns drove the native ships off and the voyagers reached sea safely. Outside the port they came upon a large junk carrying 100 men, five women, and a child; they captured it, taking the crew and passengers prisoner. Carvalho discovered that among his captives was one of the Rajah of Borneo's generals, a young man who was the son of the ruler of the important Philippine island of Luzon. Carvalho sent word to shore that he would exchange this hostage for his boy and the two men captured with him, but the rajah refused, and after blockading the harbor for some days, Carvalho put out to sea, leaving his son behind.

Now he embarked on a campaign of frank piracy. Through the whole month of August he cruised the coast of Borneo, looting and destroying any vessel he encountered, whether Chinese junk, Malay *prau*, or Arab merchantman. Like any pirate captain, he kept mistresses, choosing three women from the first junk as his private harem. Discipline vanished altogether once women were permitted aboard the ships; but the sight of Carvalho indulging his lusts in Magellan's own cabin so scandalized the other officers that they deposed him on the grounds that he "was pursuing his own advantage and not that of His Majesty." Gonzalo de Espinosa, whose conduct throughout the entire voyage had been exemplary, became the new captain-general, which carried with it command of the flagship, the *Trinidad*. Juan Sebastian del Cano now replaced Espinosa as captain of the *Victoria*. And so this Basque mariner, who had earned a commuted sentence of death from Magellan for his part in the Port San Julian mutiny, rose to the second highest position in the expedition.

Espinosa brought the fleet to an island north of Borneo, where they halted 42 days to careen and repair the ships, a job they had not managed to finish at Brunei. There was wood here, which they had to haul at great discomfort from thorny thickets, and here Pigafetta made the most extraordinary of his biological discoveries, the famous walking leaves, which began to crawl when they fell to the ground: "These leaves," he asserted, "resemble those of the mulberry tree, except in not being so long. Their stalk is short and pointed; and on each side of the leaf, near the stalk, they have some sort of organs, which look like two short pointed feet, yet if they were cut off, neither blood nor sap drips from the wound. Upon being touched they crawl away. I preserved one of these leaves in a bowl for eight days, but when I tried to touch it, it began to run about in the bowl. I fail to understand what these leaves live on. I assume it is on air." Crocodiles, gigantic oysters, horned fish, and other marvels caught his attention also on this island.

Espinosa, who was an honest man, though illiterate, restored discipline aboard the ships but continued the policy of attacking merchant shipping. Late in October, on an island called Sarangani, they captured two Malays in one of these pirate raids and found that one of the men came from the Moluccan island of Ternate. He knew of Magellan's old comrade, Francisco Serrão, and informed them that Serrão had recently died. Espinosa forced the Moluccan to serve as their pilot, and reluctantly he guided them through the sea in which they had wandered for nearly six months, until, Pigafetta writes, "On Wednesday the 6th of November we sighted four lofty islands. . . . The pilot told us that those four islands were Maluco [The Moluccas]. Therefore we thanked God and for joy we discharged all our artillery. It was no wonder that we were so glad, for we had passed twenty-seven months less two days in our search for Maluco."

10

Now finally they were at their goal, having spent twice as long getting from the Philippines to the Moluccas as they had taken to cross the thousands of miles of the open Pacific. On November 8 they entered the port of the island of Tidore and fired an artillery salute. The next morning Sultan Almanzor, the handsome and affable Moslem ruler of the island, came out in his canoe, seated under a silk umbrella, and was rowed around the ships. Almanzor had dreamed that voyagers would come to Tidore from a great distance, and he offered a hearty welcome. When he came aboard the flagship at Espinosa's request, he momentarily showed the distaste of a good Moslem for the hogs on board, and he had to enter the captain-general's cabin through a hatch in the roof, since the Sultan of Tidore could not stoop, as was required in order to go in the usual way. Upon learning that the visitors were Spaniards he expressed great delight, since the Portuguese had not made themselves popular in their occupation of the neighboring island of Ternate. Soon Almanzor was pledging allegiance to Emperor Charles, and even, so Pigafetta says, decreeing that henceforth his land should be known not as Tidore but as Castile, "in proof of the great love he bore to our king and master."

Here was paradise indeed. The Portuguese had spread rumors that the Moluccas were arid, fog-bound islands surrounded by deadly reefs, but this was meant only to discourage the ships of other nations, and to their relief the Spaniards found Tidore idyllic. Pigafetta says, "Cloves, sago, ginger, coconuts, rice, almonds, bananas, sweet and sour pomegranates, sugar cane, nut and sesame oil, cucumbers, pumpkins, and pineapples—an extraordinarily refreshing fruit about the size of our watermelons—could be found here, as well as a peachlike fruit called guava, and many other edible plants. Furthermore, there were goats and poultry in abundance, and honey, gathered by bees the size of ants in hollow trees, was plentiful. White and colored parrots flocked in the trees; the red ones were most sought after, not because they were edible, as one might have supposed, but because they were the quickest to learn to speak." The women of the island, though, appeared ugly to him; the men guarded them so jealously nevertheless that it seemed "that they were possessed by the devil." Pigafetta got close enough to the women to discover that "the venereal plague was more widespread here than anywhere else in the world," owing to "the lechery which these poor heathens practice."

The chief product of Tidore was cloves, which grew in the mountains on a tree that had fragrant leaves, bark, and wood. The cloves, found in clusters of 10 to 20 at the ends of the smaller branches, were white at first, red as they ripened, and black when dried; they were gathered twice a year, in June and December. As at Cebu, the Spaniards set up shop on shore and proceeded to trade linen, knives, and trinkets for local goods. The holds of the two vessels rapidly filled with cloves and cinnamon, but not rapidly enough to suit the Spaniards, who suspected that spices were in better supply on Ternate or one of the other islands. This was confirmed on November 13 by a Portuguese, Pero Affonso de Lorosa, who came over from Ternate upon hearing that Spaniards had arrived. Lorosa reported that Ternate was the best place to get cloves; that Francisco Serrão was indeed dead, having been poisoned eight months earlier at the instigation of the Sultan Almanzor; that the Sultan of Ternate had been poisoned at the same time; that Serrão's hoard of spices had been dissipated; and that seven Portuguese who had gone to collect cloves on the island of Bachan had lately been slain by the natives for taking liberties with their women. Lorosa himself, who had come to the Moluccas with Serrão in 1512, asked and was granted permission to return to Europe aboard the Spanish ships.

It was disturbing to hear that Almanzor had had a hand in Serrão's death, for the Spaniards had learned at Cebu and at Borneo not to trust seemingly friendly monarchs, and the sultan's attitude was so warmly effusive that it had already kindled some uneasiness. He went so far as to fetch a cargo of cloves from the large island of Halmahera for them, saying that he did not want them to go to the trouble of leaving his land. He seemed to have a rational motive for his excessive friendliness, for he informed them that he would like Spanish military aid in settling an old feud with Ternate. Almanzor had recently established a shaky protectorate over Ternate and hoped that the Spaniards would help him maintain his nephew on Ternate's throne. However, the Spaniards continued to mistrust him, even while they were accepting his immense hospitality and discussing the details of the treaty between Tidore and Spain.

On November 25 Almanzor's cloves arrived from Halmahera; now the Spanish ships were fully laden, and Espinosa, nervous about a possible trap, was in a hurry to be off. But on the 26th came an invitation from Almanzor to a feast on shore to celebrate the arrival of the cloves and also that of the Sultan of Bachan, who was paying a state visit. To the tense Spaniards this seemed all too reminiscent of the fatal banquet at Cebu. Espinosa refused the invitation in such a jittery way that Almanzor realized the Spaniards feared some sort of treachery. The sultan's intentions were quite peaceful, however, and to reassure his guests he went aboard the *Trinidad* in grand style, pleading with Espinosa not to rush off so precipitously, for November was a poor month for navigation in these seas. Espinosa still seemed eager to depart, whereupon Almanzor brought forth a Koran and swore elaborately that he meant no harm. Espinosa relaxed enough to delay the sailing for several weeks.

During this time, the sultans of the other Moluccan islands did their best to win Spanish favor. Delegations came from Halmahera, Bachan, and Ternate, bearing gifts for Emperor Charles, and offered such a quantity of cloves that the market became glutted; a couple of little brass chains would buy a hundred pounds of them. The Spaniards had exhausted their trade goods and began to sell their cloaks and their shirts for spices. Every cranny of the ships held bales of cloves; the ships were so overladen that they threatened to capsize every time the Spaniards fired a salute in honor of the royal delegations, and the salutes had to be discontinued. There was not even room for all of the gifts of the sultans, though among the rarities that did get aboard were the skins of two birds of paradise, sent by the Sultan of Bachan and described by Pigafetta as being of marvelous beauty.

The time set for departure was Wednesday, December

18. Three island sultans and a royal prince came aboard to pay farewells and proposed to accompany the Spaniards as far as a small island near Tidore. But the *Trinidad*'s anchor stuck in the mud, and when it was finally drawn up, the ship sprang a leak somewhere below the waterline; the hold began to flood, and the sailing had to be postponed. Sultan Almanzor provided divers to examine the ship's hull. They wore their hair long and loose, says Pigafetta, so that as they swam about the ship their tresses would be sucked toward the leak, indicating its location. They could not find it, though, and it became clear that the *Trinidad* would have to undergo extensive repairs, which would take several months. "Who will go to take news of me to King Charles our lord?" Almanzor lamented.

Captains Espinosa and Cano conferred, and it was agreed that Cano would take the *Victoria* back to Spain right away, while Espinosa would remain with the *Trinidad* at Tidore until she was ready. Since the monsoon from the east was now blowing, Cano's route was dictated by the winds: he would have to go by way of the Cape of Good Hope, and so would complete a circumnavigation, something that had not been part of the original plan. To avoid Portuguese shipping, Cano would have to keep far to the south of the usual route, stealthily crossing the Indian Ocean and swinging wide of Africa without touching port. The *Victoria* went on her way late in December, bearing 47 Europeans, 13 Moluccans who had signed on as crewmen, and 26 tons of cloves; an additional two tons of cloves had to be unloaded and left behind for the sake of safety.

Sultan Almanzor supplied several hundred carpenters, who went to work on the leaky *Trinidad*. But her hull was not repaired until early April, and by then the prevailing winds had changed; the monsoon from the west now ruled, robbing the loyal and goodhearted Espinosa of his circumnavigation. He would have to go back to Spain by recrossing the Pacific and passing eastward through the Strait of Magellan, as originally planned. The *Trinidad* set out from Tidore on April 6, 1522, with 53 men and a cargo of 50 tons of cloves. But she had a muddled, unhappy voyage, for Espinosa was no navigator, and he was not far east of the Moluccas when he ran into unexpected difficulties: in place of the monsoon from the west, he found his ship buffeted by strong winds out of the east. It was not yet realized that in the great zone of ocean between the two Tropics the winds blow always from the east, making the sea a one-way street. In a roundabout manner Espinosa sought a favorable wind, going northward until he was in 42°N., the latitude of Japan. Here the wind did permit an eastward voyage, but his men suffered bitterly from the cold, and he descended to lower latitudes again, where the winds were contrary. Valiantly he struggled eastward as far as the Ladrones, while his crew weakened and sickened, and some deserted, preferring the unknown life of a remote island to the harshness of a journey to Spain. A tempest lasting five days carried away the mainmast, so that there could be no further thought of guiding the patched, battered ship safely through such an intricate passage as the Strait of Magellan; abandoning hope of an immediate return to Spain, Espinosa tried now to sail to the Spanish ports on the west coast of Panamá, but even that proved beyond his abilities. Twenty-seven of his crewmen had perished before he decided to turn around in mid-Pacific and go back to the Moluccas.

The poor *Trinidad* arrived in the Moluccas six months after she had set out for home. By ill luck or mismanagement, Espinosa landed at Ternate, not Almanzor's Tidore, and in the interval the Portuguese had reoccupied Ternate, building a fort there and ending Almanzor's brief period of control over that island. The despondent Espinosa surrendered to the Portuguese commander, who promptly seized the ship, her cargo, and all her charts and journals. Her surviving crewmen were sent as prisoners to Malacca, and thence to India, where they remained in captivity for four years as punishment for having trespassed on Portugal's sector of the world. By 1526 only Espinosa and four others were still alive; they were released then and returned to Spain, where Emperor Charles V raised Espinosa to the nobility, gave him a substantial pension, and appointed him to a high rank in the Spanish navy.

Juan Sebastian del Cano's voyage homeward in the *Victoria* was more successful, though no less arduous. Pigafetta, who was on board, supplies a detailed though confusing itinerary of a two-month journey southward through a host of islands to Timor, at the lower end of the Indonesian group; this route into the Indian Ocean was necessary because the far simpler westward route via the Straits of Malacca was controlled by the Portuguese. The Moluccan pilots provided by Sultan Almanzor found Pigafetta a willing listener to their tales of wonder; he set down accounts of the island of Arucete, where the people are 18 inches long and have ears as long as their bodies, so that when they slept they used one ear as a mattress and the other as a coverlet; of an island in the South China Sea, where there were birds so great they could seize elephants in their talons and fly off with them; of China, where the king is never seen by commoners, and who, when he travels about in his peacock-shaped chariot, is accompanied by six ladies of the court, all dressed in robes identical to his so that none might know which was truly the king. Pigafetta accepted all these reports at face value, although he found it impossible to believe the Hindu custom of letting widows throw themselves upon their husbands' funeral pyres.

At Timor, where the *Victoria* remained for several

weeks, there was some sort of uprising against Captain Cano. Pigafetta says nothing about it, but Herrera, a generally reliable chronicler, asserts that two men were put to death at the captain's orders. Others apparently deserted. It is possible that some of these dissidents were men still loyal to the memory of Magellan who were unwilling to take orders from the condemned mutineer Cano. On February 11, 1522, the *Victoria* left Timor and entered the Indian Ocean, making a wide detour around Sumatra, which the Portuguese had reached. The provisions obtained at Timor speedily began to rot, for salt to preserve them had been unavailable there; the pork had to be thrown overboard, and the men lived on rice and water. They suffered greatly from scurvy, and one by one began to die. Pigafetta relates that, as the dead bodies were committed to the sea, "we observed that the Christians always descended with their faces towards Heaven, and the Indians [Moluccans] sank with their faces downward." Stricken with disease and famine, the crewmen urged Cano to make for the Portuguese ports on Africa's eastern coast, where they would lose their ship, their cargo, and possibly their freedom, but at least retain their lives. Cano resisted the suggestion; in his own way he was as determined a man as Magellan, and he was going to bring the ship safely to Spain even if it had to be manned by a crew of corpses.

Twenty-one sailors died on the Indian Ocean crossing. As Cano tried to complete the great arc that would take him around Africa, he encountered heavy weather, gales from the northwest, the same strong winds that had for so many years sped Portuguese vessels southward down Africa's western coast. Now he fought to make headway against those winds on his northward journey. Not until May 6 did the *Victoria* finally round the Cape of Good Hope and enter the Atlantic, and in the rounding of that terrible cape she lost her foretopmast and had to stop at an uninhabited island for repairs. Food was so low now that the men were reduced to nibbling at cloves, which provided no nourishment and greatly intensified their thirst. As starvation neared, Cano was compelled to take the desperate step he had rejected a few months earlier: he approached a Portuguese harbor, São Tiago in the Cape Verde Islands, on July 9.

Such a move was a sign of great extremity, for here was a Spanish ship coming home through Portuguese waters laden with cloves from Portugal's Moluccas, and any hint of the truth would bring certain arrest. Cano therefore sent a boatload of men ashore to buy food from the Portuguese, instructing them to say that they were coming back in a crippled ship from the coasts of America and needed aid. This worked well enough; the Portuguese were generous to mariners in distress, so long as they did not happen to be trespassers. When the shore party returned, it bore the news that the date in São Tiago was Thursday, July 10. Pigafetta was puzzled, for he had kept careful entries in his journal; by his reckoning it was only Wednesday, July 9, and he knew he had made no mistake. The truth dawned only slowly: that by sailing continuously westward around the world, they had lost a day somewhere. This had been realized in theory for several centuries, since Arab geographers had noticed that the time of sunrise varied by four minutes for each degree of longitude; the variation for a complete global circuit of 360° would thus be 1,440 minutes, or one full day. There was no more dramatic proof possible that they were circumnavigators, nor none that could have been more disturbing—for they saw now that for some time past they had been eating meat unknowingly on Fridays, celebrating the Sabbath on Saturdays, and otherwise failing to observe their religious obligations properly.

A more immediately serious problem developed when

Cano sent his men back to São Tiago for a second load of provisions. This time one Spaniard was so foolish as to offer a handful of cloves in payment for goods. The Portuguese authorities quickly seized the 13 men of the shore party and made caravels ready to attack the *Victoria*. Seeing that his men had not come back, Cano did not wait to be captured, but raised sail at once and left the island. Now just 18 Europeans and four Moluccans remained to man the *Victoria* as the leaky, rotting ship limped for home. Any good storm would have sent the overloaded vessel down, but she wobbled northward all the month of August. On September 4 Cape St. Vincent, Europe's southwestern tip, came into sight. Two days later they reached the coast of Spain, after an absence of three years less two weeks, and on Monday, September 8, 1522, Juan Sebastian del Cano brought the *Victoria* into Seville, successfully carrying out the longest voyage in the history of man.

They had come home, and Pigafetta brought his journal to its close by writing, "These were mariners who surely merited an eternal fame, more justly than the Argonauts of old, who sailed with Jason in search of the golden fleece, into the region of Colchis, and entered the river Phasis, from the sea of Pontus. The ship too, undoubtedly, deserved far better to be placed among the stars than their ship *Argo*, which, from Greece, discovered that great sea. For this our wonderful ship, taking her departure from the Straits of Gibraltar, and sailing southwards through the great ocean towards the Antarctic Pole, and then turning west, followed that course so long that, passing round, she came into the east, and thence again into the west, not by sailing back, but by proceeding constantly forward; so compassing about the globe of the world, until she marvelously regained her native country Spain, and the port from which she departed, Seville."

On the next day, the 18 survivors, gaunt, withered, old

ahead of their years, walked barefoot with lighted candles in their hands to give thanks for their deliverance at Magellan's own favorite shrine, Santa Maria de la Victoria, Our Lady of Victory. Where was Magellan? Our Lady had brought him no victory, and his bones lay on distant Mactan. Where were the proud captains, Cartagena, Mendoza, Quesada? Where was Duarte Barbosa? Juan Serrano? Antonio de Coca? Carvalho, the pilot who had become captain-general, had died in the Moluccas after his downfall. Espinosa, the master at arms who had become captain-general, was on his confused way back across the sea to Ternate and four years of imprisonment. Astrologer San Martín? Dead. Two hundred seamen and marines? Dead. Dead. Dead. The roster of the 18 circumnavigators survives: Miguel de Rodas, Martin de Judicibus, Miguel Sanchez, Nicolas the Greek, Hans of Aachen, Juan de Arriata, Juan de Zubileta, Antonio Hernández Colmenero, Juan de Santandres, Francisco Rodrigues, Vasco Gomes Galego, Hernando de Bustamente, Juan de Acurio, Francisco Alvo, Juan Rodríguez, Diego Carmona, all of them names that meant little when the grand armada set sail in 1519, and also a certain "Antonio Lombardo," who is our friend Antonio Pigafetta of Vicenza, and Juan Sebastian del Cano, mutineer, former master of the *Concepción*, ultimately captain of the *Victoria*, and in a sense the first captain to circumnavigate the world.

11

And so it was over. Magellan, that most single-minded of men, had his triumph after death, for no one now could doubt that the world was round, that it was circumnavigable, or that a strait in South America gave Spain access to the Pacific, greatest of seas. He was gone, but if he had lived to come home, he would have found his wife and his only child in their graves, and he would have taken small pleasure in learning that his old nemesis, King Manoel of Portugal, had not lived to see 1522.

To Juan Sebastian del Cano went much of Magellan's glory, not altogether undeservedly, for Cano played a real part in bringing the voyage to its conclusion. But Pigafetta, mindful of the true hero of the enterprise, supplied a stirring epitaph for Magellan in his account: "I hope that the renown of such a noble and valiant captain will never be extinguished or pass into oblivion in our time. For among other virtues were his constancy and perseverance even in the most difficult situations. He bore hunger better than all the rest of us. He was expert in navigation and in the making of nautical charts. That this is the truth is apparent, since no one else had so much natural genius and fortitude, all the knowledge that enabled him to circumnavigate the world—for he had as good as completed his aim when he died—no man having preceded him in this."

Cano received a letter on September 13 from Charles V, who was at his court in Valladolid; the emperor offered his "infinite thanks" for bringing his ship safely home, and requested Cano to come at once to court to give a personal account of the voyage, bringing with him "two of the most reliable and best-informed men." Curiously, Cano chose Francisco Alvo, the pilot, and Hernando de Bustamente, the barber; he did not pick Pigafetta, possibly because the Italian, strongly pro-Magellan, might say the wrong things about the mutiny of Port San Julian.

Charles V was already considerably perplexed about that mutiny, for the *San Antonio* had returned to Spain in the spring of 1521 after Estevão Gomes and Geronimo Guerra had done their turnabout in the strait, and those two had been spreading malicious tales of Magellan's high-handed, arbitrary ways. On October 18, 1522, a royal commission of inquiry began investigating the events of the voyage. Cano testified that Magellan had failed to consult Juan de Cartagena on a number of major decisions, as he was bound to do by his orders, and that this had led to dissension and the uprising. Magellan's own log had vanished—very likely destroyed after the captain-general's death by those it incriminated—and Cano successfully concealed his own role in the mutiny, so that in the end there was no official placing of blame, no sorting out of rights and wrongs. The officers of both factions were dead, and so be it, and Cano, as the last of the captains, carried off the honors. He attended a grand reception at court, along with his 17 fellow survivors from the *Victoria*, and the 13 men captured at the Cape Verde Islands, who had been freed by Charles V's intervention. Cano was awarded a pension of 500 ducats a year for life, and the right to use a handsome coat of arms bearing a globe for a crest, and the motto, *Primus me circumdedisti* ("You first circumnavigated me").

Pigafetta also became a celebrity. He paid his own visit to Charles V, presenting a copy of his lively journal, expurgated to remove many of the details of the controversies of the voyage. Then he went on to Portugal for an audience with the new king, João III, who requested his presence to hear his tale of wonders; next he was summoned to the French court to tell his story, and in December 1523 Pope Clement commanded him to Rome for the same purpose. Graceful, charming, witty, Don Antonio delighted these great princes hugely, and for a while was the most lionized man in Europe; fortunately, he made manuscripts of his journal available to each of the monarchs whom he visited, so that several copies survive. Eventually he wearied of attention and, in October 1524, applied for admission to an ascetic monastic order, the Knights Hospitaller of St. John of

Jerusalem—whose grand master also insisted on having a copy of his journal. He took his vows and in 1530 followed his order to the island of Malta, which Charles V had granted it, and there he died bravely in 1536, defending Malta against Turkish attack. In that same year his work on the circumnavigation finally was published, and it has never ceased to entertain.

Those two key figures in organizing the voyage, Cristóbal de Haro and Bishop Fonseca of Burgos, had varying fates.

Fonseca's health was broken by the news of the marooning and likely death of his heir and protégé, Juan de Cartagena, but he had strength left for one final power play, attempting to replace Hernando Cortés as governor of the newly conquered land of the Aztecs with the husband of his own bastard daughter. Cortés was able to win the support of Pope Adrian VI, who knew Fonseca well from his days in Spain, and in the inquiry that followed, the bishop's infinite rascalities were exposed and he was discharged by Charles V from all his posts of power. Retaining only his bishopric, he retired from active life and devoted himself thereafter to scholastic controversies.

Cristóbal de Haro, on the other hand, had prospered in Spain during the three-year absence of the Magellan expedition, and he grew even wealthier on the proceeds of the venture. Though the *Trinidad*'s cargo had been lost, the *Victoria* reached Spain with her 26 tons of spices mostly intact and in good condition. This cargo, worth some 675,000 dollars, more than repaid the cost of outfitting the ships, and Haro obtained his fair share of the profits, and then some. (The only claimant for Magellan's share was his father-in-law, old Diogo Barbosa, who filed suit jointly with his son Jaime. But Diogo was dead before a favorable verdict was handed down in 1525, and Jaime was unable to enforce it. No one ever succeeded in receiving the captain-general's portion of the expedition's yield.)

Now that Magellan's great voyage had given Spain the route to the Moluccas, Haro began to think of sending a second expedition, which, avoiding the delays and conflicts of the first, would go directly to Tidore, take on a load of spices, and return swiftly and profitably to Spain via the strait. One did not need a monomaniacal Magellan to carry out such an enterprise, now that the way was known. A Sebastian del Cano was sufficient, and Haro approached Cano, sounding him out about a second Molucca voyage. While this was taking place, the governments of Spain and Portugal were trying to settle the vexed question of the eastern extension of the papal line, so that it could be determined which nation had the right to exploit the Moluccas. In March 1524 a remarkable group of judges assembled on the border of Spain and Portugal between the towns of Badajoz and Yelves to decide the issue. Those who took part included Juan Sebastian del Cano, Estevão Gomes, and Sebastian Cabot; Ferdinand Columbus, son of Christopher, and Juan Vespucci, son of Amerigo; Diogo Lopes de Sequeira, a former governor-general of Portuguese India; and several other great geographers and explorers. But the meeting was futile, for the high commissioners could not agree even on which of the Cape Verde Islands to base the demarcation line's Atlantic side: the Portuguese insisted on the easternmost island, the Spaniards on the westernmost, for the farther east the line ran in the Atlantic, the farther east it would lie in the Pacific, and each side was willing to give up a segment of the New World to insure having the Spice Islands in its half of the globe. Nor did the testimony of the *Victoria* survivors impress the Portuguese much, since Cano and his men were in Spanish pay and hardly objective when they placed the Moluccas east of the dividing line. Besides, as everyone knew, reckonings of longitude made at sea were virtually worthless. After two months of deadlock the conference ended with both nations claiming the Moluccas.

Plainly nothing but actual possession would legitimize any claim, and the Portuguese already had their fort on Ternate; the Spaniards hurried to get their own new Molucca expeditions on their way. The first to go to sea was Estevão Gomes, who believed that a better strait than Magellan's could be found north of the Isthmus of Panamá. He based this on a report of the voyage of the Florentine Giovanni da Verrazzano, who had traversed the North American coast from North Carolina to Maine in 1523–24, discovering New York Harbor in the process. Verrazzano had tricked himself into thinking that Cape Hatteras was a narrow neck of land separating the Atlantic and the Pacific; but Gomes followed the coast from Nova Scotia to the Caribbean without finding a strait. This expedition was financed half by Charles V, half by private investors.

Cristóbal de Haro, who preferred sure things, outfitted seven ships to go to the Moluccas by way of Magellan's strait. As co-captains he hired Sebastian del Cano and a knight named Garcia Jofre de Loaysa; the ships did not include that grand veteran, the *Victoria*, which had been sent on a voyage to the West Indies and was lost on her return trip to Spain. The Loaysa-Cano expedition sailed from the Spanish port of La Coruña in July 1525; the vessels were large and well equipped, and expectations were high. Cano was to have charge of the naval affairs, while Loaysa would remain as Spain's governor in the Moluccas.

But the voyage was a succession of mishaps. The weather was unfavorable from the start; the squadron was separated repeatedly; Cano's ship was wrecked near the strait, though he and most of the others survived; two more vessels were so badly damaged that they had to return to

Spain. It was April before the four remaining ships entered the strait, and the southern hemisphere's winter was coming on. Driven in and out of the strait several times, they did not escape into the Pacific until May 26; six days later they were scattered by a tempest and never reunited. The fate of two ships is unknown. A third reached Mexico after its men suffered terrible privations; they were taken before Cortés and told him the story of the disastrous voyage. The fourth ship, which was the flagship and now bore both Loaysa and Cano, sailed westward through the empty Pacific with nearly all hands wasted by disease, undergoing hardships similar to those of Magellan's passage of 1521. Loaysa died on July 30, 1526, and Cano survived him by less than a week. Those who still lived took the ship to the Ladrones in September, 98 days out from the strait—the same span, to the day, that the voyage had taken Magellan. A month later they reached Tidore in the Moluccas.

There they learned that the Portuguese entrenched at Ternate had recently burned Tidore's capital as punishment for the cordial reception Sultan Almanzor had given the Spaniards in 1521. Almanzor was dead and had been succeeded by a thirteen-year-old son. The weary Spaniards established themselves at Tidore and held out sturdily against attacks by the Portuguese of Ternate, but their numbers rapidly diminished through death and desertions.

Meanwhile, Cortés sent a rescue party from Mexico: three ships commanded by his kinsman Alvaro de Saavedra. This fleet left Mexico's Pacific shore late in 1527; two ships evidently were wrecked in Hawaii, but the third, under Saavedra, reached the Moluccas in March 1528. Saavedra could do little to help the 120 survivors of Loaysa's fleet against the Portuguese, and he simply collected a cargo of cloves and set out again for Spain, planning to make an eastward crossing of the Pacific. He met with the same difficulty that had stopped Espinosa in 1522—the prevailing winds blowing from the east—and, baffled, had to turn back. After visiting New Guinea (which a Portuguese captain, Jorge de Meneses, had discovered in 1526), he eventually returned to Tidore and joined forces with the stranded Spanish garrison from Loaysa's expedition. There the Spaniards remained, harassed by an increasing number of Portuguese who came out from Malacca. By 1530, when only 40 Spaniards were left, they surrendered to the Portuguese, but stayed on for another four years in a kind of peaceful accommodation. At length the Portuguese offered to send them home by way of India; they were transferred to Cochin in 1534 but ran into administrative difficulties there and were stranded again. A few of Saavedra's and Loaysa's men finally reached Spain in 1537, thereby completing a circumnavigation, of sorts, that had taken about a dozen years.

They arrived to find that Spain no longer was seeking to reach the Spice Islands. The failure of the Loaysa-Cano expedition and the inability of Saavedra to carry out an eastward crossing of the Pacific had caused Charles V to lose interest in the Moluccas. (He had also sent out another Molucca-bound fleet in 1526, under Sebastian Cabot, which got sidetracked on the eastern coast of South America. Calling at the estuary of the Plata, Cabot picked up some survivors of the calamitous Solís expedition of 1515–16, heard from them of a wondrous land of gold and silver somewhere inland, and, forgetting his orders entirely, sailed upriver for a thousand miles, finding nothing of note. He turned back to Spain in 1529 without ever seeing the Pacific.) The Moluccas were of no use to Charles V unless some way could be found to bring goods back to Spain without infringing on Portugal's rights. Since the Pacific's merciless trade winds apparently made an eastward voyage impossible, Charles decided to cut his losses, and in 1529, when he was in even greater need of ready cash than usual, he repudiated all Spanish claims to the Moluccas in return for the payment by Portugal of 350,000 ducats, or about 5,000,000 dollars. It was only a provisional repudiation, pending some accurate determination of the longitudes, but its effect was to cut Spain off permanently from the Spice Islands. This was particularly bothersome to Cristóbal de Haro, who was then about to send a new *armada de Maluco* to sea and was forced to cancel it. He sued Emperor Charles for his expenses, won his case, and thereafter flourished in different and less risky enterprises.

What, then, had Magellan accomplished? He had, as promised, found a westward route to the Spice Islands, but it was a one-way route, as many men had died to discover. The Moluccas were still Portugal's to exploit. His great geographical achievement, the finding of the strait, held little practical value, for the strait was remote and formidable, and there was small point in daring it when nothing but the emptiness of the Pacific lay beyond. The Spaniards concentrated instead on mining their twin treasurehouses of Mexico and Peru. As of 1530, it appeared that Magellan had demonstrated certain facts about the shape of the world and about the capabilities of the human spirit, but not that he had brought profit to Spain.

[4]

DRAKE

HE SPANIARDS COULD NOT ALTOGETHER FORget the ocean Magellan had given them. Even after Charles V's pawning of the Moluccas, a few tentative Spanish probes of the Pacific were made. In 1537 Cortés sent two vessels from Mexico under the command of Pedro de Alvarado and Hernando Grijalva to search along the equatorial line for certain islands thought to abound in gold. They discovered a number of islands, including the Gilberts, but found no gold, and the crew mutinied, slew Grijalva, and suffered shipwreck off New Guinea. Seven survivors reached the Moluccas and were taken into Portuguese custody. In 1542 Spain belatedly remembered the "Islands of St. Lazarus" that Magellan had given his life to find. Again an expedition went out from western Mexico—no one was using Magellan's strait in these years—led by Ruy Lopez de Villalobos. Upon reaching the island of Mindanao, Villalobos changed the name of the archipelago to the Philippine Islands, in honor of the son of Charles V, and formally claimed the group for Spain. Though it was necessary to subdue the Mindanaoans by force, the Spaniards soon were enjoying friendly commerce

DRAKE'S VOYAGE 1577-1580

with the inhabitants of several islands. This aroused the Portuguese, who sent word from the Moluccas that all Pacific islands belonged to Portugal; Villalobos' reply conceded only the Moluccas to the Portuguese. After a year in the Philippines, he embarked on a bungled voyage of exploration that eventually brought him to Tidore, where he became involved in intricate and treasonous negotiations with the Portuguese and with the native rulers. During this time he sent one of his captains, Ynigo de Retez, on a voyage to Mexico. Retez sailed 230 leagues along the north coast of the large island of New Guinea, to which he gave that name, but he could not make headway eastward across the Pacific and returned to the Moluccas. In the end the Portuguese shipped Villalobos and his men to India, but he died en route in 1547 on the island of Amboina.

This attempt to take permanent possession of the Philippines thus came to nothing; but Philip II was determined to have a Pacific empire for Spain and ordered the Viceroy of Mexico to undertake the conquest and colonization of the Philippines. The expedition was planned by Andres de Urdaneta, who had sailed on the dismal Loaysa-Cano venture of 1525 and who had been the first survivor of that voyage to return to Spain in 1537. Urdaneta had since become a monk whose special study was geography, and since his professor forbade him to hold any secular rank, command of the Philippines enterprise went to Miguel López de Legaspi. With Urdaneta as his pilot, Legaspi took four ships westward from Mexico in November 1564, passed quickly through the Ladrones to the Philippines, and, exercising great tact and diplomatic skill, won the loyalty of several island chiefs and founded a permanent settlement on Cebu. Thereby the Philippines entered upon four centuries of Spanish rule until the United States seized them in the Spanish-American war in 1898.

Urdaneta soon produced a geographical achievement even more significant than Legaspi's political one. He volunteered to carry the news of Legaspi's success back to Mexico by an eastward route. Avoiding the winds and currents that had stymied other pilots, Urdaneta crossed the Pacific in a sweeping northerly arc that took him above 40°N. There he picked up a wind from the west and crossed to Mexico. The discovery of what became known as Urdaneta's Passage transformed Pacific commerce, for now it was no longer necessary that every westward voyage to the Orient be a circumnavigation of the globe, and, with a return route available, Spain was at last able to exploit the great ocean. Magellan's forbidding strait was still avoided; it was easier to transport men and goods by land over the Isthmus of Panamá than to risk that bleak southern waterway. A network of ports sprang up along the Pacific coasts of South and Central America and Mexico, and regular trade began between those Spanish harbors and the Philippines. The most reliable of contacts was the annual Acapulco galleon, which left Manila, Spain's new Philippine capital, every June with a load of silks and spices and arrived in Acapulco, Mexico, via Urdaneta's Passage by December. The Acapulco galleon shuttled on this route for more than two centuries.

This trans-Pacific highway was a narrow one, for all pilots kept to the known paths. Magellan's northwesterly route through emptiness to the Ladrones and the Philippines was the standard outbound way, and Urdaneta's Passage through even emptier seas was the standard means of return. The relatively isolated Hawaiian Islands remained undiscovered, though they lay virtually in the latitude of Acapulco, and almost nothing was known of the numerous archipelagoes that lay south of Magellan's track. Some rumors of those isles of the South Pacific had reached the Spanish conquerors of Peru, however, and geographers suggested that they might be outlying outposts of the great unknown southern continent. (Belief in *Terra Australis* had never waned; it was still thought to begin just south of the Strait of Magellan and to stretch westward for thousands of miles at the bottom of the world, with such vaguely known places as New Guinea representing its northern coast.) The only two expeditions that had succeeded in traversing the Strait of Magellan—that of Loaysa and Cano, and that of Magellan himself—had ignored the question of *Terra Australis* by turning north immediately upon reaching the Pacific. Hungry for new worlds, the Spaniards persuaded themselves that the unknown continent reached as high as 15°S. and came within 600 leagues of Peru in the South Pacific. In 1567 they went looking for it.

The voyage was inspired by Pedro Sarmiento de Gamboa, a vigorous and unusual character who was expert in mathematics and astronomy, had studied Inca traditions deeply, and had investigated the black arts to the extent that the Inquisition had given him some notice. Sarmiento aroused the interest of his friend the Viceroy of Peru in the quest for *Terra Australis*, and the viceroy authorized the use of two small ships, optimistically provisioned for a voyage of only 600 leagues. The viceroy's young nephew, Alvaro de Mendaña, was given nominal command and instructed "to convert all infidels to Christianity."

They sailed from the Pacific port of Callao late in 1567, passed westward between the Marquesas and the Tuamotu Archipelago without sighting land, and, after discovering and stopping in the Ellice Islands, came, on their eightieth day at sea, to a rugged shore which they believed to be the coast of *Terra Australis*. Exploration showed it to be an island, one of a major group which they named the Solomon Islands, since they had convinced themselves that King Solomon's fabled gold mines had been located in the South Pacific. After a six-month stay and a good deal of trouble with the natives, they turned back, reaching Callao in August 1568 after a stormy and famine-ridden crossing of Urdaneta's Passage. Mendaña returned inflamed with visions of discovery, but not until 1595 did he get a second chance to look for *Terra Australis*. In the 27 years between Mendaña's two voyages, the Spaniards of the New World had other concerns than searching for unknown continents, for their monopoly of Pacific navigation was broken, and broken most expensively, by the arrival on the scene of Queen Elizabeth's lusty privateers.

2

England had been slow to become a seafaring nation. Though they were island folk, the English had no tradition of an open sea; their chief source of foreign exchange was the export of wool, and later of woolen cloth, and generally they used foreign shippers to take their goods abroad. Such shipping as they did themselves went only as far as Flanders or Portugal or France, for the cold seas off their shores did not encourage far voyaging. While Italian merchants journeyed to China and Portuguese mariners were finding the Cape of Good Hope, the English stayed home, preoccupied first with their seemingly endless war with France, then with that generation-long civil convulsion, the Wars of the Roses.

Very gradually they began to look outward, once Henry VII had come to the throne to put his Tudor dynasty in the place of warring Lancaster and York. Fishermen from Bristol sailed to Iceland; the Cabots in 1497 got as far west as Newfoundland; a few pioneering British geographers began to spread word early in the sixteenth century of the discoveries of Columbus and Vasco da Gama, so that the English realized what vast claims were being staked by Spain and Portugal. There were some tentative attempts to follow up the Cabot discoveries, but little came of these.

About 1530 the geographer Roger Barlow and the merchant Robert Throne, who had lived in Seville, composed their *Declaration of the Indies*, the first resounding manifesto of English maritime expansion. This document, which was submitted to Henry VIII in 1540, urged the discovery of an English route to the Spice Islands by the only path that would not interfere with the claims of Spain and Portugal: over the North Pole and westward through the supposed Strait of Anian across North America into the Pacific. "With a small number of ships there may be discovered divers new lands and kingdoms," they wrote, "in the which without doubt your Grace shall win perpetual glory, and your subjects infinite profit. To which places there is left one way to discover, which is into the North: for that of the four parts of the world, it seemeth three parts are discovered by other princes. For out of Spain they have discovered all the Indies and Seas Occidental, and out of Portugal all the Indies and Seas Oriental: so that by this part of the Orient & Occident, they have compassed the world. For the one of them departing to the Orient, and the other toward the Occident, met again in the course or way of the midst of the day, and so then was discovered a great part of the same seas and coasts by the Spaniards."

But was there such a northern route? The *Declaration of the Indies* replied with a phrase of affirmation that might well stand as a motto for the entire sixteenth century: "There is no land uninhabitable, nor sea innavigable." What the English must do was pass the North Pole, which would be no more impassable by reason of ice than the equator had turned out to be impassable by reason of extreme heat; then, the authors of the *Declaration* said, ships might sail southwest along "the back side of the new found land . . . and then decline towards the lands and islands situated between the Tropics, and under the Equinoctial," where without doubt "they shall find the richest lands and islands of the world of gold, precious stones, balms, spices, and other things that we here esteem most: which come out of strange countries, and may return the same way."

By the 1550s England was making regular northern voyages—through the Northeast Passage, though, and not the Northwest. Sebastian Cabot, that servant of many kings, had advocated reaching Asia by skirting the Arctic Circle going east. Three ships sailed in 1553, hoping to reach China, but unexpectedly discovered a useful route to Russia instead. England organized the Muscovy Company and engaged in steady and profitable trade with Russia for a generation without seriously trying to get to the Orient at all. But the Northwest Passage was the object of renewed interest after 1576, when Martin Frobisher went in search of the Strait of Anian, the first of a number of English voyagers to make the attempt.

The success of the Russian enterprise drew England more eagerly into maritime development; the Russians provided a good market for English textiles, and it was reasonable to look for other markets elsewhere. (By contrast, Spain and Portugal had little to export, and Spain in particular founded her overseas empire on the desire for plunder, not for trade.) To expand their commerce, the English looked toward the West Indies, where cloth was in good demand and could not be supplied by the Spaniards who controlled the region. The English also proposed to bring a second commodity to the Spanish masters of the Caribbean: African slaves. The natives of the West Indies did not make suitable slaves for the mines and plantations of the Spanish Indies; some, like the Caribs, were fierce and intractable, while the docile ones were rapidly dying out from imported European diseases. The Spaniards needed husky African blacks, but could not easily obtain them because of Portugal's control of Africa's western coast. The English, who rejected the authority of the pope and had no concern with the line of demarcation, were unhampered by the necessity of staying out of Portugal's allotted waters, and were able to go into business as purveyors of slaves to Spanish America.

This commerce sprang up in a highly unofficial way about 1530, when William Hawkins of Plymouth intruded himself as an unwanted middleman between the Portuguese of Guinea and the Portuguese of Brazil. He made three voyages in which he picked up blacks in West Africa—stealing them from the Portuguese there who were trying to monopolize the slave trade, and selling them to the settlers who were just starting to colonize Brazil for Portugal. These trans-Atlantic voyages continued for many years, though the English soon abandoned Brazil as their market in favor of the Spanish settlements on Hispaniola and other Caribbean islands. The Hawkins family remained central to the triangular England-Guinea-Hispaniola slave trade; and the boldest member of this great seafaring line was William's son, John Hawkins, whom Queen Elizabeth eventually knighted for his prowess as a slaver.

John Hawkins made his first voyage for his own account in October 1562. With three ships and 100 men he raided Sierra Leone in Portuguese Guinea, rounded up 300 blacks, and carried them to Hispaniola. Though England and Spain differed sharply in matters of religion, they were then not at all so hostile to one another as they later became, and Hawkins was welcome in the Spanish Indies; he even had the services of a Spanish pilot in crossing the Atlantic. Blandly overlooking the fact that they were buying property stolen from Portugal, the Spaniards were glad to have Hawkins' blacks and paid for them handsomely in hides, ginger, sugar, pearls, and other commodities. Some of this Hawkins sent directly to England; the rest, strangely, he shipped aboard two chartered vessels for sale in Spain. The Spanish authorities at Cádiz could not abide such outrageousness; they did not mind so much that Hawkins had obtained his cargo by selling stolen blacks, but there were strict rules prohibiting vessels other than Spanish ones from trading in the West Indies. The goods were confiscated, but Hawkins still showed a fine profit on his venture. (Among his backers was Queen Elizabeth, as a secret shareholder.)

Hawkins was determined to trade in the Spanish Indies regardless of Spain's restrictions, and in 1564 he led a second expedition, of five ships, including the *Jesus of Lubeck*, a 700-ton vessel of the English navy lent him by Elizabeth. Loading slaves at Guinea again, he made a difficult crossing of the Atlantic but brought his live cargo to the ports of the Spanish Main, as South America's Caribbean shore was known. Slaves were so coveted there that the port officials winked at the regulations forbidding foreigners to trade in the New World, and through connivance and chicanery Hawkins was able to make another good profit. The Spanish government, however, protested to Queen Elizabeth, who, though privately an investor in Hawkins' venture, piously disowned it publicly and made a great show of forbidding Hawkins to go to the Indies again, thus averting an undesired crisis in her relations with Spain. Nevertheless, in 1566 Hawkins was able to send one of his captains, John Lovell, on another slaving voyage—an expedition noteworthy because it was the first important experience at sea of England's noblest mariner, Francis Drake.

The story of Drake's early life is as hazy as that of Magellan: we have a few facts and a great deal of conjecture, much encrusted by apocryphal myth. He was born at Tavistock in Devonshire between 1539 and 1545—1541 seems like the most plausible date—and was, it appears, one of the 12 sons of the Reverend Edmund Drake, a seaman turned preacher. Edmund Drake belonged to the class of gentlemen, which is to say that he was a respectable commoner with the right to bear arms; he lived on the land of Lord Francis Russell, the son of the first Earl of Bedford, who stood godfather for his tenant's son Francis and gave him his own name. The elder Drake followed Henry VIII out of the Church of Rome and became fiery in his anti-Catholicism, a trait inherited by Francis. Edmund's extreme Protestant views caused him great trouble when Mary, the Catholic daughter of Protestant Henry, came to the throne in 1553, for he refused to relapse to the old faith when his neighbors did, and they persecuted him severely for it. This much we know about Francis Drake, then: that he came from a poor but honorable family and that he grew up with good reason for hating Catholics. (And for hating Spaniards, since Queen Mary's husband was King Philip II of Spain, and her mother, Catherine of Aragon.)

Edmund Drake's religious views evidently cost him his livelihood during Mary's reign and reduced the family to poverty. It was natural for the Drake boys then to seek employment at sea, for not only did they spend their adolescence in a seafaring town (their father had moved to the English Channel port of Gillingham, in Kent, to avoid religious oppression), but they were related in some way to the famous Hawkins family. It may have been that old William Hawkins of Plymouth was Francis Drake's uncle, for William's sons, John and William, referred to Drake as their cousin. As a boy apprentice Francis served on a Channel coaster which he inherited from her owner when he was only eighteen but soon was forced to sell when Channel trade diminished. By now he knew more than a little about seamanship, and he signed on to sail for the Hawkinses in 1564.

His character seems to have been fairly well fixed by then. He was energetic, daring, ambitious, and strong-willed; he was kindhearted, lively, and good-natured; he was intelligent, courageous, resourceful, patient, and hearty. That is, he was ideally suited to become a legendary hero of romance. In addition, he had, like any great man, a set of driving obsessions: he was a vigorous Protestant, which was permissible now that Protestant Elizabeth had replaced her Catholic half-sister, Mary, and he detested Spaniards and Catholics with all his will. These prejudices were reinforced by his first voyage with the younger William Hawkins, in which he sailed to San Sebastian in the Bay of Biscay to rescue some Plymouth seamen who had been in the grip of the Spanish Inquisition. This gave him a clear and chilling view of that dark cruelty so deeply embedded in the Spanish character. In 1566, when he embarked on his slaving voyage under Captain John Lovell, he gained another reason to loathe Spaniards: Lovell, a poor businessman, was bilked of his slaves at the Spanish Main port of Río Hacha, and because of this Spanish slyness, Drake came home with no earnings from his voyage.

Drake had been only a purser on Lovell's ship, but almost at once he found himself a higher post in another slaving expedition ready to depart from England. John Hawkins, who had been idle since 1565 by Queen Elizabeth's command, had persuaded the queen to let him make a third voyage to Africa and America. Again Elizabeth made a private investment in the venture while outwardly claiming to know nothing about it. The project was risky, for Philip II had grown irate at the way his own officials in the Caribbean were covertly doing business with the English; he had prosecuted some of them and had issued strong orders to the others to prevent English intrusion in the Indies. Hawkins still believed that he could prevail upon the Spaniards of the Indies to buy his slaves, but took the precaution to arm his five ships heavily. Young Francis Drake, then in his early twenties, was taken on as a pilot, or second in command, but shortly was transferred to command of the 50-ton *Judith.*

Hawkins' fleet left England in October 1567 and collected slaves as usual in Guinea, plundering several Portuguese slave ships in the process. Then the English carried their cargo to the Spanish Main, where the reception was icy. Fearful of King Philip, the authorities in the ports refused to let Hawkins do business, though the plantation owners were as willing as ever to purchase his slaves. The English sold some of their blacks at Santa Marta, on the coast of what is now Colombia, but at Río Hacha they had to storm the town in order to gain permission to trade. Hawkins, aided by Drake, drove the port officials out and kept them away while finding purchasers for the slaves. At Cartagena, too, the English met with official hostility and had to force their trade upon the Spaniards by bombarding the port. At length the work was done, and, laden with gold and pearls, Hawkins began the homeward voyage.

Hurricanes struck as the ships were passing through the channel between Yucatán and Cuba. They were badly damaged, and Hawkins was forced to run for San Juan de Ulúa, a harbor on the Mexican coast near Vera Cruz. This was embarrassing to him, for officially he had no business in these waters at all, and he had to ask politely for leave to call at a port where English shipping was forbidden. It was equally awkward for the local authorities, for San Juan de Ulúa happened to be the port from which Mexican silver was shipped to Spain, and at the moment 12 Spain-bound ships

[*246*]

were there, bearing a load of ingots worth millions of dollars. They knew that Hawkins knew the treasure fleet was there. If he chose to seize it, they probably could not stop him. But Hawkins hesitated to commit such a flagrant act of war, and so he and the authorities at San Juan de Ulúa struck an uneasy deal: they would let him repair his ships, and he would refrain from pirating the treasure fleet.

Unfortunately, another fleet of 13 ships arrived the next day, several weeks ahead of schedule, bringing from Spain the new Viceroy of Mexico, Don Martín Enriquez. The viceroy was astounded to find five English ships in the harbor— and, moreover, occupying such a strategic position that they controlled the port. Hawkins allowed the newcomers to enter the harbor, for to prevent them would also be an act of war, and Enriquez learned from the shamefaced port officials of the deal that had been made. Local colonial officials might feel free to ignore the orders of King Philip, but the viceroy could not; he had been sent from Spain specifically to uphold those orders and to keep English shipping away from Mexico. However, he was aware of Hawkins' superior position, and so he sent word to the English captain that the truce would be honored. For several days the five English ships anchored peacefully in the harbor while being refitted, and their crewmen mingled amiably with the Spaniards. Then, at a signal, the Spaniards attacked the partly dismantled English fleet by surprise. The *Jesus of Lubeck*, the largest vessel, was captured, along with two others. The Englishmen on shore were murdered. Hawkins and Drake succeeded in fighting their way out of the harbor, Hawkins on the *Minion*, Drake on his *Judith;* both ships were terribly overcrowded with survivors from the other vessels, and their voyages home were marked by extraordinary suffering. The *Minion* took so many men aboard that it could scarcely stay afloat, and 100 volunteers went ashore in the Gulf of Mexico, where they were seized by Spaniards and subjected to the worst torments of the Inquisition.

In January 1569 the *Minion* and the *Judith* came separately into port at Plymouth, and soon all England was aflame with news of Spanish infamy. The effect was precisely that of the Pearl Harbor attack on the United States: an angry nation demanded war. Francis Drake, who had seen the treachery of San Juan de Ulúa at first hand, was the least forgiving of all. He pledged himself to take vengeance on Spain and went on to make the Spaniards pay many times over for their trick. Although Queen Elizabeth, politically overextended on too many other fronts, refused to declare war on Spain, she hinted broadly that she would countenance unofficial acts of reprisal. The years of Anglo-Spanish friendship were over; there could be no more of the irregular but lucrative commerce in slaves along the Spanish Main; the two nations were set now on the path that took them toward the clash of 1588, the year of the Spanish Armada. The perfidy of Don Martín Enriquez loosed upon Spain a demon in Francis Drake—"the Dragon," the Spaniards called him, grimly punning on *Draco*, the Spanish form of his name. Now he cruised the seas inspired by a vindictiveness that knew no soothing, carrying on his private war with Spain. His revenge was thorough and effective, and his exploits grew more spectacular until, a decade after San Juan de Ulúa, his thirst for vengeance carried him around the world in Magellan's track and placed him in the ranks of the circumnavigators.

3

In the summer of 1569 Drake took a wife, Mary Newman, and then commenced his campaign against Spain. He led secret voyages of reprisal to the West Indies in 1570 with the *Dragon* and the *Swan*, and in 1571 with the *Swan* alone. Little is known of these expeditions; he captured a few ships off the Spanish Main, relieving them of their merchandise, but primarily he seems to have been scouting the territory. He paid particular attention to the Isthmus of Panamá, for all the treasure looted in Peru had to cross this narrow neck of land to be shipped to Spain, the sea route via the Strait of Magellan remaining unused. Drake made contact with the *Cimarrones*, or Maroons, a tribe of runaway Negro slaves and Indian women who lived in the jungles of the Isthmus and defied all Spanish attempts to bring them under control. They hated the Spaniards as vehemently as Drake did and conspired with him to intercept the mule trains that carried Spanish bullion from the Pacific to the Atlantic side of the Isthmus. Operating out of a secret base that he called Port Plenty, in the Gulf of Darien, Drake harassed the Spaniards with great success and soon was planning a surprise attack on the major treasure-shipping port of Nombre de Dios.

Drake was back in England by 1572, and in May of that year he set out with two ships, the *Pasha* and the *Swan*, to make his bold raid on Nombre de Dios. Two of his brothers, John and Joseph, joined him in this venture. At Port Plenty they assembled some pinnaces, or small schooner-rigged vessels, which they had brought in sections from England. Quietly they moved along the coast toward Nombre de Dios, Drake undaunted even after learning that the town was on guard against an expected attack by the Maroons and its garrison had lately been reinforced. With only 73 men he fought his way into Nombre de Dios by night, routed the defenders and seized the royal treasury. But a tropical downpour wet the English gunpowder, and Drake himself was wounded and collapsed; trapped in the treasury with silver bullion all about them, his men left the heavy ingots behind and escaped with their fallen commander. Recovering at Port

Plenty, Drake realized he could never carry out a second such raid on Nombre de Dios, and fell back on his alternate plan of seizing the overland bullion convoy as it crossed the Isthmus.

It was the rainy season, and no bullion would be shipped for several months. Drake spent some of this time marauding along the Spanish Main; he swooped in and out of the harbor of Cartagena at will, seizing large Spanish ships and disrupting commerce along the entire coast; he mystified the Spaniards by his unpredictable comings and goings; and he diverted Peruvian treasure in great amounts from Spain to England. During this period, Drake scuttled the *Swan*, for he no longer had enough men to sail her. Returning to Port Plenty, he learned that his brother John had been killed in a bold but foolhardy raid on the Spaniards, and now tropical fevers assailed Drake's camp, causing the loss of many lives, including that of Joseph Drake.

When the Maroons brought him word that a shipment of treasure had arrived at the city of Panamá, the port on the Pacific side of the isthmus, Drake set out across the isthmus to capture it. On this journey he had his first view of the Pacific, an event described by one of his companions and first published in 1626 in a volume called *Sir Francis Drake Revived:* "It gave a special encouragement unto us all, that we understood there was a great tree about the midway, from whence we might at once discern the North Sea [Atlantic] from whence we came, and the South Sea [Pacific] whither we were going. The fourth day following, we came to the height of the desired hill, (lying east and west, like a ridge between the two seas,) about ten of the clock; where the chiefest of the Symerons [Maroons] took our Captain [Drake] by the hand, and prayed him to follow him. Here was that goodly and great high tree, in which they had cut and made divers steps to ascend near to the top, where they had made a convenient bower, wherein ten or twelve men might easily sit; and from thence we might see the Atlantic Ocean we came from, and the South Atlantic [sic] so much desired. South and north of this tree, they had felled certain trees, that the prospect might be the clearer.

"After our Captain had ascended to this bower, with the chief Symeron, and having, as it pleased God at this time by reason of the breeze, a very fair day, had seen that sea of which he had heard such golden reports; he besought Almighty God of his goodness, to give him life and leave to sail once in an English ship in that sea."

The carelessness of a drunken English seaman prevented Drake at the last moment from seizing the Spanish gold, and he returned to the Atlantic side of the isthmus. There he joined forces with a French pirate and captured a second Spanish treasure convoy almost in the harbor of Nombre de Dios. He sacked several other towns along the coast, gaining a reputation as a corsair whose movements could be neither predicted nor halted, and also winning fame as a gentle raider who respected ladies in distress and gallantly released prisoners unharmed. The Spaniards thus were never able to hate Drake properly; they dreaded him, but they regarded him always with uneasy respect and reluctant admiration.

In August 1573 he arrived at Plymouth, sailing a captured Spanish ship laden with the spoils of 15 months of privateering. Several times on the voyage he had come close to losing all his booty, but his resourcefulness, energy, and remarkable luck saw him safely through. He had done so well, in fact, that he was an embarrassment to Queen Elizabeth, who was still trying to avoid war with Spain. Though secretly proud of Drake's lightning raids, his triumphant achieving of the impossible, his quickness of action, his cheerfully insouciant heroism, she made open show of disapproving his piracies, and for the next several years Drake was forced into obscurity, his patriotic lust for war against the Spaniards thwarted.

So it fell to another Englishman to be the first to sail that great South Sea that Drake had prayed to reach. John Oxenham of Plymouth, who had stood beside Drake by that tall tree in Panamá and vowed to follow his captain to the Pacific, reached it before him. Oxenham, an officer aboard the *Pasha* in Drake's 1572 expedition, went on his own privateering voyage in the West Indies in 1575 with a 120-ton ship and 70 men. After landing at Port Plenty, he camouflaged his ship and set out through the isthmus accompanied by Maroons. At an inland river he built a 45-foot pinnace and went downriver to the Pacific, becoming the first of his nation to enter that ocean other than one John Chilton, who in 1572 had sailed from Panamá to Peru as a passenger aboard a Spanish ship. Oxenham raided the Pearl Islands south of Panamá and captured two vessels from Peru bearing a rich cargo of silver and gold; but when the Spaniards learned that an English pirate was loose in the ocean they regarded as their private lake, a general alarm went out, and Oxenham was driven ashore, trapped in the isthmus, and captured with all his men. Taken to Lima for interrogation, Oxenham admitted that he had undertaken piracy upon his own authority and at his own risk, and he was hanged.

The Spaniards were within their rights in putting Oxenham to death, but in 1576 Spain committed several open acts of aggression against British ships on the high seas, and England's mood became warlike again, with Drake as usual the most belligerent of all. Early in 1577 he obtained the queen's blessing for a major undertaking: a full-scale English intrusion into the Pacific. Drake knew of Oxenham's voyage, although not yet of his friend's tragic fate, and apparently hoped to join forces with him in the Pacific. But while Oxenham's Pacific venture had been nothing more than a casually conceived raid, a quick piratical thrust along the western side of the isthmus, Drake proposed an extensive voyage combining geographical discovery with a lucrative raid on Spain's Pacific ports. Like Magellan, Drake did not originally intend a circumnavigation. The initial plan called for a 13-month voyage in which he would sail into the Pacific via the Strait of Magellan, attack Spanish shipping along the coasts of Chile and Peru, and return to England by way of the strait. The main geographical project was the discovery of *Terra Australis Incognita*, which now was thought to run northwest from the Strait of Magellan to a latitude of 30°S. Drake was to spend five months in the newly found southern continent, entering into friendly relations with its natives, arranging for the marketing of English textiles, and learning whether gold, silver, and spices could be obtained there. However, Drake did not care to have the profits of his expedition turn on the hypothetical existence of an unknown continent in the Southeast Pacific and amended his proposal with a considerable expansion. After exploring *Terra Australis*, or in the event that *Terra Australis* did not exist, he would cross the Pacific to the Moluccas and then turn north, annexing any promising islands not yet controlled by Spain or Portugal. He would visit Cathay and Cipangu—China and Japan—and open trade with them. Then, when he had reached the northwestern corner of the Pacific, he would seek for the Strait of Anian and sail eastward through it back to the Atlantic. There was no intention at all of continuing westward from the Moluccas to come home by way of the Indian Ocean and the Cape of Good Hope.

This grandiose plan aroused great controversy in England, for a substantial peace faction opposed any infringement on Spain's rights in the Pacific. The Lord Treasurer of England, Lord Burghley, was Drake's chief opponent; Sir

Christopher Hatton, Elizabeth's vice-chamberlain and a member of her Privy Council, was Drake's most enthusiastic advocate before the queen. Elizabeth allowed herself to be swayed by Hatton and not only approved the project but once again made a private investment in it; to avoid trouble with the powerful Lord Burghley, she ordered that he not be told of the enterprise until Drake was safely on his way. However, Hatton's own private secretary, a brilliant but treacherous courtier named Thomas Doughty, informed Burghley of the plan. Unable to halt the expedition, Burghley arranged for Doughty to accompany it in a position of trust and secretly work toward the overthrow of Drake and the frustration of the scheme to attack the Spanish ports. So Drake, like Magellan, was the subject of conspiracies before he went to sea; and Drake, like Magellan, would have to deal with a mutinous captain far from home.

The queen gave Drake wholehearted support. According to one near-contemporary account of the voyage, she had presented him with a sword before his departure, declaring, "We do account that he which striketh at thee, Drake, striketh at us." Money, ships, and men for the expedition were amply forthcoming. For reasons of security, Drake pretended that the intended destination of the enterprise was Alexandria, Egypt; but while this may have confused and deceived the Spaniards, it was well known in England that he was embarking on a far more ambitious voyage, and men of the highest families vied for places aboard his ships. Thus a good many "gentleman adventurers" entered Drake's complement, some of them as dependable and useful as any professional mariner, others—like the sly Thomas Doughty—destined to be troublemakers: headstrong, unreliable, and insubordinate.

There were five ships. Drake's flagship was the *Pelican*, a 100-ton vessel armed with 18 guns. The 80-ton, 16-gun *Elizabeth* was the "vice-admiral" or second most important ship; she was commanded by John Winter, thought to be the nephew of Sir William Winter, Elizabeth's Admiral of the Sea. A gentleman adventurer, John Thomas, was made captain of the 30-ton bark *Marigold*, with 16 guns. Another of these well-born adventurers, John Chester, was placed in command of a 50-ton, 5-gun "flyboat" or storeship, little more than a floating hold designed for efficient carrying of large cargoes; she was called the *Swan*, after the little ship that Drake had had to scuttle in the Caribbean in 1573. Thomas Moone, the carpenter who had had charge of the scuttling of the original *Swan*, was captain of the fifth ship in Drake's fleet, a 15-ton pinnace named the *Christopher*. Thomas Doughty held the post of Captain of the Land Soldiers; his half-brother, John Doughty, was among the gentleman adventurers. The total complement of the five ships was 150 men and 14 boys; Drake had with him his youngest brother, Thomas, his young cousin, John Drake, and two gentleman adventurers named William and John Hawkins, who probably were the nephews of the famous Sir John Hawkins in whose service Drake had first gone to sea.

The ships were sumptuously equipped. The standard account of the voyage, published in 1628 and based on the diary of Drake's chaplain, Francis Fletcher, is a volume called *The World Encompassed by Sir Francis Drake*, from which we learn that the vessels were furnished "with such plentiful provision of all things necessary, as so long and dangerous a voyage did seem to require; and amongst the rest, with certain pinnaces ready framed, but carried aboard in pieces, to be new set up in smoother water, when occasion served. Neither had he omitted to make provision also for ornament and delight, carrying to this purpose with him, expert musicians, rich furniture (all the vessels for his table, yea, many belonging even to the cook-room being of pure silver), and divers shows of all sorts of curious workmanship, whereby the civility and magnificence of his native country might, amongst all nations whithersoever he should come, be the more admired." On November 15, 1577, this grand fleet put to sea from Plymouth. Thus commenced what *The World Encompassed* called "that valiant enterprise, accompanied with happy success, which that right rare and thrice worthy Captain, Francis Drake, achieved, in first turning up a furrow about the whole world."

4

Drake kept an illustrated journal of his circumnavigation, as we know from the narrative of a Portuguese pilot named Nuno da Silva, who was captured by Drake early in the voyage and involuntarily accompanied him much of the way. Silva, who gives us the useful and interesting fact that one of the three books Drake brought with him on the voyage was Pigafetta's journal, relates that "Francis Drake kept a book in which he entered his navigation and in which he delineated birds, trees, and sea-lions. He is an adept in painting and has with him a boy, a relative of his cousin, John Drake, who is a great painter. When they both shut themselves up in his cabin they were always painting." A letter preserved in the British Museum from the Spanish Ambassador to England to King Philip II of Spain dated October 16, 1580, says, "Drake has given the queen a diary of everything that happened to him during the three years he was away." This invaluable document must have disappeared almost at once, for it was not included in the first edition of Richard Hakluyt's great collection of narratives of English voyages, which appeared in 1589, nor did it appear in Hakluyt's vastly expanded second edition of 1598–1600.

However, even in the absence of Drake's own account, there is no shortage of primary sources for the circumnavigation. The first to be published was an anonymous account, considered to be the work of a mariner named Francis Pretty, which Hakluyt included in his volumes. It was withdrawn from the 1589 edition at the request of friends of Drake who claimed to be preparing their own account and did not wish to be forestalled, but was inserted into some copies of that text and, when the other account did not appear, was openly printed in Hakluyt's second edition. The second edition also includes a translation of Nuno da Silva's deposition before Spanish authorities in Mexico and a relation of the voyage of Drake's second in command, John Winter, with the *Elizabeth*, written by a seaman named Edward Cliffe. At least two other members of the expedition kept journals: a seaman named John Cooke, and the chaplain, Francis Fletcher. Neither of these was published until the nineteenth century, but they were used as the basis for the 1628 work, *The World Encompassed by Sir Francis Drake*, which was compiled by the circumnavigator's nephew and namesake, Sir Francis Drake, Bart., the son of his brother Thomas. *The World Encompassed* is essentially Francis Fletcher's narrative, greatly revised and polished, and supplemented in places with details from Cooke and others; Fletcher can fairly be called Drake's Pigafetta. Evidently he was conscious of his role, for he knew Pigafetta's book and seems to have based parts of his own account on it. In addition to these works by members of the expedition, a great many Spanish official documents bearing on the voyage have been discovered, most of them reflecting dismay at Drake's piracies in the Pacific or describing the ineffectual attempts to halt his giddy progress through Spanish waters. These papers, most of which remained buried in the archives of Spain until 1914, confirm in a number of respects the details of the various English accounts.

The voyage made a poor start. Contrary winds forced the fleet to take refuge at the port of Falmouth on its second day out, November 16, 1577, and storms on the 17th and 18th so injured the ships that they put back to Plymouth for repairs and did not set forth again until December 13. While the ships were being refitted, Thomas Doughty began to stir up dissension in the crew; Drake seemed unaware of the real source of the trouble and singled out one of Doughty's henchmen, James Syday, whom he dismissed from the voyage even though they were old friends who had seen military action together.

When the expedition finally succeeded in getting out to sea, Drake ended the pretense of a cruise down the Mediterranean to Alexandria by setting his course for the Atlantic and announcing that the first point of rendezvous in case the ships were separated would be the "island" (actually a cape) of Mogador on Africa's northwestern coast. By December 27 the fleet was anchored in harbor at Mogador. During a four-day stay at this uninhabited desert headland, the voyagers gathered firewood and assembled one of the four prefabricated pinnaces they had brought with them, and received a friendly visit from some Moroccan natives who came to the ships riding on camels. Drake entertained and feasted them and gave them some linen, shoes, and a javelin; the Moroccans promised to come back the next day for an exchange of merchandise, and when they appeared Drake sent a shore party to meet them. However, the first man to step ashore, a man named John Fry, was seized and carried off by the Moroccans before the astounded Englishmen could act.

Furious at this breach of hospitality, Drake led a band of his men inland, but found neither Fry nor any native to take as a hostage. There was still no sign of Fry when the fleet was provisioned and ready to go; and on December 31 the ships departed without him. Fry, meanwhile, had been taken before the local ruler, who had declared his country independent of Portugal and feared that the ships at

Mogador were a Portuguese fleet of war. Upon learning that they were English, and so no threat to his independence, the Moorish monarch apologized to Fry, gave him presents, and sent him back bearing a conciliatory message for Drake. But Fry reached Mogador to find the fleet gone, and for him the voyage ended at that point; he stayed as guest of the Moroccans for some time and eventually went home aboard an English merchant vessel that called at Mogador.

The fleet continued down the African coast. Drake now frankly admitted to his men what they had already suspected: that they were bound toward the Pacific via the Strait of Magellan, which no ship had entered in 50 years and which, according to one rumor, had "closed up" in the interval. On January 7, delayed by foul weather, they halted again on the Moroccan coast at Cape Ghir, where, says *The World Encompassed*, "we lighted on 3 Spanish fishermen called *caunters* [fishing vessels known as *canteras* in Spanish, as large as 40 tons], whom we took with our new pinnace, and carried along with us till we came to Rio de Oro, just under the Tropic of Cancer, where with our pinnace also we took a caravel. From hence till the fifteenth day [of January] we sailed on towards Cape Barbas, where the *Marigold* took a caravel more, and so onward to Cape Blanco." The pattern of genial piracy was taking form. Drake meant no harm to the crews of these Spanish fishing vessels and let both the men and the ships go at Cape Blanco, after taking from them such things as he found useful for his own voyage. Only one of the *canteras* was retained, the largest, which he added to his fleet; but he recompensed her captain by giving him the 15-ton pinnace *Christopher* in exchange, rechristening his Spanish prize with that name.

At Cape Blanco the English laid in a stock of fresh fish and carried out some minor repairs on their ships. Drake had also hoped to obtain a supply of fresh water, but there was none to be had; in fact, a delegation of natives came to him seeking to buy water. They offered a bony, exhausted woman and her half-starved child as slaves, but, says Fletcher's account, Drake would not deal in that sort of merchandise. "But they also had ambergris, with certain gums of some estimation, which they brought to exchange with our men for water (whereof they have great want). . . . A very heavy judgment of God upon that coast! The circumstances whereof considered, our general would receive nothing of them for water, but freely gave it them that came to him, yea, and fed them also ordinarily with our victuals, in eating whereof their manner was not only uncivil and unsightly to us, but even inhuman and loathsome in itself."

Thomas Doughty took his company of soldiers ashore at Cape Blanco to drill them, and used the opportunity to spread anti-Drake propaganda among them. Though some reports of this reached Drake, he took no notice. After six days the fleet departed for the Cape Verde Islands, which were Portuguese. Here it was absolutely necessary to get fresh water, for Drake, with characteristic boldness, was planning "from thence to run a long course (even to the coast of Brazil) without touch of land," rather than following the usual route around Africa's hump to minimize the period of open-sea sailing before turning west. Passing through the Cape Verdes, they skipped the island of Boavista, which looked unpromising, and called at Maio, a small island west of the group's main island, São Tiago. Maio proved to be a desolate, ramshackle place whose inhabitants lived in dread of pirates. They salted the wells and fled inland when the English appeared. Drake sent men through the island, past extensive plantations of coconuts, plantains, figs, and grapes, but the only good water supply they found was so far from the harbor that it was impossible to make use of it. So they moved westward on January 31 toward São Tiago. "In sailing along this island," wrote Francis Fletcher, "we perceived the inhabitants were too superstitious according to the Pope's anti-Christian tradition, for upon every cape and small head they set up a cross, on most whereof is engraven an evil faced picture of Christ. One of the crosses myself and other did break down, but with great dislike as well to some of our own company, being so much addicted to that opinion as the Portugals themselves."

São Tiago was well defended, and Drake did not risk an incursion; as his ships passed by without entering the harbor, the shore batteries fired a salute, ostensibly in Drake's honor but also intended to warn him away. Off the southwest coast of the island the English captured an important prize: the *Santa Maria*, a Portuguese ship bound for Brazil with a cargo of wine and textiles. Drake did not thirst for vengeance against Portugal as he did for Spain, but he regarded Portuguese shipping as fair prey and raided it indiscriminately with that of Spain, merely because he looked upon all Catholics with equal contempt and thought of the Portuguese as a species of Spaniards. Imprisoning the *Santa Maria*'s men, Drake sent a prize crew of 28 mariners aboard her, with Thomas Doughty as captain, and renamed the ship the *Mary*.

Still looking for water, Drake sailed past the island that the Portuguese called Fogo, "fire," because of its active volcano, and stopped at the "most sweet and pleasant island" of Brava nearby, where "from the banks into the sea do run in many places the silver streams of sweet and wholesome water, which with boats or pinnaces may easily be taken in." Brava was inhabited only by a hermit who hid when the English arrived, "leaving behind him the relics of his false worship; to wit, a cross with a crucifix, an altar with his superaltar, and certain other idols of wood with rude workmanship." Here on February 1 they took on board a small supply of water, a task complicated by the absence of any anchorage by which they could approach the shore with their ships. Somewhat to the displeasure of some of his men, Drake behaved with his usual generosity toward the Portuguese from the *Santa Maria*, releasing them and giving them, in return for their ship, the new pinnace assembled at Mogador. He supplied them also with food, wine, and clothing before letting them go. Drake kept only a Portuguese pilot, Nuno da Silva, whom the Englishmen called Sylvester. Silva had had experience on the Brazilian coast and, Fletcher insists, "when he heard that our travel was into Mare del Zur, that is, the South Sea, was willing to assist." How voluntary Silva's enlistment really was is a matter for some skepticism, since in his own account he plainly states that he was a prisoner; but he served Drake faithfully and was treated well throughout his stay with the English voyagers.

At Brava, Drake had his first overt trouble with Thomas Doughty. Now that he was captain of the prize ship *Mary*, Doughty began to exert authority in a swaggering way, accusing Drake's brother Thomas of pilfering from the *Mary*'s cargo. An investigation followed which exonerated Thomas Drake and plainly showed that Doughty was engaging in schemes against his captain-general, whereupon Drake removed him from command of the *Mary* and sent him aboard the flagship, the *Pelican*. Drake himself took charge of the *Mary*, and Thomas Hord, a gentleman adventurer who was master of the *Pelican*, became her captain for the time being. Soon Doughty was claiming command of the flagship himself, as well as troubling the sailors by his experiments in sorcery, and Drake had to send him in disgrace onto the little storeship, the *Swan*. Even there Doughty continued to agitate against Drake.

On February 2 the fleet, now consisting of six ships, began its Atlantic crossing, in which 63 days went by without sight of land. *The World Encompassed* says that it would have been agreeable to report that during the "long passage on the vast gulf, where nothing but sea beneath us and air above us was to be seen," God had given them "a particular taste of His fatherly care over us all the while," but in truth "we often met with adverse winds, unwelcome storms, and to us (at that time) less welcome calms, and being as it were in the bosom of the burning zone, we felt the effects of sultring heat, not without the affrights of flashing lightnings, and terrifyings of often claps of thunder." But at least the almost daily rain kept them well supplied with water, and they were entertained by the sight of pale, glistening flying fish soaring through the air, and other wonders of the sea, "the most excellent works of the eternal God." The fleet kept together well on the ocean, though the *Mary* was lost for a day, March 28–29.

On April 5 they reached the coast of South America at about 31°30′S. and saw the great fires of the natives on the shore; but there was no harbor, and they followed the land southward. A violent storm separated the *cantera Christopher* from the other ships on April 7, and it was not seen again for more than a week. On April 14 Drake reached the estuary of the Río de la Plata, anchoring by a headland that he named Cape Joy a few days later to mark his relief at the reappearance of the *Christopher*. Southerly gales kept the fleet in and about the estuary for nearly two weeks. Drake returned to the *Pelican* and made his brother Thomas captain of the *Mary*. The sailors killed a great many seals, which, said Fletcher, they found "not only good meat . . . but profitable in respect of their fatness yielding abundance of oil." The only efficient way to kill them, he noted, was "to strike them upon the nose with a cudgel, for no other place can hurt them." Fletcher was very much on the lookout for the Patagonian giants of which Pigafetta had written and hoped to find some here, though they still were well north of Patagonia. The best he could report, though, was giant footprints in the soft ground, "the breadth whereof was the length of one of our men's feet of largest size, which could be no other than the foot of a giant." From this he conjectured that the South American mainland must be inhabited by giants all the way from the Plata to the Strait of Magellan.

The fleet went to sea again on April 27, and almost at once the storeship *Swan* was separated from the company. Drake began to realize that he had too many ships and decided to consolidate his fleet at the next good harbor; but meanwhile the *Swan* did not show up, and on May 8 the *Mary* too was severed from the fleet. The other four vessels came to anchor on May 12 in 47°S., at a headland which Drake named Cape Hope. The next day Drake went in an open boat to investigate the bay within the cape. When he was near the shore, says *The World Encompassed*, "One of the men of the country showed himself unto him, seeming very pleasant, singing and dancing, after the noise of a rattle which he shook in his hand, expecting earnestly his landing. But there was suddenly so great an alteration in the weather, into a thick and misty fog, together with an extreme storm and tempest, that our General, being now three leagues from his ship, thought it better to return, than either to land or make any other stay." The fog thickened so much, though, that Drake lost his way, and he was rescued only by the bravery of Captain Thomas of the *Marigold*, who entered the bay despite the storm to pick him up in his ship. The missing *Mary* had turned up just before the storm, after an absence of six days, but disappeared once more in the gale and was not seen again for a long while. The rough weather of the Patagonian coast was hurling Drake's little vessels about like toy ships; so far, none had been lost, but he felt great distress at each disappearance and rested poorly until the ship returned.

When the weather cleared Drake went ashore, hoping to have some contact with the natives. They could be seen at a distance—evidently they were of ordinary stature—but they fled when the English approached. Drake discovered a storehouse containing some 50 dried "ostriches"—they were South American rheas, related to the somewhat larger African ostrich—that were being prepared for eating. "The ostriches' thighs were in bigness equal to reasonable legs of mutton," declares *The World Encompassed*. "They cannot fly at all; but they run so swiftly, and take so long strides, that it is not possible for a man in running by any means to take them, neither yet to come so nigh them as to have any shot at them either with bow or piece." Fletcher described how the Indians catch these ostriches by sneaking up on them wearing ostrich costumes and driving them into nets, turning dogs upon them for the kill.

The harbor at Cape Hope was not considered suitably safe, nor were food, wood, and fresh water easily available, so on May 15 the fleet left and moved on to a "fair, safe and beneficial" bay in 47° 30′S. The ships anchored there on May 18 and remained for 15 days; Drake named the place Seal Bay, though later mariners would make it famous as Port Desire. His first thought was of his missing ships and immediately upon arrival at Seal Bay sent John Winter in the *Elizabeth* south along the coast to look for the *Swan* and the *Mary*, while he took his *Pelican* north to do the same. Drake found the *Swan* not far above Seal Bay and brought her into the harbor; she was in poor condition, and Drake now began to implement his policy of consolidating the ships, breaking the *Swan* up and salvaging her iron, making firewood of the rest. Thomas Doughty and his half-brother John, who had been in a kind of detention aboard the *Swan*, were put aboard the *Pelican*, but commenced their usual practice of covertly inciting the men to mutiny. Drake continued to show great tolerance to this troublesome pair whom another captain might have cast overboard weeks before; he simply rebuked them and, to get them away from him, transferred them to the *Christopher*, whose captain, the salty old ex-carpenter Thomas Moone, would keep close watch on them.

At Seal Bay the voyagers were visited by Patagonian Indians, who, according to Edward Cliffe's account, came within 100 paces of the Englishmen and "set themselves in array very orderly, casting their company into the form of a ring, every man having his bow and arrow. . . . Then the country people . . . approached nearer to our men, showing themselves very pleasant, insomuch that Mr. Winter danced with them. They were exceedingly delighted with the sound of the trumpet, and viols. . . . They be much given to mirth and jollity, and are very sly, and ready to steal anything that comes within their reach: for one of them snatched our General's cap from his head (as he stooped) being of scarlet with a golden band: yet he would suffer no man to hurt any of them."

The version of this encounter in the manuscript of Francis Fletcher's journal is quite different. Cliffe makes a point of remarking that the natives "be of a mean stature," but Fletcher speaks of them as giants, and describes them in terms so similar to Pigafetta's that he seems almost to be paraphrasing the Italian: "The inhabitants showed themselves in divers companies upon several hills not far from us with leaping, dancing, and great noise, and cries with voices like the bulls of Bashan." Fletcher relates how the Patagonians sought oracular advice "from their God Settaboth [Setebos] that is the Devil whom they name their great God," and how they seemed to receive a warning from Setebos, for they grew more menacing after their priest had conferred with his deity; Drake sounded a trumpet call of retreat and left bead bracelets tied to a pole in the earth as a sign of good will. Soon the attitude of the giants changed, though, and relations grew so friendly that there were daily visits and some exchange of English goods for native arrows and other souvenirs. Fletcher tells the story of the theft of Drake's cap a little differently, too: "One of them standing by the General and seeing upon his head a scarlet sea cap and seeming to be delighted in the color, he boldly took it from his head and put it upon his own who fearing lest the General should dislike with him for it presently took an arrow and setting out his leg did deeply wound the calf of the same with it and receiving the blood in his hand offered it to the General seeming thereby to signify to him that he loved him so dearly that he would give his blood for him: and that therefore he should not be angry for so small a matter as a cap." Another of the giants, says Fletcher, standing with some Englishmen who were taking their morning glasses of wine, "would do as they did," and, "taking the glass in his hand (being strong Canary wine) it came not to his lips when it took him by the nose and so suddenly entered into his head that he was so drunk or at least so overcome with the spirit of the wine that he fell flat upon his buttocks not able [to] stand any longer." The other Patagonians were startled, thinking he had been slain, but the fallen man sat up tipsily, still gripping the glass of wine unspilled, and sniffed it cautiously to see "if he could have any better luck sitting than standing. He smelled so long and tasted so often that at the last he drew it to the bottom, from which time he took such a liking to wine that having learned the word every morning he would come down the mountains with a mighty cry, Wine, Wine, Wine, till he came to our tent and would in that time have devoured more wine at a time than 20 men could have done, never ceasing until he had his draught every morning."

Both men and women go naked but for fur mantles which they wear about their shoulders or their loins or not at all as the mood takes them, Fletcher asserts. Men let their hair grow long; women shave theirs with stone razors. "The men in height and greatness are so extraordinary that they hold no comparison with any of the sons of men this day in the world," he says, and "the women are answerable to them in stature and proportion every way." The meat of ostriches and seals is their chief food; they "cast it by bits of six pounds' weight into the flame till it be a little scorched and taking it out tear it in pieces like lions with their teeth, both men and women, whose breasts, bellies, and all to the feet are so beblubbered and basted with water and blood falling from their mouths out of the crude and raw flesh that it is loathsome to behold."

Since none of the other accounts of the voyage speaks of the Seal Bay people as giants, the compiler of *The World Encompassed* sidestepped the point by making no references to their size. *The World Encompassed* supplies one ingenious suggestion concerning the Patagonians' habit of painting their bodies: "Some wash their faces with sulphur, or some such like substance: some paint their whole bodies black, leaving only their necks behind and before white, much like our damosels that wear their squares [bosoms], their necks and breasts naked. Some paint one shoulder black, another white; and their sides and legs interchangeably, with the same colors, one still contrary to the other. The black part hath set upon it white moons, and the white part black suns. . . . They have some commodity by painting of their bodies, for the which cause they use it so generally: and that I gather to be the defense it yieldeth against the piercing and nipping cold. For the colors being close laid on upon their skin, or rather in their flesh, as by continual renewing of those juices which are laid on, soaked into the inner part thereof, doth fill up the pores so close that no air or cold can enter, or make them once to shrink."

By June 3 Drake was ready to leave Seal Bay, though the *Mary* was still missing. They had loaded much fresh meat—the seals were so abundant that 200 were killed in the space of a single hour—and were well prepared to face the advancing winter. Still regrouping his ships, Drake decided on June 12 to abandon the Spanish prize ship he had named the *Christopher;* in the redistribution of men the Doughty brothers were put with Captain Winter on the *Elizabeth.* Five days later, the fleet anchored in a bay in 50°20'S., probably the Santa Cruz estuary discovered by Juan Serrano in 1520. Drake's study of maps based on the Magellan voyage showed him that he was now scarcely more than 200 miles from the strait, but he could not enter without making one last attempt at finding his Portuguese prize, the *Mary.* Therefore on June 18 he put to sea again with his three other ships, prepared to sail all the way back up the coast if necessary before abandoning the search. But the next day the long-lost vessel came into sight only a short distance to the north, "far out of order, and very leaky, by reason of extremity of weather which she had endured," according to *The World Encompassed.* Seeing her in this condition, Drake decided to lead the entire fleet into the nearest harbor, a bay whose latitude he calculated at 49°30'S. And so, on June 20, the voyagers entered Magellan's Port San Julian, that place of ill omen where mutiny had been thwarted and Spanish captains put to death 58 years before.

5

Magellan was well remembered here, if we can give credit to a passage in the narrative of the Portuguese pilot Nuno da Silva. On June 22, after the ships were secured, Drake led a shore party to search for fresh water, taking with him his brother Thomas, Captain John Thomas of the *Marigold*, a gentleman volunteer named Robert Winter, and three others, including Mr. Oliver, the flagship's master gunner. Silva says that "before they left on land, four of the Indians came unto their boat, to whom the Englishmen gave bread and wine: and when the Indians had well eaten and drunk, they departed thence: and going somewhat far from them, one of the Indians cried to them, and said, *Magallanes, Esta he minha Terra*, that is, 'Magallanes, this is my country.'"

It is doubtful that the Patagonians could speak even one sentence of Portuguese, and equally unlikely that they were the giants Francis Fletcher says they were. Fletcher's journal calls them "old and grim weather-beaten villains" of great size, but again *The World Encompassed* rejects his testimony, for Edward Cliffe's narrative denies it most explicitly. Cliffe says, "These men be of no such stature as the Spaniards report, being but of the height of English men: for I have seen men in England taller than I could see any of them. But peradventure the Spaniard did not think that any English men would have come thither so soon to have disproved them in this and divers others of their notorious lies: wherefore they presumed more boldly to abuse the world." The compiler of *The World Encompassed* follows Cliffe, and embellishes his words to mock the Spaniards even more by attributing to Magellan a fanciful etymology for the name *Patagones*, supposedly derived from the imagined height of the giants the Spaniards claimed to have seen: "Magellan was not altogether deceived in naming them Giants, for they generally differ from the common sort of men, both in stature, bigness, and strength of body, as also in the hideousness of their voice; but yet they are nothing so monstrous or giant-like as they were reported, there being some English men as tall as the highest of any that we could see, but peradventure the Spaniards did not think that ever any English men would come thither to reprove them, and thereupon might presume the more boldly to lie; the name *Pentagones*, *Five cubits*, viz., 7 foot and half, describing the full height (if not somewhat more) of the highest of them." Magellan's name had referred to the large feet of the giants.

But all accounts agree on what took place between the Patagonians and the shore party. Drake offered them presents, which they received with satisfaction, and then Oliver, the gunner, demonstrated the range and power of an English bow for them. The Patagonians tried to equal Oliver's prowess using their own bows, but could not reach nearly so far and were impressed and awed. Then another native arrived, "of a sourer sort," says *The World Encompassed*, "for he misliking of the familiarity which his fellows had used, seemed very angry with them, and strove earnestly to withdraw them, and to turn them to become our enemies; which our general with his men not suspecting in them, used them as before." Robert Winter, the gentleman adventurer, took the bow from Oliver to provide a display of archery for the newcomer; but the string of his bow broke, and the Patagonians, not realizing that the swords and guns carried by the Englishmen were also weapons, concluded that the strangers now were vulnerable to attack without their mighty bow. As Winter was restringing the bow, the natives drew their own and wounded him first in the shoulder, then in the lungs, but he did not fall. Oliver seized his gun but it misfired, and he was slain by the arrows of the Patagonians.

"In this extremity," says *The World Encompassed*, "if our general had not been both expert in such affairs, able to judge, and give present direction in the danger thereof, and had not valiantly thrust himself into the dance against these monsters, there had no one of our men, that there were landed, escaped with life. He therefore, giving order that no man should keep any certain ground, but shift from place to place, encroaching still upon the enemy, using their targets [shields] and other weapons for the defense of their bodies, and that they should break so many arrows as by any means they could come by, being shot at them, wherein he himself was very diligent, and careful also in calling on them, knowing that their arrows being once spent, they should have these enemies at their devotion and pleasure, to kill or save." By this stratagem Drake induced the Patagonians to exhaust their arrows, and then, himself taking up the gun Oliver had been unable to discharge, shot the man who had slain the master gunner. At his terrible dying cry, the Patagonians rushed in fright to the woods, permitting the Englishmen to make their escape, carrying the wounded Robert Winter. Winter died two days later; and when Drake went ashore again to recover Oliver's body, he found it lying where it had fallen, but stripped of its upper garment, and with an English arrow thrust into the right eye.

There was no further trouble with the natives during the two months spent gathering wood and water at Port San Julian. But in this time the agitations of Thomas Doughty reached an intolerable point, and Drake, thoroughly conscious of the precedent set here by Magellan, finally turned upon him on June 30 and brought him to trial before an improvised jury of about 40 men. Edward Cliffe's narrative is most concise: "The last of June Mr. Thomas Doughty was brought to his answer, was accused, and convicted of certain articles, and by Mr. Drake condemned. He was beheaded the 2 of July 1578."

This is the most controversial incident of Drake's voyage; for Doughty, like his marooned predecessor, Juan de Cartagena, had powerful friends in his homeland who never ceased to regard his fate as a case of judicial murder by an arrogant and dictatorial commander. Therefore both pro-Drake and anti-Drake versions of Doughty's trial exist. The journal of Francis Fletcher speaks favorably of Doughty, apparently because the chaplain quarreled with Drake later in the voyage and came to dislike him. Fletcher asserts that Doughty denied all guilt, and says of him that "he feared God, he loved his word, and was always desirous to edify others and confirm himself in the faith of Christ. . . . Long before his death he seemed to be mortified and to be ravished with the desire of God's kingdom, yea to be dissolved and to be with Christ. . . ."

Far more hostile to Drake is the narrative of John Cooke, who served under Captain John Winter in the *Elizabeth*. As we will see, Winter and the men of the *Elizabeth* had their own reasons for wishing to paint Drake in the blackest possible colors, and Cooke's journal, in the British Museum, shows signs of having been doctored by some literary man eager to emphasize the anti-Drake position. The journal says that at Port San Julian Drake "spewed out against Thomas Doughty all his venom, here he ended all his conceived hatred, not by courtesy or friendly reconcilement, but by most tyrannical blood-spilling." Cooke declares that Drake seized Doughty, had his arms bound, and accused him not merely of mutinous schemes but of a variety of crimes preceding the voyage. Doughty replied, "Let me live to come into my country, and I will there be tried by Her Majesty's laws." To which Drake responded, "Nay, Thomas Doughty, I will here impanel a jury on you to inquire farther of these matters that I have to charge you with." The jury was called, with Captain John Winter as foreman; Drake recited Doughty's alleged treacheries, including his betrayal of the plan of the voyage to Lord Burghley and his supposed attempts at inciting mutiny at sea. The jury, plainly intimidated by Drake's forceful manner, quickly brought in a verdict of guilty, and Drake called for a sentence of death. Out of fear of Drake the jury agreed, although Cooke claims that many privately felt the sentence too harsh; and so Doughty was done to death, a victim of Drake's spite and insecurity.

Cooke's version can probably be dismissed as a self-serving document. On the other hand, the events related in *The World Encompassed* appear to have suffered the opposite distortion, with Drake's nephew tampering with them half a century after the fact in order to justify Doughty's execution. For, while Fletcher's journal states that Doughty claimed innocence to the last, *The World Encompassed*, though based liberally on Fletcher's own words, departs here from them and claims that Doughty, after hearing the accusations against him, was "stricken with remorse of his inconsiderate and unkind dealing," and "acknowledged himself to have deserved death, yea many deaths; for that he conspired, not only the overthrow of the action [the voyage], but of the principal actor also, who was not a stranger or ill-willer, but a dear and true friend unto him; and therefore in a great assembly openly besought them, in whose hands justice rested, to take some order for him, that he might not be compelled to enforce his own hands against his own bowels, or otherwise to become his own executioner."

The World Encompassed goes on to describe the trial, held on an island in the bay at Port San Julian: when the jury had fully discussed the evidence against Doughty, they all adjudged that "he had deserved death: and that it stood, by no means with their safety, to let him live: and therefore, they remitted the manner thereof, with the rest of the circumstances, to the General." The island supposedly was given the name of True Justice and Judgment in memory of this verdict, although Fletcher's journal says, "We named the island the Island of Blood in respect of us and Magellan."

Drake then confronted Doughty with the verdict, *The World Encompassed* continues, and offered him a choice: to be executed on this island, to be marooned on the mainland after the fashion of Juan de Cartagena, or to return to England to submit to Queen Elizabeth's high court. Doughty "humbly thanked the General for his clemency" and the next day made his answer. As a good Christian, he said, he did not wish to jeopardize his body among heathen savages, where there would be no one to perform the last rites for him or to give him a fitting burial. As for returning to England, he doubted that any man would wish to escort him on such a journey, and also "the very shame of the return would be as death, or grievouser if it were possible: because he would be so long a dying, and die so often." Therefore he chose to be put to death on the island, asking only that he be allowed first to take communion together with Drake, and "that he might not die other than a gentleman's death."

On the next day Francis Fletcher celebrated a communion in which Drake took part, along with Doughty, "this condemned penitent gentleman, who showed great tokens of a contrite and repentant heart, as who was more deeply displeased with his own act than any man else. And after this holy repast they dined, also at the same table, together, as cheerfully in sobriety, as ever in their lives they had done aforetime: each cheering up the other, and taking their leave, by drinking each to other, as if some journey only had been in hand." After dinner the executioner came—not Drake, as a Spanish rumor later insisted—and Doughty meekly presented his neck to the axe. The compiler of *The World Encompassed* expresses his astonishment at the coincidence that both the first and second circumnavigations of the globe should have seen the execution of mutineers at Port San Julian, "a new pair of parallels to be added to Plutarch's: in that same place, near about the same time of the year, witnessed the execution of two gentlemen, suffering both for the like cause, employed both in like service, entertained both in great place, endued both with excellent qualities, the one 58 years after the other."

Francis Fletcher, who, as we have already seen, was so conscious of Pigafetta's narrative that he went to the trouble of finding giants in Patagonia where none of Drake's other men saw them, even inserting the salient details of Pigafetta's account into his own journal, here provides an appropriately grisly touch by commenting that, on the mainland at Port San Julian, they found the gibbet on which Magellan had mounted the quartered bodies of the mutineers, and even their bones—presumably those of Quesada and Mendoza. This story found its way into *The World Encompassed*, where, however, the incorrect assumption was made that the bones were those of "John Carthagene, the Bishop of Burgos' cousin." The entire story might be as suspect as Fletcher's tale of giants, except that the finding of the gibbet and the bones is described in the accounts of John Cooke and the anonymous mariner in Hakluyt's collection.

The great question at issue in the execution of Thomas Doughty was whether Drake held the right to put him to death. No one questioned his power to execute an insubordinate seaman, but Doughty was a gentleman adventurer, and his partisans insisted loudly thereafter that the proper course in dealing with a man of such rank was to bring him back to England for trial. They subjected Drake to much abuse on this score after his return. That Drake felt he was acting properly is indicated by the only firsthand account by a wholly impartial observer: Nuno da Silva, the Portuguese pilot. In the log that he kept of the voyage, Silva notes for June 30 merely, "They passed sentence that he was to die," and for July 2, "They cut off his head." But Silva was interrogated by the Spaniards the following May, after Drake had released him in a Mexican port, and at that time he declared that when Drake "beheaded the said English gentleman,

who was named Master Doughty, the said Master Doughty
challenged him to show whence and by what power he could
behead him, and then the said Francis Drake assembled all
his men, without omitting a single one. Placing himself in a
more elevated position than the others, he took out some papers, kissed them, put them on his head, and read them in a
loud voice. After reading them he showed them to the others
and all saw and inspected them. After the head had been severed, he took the head in his hand, showed it and cast it away,
saying, 'Long live the Queen of England.' All present said
that those papers were from her and that it was with her authority that he was executing [Doughty] and making the
voyage."

John Cooke's narrative indicates the position of Drake's
enemies in its opening sentence: "The XV November in the
year above written [1577] Francis Drake, John Winter, and
Thomas Doughty, as equal companions and friendly gentlemen with a fleet of five ships and to the number of 164 men,
gentlemen and sailors, departed Plymouth. . . ." If Drake,
Winter, and Doughty actually were "equal companions and
friendly gentlemen" at the outset, then obviously Drake, as
first among equals, had overstepped his authority by putting
Doughty to death. This must have been much discussed in
the weeks following the execution, for Drake found it necessary to make a dramatic affirmation of his own supreme authority in the enterprise, as well as settling at last the problem of the relative positions of sailors and gentlemen aboard
his ships. His speech is given in John Cooke's narrative, and
it is one of the classics of the English seafaring literature of
the sixteenth century.

According to Cooke, Drake called all his men ashore at
Port San Julian on Sunday, August 15, "for that he had
some matter of importance to say to them." The men assembled, and Francis Fletcher offered to deliver a sermon. "Nay,

soft, Master Fletcher," Drake replied, "I must preach this
day myself, although I have small skill in preaching." Commanding each ship's company to stand in a group, Drake
said, "My masters, I am a very bad orator, for my bringing
up hath not been in learning, but what so I shall here speak,
let any man take notice of what I shall say, and let him write
it down if he list, for I will speak nothing but I will answer it
in England, yea, and before her Majesty, and I have it here
already set down. Thus it is, my masters, that we are very far
from our country and friends, we are compassed in on every
side with our enemies, wherefore we are not to make small
reckoning of a man, for we cannot have a man if we would
give for him ten thousand pounds. Wherefore we must have
these mutinies and discords that are grown amongst us re-
dressed, for by the life of God it doth even take my wits from
me to think of it; here is such controversy between the sailors
and the gentlemen, and such stomaching between the gentlemen and sailors, that it doth even make me mad to hear it.
But, my masters, I must have it left; for I must have the gentleman to hale and draw with the mariner, and the mariner
with the gentleman. What, let us show ourselves all to be of a
company, and let us not give occasion to the enemy to rejoice
at our decay and overthrow. I would know him that would
refuse to set his hand to a rope,—but I know there is not any
such here; and as gentlemen are very necessary for government's sake in the voyage so have I shipped them for that,
and for some farther intent, and yet I know sailors to be the
most envious people of the world, and so unruly without government, yet may I not be without them. Also, if there be any
here willing to return home, let me understand of them, and
here is the *Marigold*, a ship that I can very well spare; I will
furnish her to such as will return with the most credit I can
give them, either by my letters or any way else; but let them
take heed that they go homeward; for if I find them in my

way I will surely sink them; therefore you shall have time to consider hereof until tomorrow; for, by my troth, I must needs be plain with you, I have taken that in hand that I know not in the world how to go through withal; it passeth my capacity, it hath even bereaved me of my wits to think on it."

No one spoke for going home; with the smashing of Doughty's conspiracy, the voyage would continue as planned through the Strait of Magellan, and the Spanish shipping along the western coast of South America would be raided despite the attempts of England's antiwar faction to prevent it. Drake now asked his men if they followed him with good will, and they said they did. Now he turned to the officers of his three ships. (A few days earlier he had had the leaky and troublesome Portuguese prize, the *Mary*, unloaded and broken up.) Drake said, "Master Winter, I do here discharge you of your captainship of the *Elizabeth*; and you, John Thomas, of the *Marigold*; and you, Thomas Hood, of your mastership in the *Pelican*; and you, William Markham, of the *Elizabeth*; and Nicholas Antony, of the *Marigold*; and, to be brief, I do here discharge every officer of all offices what so ever."

After a moment of astonished silence, John Winter and John Thomas asked why he had stripped them of their captaincies. Was there any reason, Drake replied, why he should not do so? While they stood baffled and crestfallen by this, he singled out certain specific men before him, criticizing them for opposing him, and accepting now their oaths to be obedient. Then he reviewed the origin of the voyage, examining and dismissing the belief that this was some private venture of "equal companions" for individual profit. It was Queen Elizabeth herself, he claimed, who had instigated this expedition and chosen him as its commander, sending for him privately and declaring, "Drake, I would gladly be revenged on the King of Spain, for divers injuries that I have received." He held up a receipt for the queen's own investment in the voyage of 1,000 crowns and said that she had sworn that if anyone sent word to the King of Spain of her involvement in the project, that man would lose his head.

Drake went on, "And now, my masters, let us consider what we have done. We have now set together by the ears three mighty princes, as first her Majesty, the Kings of Spain and Portugal, and if this voyage shall not have good success, we shall not only be a scorning, or a reproachful scoffing-stock, unto our enemies, but also a great blot to our whole country for ever; and what triumph will it be to Spain and Portugal: and never again the like will be attempted." Now he restored the officers to their former ranks, making it clear that they would be servants of the queen under her chosen commander, Francis Drake, and promising that they would be well paid even if he had to sell his shirt. "For," he said, "I have good reason to promise, and am best able to perform it, for I have somewhat of mine own in England, and, besides that, I have as much adventure [investment] in this voyage as three of the best whatsoever; and if it so be that I never come home, yet will her Majesty pay every man his wages, whom indeed you and we all come to serve; and for to say you come to serve me, I will not give you thanks, for it is only her Majesty that you serve, and this voyage is only her setting forth."

Drake had taken an enormous risk by revealing the queen's complicity in the enterprise to his men, for she would ultimately learn what he had done and might well be angered by it, and Elizabeth did not hesitate to behead courtiers who angered her. But he awed his men and his officers into renewed loyalty; they saw the purpose of the voyage a new way now and ceased to question Drake's authority. On August 17, two days later, the three ships departed from Port San

Julian, though winter was not yet done. Unlike Magellan, who had left the same port on August 24, 1520, only to spend the next two months camped unknowingly just north of the still undiscovered strait, Drake made immediately for that waterway and within four days arrived at the headland Magellan had called the Cape of the Eleven Thousand Virgins, now known simply as Cape Vírgines. Just beyond lay the steep gray cliffs marking the entrance to Magellan's strait.

6

At Cape Vírgines, Drake formally changed the name of his flagship from the *Pelican* to the *Golden Hind*, to honor his friend and sponsor, Sir Christopher Hatton, whose coat of arms displayed a gleaming deer. Then he struck boldly into the strait, which, Hakluyt's anonymous voyager wrote, "we found to have many turnings, and as it were shuttings up, as if there were no passage at all, by means whereof we had the wind often against us, so that some of the fleet recovering a cape or point of land, others should be forced to turn back again, and to come to an anchor where they could."

On August 24 they came upon three islands within the strait. It was St. Bartholomew's Day, and Drake named one island St. Bartholomew, one St. George, and the third after his queen. Here the voyagers found, says *The World Encompassed*, "great store of strange birds, which could not fly at all, nor yet run so fast as that they could escape with their lives; in body they are less than a goose, and bigger than a mallard, short and thick set together, having no feathers, but instead thereof a certain hard and matted down; their beaks are not much unlike the bills of crows." Edward Cliffe's account identifies these flightless birds unmistakably: "They have no wings, but short pinions which serve their turn in swimming. Their color is somewhat black mixed with white spots under their belly, and about their neck. They walk so upright, that afar-off a man would take them to be little children." And Francis Fletcher gives them the name by which we know them: "The fowl which the Welshmen name Penguin, and Magellan termed . . . geese." There are no penguins north of the equator; but the flightless aquatic bird of the north, the great auk, was also a fat black and white bird that waddled upright on land and swam rapidly in water. The great auk was known as a "penguin" long before Magellan's voyage; some say that the fishermen of Brittany gave it a Celtic name, *pen-gwyn*, "white head," and others hold that the name is derived from the Latin *pinguis*, meaning "fat." There is no longer any confusion between the penguins of the south and those of the north, because the great auk, hunted mercilessly for its meat, eggs, and fat, has been extinct since 1844.

Drake's men found the southern penguin good hunting, too: in a single day they killed 3,000 of them, says *The World Encompassed*, which adds, "it is not to be thought that the world hath brought forth a greater blessing, in one kind of creature in so small a circuit, so necessarily and plentifully serving the use of man; they are a very good and wholesome victual." Edward Cliffe describes the hunting as hard work, though: "If a man approach anything near them, they run into holes in the ground (which be not very deep) whereof the island is full. So that to take them we had staves with hooks fast to the ends, wherewith some of our men pulled them out and others being ready with cudgels did knock them on the head, for they bite so cruelly with their crooked bills that none of us was able to handle them alive."

As they passed through the strait, the true geography of the region became apparent to them, as it had not to Magellan. The Spaniards, still encumbered with medieval ideas, looked upon the north coast of Tierra del Fuego as the coast of *Terra Australis;* but Francis Fletcher states, "In passing alongst we plainly discovered that the same *terra australis* left and set down to be *terra incognita* before we came there to be no continent . . . but broken islands." Of course the possibility still remained, for the moment, that south of the islands might lie some unknown mainland. The strait itself was a somber, awe-inspiring place. *The World Encompassed* speaks of mountains that "arise with such tops and spires into the air, and of so rare a height, as they may well be accounted amongst the wonders of the world," and Edward Cliffe says, "The land on both parts is very high: but especially toward the South Sea, monstrous high hills and craggy rocks do exalt themselves, whose tops be all hoary with snow, in the months of August, September, and October. Notwithstanding," Cliffe goes on, "the lower parts of the hills are replenished and beautified with impenetrable thick woods of strange and unknown trees, flourishing all the year long."

Nearing the Pacific end of the strait, they observed so many channels opening to the south that they were not sure of the proper route, nor did Magellan's account help them. They now were passing along the notched and serried northern coast of Santa Inés Island, cut by many misleading inlets. Repeatedly Drake had to anchor the ships and send a scout boat ahead. At one point his scouts encountered a canoe full of Patagonians, whom *The World Encompassed* says were "of a mean stature, but well set and compact in all their parts and limbs." Not even Fletcher in his journal calls them giants; but he made careful studies of their tools (hatchets and knives made of sharpened mussel shells a foot long), their nomadic customs, and their styles of body painting.

On September 6, 1578, Fletcher wrote, "God in mercy at the last brought us through this labyrinth we so long had entangled us with so many extremities and imminent dangers, to that which we so long desired, that is, to the southerly cape of America entering into the South Sea." Drake's traverse of the strait had required only 17 days. Magellan had required a month, but he was pioneering an unknown trail and had to waste many days in the fruitless search for the deserting *San Antonio.* Drake had planned to set up a monument to Queen Elizabeth at Cape Deseado, looking out upon the Pacific; however, he found no anchorage, and strong winds swept him onward without halting for the ceremony. The plan of the voyage called for them now to search the Pacific up to 30°S. for *Terra Australis;* but to have done this they would have had to sail due west from the strait, and that meant a further exposure to the wintry temperature of these high latitudes. Hence Drake abandoned the quest for the southern continent as soon as he entered the Pacific and resolved to follow Magellan's track up the coast of South America, and then northwest across the great ocean. He had perceived, says *The World Encompassed,* that "the nipping cold, under so cruel and frowning a winter, had impaired the health of some of his men," and "meant to have made the more haste again toward the line [the equator], and not to sail any farther toward the pole Antarctic, lest being farther from the sun, and nearer the cold, we might happily be overtaken with some greater danger of sickness." But this plan miscarried at first; Edward Cliffe reports, "Running along towards the northwest about 70 leagues, the wind turned directly against us, with great extremity of foul weather, as rain, hail, snow, and thick fogs which continued so more than three weeks, that we could bear no sail."

The gods of storm unleashed raging tempests and surging seas. The sun was rarely seen; the moon was eclipsed one night; the fleet was scattered. Says *The World Encompassed,* in one of those magnificent flourishes of late-Elizabethan style, "The winds were such as if the bowels of the earth had set all at liberty, or as if all the clouds under heaven had been called together to lay their force upon that one place.

The seas, which by nature and of themselves are heavy, and of a weighty substance, were rowled up from the depths, even from the roots of the rocks, as if it had been a scroll of parchment, which by the extremity of heat runneth together; and being aloft were carried in most strange manner and abundance, as feathers or drifts of snow, by the violence of the winds, to water the exceeding tops of high and lofty mountains. Our anchors, as false friends in such a danger, gave over their holdfast, and as if it had been with horror of the thing, did shrink down to hide themselves in this miserable storm, committing the distressed ship and helpless men to the uncertain and rowling seas, which tossed them, like a ball in a racket."

The ships were driven back toward the strait, but could not find an anchorage in the unending storm. It buffeted them without a break until the end of September, while they bobbed within sight of land, unable to reach shore. On September 30, in one of the most terrible of these gales, the *Marigold* was carried away and went down with all hands. The *Golden Hind* and the *Elizabeth* struggled on October 7 into a bay near the western end of the strait, hoping to find shelter. They succeeded in anchoring, but within a few hours the *Golden Hind*'s cable broke, and she was swept out to sea in the night.

The *Elizabeth*, John Winter's ship, clung fast during that stormy night. "The next day," wrote Edward Cliffe, "very hardly escaping the danger of the rocks, we put into the straits again, where we anchored in an open bay for the space of two days, and made great fires on the shore, to the end that if Mr. Drake should come into the straits, he might find us. [Afterwards] we went into a sound, where we stayed for the space of three weeks and named it The Port of Health, for the most part of our men being very sick with long watching, wet, cold, and evil diet, did here (God be thanked) wonderfully recover their health in short space. Here we had very great mussels (some being 20 inches long) very pleasant meat, and many of them full of seed-pearls.

"We came out of this harbor the first of November, giving over our voyage by Mr. Winter's compulsion (full sore against the mariners' minds) who alleged, he stood in despair, as well to have winds to serve his turn for Peru, as also of Mr. Drake's safety. So we came back again through the straits to St. George's Island, where we took of the fowls before named, and after departed."

Winter's desertion of his commander—for such it was— provided a second strange parallel with Magellan's voyage. Once again a captain had shaken off his vows and had abandoned a great enterprise in the Strait of Magellan to return alone to Europe. The circumstances were somewhat different, since those who had seized control of the *San Antonio* in 1520 were Magellan's avowed enemies, while John Winter had been loyal throughout. Winter's cowardice must have stemmed from exhaustion: the passage of the strait and the subsequent weeks of storm had been enough for him, and he could not face the prospect of further months of Pacific voyaging. It seemed to him that continuing was hopeless, for winds from the west and the north converged on the western end of the strait, as though to keep any mariners from getting past it. And perhaps he had persuaded himself that Drake was dead, after having waited nearly a month for his return. So, making no attempt to search for the *Golden Hind*, Winter swung about. By January the *Elizabeth* was at Brazil, purchasing fruit and meat from the Indians and getting an unfriendly welcome from the Portuguese settlers. In March the voyagers began their Atlantic crossing, which was a slow one, for by the first week in May they were still south of the Tropic of Cancer in what Cliffe calls "the sea of Weeds"— the Sargasso Sea—and on June 2, 1579, they arrived in England. Winter found it necessary to cover the embarrassment of his return by assailing Drake, and so the parallels with Magellan's voyage were extended, for here were some of Drake's men home well ahead of him and telling lies about him, as the *San Antonio*'s men did for Magellan. Winter bore news of the execution of Thomas Doughty, offering it as an example of Drake's tyrannies as though they excused his own defection. The manuscript credited to John Cooke was circulated, depicting Drake as a villainous and overbearing commander under whom it had become impossible to serve. And there were other calumnies, causing Queen Elizabeth to wonder what manner of man she had entrusted with this difficult mission.

Drake, meanwhile, unaware of the sinking of the *Marigold* and the desertion of the *Elizabeth*, was hoping to make rendezvous with his missing ships off the coast of Peru. But when he was swept out to sea on October 7, away from the anchorage he called the Bay of Parting of Friends, the winds carried the *Golden Hind* to the southeast, below the strait and away from Peru: the ship was "as a pelican alone in the wilderness," says *The World Encompassed*. When the winds relented, he found himself at about 55°S., in the island group off the continent's tip. Here they anchored and rested for two days; but the winds "returning to their old wont, and the seas raging after their former manner, yea everything as it were setting itself against our peace and desired rest, here was no stay permitted us, neither any safety to be looked for."

Willy-nilly the *Golden Hind* was thrust still farther southward, so that her men contemplated being swept all the way to the icy pole. During an interlude of calm, Drake ordered eight men into a small pinnace, evidently to fetch provisions from a nearby island. They included a Dutch trumpeter, several of John Hawkins' servants, and a Cornishman named Peter Carder who wrote an account of their strange and harrowing adventures. The men in the pinnace carried with them only one day's victuals and no charts or compasses, for they were not expected to be gone long. But, says Carder, "In the night time by foul weather suddenly arising we lost the sight of our ship, and though our ship sought us and we them, for a fortnight together, yet could we never meet together again. Howbeit within two days after we lost them, we recovered the shore, and relieved ourselves with mussels, oysters, crabs, and some sort of roots in the woods, and within a fortnight after the loss of our consorts, we returned back into the Straits of Magellan, and in two places came on land in the main of America, where we found oysters, mussels, and crabs as before, and filled our barricoes [kegs] with fresh water, and in one of these places we found savages, but they fled from us."

There followed one of the severest ordeals in that era of strenuous explorations. Eight men in a small boat made their way along a hostile coast, pausing in the strait to kill, salt, and dry some penguins, halting at Port San Julian to fish for bream and mackerel, slaying and roasting seals near the Plata estuary. While hunting in the woods on the Uruguayan side of the Plata they were ambushed by Indians, who wounded them all and captured four. The survivors fled to the pinnace and made toward an island some three leagues from shore. Two of the wounded men died on this journey, and the pinnace was wrecked on the island's rocky coast. Carder and one William Pitcher of London, the only ones remaining, spent two months on the island, eating crabs, eels, and fruit. Carder wrote, "In all this island we could not find any fresh water in the world, insomuch, that we were driven to drink our own urine, which we saved in some sherds of certain jars, which we had out of our pinnace, and set our urine all night to cool therein, to drink it the next morning, which thus being drunk often, and often voided, became in a while exceeding red." Making a raft of driftwood, they loaded it with food and headed for the mainland, using two poles instead of oars. The trip took them three nights and two days. "At our coming first on land, we found a little river of very sweet and pleasant water," wrote Carder, "where William Pitcher my only comfort and companion (although I dissuaded him to the contrary) overdrank himself, being pinched before with extreme thirst, and to my unspeakable grief and discomfort, within half an hour after died in my presence, whom I buried as well as I could in the sand."

Alone now, Carder met friendly Indians who took him to their town and treated him to armadillo meat and other delicacies. He stayed with them some months, learning their language and helping them in a war with a neighboring tribe by teaching them how to make shields; the Indians were cannibals who broiled and ate their enemies, and among those consumed were two Portuguese and some Negroes who, having heard that an Englishman was living with the Indians, had come to capture him. When he had wearied of savage life, Carder set out for the coast, hoping to find some passing English or French ship that would take him home. Instead, he fell into the hands of the Portuguese, one of whom, however, was an Anglophile who protected and sheltered him. The authorities decided to write to Lisbon for instructions on dealing with Carder. Meanwhile, his Portuguese friend employed him as overseer for a sugar plantation. After two years word came from Lisbon that Carder was to be shipped to Portugal as a prisoner; but, aided by his friend, he avoided capture and eventually found his way aboard a Portuguese merchant ship bound for Europe. This was seized near the Azores by two English ships of war, and at the end of November 1586 Carder reached his native land, nine years and 14 days after his departure with Drake's fleet. Interestingly, after all this time the queen was still seeking information about the trial of Thomas Doughty, for Carder was taken before her, and, he says, "It pleased her to talk with me a long hour's space of my travails and wonderful escape, and among other things of the manner of Mr. Doughty's execution; and afterward bestowed 22 angels [gold pieces] on me. . . . With many gracious words I was dismissed; humbly thanking the Almighty for my miraculous preservation, and safe return into my native country."

After losing sight of the pinnace in which Carder and his comrades were riding, the *Golden Hind* continued to run helplessly before the gale, until, according to *The World Encompassed*, on October 28, 1578, "We fell with the uttermost part of land towards the South Pole, and had certainly discovered how far the same doth reach southward from the coast of America. . . . The uttermost cape or headland of all these islands stands near in 56°, without which there is no main or island to be seen to the southwards, but that the Atlantic Ocean and the South Sea meet in a most large and free scope."

Drake had come, in fact, to the southernmost point of the continent, which later would be called Cape Horn. Some authorities doubt that Drake actually was the discoverer of the Horn and believe that he made his southernmost landing on Henderson Island, about 50 miles northwest of the cape. At least one author, Felix Reisenberg, asserted in his 1941 book *Cape Horn* that Drake had found an island that has since disappeared. Wherever he may have actually been, Drake certainly was able to look to the south and see nothing but the open water of what now is known as Drake Passage. Thus he shares with Bartholomeu Dias the honor of having sliced away a lobe of *Terra Australis Incognita*, for his unintended discovery proved that South America did come to a definite end and was not joined below the Strait of Magellan to a southern continent. Going ashore, he dropped full length to the ground upon a grassy promontory and stretched his arms as widely as possible, as though taking possession of "the uttermost part of land" in Queen Elizabeth's name. Francis Fletcher reports that he "did with my boy travel to the southernmost point of the island to the sea on that side. Where I found that island to be more southernly three parts of a degree than any of the rest of the islands. Where having set up on end a stone of some bigness and with such tools as I had of purpose ever about me when I went on shore, had engraven her Majesty's name, her Kingdom, the year of Christ and the day of the month. I returned again in some reasonable time to our company."

The storm, which with intermissions had lasted 51 days, now abated, and so the voyagers took their leave of the southernmost region, changing its name, Fletcher said, "from *terra incognita* to *terra nunc bene cognita*"—"land now well known." No reason remained to seek the unknown continent in the lower Pacific, and, finding the winds at last favorable, Drake stood to the northwest, and then to the north, clinging to the rocky, barren Chilean coast as he began England's first reconnaissance of the Pacific.

7

Neither harbors nor settlements presented themselves until they were in 37°S., far up the coast, and came to the isle of Mocha. They cast anchor, and Drake with ten men led a shore party. (It was his risky custom to go in person on such missions whenever possible.) The island was occupied by Indians who had taken refuge there from the cruelties of the Spanish conquerors of the mainland, and, Hakluyt's anonymous author declares, "The people came down to us to the waterside with show of great courtesy, bringing to us potatoes, roots, and two very fat sheep, which our General received and gave them other things for them." Drake communicated that they were in need of water, and the Indians agreed to lead them to a spring the next day. During the course of this visit, though, some of Drake's men, while asking about water, used the Spanish word *agua*, thinking that the Indians were more likely to understand it. Not only did they understand it, they concluded that the mariners must be Spaniards, and repented at once of their former hospitality.

The next morning Drake sent two men to shore to fill the water casks. The Indians led them halfway to the spring, then fell upon them and slew them. Drake, who was waiting in his boat with the empty casks, saw the assault and rushed ashore with nine men in a rescue attempt. Hundreds of armed Indians came out from behind rocks, and in the ambush all of the Englishmen were wounded. "The General himself was shot in the face," says *The World Encompassed*, "under his right eye, and close by his nose, the arrow piercing a marvelous way in under *basis cerebri*, with no small danger of his life; besides that, he was grievously wounded in the head. The rest, being nine persons in the boat, were deadly wounded in divers parts of their bodies, if God almost miraculously had not given cure to the same. For our chief surgeon being dead, and the other absent by the loss of our Vice-Admiral [the *Elizabeth*], and having none left us but a boy, whose good will was more than any skill he had, we were little better than altogether destitute of such cunning and helps, as so grievous a state of so many wounded bodies did require."

Somehow Drake and his companions reached their boat alive, and their wounds proved less serious than they appeared, for that afternoon Drake was in command as the *Golden Hind* hurried away from the island. He refused to attempt any punitive expedition, saying that he would rather preserve one of his own men alive than to destroy a hundred of his enemies; and, knowing that the Indians had mistaken them for Spaniards, he rather approved of their ferocity even though he had been its unwitting victim.

Four days later, on November 30, they were anchored in a bay at about 32°S. when they met a good-natured Indian in a canoe whom they gave some linen, a butcher's chopping knife, and some other things. He was so pleased that he went to his village and showed the gifts to friends, who brought out hens, eggs, a fat hog, and other provisions for Drake. Another Indian, evidently the chief of the tribe, spoke Spanish and, not realizing that the English were enemies to the Spaniards, told Drake (who was fluent in Spanish) that the port of Valparaiso was a short distance down the coast, and that a Spanish ship laden with treasure was at anchor there. Concealing his glee, Drake arranged for the Indian to serve as their pilot, and on December 5 he led them to Valparaiso, then a mean town housing some nine families.

Hakluyt's chronicler declares, "When we came thither, we found indeed the ship riding at anchor, having in her eight Spaniards and three Negroes, who thinking us to have been Spaniards and their friends, welcomed us with a drum, and made ready a *botija* [jug] of wine of Chile to drink to us: but as soon as we entered, one of our company called Thomas Moone began to lay about him, and struck one of the Spaniards, and said unto him, Abaxo Perro, that is in English, Go down dog. One of these Spaniards seeing persons of that quality in those seas, all to crossed, and blessed himself; but to be short, we stowed them under hatches all save one Spaniard, who suddenly and desperately leaped overboard into the sea, and swam ashore to the town . . . to give them warning of our arrival."

The appearance of an English ship at a Chilean port bore the impact of an earthquake. Except for Oxenham's brief and unsuccessful raid near Panamá, no Englishmen had penetrated the Pacific, and Oxenham had come by land over the Isthmus of Panamá, building his vessel there. Here was Drake coming the other way, through the almost forgotten Strait of Magellan, bursting into an empire that had been the exclusive domain of Spain since the conquests by Pizarro and Valdivia nearly half a century earlier. It was as though a mighty trumpet blast had sounded the end of the Spanish monopoly of the Pacific. The people of Valparaiso, forewarned, abandoned their town without waiting to test Drake's mercies; all up the coast the reaction would be similar, either wild flight or the paralysis of panic as the English buccaneers approached.

At their leisure, Drake's men checked through the warehouses on shore, finding a great deal of Chilean wine and some cedarwood boards. They took all the wine to the *Golden Hind*, and some of the lumber as well, for firewood. Also they rifled and desecrated the church, taking from it a silver chalice, two cruets, and an altar cloth, which Drake gave to Francis Fletcher. They rewarded their Indian pilot and put him ashore and freed the crew of their Spanish prize ship, keeping only one Juan Griego, a Greek, to serve as their pilot as they proceeded along the coast. On December 8 they sailed, taking the prize with them.

Once at sea, Drake examined the Spanish ship, which according to *The World Encompassed* was called the *Captain of Moriall*, or the *Grand Captain of the South, Admiral to the Islands of Solomon*. Her cargo was mainly wine, but she was laden with gold to the value of 37,000 Spanish ducats and "a great cross of gold beset with emeralds, on which was nailed a god of this same metal." Though no state of war yet existed between England and Spain, Drake deemed it quite proper for him to seize such cargo as part of the reparations he meant to exact for the treachery at San Juan de Ulúa 11 years previously. This casual assumption of righteousness is reflected in *The World Encom-*

passed, which describes each of Drake's piracies with heavy-handed joviality; thus it speaks of "easing this ship of so heavy a burden."

Looking for a place to refit his ship and assemble another pinnace, Drake sailed on December 19 to the mouth of the Coquimbo river, at about 29°30′S. Here he sent 14 men ashore to fetch water and explore the terrain; he did not realize that a large Spanish garrison was stationed just north of the river, and, notified by Indian spies, the Spaniards sent a large cavalry force to attack. Drake had posted lookouts who saw the horsemen advancing, and the English were able to withdraw in time. One man, Richard Minivy, was foolhardy enough to hold his ground and killed a Spanish horse with his halberd before he was speared and slain. This place was clearly unsuitable, "nor the entertainment such as we desired," and Drake moved on to a more agreeable harbor in 27°55′S. As soon as the pinnace was set up, he chose a capable crew and set out in her to search for the *Marigold* and the *Elizabeth*, for he had not yet abandoned hope that those vessels would join him in the vicinity of 30°S. This gallant but misguided voyage lasted only a single day; the steady wind blowing from the south made progress impossible, and Drake had to return to the *Golden Hind*.

Leaving their anchorage on January 19, 1579, they continued north. At a place called Tarapacá, while looking for water, they came upon a sleeping Spaniard with 13 silver ingots lying beside him. Without awakening him, "we freed him of his charge, which otherwise perhaps would have kept him waking," says *The World Encompassed*. "Our search for water still continuing, as we landed again not far from thence, we met a Spaniard with an Indian boy, driving eight lambs or Peruvian sheep [llamas]: each sheep bore two leather bags, and in each bag was 50 pound weight of refined silver, in the whole 800 weight; we could not endure to see a gentleman Spaniard turned carrier so, and therefore without entreaty we offered our service and became drovers."

A little to the north, in 22°30′, they reached the large Indian town of Mormorena, subject to the Spaniards and ruled by two Spanish administrators. Drake would not raid an Indian town, but he wished to engage in trade there, and the two Spaniards did not dare object. Exchanging knives and mirrors for fish and meat, the English also obtained a few llamas, which Francis Fletcher described with care: "Their height and length was equal to a pretty cow, and their strength fully answerable, if not by much exceeding their size or stature. Upon one of their backs did sit at one time three well grown and tall men, and one boy, no man's foot touching the ground by a large foot in length, the beast nothing at all complaining of his burden in the mean time. These sheep have necks like camels, their heads bearing a reasonable resemblance of another sheep. The Spaniards use them to great profit. Their wool is exceeding fine, their flesh good meat . . . and besides they . . . serve to carry over the mountains marvelous loads for 300 leagues together, where no other carriage can be made but by them only."

Of the richness of this region Fletcher was willing to believe anything, for he says, "Hereabout, as also all along, and up into the country throughout the Province of Cuzco, the common ground; wheresoever it be taken up, in every hundred pound weight of earth, yieldeth 25s. of pure silver, after the rate of a crown an ounce." Drake attempted to appropriate as much of this treasure as possible: arriving at the port of Africa in 20°S. on February 7 and finding two Spanish ships abandoned there by their frightened crews, they came on "some forty and odd bars of silver (of the bigness and fashion of a brickbat, and in weight each of them about 20 pounds), of which we took the burden on ourselves to ease them." At the next port they discovered a third ship which had been transporting 800 bars of silver, but news of Drake's rampage was beginning to precede him, and this vessel had been unloaded before he could seize its cargo.

His destination now was Callao, the port for Lima, capital of Spanish Peru, at 12°30′. Fifteen or 20 Spanish ships were in harbor at Callao when Drake arrived on February 15, but most of these were moored and without their sails, as though it were beyond all possibility that an enemy might enter the harbor. Just outside Callao, Drake captured a small Spanish ship and compelled her pilot, Gaspar Martén, to guide him under cover of darkness into the port. Drake questioned Martén about the whereabouts of the *Marigold* and *Elizabeth*, but the Spaniard knew nothing of those vessels. Martén gave Drake some useful information about the movements of the Spanish treasure fleet: a vessel called *Nuestra Señora del' Valle*, belonging to a well-known captain named Miguel Angel, was now in Callao to load a cargo of 1,500 silver ingots, along with silks, linens, and silver coins; and another ship, the *Çacafuego*, had passed through Callao two weeks earlier, taking on a great deal of gold and silver to carry to Panamá. Drake also learned that his friend Oxenham was imprisoned at Lima with other Englishmen, and he caught up on world events, hearing of the death of King Sebastian of Portugal in a war with Morocco and of the passing at about the same time of King Henry III of France and Pope Gregory XIII (who, in fact, had ten and six years, respectively, yet to live, despite the news circulating in Callao).

Coolly anchoring in the midst of the Spanish ships in the harbor, Drake quickly began operations by boarding Miguel Angel's vessel, only to find that her cargo of treasure had not yet been loaded. Next, he attacked the *San Cristóbal*, which had just arrived from Panamá and was laden with general merchandise. One Englishman was killed in this encounter, but in general the Spaniards made little resistance, regarding Drake as a devil set loose among them. After ransacking every ship in the harbor without finding much of value, Drake took the cargo of the *San Cristóbal*, cut the anchor cables of all the Spanish vessels, disabled the two largest by cutting away their masts, and left them to drift in confusion. Then, on the morning of February 16, he set out in pursuit of the *Çacafuego* and her booty.

While this escapade was taking place, news had come of it at midnight to the palace in Lima of Don Francisco de Toledo, the Viceroy of Peru. This energetic and forceful Spaniard who won an unhappy place in history by ordering the execution of Tupac Amaru, last of the Incas, determined to deal with the buccaneer immediately and sent two ships after him. "Although they left the port on the same day and chased the Corsairs," declares an official Spanish document of February 18, "they were not able to reach them and accomplished nothing, for during the time when they were preparing the said ships the enemy outdistanced them. Nor could they venture to pursue them for many days, because, owing to the hàste with which the ships were made ready, they did not carry a sufficient amount of provisions. Therefore they returned to this port in order to provide themselves with what was necessary." To slow his pursuers, Drake released the merchant vessel *San Cristóbal*, which he had taken with him as a prize. He left the Greek pilot Juan Griego on board, and from him the Spaniards learned the name of their demonic adversary: "Captain Francisco Andreque." Viceroy Toledo decreed that ships be sent at royal expense to warn all ports along the coast of "Andreque's" depredations.

On February 20 Drake reached the port of Paita and entered it looking for the *Çacafuego*. She was not there, but in the course of plundering some ships in the harbor Drake found out that the treasure vessel had called at Paita only two days before. Outside Paita he seized another ship from

Panamá and, to gain information about a supposed hidden cache of bullion, gave the supercargo some rough treatment, stringing him up from the yardarm and dropping him into the sea. In Nuno da Silva's account of the voyage this came out, "The next day they hanged a man of the ship, because he would not confess two plates of gold that he had taken, which after they found about him," and Spain later lodged a stiff protest at this alleged atrocity. However, in the inquiry that followed, a deposition by the "hanged" man, Francisco Jacome, was discovered in the records of the Royal Court of Panamá: "As deponent had not hidden anything whatsoever and was unable to reveal anything to them, they hanged him by the neck with a cord as though to hang him outright, and let him drop from high into the sea, from which they fetched him out with the launch and took him back to the ship on which he had come. It was thus he parted from them." Jacome's experience was frightening and painful, but not fatal, and so Drake must be absolved of the charge, so improbable for a man of his character, of cold-blooded murder.

Hastening northward, the Englishmen searched the horizon for the *Çacafuego* so that, as *The World Encompassed* puts it, they could do her captain "a kindness, in freeing him from the care of those things with which his ship was loaden." The anonymous account in Hakluyt says, "Our general promised our company, that whosoever could first descry her, should have his chain of gold for his good news. It fortuned that John Drake going up into the top, descried her about three of the clock [on March 1, 1579], and about six of the clock we came to her and boarded her." Nuno da Silva adds a curious detail: by now, he says, the *Golden Hind* was so heavy with Spanish treasure that she was unbalanced and sailed poorly; to remedy this, once the *Çacafuego* had been sighted, Drake had some empty Chilean wine jars filled with water and hung at the stern, after which she was more graceful again. But Julian Corbett, whose 1898 biography of Drake is still a standard work, feels that either Silva or his sixteenth-century translator was mistaken, and that Drake was enploying a common device of pirates of this time for deceiving their prey: "If any ships stand in after them, they have out all the sail they can make and hang out drags to hinder their going, that so the other that stand with them might imagine they were afraid and yet they shall fetch them up." Corbett means that the wine jars enabled Drake to keep up his sail without moving forward, so that he would not overtake the *Çacafuego* before dusk but would be ready to maneuver quickly if necessary.

The captain of the *Çacafuego* was San Juan de Anton, a man of Biscay who, according to Nuno da Silva, had been reared in England. His ship was unusually large and heavily laden with treasure; the Spanish accounts refer it to sometimes simply as the *Nao Rica*, "rich ship," though her true name seems to have been *Nuestra Señora de la Concepción*. *Çacafuego* was actually a nickname, usually given in English as "spitfire," although "fartfire" would be a more accurate translation. A few weeks after his encounter with Drake, San Juan de Anton appeared before the Royal Court of Panamá to tell his story, and also gave an account of it to Pedro Sarmiento de Gamboa, the discoverer of the Solomon Islands, who published it. Sarmiento's version declares:

"At noon on Sunday, the first of March, San Juan de Anton, being out at sea in his ship . . . saw, close to land, a ship which was going the same way, bound for Panamá. He thought she was a bark from Guayaquil and bore towards her. At about nine o'clock at night, the English ship crossed the course of San Juan's vessel and immediately came alongside. San Juan saluted but the corsair did not return the salute. Believing her to be a ship from Chile which was then in rebellion, Master de Anton came to the side. By that time the

English were already grappling his ship shouting: 'Englishman! Strike sail!' Someone said: 'Strike sail, Mr. Juan de Anton; if not, look out, for you will be sent to the bottom.'

San Juan answered: 'What England is this [which gives me orders] for striking sail? Come on board to strike sail yourselves!' On hearing this they blew a whistle on the English ship and the trumpet responded. Then a volley of what seemed to be about sixty arquebuses was shot, followed by many arrows which struck the side of the ship, and chain-balls shot from a heavy piece of ordnance carried away the mizzen and sent it into the sea with its sail and lateen yard. After this the English shot another great gun, shouting again 'Strike sail!' and, simultaneously, a pinnace laid aboard to port and about forty archers climbed up the channels of the shrouds and entered San Juan de Anton's ship, while, at the opposite side, the English ship laid aboard. It is thus that they forced San Juan's ship to surrender. They inquired for the pilot and captain from the selfsame San Juan de Anton, who was alone on deck. He would not answer them. Not seeing any other person on deck, they seized him and carried him to the English ship, where he saw the corsair Francis Drake, who was removing his helmet and coat of mail. Francis Drake embraced San Juan de Anton, saying: 'Have patience, for such is the usage of war,' and immediately ordered him to be locked up in the cabin in the poop, with twelve men to guard him."

At nine the next morning Drake went aboard the *Çacafuego* to take breakfast, leaving word with his chief sergeant to prepare his own table for San Juan de Anton as though it were for himself. Until noon Drake examined the treasure he had seized; then he gave orders for sailing, and both vessels moved together toward the northwest. Over the next three days Drake's pinnace fetched riches from the *Çacafuego* to the *Golden Hind*. The yield was immense, says *The World Encompassed:* "A certain quantity of jewels and precious stones, 13 chests of reals of plate [silver coins], 80 pound weight in gold, 26 ton of uncoined silver, two very fair gilt silver drinking bowls, and the like trifles, valued in all about 360,000 pesos." A boy in the Spanish ship's crew commented, "Our ship shall be called no more the *Ça-cafuego* [fartfire] but the *Çacaplata* [fartsilver]," which gave Drake's men great amusement then and long after.

Drake's treatment of his Spanish prisoners was exemplary. Sarmiento's account says that "the Englishman made several gifts to those whom he had robbed. He gave thirty or forty pesos in cash to each. To some he gave pieces of stuff from Portugal, and agricultural implements, such as hoes and pruning-knives; to others, two of his own cloaks adorned with trimmings. . . . To San Juan de Anton he presented a firelock saying that it had been sent him from Germany and that he prized it highly. To the clerk he gave a steel shield and a sword saying that he did this so that the clerk might appear to be a man-at-arms. . . . To a merchant named Cuevas he gave some fans with mirrors, saying that they were for his lady. And to San Juan de Anton he gave a silver-gilt bowl, in the center of which his name, 'Francisqus Draqus,' was inscribed."

In his conversations with San Juan de Anton, Drake spoke of the betrayal at San Juan de Ulúa, complaining of the faithless Viceroy Martín Enriquez and saying that 300 Englishmen had been killed by his treachery, Drake himself losing 7,000 pesos. He begged the Spanish captain to intercede with the Viceroy of Peru on behalf of John Oxenham and the other English prisoners at Lima. San Juan assured him, wrongly, that Oxenham would not be put to death, and "Francis rejoiced greatly on hearing this and became pacified; for he displayed much anger whenever he spoke about them." Drake even discussed his homeward route with his fellow captain, observing that there were four possible routes for him to take from the Pacific to England: "One was by the Cape of Good Hope and India; another by Norway; another by the Strait of Magellan. He would not name the fourth." Sarmiento's guess was that he meant the Strait of Anian, leading from the coast of China over the North Pole. Drake told San Juan de Anton that he expected to be back in England within six months; but the other told him he would not be able to return in less than a year.

Drake set San Juan de Anton and his stripped vessel free, with all her crew, on March 7. He still believed that his *Marigold* and *Elizabeth* were following him, and so that the *Çacafuego* would not be seized and robbed all over again by the other two English ships, he gave San Juan a safe-conduct signed in English. The original of this interesting document has been lost, but its text has come down to us in an involved way: it came into the hands of the Inquisition in Lima, where Oxenham and his men were then being interrogated, and one of the English prisoners, a man named John Butler, translated it into excellent Spanish for the benefit of his captors. This Spanish version was entered in the records of the Inquisition, which have been preserved, and, retranslated, reads:

"Mr. Winter. If it please God that by a favorable chance Your Honor should meet San Juan de Anton, I pray you to treat him well, in accordance to the word I have given him. If Your Honor should be lacking in any of the things that San Juan de Anton carries, pay him double their value in the merchandise that Your Honor carries. Give orders that none of your soldiers are to do him harm or wound him. What we determined about the return to our country will be carried out if God so wills, although I greatly doubt whether this letter will reach your hands, I abide as God knows, constantly praying to the Lord who holds you and me and all the world in His keeping to save or to damn. I give him thanks always. Amen.

"This my writing is not only for Winter but also for . . . all the other good friends whom I commend to Him who redeemed us with His Blood. I have faith in God that he will not inflict more toils upon us but will help us in our tribulations. I beseech you for the love of Jesus Christ, that if God permits you to suffer afflictions you do not despair of the great Mercy of God, for the great Prophet says that the Lord grants and gives new life. May God thus have mercy and show his compassion—to Him be glory, honor, power and empire, for ever and ever, amen, amen.

"I, the mournful captain whose heart is very heavy for you,

"FRANCIS DRAKE"

The taking of the *Çacafuego* had satisfied Drake's lust for Spanish treasure, and now he began to think about quitting the South American coast to undertake the next phase of his voyage. But he was uncertain whether to go out to the Moluccas and China or simply to sail up the western coast of America until he found the Strait of Anian, which would take him home. While he deliberated, he continued to go north, continuing, almost by force of habit, to raid Spanish shipping. Having come to South America's westernmost point, he did not follow the coast inland along Colombia, but struck for the northwest and Nicaragua. On the way he seized a ship that carried a valuable collection of charts of the Pacific, copied from those of Urdaneta. A few days later, on March 16, the *Golden Hind* reached the island of Caño off the Nicaraguan coast; there Drake remained for eight days, refitting, reprovisioning, and constructing another pinnace. After enduring a severe earthquake without harm, he set out on March 24 toward Mexico, which still was ruled by his old enemy, Don Martín Enriquez.

On April 4, about an hour before dawn, still off the Nicaraguan coast, Drake came upon a Spanish ship. Aboard her was Don Francisco de Zarate, a gentleman of high birth whose report to Don Martín Enriquez on his capture casts light on Drake's personality. "We saw, by moonlight, a ship very close to ours. Our steersman shouted that she was to get out of the way and not come alongside of us. To this they made no answer, pretending to be asleep. The steersman then shouted louder, asking them where their ship hailed from. They answered, 'from Peru,' and that she was 'of *Miguel Angel*,' which is the name of a well-known captain of that route." Drake had compelled a Spaniard he had recently taken from another ship to give this answer. Suddenly, in a moment, Zarate wrote, "she crossed our poop, ordering us 'to strike sail' and shooting seven or eight arquebus shots at us. We thought this as much of a joke as it afterwards turned out to be serious. On our part there was no resistance, nor had we more than six of our men awake on the whole boat, so they entered our ship with as little risk to themselves as though they were our friends. They did no personal harm to anyone, beyond seizing the swords and keys of the passengers."

This reveals how Drake's piracies were so successful, even against larger and better-equipped ships: he struck by surprise, so audaciously that almost invariably he caught his foes off guard. Never did he succumb to the temptation of a foolhardy attack against a well-prepared enemy, but, pouncing swiftly and unpredictably, he demoralized and bewildered the Spaniards completely, so that there were scarcely any casualties on either side in his buccaneering career up the Pacific coast. (He does not seem to have killed a single Spaniard, and his only recorded loss was one man slain at Callao.)

Zarate says that Drake is "a nephew of John Hawkins, and is the same who, about five years ago, took the port of Nombre de Dios. He is called Francisco Drac, and is a man about 35 years of age, low of stature, with a fair beard, and is one of the greatest mariners that sails the seas, both as a navigator and as a commander. His vessel is a galleon of nearly four hundred tons [a fourfold exaggeration] and is a perfect sailer. She is manned with a hundred men, all of service, and of an age for warfare, and all are as practiced therein as old soldiers from Italy could be. Each one takes particular pains to keep his arquebus clean. He treats them with affection, and they treat him with respect. . . . He is served on silver dishes with gold borders and gilded garlands, in which are his arms. He carries all possible dainties and perfumed waters. . . . He dines and sups to the music of viols."

Drake was courteous to Zarate, who had no gold to offer him. He asked the Spaniard if he knew Don Martín Enriquez. "I said, 'Yes.' 'Is any relative of his or thing pertaining to him on this ship?' 'No, sir.' 'Well, it would give me a greater joy to come across him than all the gold and silver of the Indies. You would see how the words of gentlemen should be kept.' " When he released the Spaniards, giving each man a handful of silver reals as a present, he earnestly beseeched Zarate "to tell certain Englishmen who were in Lima that I had met him and that he was well. From this it is to be inferred that he has spies in all this realm and in Peru." Zarate did not realize that the "spies" in Peru were Oxenham and his men, awaiting execution.

About April 15 Drake came to the port of Guatulco, or Aquatulco, in 15°40'N. The narrative published by Hakluyt says, "We went presently to the town, and to the townhouse, where we found a judge sitting in judgment, being associate with three other officers, upon three Negroes that had conspired the burning of the town: both which judges and prisoners we took, and brought them on shipboard, and caused the chief judge to write his letter to the town, to command all the townsmen to avoid, that we might safely water here." They ransacked the town, collecting some treasure and desecrating a Catholic church. Here Drake released all his prisoners, including Nuno da Silva, whom he had captured more than 14 months earlier in the Cape Verde Islands. Silva made his way to Mexico City, where he incautiously admitted to Don Martín Enriquez that he had taken Protestant communion several times aboard the *Golden Hind*. Although he insisted that this had been done under compulsion, he was called before the Inquisition and accused of intentionally committing heresy. This he denied under torture, though the Inquisitors, mindful of Drake's gentle treatment of other prisoners, refused to believe that the Portuguese pilot could have been subjected to Protestantism against his will; he was sentenced to make public confession of his sins and to "perpetual exile from the Indies." It appears that ultimately Silva settled in England and as late as 1593 was part of a buccaneering expedition to the Brazilian coast.

At Guatulco, Drake concluded that he was done with piracy and addressed himself to the problem of his next destination. He seriously considered dropping the Moluccas voyage and returning at once to England with his booty; but by which route? To go south, back to the Strait of Magellan, meant that he would almost certainly fall into the hands of Spanish squadrons now scouring the South American coast for him, and he was not eager either to taste the fury of Antarctic storms again. To go north to the supposed Strait of Anian meant to search for the unknown, and he hesitated now to do this. That left only the Moluccas, but when he attempted to turn west in the latitude of Nicaragua, Drake found himself becalmed, and therefore he had no choice but

to keep going north, along what the Elizabethans called "the
back side of America." Keeping well out to sea, he paralleled
the coast of Mexico and went up the coast of Baja California,
still without finding a favorable breeze to carry him westward; by this time he was so far to the north that he decided
to look for the Strait of Anian after all.

The Spaniards too were speculating on Drake's intended route. The nervous documents that went fluttering
through their official channels in the early months of 1579
reflect their concern and their bafflement. In February, at
Callao, Drake had given out that he planned to return to
England "by China and the route of the Portuguese," that is,
make a circumnavigation via the Cape of Good Hope. But a
report to King Philip II filed in April indicated that the Spaniards considered him deliberately to be trying to mislead
them. This report considered the various possibilities, elimi-
nating the Strait of Anian (called here the strait *de los bacal-
laos*, "of the codfish"), "because this is a strait which has
never been navigated and is not known to exist." Nor could
Drake really be planning to go home by way of the Portuguese route, for "The navigation is so long and troublesome,
as he would have to pilot and coast the entire world in order
to return to England. . . . He cannot convey, in one ship
only, the provisions sufficient for the 80 men he carries, during such a long voyage, even if his ship were to carry no
other cargo but victuals. . . . He would have to touch at, or
pass in sight of, Portuguese ports, where he would certainly
run the risk of being seized and severely chastised by the armadas that are there. On reaching Asia, he would also run
the risk of the Turks. . . . As, ever since he came out
through the Strait of Magellan, he has been proclaiming that
he intended to return by the route of China, we must believe
the contrary. For soldiers, when it suits their purpose, and in

order to put their enemy off their guard, are apt to proclaim what they do not intend doing." Furthermore, if Drake meant to go that way, why had he released the skilled pilot Nuno de Silva? "The return by the same Strait of Magellan seems the most likely," the report concluded. Having proven to their own satisfaction that Drake would soon be coming back down the coast of South America, the Spaniards got ready to intercept him.

8

The *Golden Hind* left Guatulco on April 16, 1579, and sailed to the northwest without sighting land until, by June 3, she was in 42°N., or somewhere off the coast of Oregon. Here, says *The World Encompassed*, "we found such alteration of heat, into extreme and nipping cold, that our men in general did grievously complain thereof. . . . The very ropes of our ship were stiff, and the rain which fell was an unnaturally congealed and frozen substance, so that we seemed rather to be in the frozen zone than any way so near unto the sun, or these hotter climates." The cold weather continued for several days, with harsh effects on men who had been in the tropics for many months. On June 5 contrary winds forced the ship to run to shore, which emerged unexpectedly, for they had not thought that America extended this far to the west. They anchored in an open, poorly sheltered bay, reckoning their position as 48°N., or about the latitude of Vancouver Island. The gale that had assailed them died down, but was succeeded by "most vile, thick, and stinking fogs." The cold weather persisted, and even more discouraging was the wind out of the north, which seemed to bar any further search for the Strait of Anian and the Northwest Passage. Therefore they turned back, going south down a coast where, even in June, the hills were crested with snow, and on the 17th of the month "fell with a convenient and fit harbor" in 38°30′N. Here they landed to begin a visit of more than a month.

They had come to San Francisco Bay.* This was not the first visit of Europeans to California. Supposedly a Portuguese expedition had crossed the Pacific from the Moluccas in 1520 and discovered the coast of North America, though there seems little truth in this story, but beyond doubt Spaniards led by Juan Rodríguez Cabrillo had carefully explored the entire coast as far as 44°N. in 1542–43. Drake seemed unaware of Cabrillo's work and regarded himself as the discoverer of the territory: "The Spaniards never had any dealing, or so much as set a foot in this country, the utmost of their discoveries reaching only to many degrees southward of this place," claims *The World Encompassed*.

The English found summer in San Francisco unaccountably harsh; it was so cold that they would have had to wear winter clothes if "violent exercises of our bodies, and busy employment about our necessary labors" had not kept them warm. Nor was this entirely a matter of failing to adjust to a temperate climate after a sojourn in the tropics, for they shortly were greeted by Indians "who had never been acquainted with such heat, to whom the country, air, and climate was proper, and in whom custom of cold was as it were a second nature; yet [they] used to come shivering to us in their warm furs, crowding close together, body to body, to receive heat of one another." Some of Drake's sailors had seen service on the Northeast Passage run and insisted that they found it colder here in June than at 72°N. off the northern coast of Norway in the same season. This mysterious frigidity has puzzled later geographers, since it is so contrary to the usual moderation of the climate there; but those who

---

* Some geographers hold that Drake missed the Golden Gate in fog, and made his landfall to the north at the place now known as Drake's Bay.

know the fogs of San Francisco will recognize the accuracy of Francis Fletcher's statement, "Neither could we at any time, in whole fourteen days together, find the air so clear as to be able to take the height of sun or star."

The day after they anchored a number of natives appeared on the shore, and one man in a canoe paddled toward them. While still at a great distance he began to speak to those on board, and when he was close, he halted and commenced "a long and tedious oration," with many gestures, signs, and indications of reverence, after which he returned to shore. Soon after, he came a second time in the same manner, and then a third, this time bringing the gift of some black feathers on a string and a little basket of woven rushes containing an herb called *tobáh*. (In the Hakluyt account, the name of this herb is erroneously given as tobacco; but tobacco had been known in England since 1565, and *tobáh* was clearly something new to Drake's men.) He tied these gifts to a short stick and cast them into the ship's boat. Drake would have given him presents in return, but he ignored some things floated toward him on a plank and took only a hat thrown from the ship into the water, and made his return to land. It seemed to the English that they were being looked upon as gods.

The *Golden Hind* had sprung a leak at sea, and to lighten her for repairs Drake had her anchored close to shore and unloaded of most of her provisions and cargo. A party of men put up tents and began to build a fort; while this was going on, a large number of Indians collected, watching the proceedings in awe and amazement. Though they were armed, they put aside their bows and arrows at a sign from Drake, who was cautious and watchful despite the seemingly childlike innocence of these Californians.

The men were naked; the women wore only loose garments of rope around their waists and deerskin mantles over their shoulders. Seeking to maintain the friendly tone of the encounter, Drake gave them shirts and linens, "bestowing upon each of them liberally good and necessary things to cover their nakedness," says *The World Encompassed*, "withal signifying unto them we were no gods, but men, and had need of such things to cover our own shame; teaching them to use them to the same ends, for which cause also we did eat and drink in their presence, giving them to understand that without that we could not live, and therefore were but men as well as they."

Nevertheless, the Indians persisted in looking upon the English as gods, and soon the visitors had a view of a less childlike side of these people, for when they returned to their houses, some three-quarters of a mile from the harbor, they began a strange religious ceremony, setting up "a kind of most lamentable weeping and crying out; which they continued also a great while together . . . the women especially extending their voices in a most miserable and doleful manner of shrieking."

Two days passed without contact with the Indians; then a great assembly of them gathered, bearing feathers and bags of *tobáh* as offerings to the new gods. They mounted the hill at the foot of which the English had built their fort, and another orator came forth to deliver a loud and tempestuous speech, "his voice being extended to the uttermost strength of nature, and his words falling so thick one in the neck of another, that he could hardly fetch his breath again." (The descriptions here and following are those of *The World Encompassed*.) When he had done, the others bowed "in a dreaming manner" and cried out as if agreeing with all he had said; the men then laid down their bows and descended the hill to make their offerings to Drake. "In the meantime the women, as if they had been desperate, used unnatural violence against themselves, crying and shrieking piteously, tearing their flesh with their nails from their cheeks in a monstrous manner, the blood streaming down along their breasts, besides despoiling the upper parts of their bodies of those single coverings they formerly had, and holding their hands above their heads that they might not rescue their breasts from harm, they would with fury cast themselves upon the ground, never respecting whether it were clean or soft, but dashed themselves in this manner on hard stones, knobby hillocks, stocks of wood, and pricking bushes. . . ."

Drake was dismayed by the violence of the women's manner of worship. Calling his own men to prayer, he besought God "to open by some means their blinded eyes, that they might in due time be called to the knowledge of Him, the living God." The singing of psalms and reading of Biblical chapters so pleased the Indians that in all later meetings they requested the English to sing again as the first order of business. At the end of the ceremony Drake presented gifts to the Indians, who politely declined them as though "thinking themselves sufficiently enriched and happy that they had found so free access to see us."

Three days later, on June 26, an even greater gathering of Indians collected, as though they were coming from all outlying provinces to view the English. This time the king himself arrived, with a bodyguard of 100 warriors. He was preceded by two heralds who came to the English fort and announced by speech and gestures that their *hióh*, or ruler, wished to visit Drake and desired first to have some token of peace and friendship sent to him. Drake complied, and in a little while the royal train appeared, led by "a man of a large body and goodly aspect" who carried a scepter of black wood, to which were affixed two feather crowns and three chains made of links of bone, and a bag of the herb *tobáh*. Next to this official walked the hióh, wearing a knit crown and a cloak of rabbit skins; his bodyguard also was in uniform, and their faces were painted each in a different pattern. Commoners, naked but wearing plumes of feathers in their hair, followed, and the last part of the procession was a band of women and children carrying baskets of *tobáh*, a root called *petáh*, broiled fish, seeds, and other such things. The description of these baskets in *The World Encompassed* clearly identifies Drake's Indians as the Pomo or a kindred tribe: "Their baskets were made in fashion like a deep bowl, and though the matter were rushes, or such other kind of stuff, yet was it so cunningly handled, that the most part of them would hold water: about the brims they were hanged with pieces of the shells of pearls, and in some places with two or three links at a place, of the [bone] chains forenamed: thereby signifying that they were vessels wholly dedicated to the only use of the gods they worshipped; and besides this, they were wrought upon with the matted down of red feathers, distinguished into divers works and forms."

Drake, still wary, kept his men armed and ready as the hióh drew near. But the Indians meant no harm: the scepter-bearer launched an oration of half an hour's length, repeating "with an audible and manly voice" words whispered to him by another official; this was followed by stately singing and dancing, though the women, whose breasts were scratched and bodies bruised by injuries self-inflicted during the march, danced without joining the songs. At the conclusion of these extensive ceremonies, the hióh made signs to Drake to sit down. He then placed a feather crown on Drake's head, garlanded his neck with many-linked bone chains, offered him other gifts, and saluted him by the name of "hióh."

It may have been that the native monarch was merely indicating by all this that he regarded Drake as a man of status equal to his own, and thus worthy of reverence. Perhaps by calling him "hióh" he was initiating a ceremonial exchange of names, and expected Drake to reciprocate by hailing him as "Drake." To the English, unschooled in ethnological subtleties, the hióh's actions were wholly without ambiguity, and were "supplication that he [Drake] would take the province and kingdom into his hand, and become their king and patron: making signs that they would resign unto him their right and title in the whole land, and become his vassals in themselves and their posterities." And the dance that followed the hióh's words was interpreted as an expression of joy that "the great and chief God was now become their God, their king and patron."

Drake could not refuse such generous homage. So "he took the scepter, crown, and dignity of the said country into his hand; wishing nothing more than that it had lain so fitly for her Majesty to enjoy, as it was now her proper own." While Drake and the hióh sat side by side, new dances began; the Indians clustered about the English, favoring the youngest and most handsome of them, and offered the herbs and seeds they had brought, "crying out with lamentable shrieks and moans, weeping and scratching and tearing their very flesh off their faces with their nails; neither were it the women alone which did this, but even old men, roaring and crying out, were as violent as the women were." The English "groaned in spirit to see the power of Satan so far prevail in seducing these so harmless souls," and began prayers and psalms of their own, not in any naïve hope that the Indians would understand, but only so that the solemnity of their voices might halt the wild, frightening, and, to a European, incomprehensible displays of self-destructive fervor.

In the days that followed, the Indians came frequently to the English fort. It became clear that "they are a people of a tractable, free, and loving nature, without guile or treachery; their bows and arrows (their only weapons, and almost all their wealth) they use very skillfully, but yet not to do any great harm with them, being by reason of their weakness more fit for children than for men." They brought gifts of fish (which they caught bare-handed, most expertly), mussels, and seals; and they displayed sores and wounds which they hoped their guests would cure by a laying-on of hands. Still trying to persuade the Indians of their mortal nature, the English attempted no mystical healing, but did apply such medicines and ointments as they had.

When the repairs to the ship were nearly finished, Drake and some of the officers and gentlemen made an inland journey. They visited the Indian village, the dwellings of which were dug in the earth and roofed over with timber and soil. They found the interior country to be far more appealing than the cold coast, fertile and warm, abounding in "very large and fat deer" and other animals. Drake gave this country, already known as California to the Spaniards, the name of New Albion, "and that for two causes: the one in respect of the white banks and cliffs, which lie toward the sea; the other, that it might have some affinity, even in name also, with our own country, which was sometime so called." As the time of departure approached, Drake set up a monument at the shore—a brass plate, nailed to a sturdy post, on which was engraved a statement of England's claim to New Albion. By way of displaying the queen's picture and coat of arms, he mounted a sixpence coin in a hole in the plate. Though this monument was long assumed to be lost, the brass plate was discovered in 1937 by Beryle Shinn, a twenty-six-year-old department-store clerk whose automobile suffered a blowout on a hillside overlooking Richardson's Bay in Marin County. Sitting down to rest on a heap of stones after changing the tire, Shinn felt something pinch him, and found a piece of brass wedged between the stones. He thought it might be useful and took it with him. Later, he was about to cut it up when he noticed a barely legible inscription. The plate was taken to the great historian Herbert E. Bolton of the University of California, who reported in astonishment that it read, "Bee it known unto all men by these presents June 17 1579, by the grace of God and in the name of herr Majesty, Queen Elizabeth of England, and her successors forever I take possession of this kingdome whose King and people freely resigne their right and title in the whole land unto herr majesty's keeping now named by me and to be known unto all men as Nova Albion. Francis Drake."

On July 23 the English were ready to leave—somewhat reluctantly, for it had been an agreeable stay, and they now were quitting one of the world's safest and most tranquil harbors for the uncertainties of the Pacific. The Indians, too, were sorrowful, protesting with bitter tears and wringing of hands that they were being deserted by their gods. They built a fire and burned a chain and a bunch of feathers, and threatened to begin another of their barbarously uninhibited frenzies: "We labored by all means possible to withhold or withdraw them, but could not prevail, till at last we fell to prayers and singing of psalms, whereby they were allured immediately to forget their folly, and leave their sacrifice unconsumed, suffering the fire to go out; and imitating us in all our actions, they fell a lifting of their eyes and hands to heavens, as they saw us do." They watched from the hills as the *Golden Hind* made her way through the Golden Gate, and their sacrificial fires could be seen when the ship was well out to sea. The next day the voyagers passed the Farallon Islands, famous for their seals, just off the coast at San Francisco. The weather was still cold, and the wind blew as before from the northwest, which cut off all hope of finding a passage to Europe by way of a northern strait; and so, "with general consent of all," Drake "bent his course directly to run with the Islands of the Moluccas." For 68 days they would travel Magellan's route through a landless sea, until, on September 30, they attained the Island of Thieves.

9

While Drake was making his Pacific crossing—a month shorter than Magellan's, and infinitely less arduous—the Spaniards of Peru were fretting over the possibility that he would descend once again on their shores. "It is a thing that terrifies one, this voyage and the boldness of this low man, the son of vile parents (for, it is said that his father was a shoemaker)," wrote General Miguel de Eraso to King Philip II on May 10, 1579. Through the months that followed, the Spaniards kept a close watch for Drake's return. Pedro Sarmiento de Gamboa, who had advocated following Drake across the Gulf of Panamá and seizing him off Nicaragua, but who was overruled, argued that Drake would go home by way of the Strait of Anian: "A man who has had the spirit to do what he has done will not be lacking in courage to persevere in his attempt, especially as he can take advantage, at present, of its being summer in the polar regions." But though Sarmiento believed that the last route Drake was likely to take back to England was the Strait of Magellan, he drew the assignment of patrolling the coast; and, when Drake had not appeared by late September, it was assumed that he had slipped by the patrol and was heading for the strait. Sarmiento was dispatched to pursue and capture him.

He set out from Callao with two ships and 108 men on October 11, 1579, instructed to search for Drake between there and the strait, to examine the strait (which no Spanish ship had entered in more than 50 years) for navigational use, and to observe where it could be fortified against further English intrusions. Despite stormy weather, Sarmiento beat his way south, finding no trace of Drake but carrying out the first detailed reconnaissance of Chile's intricate southern coast and taking possession of the offshore archipelago on November 22 in the name of King Philip. Learning from the Indians that two large ships bearing bearded men had lately been seen at anchor nearby, he assumed that they were part of Drake's squadron and hurried into the strait to seek them. They were not there—they were, in fact, imaginary, since Sarmiento's ships were the only ones near Patagonia that year—but he performed an elaborate survey of the strait and the region about it, after undergoing a good deal of difficulty finding the western mouth of the strait at all among the many channels of the archipelago. Magellan had had a far easier time locating the large and simple eastern entrance. In the strait, Sarmiento's ships were separated, and, as was by now virtually the custom on such voyages, his co-captain abandoned the enterprise after a few days, leaving the strait by the Pacific side and going swiftly back to Peru. Continuing alone, Sarmiento met many Patagonians who, according to the unreliable seventeenth-century historian of his voyage, Argensola, were nine feet tall; ten crewmen surrounded a one-eyed giant of prodigious bulk and captured him to bring to Spain. Late in February 1580 Sarmiento finally reached the Atlantic side of the strait and, in gratitude for his deliverance from the complex waterway, wrote in his journal, "Be it known to all men, that to make this voyage and discovery, we chose for our advocate and patroness, our most serene Lady the Virgin Santa Maria. . . . For which reason, and for the wonders which through her intercession have been wrought in our behalf, the name of the STRAIT DE LA MADRE DE DIOS is given to this strait heretofore called *de Magallanes*." This pious attempt to change the strait's name earned Sarmiento the contempt of later writers, such as the eighteenth-century collector of sea narratives John Callander, who called him "a vain empty man," but evidently he meant no disrespect to Magellan, and his new name was ignored by all. Upon leaving the strait, Sarmiento headed for Europe, coming in through the Cape Verde Islands, where the Portuguese settlers were unwilling to believe that he had actually sailed from the South Sea by way of the strait. He reached Spain in mid-August 1580, having heard en route that Drake had returned to England in the spring. Actually Drake was still at sea and, within a week after Sarmiento's arrival in Spain, was nearing the Azores, which Sarmiento had passed a month previously. But Drake had come there another way, not through the strait at all, but by sailing westward around the world.

10

After more than two months of traveling through the emptiness west of San Francisco, Drake's men sighted land about 8° north of the equator on September 30, 1579. From an island group came, says the Hakluyt account, "a great number of canoes, having in some of them four, in some 6, and in some also 14 men, bringing with them cocos [coconuts], and other fruits. Their canoes were hollow within, and cut with great art and cunning, being very smooth within and without . . . and on each side of them lie out two pieces of timber about a yard and a half long, more or less, according to the smallness, or bigness, of the boat." The islanders "have the nether part of their ears cut into a round circle, hanging down very low upon their cheeks, whereon they hang things of a reasonable weight."

Hakluyt's anonymous mariner says little more, but the only other account, that of Francis Fletcher as adapted for *The World Encompassed*, reads suspiciously like a plagiarism of Pigafetta. It declares that the natives were light-fingered, "for if they received anything once into their hands, they would neither give recompense nor restitution of it, but thought whatever they could finger to be their own." When "with brows of brass"—brazenly, that is—the islanders demanded yet more and were refused, they began hurling stones from their canoes. Drake ordered a cannon fired, and they all leaped into the water and swam away in fright. But soon others came and "cunningly fell a filching of what they could, and one of them pulled a dagger and knives from one of our men's girdles. . . . Neither could we at all be to rid of this ungracious company, till we made some of them feel some smart as well as terror: and so we left that place, by all passengers to be known hereafter by the name of the *Island of Thieves*." Now Fletcher must certainly have known from Pigafetta that Magellan had already given the same name to the island group containing Guam and Rota, and that Magellan's Ladrones—the Marianas—lay about 13° north of the equator, considerably northeast of the *Golden Hind*'s present position. It seems sure that Drake never saw the Ladrones, and that Fletcher's Island of Thieves was in the Palau or Pelew group. It is hard to understand why he borrowed the whole episode of thievery from Pigafetta, even for the sake of a good story, when the Italian's book was so well known at that time.

At any rate, by October 16 Drake was in the Philippines and, five days later, anchored to take water at Mindanao. Unlike Magellan, who had dallied fatally in these islands, Drake hurried on without even trying to molest the Spanish settlement at Manila on the isle of Luzon. He made his course for the Moluccas, arriving on November 3.

The history of the Spice Islands had been a stormy one since Charles V had negated all Magellan's work by selling his rights in them to Portugal in 1529. The Portuguese had never quite succeeded in entrenching themselves there as they had done while building their empire in Malacca and the Malabar Coast early in the sixteenth century. For a while they had enjoyed a strong hold on Ternate, but were always dependent on the good will of the island's sultan, which they attempted to keep by aiding him in his perpetual struggle against the rival island of Tidore. When castaway Spaniards established themselves on Tidore in the late 1520s, the Portuguese were able to encircle and eventually seize them. But the Moluccas had lost their monopoly on the clove trade, which complicated the Portuguese position. Portuguese buying had driven up the price of cloves, encouraging the development of new clove plantations on the Banda and Amboina islands. These sold their product mainly to Javanese merchants, who shipped them by way of the Moslem city of Brunei on the north coast of Borneo to China and India. Brunei became a commercial rival to Ternate; at the same time, just across from Malacca on the island of Sumatra, a sultanate called Atjeh was going into competition with Malacca for the pepper trade. The Atjenese not only cut Portugal out of much business that would normally have been routed through Malacca, but assaulted Malacca itself in 1537, 1547, and 1551, nearly dislodging the Portuguese from their strategically located fortress.

Portugal attempted to cope with these problems by establishing trade centers on the other islands of the East Indies, and by Christianizing the natives to make them more cooperative. The missionary St. Francis Xavier preached in Amboina and the Moluccas in 1546, and some superficial token conversions resulted, mainly on Amboina; elsewhere, Islam held its ground. But while the Portuguese were preoccupied with Amboina, Ternate decided to shake off the Portuguese grip altogether. Sultan Hairun of Ternate, who came to his throne in 1545, was unsuccessful in his attempts to capture the Portuguese fort on his island, but Hairun's assassination by the Portuguese precipitated a climactic war in which his son and successor, Baabullah, took the fort in

1574. The Portuguese of Goa, overextended in their attempt to control thousands of miles of the Indies, were unable to give aid.

The Portuguese influence in the East Indies was cut to the base on Amboina and, after 1578, to an outpost on Tidore, an island that had been previously linked to Spain. When Drake arrived in the Moluccas late in 1579, he found the Portuguese in poor shape and seemingly on the verge of expulsion from the entire region. Indeed, only the annexation of Portugal by Spain a few years later would save them from being driven out of the Spice Islands altogether, by giving them the support of the Spanish forces based at Manila.

Drake would have gone at once to Tidore, for he did not know of the Portuguese catastrophe at Ternate; he assumed that Tidore was under native rule and that Ternate was a hotbed of Catholicism. But on November 4, while off the island of Motir, which was subject to Ternate, Drake was met by canoes bearing officials of Ternate. They implored him to go to their island, not to Tidore; the Portuguese, they said, were now on the latter island. Drake was startled and needed some convincing before he would believe the change in political balance, but finally he accepted their assurance that Sultan Baabullah was Portugal's sworn enemy. He sent a velvet cloak to the sultan, and a message that he wished only to engage in peaceful trade. According to the report in Hakluyt, the sultan "was moved with great liking towards us, and sent to our General with special message, that he should have what things he needed, and would require with peace and friendship, and moreover that he would yield himself, and the right of his island, to be at the pleasure and commandment of so famous a prince as we served." It seems unlikely that Baabullah actually offered to become Queen Elizabeth's vassal after having spent so many years driving out the Portuguese, and more probably this was some misunderstanding similar to that in California, but on the basis of this "verbal treaty," the British East India Company later would claim, without much success, a sovereignty in the Moluccas.

Three large *praus*, or canoes, came from Ternate to greet the *Golden Hind*. Each had 80 oarsmen, who rowed to the rhythm of brass cymbals. Alongside these vessels stood soldiers armed with swords, daggers, and shields; in each was a small piece of artillery about a yard long. The greatest personages of the island, attired in white cloth of Calicut, sat beneath thin, fine mats, in the order of their dignity. As the canoes neared the ship, they rowed solemnly about it, and the notables, beginning with the highest, began to make deep bows. Then the sultan's own *prau* appeared. The sultan, says the Hakluyt account, was "accompanied with six grave and ancient persons, who did their obeisance with marvelous humility. The king was a man of tall stature, and seemed to be much delighted with the sound of our music." *The World Encompassed* calls him "very corpulent and well set together, of a very princely and gracious countenance." He listened awhile to the trumpets and other instruments; then he offered gifts of bananas, sugar cane, hens, coconuts, sago meal, and other provisions, and declared that the next day he would go aboard Drake's ship.

But the sultan did not return on the morrow. He sent his brother, who made excuses and invited Drake to go ashore, offering himself as a hostage for his safe return. Remembering some of the treacheries practiced on similar islands against Magellan, Drake hesitated, and his officers argued vehemently against his risking himself. In the end he succumbed to the pleas of the sultan's brother by sending a few of the gentleman adventurers to the palace. They were received there by another brother of the sultan and about a thousand islanders. The sultan's residence, which was near the old Portuguese fort, was magnificently draped with cloth.

While the English awaited his arrival, they met the nobility of Ternate, and also four "Romans," as they were called— ledger-keepers who handled the books of Ternate's clove trade, two Turks, an Italian, and a Spaniard. At last Sultan Baabullah appeared clad in cloth of gold with a crownlike cap of golden plates on his head, a thick golden chain about his neck, and huge diamonds, emeralds, and rubies on his hands. A page carried a fan set with eight sapphires. The meeting was satisfactory; he granted permission for the English to purchase cloves and had them carry his compliments to Drake. But he never did go aboard the *Golden Hind*, nor did Drake set foot in Ternate. Once the trade agreement was concluded, Drake gave orders for sailing, for he was growing impatient to see England and found commercial matters dreary; his cargo of stolen Spanish treasure interested him far more than taking aboard a few barrels of fragrant cloves.

Before the English left Ternate, however, an odd and improbable incident took place, probably greatly distorted as it is told in *The World Encompassed*. Among the many sightseers who came aboard the *Golden Hind* as she rode in the harbor was one not native to the Moluccas, "a goodly gentleman," accompanied by an interpreter. He announced that he was a native of China, related to the family of the reigning emperor; wrongly accused of a capital crime, he had had his sentence commuted from death to exile and was condemned never to set foot in China unless he could bring back with him "some worthy intelligence, such as his Majesty had never heard before." He questioned Drake extensively on the route he had taken thus far around the world, thinking that so wonderful a narrative might be enough to win him his pardon; "he firmly printed it in his mind, and with great reverence thanked God, who had so unexpectedly brought him to the notice of such admirable things." Then he began vigorously to implore Drake to tour China himself, "that it should be a most pleasant, most honorable, and most profitable thing for him; that he [Drake] should gain hereby the notice, and carry home the description of one of the most ancient, mightiest, and richest kingdoms in the world." He tempted Drake with tales of China's wonders, telling him of brass cannons 2,000 years old, "so perfectly made that they would hit a shilling," and other marvels. Drake could not be induced to visit China, though, "and so the stranger parted sorry that he could not prevail in his request, yet exceedingly glad of the intelligence he had learned."

On November 9, 1579, Drake left Ternate to begin his homeward run. He could not take the usual Portuguese route to the Indian Ocean via the Straits of Malacca, for that would bring him under the guns of the garrison guarding that straits. Instead, he was compelled to find his way southward through the archipelagoes of Indonesia and keep to the outside of the entire island group. He had no charts of these islands; it would have to be trial-and-error navigation.

Within five days they came to a small uninhabited island south of the Moluccas and not far north of the equator. Here they spent nearly a month refitting. "We trimmed our ship," says *The World Encompassed*, "and performed our other businesses to our content. The place affording us, not only all necessaries . . . but also wonderful refreshing to our wearied bodies, by the comfortable relief and excellent provision that here we found, whereby of sickly, weak, and decayed (as many of us seemed to be before our coming hither), we in short space grew all of us to be strong, lusty, and healthful persons. Besides this, we had rare experience of God's wonderful wisdom in many rare and admirable creatures which here we saw."

Among these creatures were "an infinite swarm of fiery-seeming worms flying in the air" at night, making such a show "as if every twig on every tree had been a lighted candle, or as if that place had been the starry sphere." Almost as wondrous as the fireflies were the huge bats, "equalling or rather exceeding a good hen in bigness. They fly with marvelous swiftness, but their flight is very short; and when they light, they hang only by the boughs with their backs downward." There were multitudes of land crabs, "of such a size, that one was sufficient to satisfy four hungry men at a dinner, being a very good and restorative meat. . . . They are, as far as we could perceive, utter strangers to the sea. . . . Some, when we came to take them, did climb up into trees to hide themselves, whither we were enforced to climb after them, if we would have them." This island they called Crab Island.

On December 12 they put out to sea on a westward course, which took them into a blind alley: the Gulf of Tomini between the two northern arms of the island of Celebes, in which they wandered for three days before realizing their error. Retracing their route, they headed south, "being entangled among many islands," and met some of the most difficult sailing of the entire voyage. Coral reefs, whose complexities and sharpness were unknown to Englishmen, lurked beneath the innocent waters; the channels were narrow; and not until January 8 did they emerge from the archipelago and find a clear passage to the west. Full sails were raised, and the *Golden Hind* raced blithely along in a brisk northeast wind, "when lo, on a sudden, when we least suspected, no show or suspicion of danger appearing to us . . . even in a moment, our ship was laid up fast upon a desperate shoal." She was impaled on coral fangs. Drake offered some inspiring prayers and led the men to pumping stations. All night they remained aground, battered by the sea, which threatened to split the ship apart or dash it more violently against the reef. The nearest land was six leagues away, so

THE LONGEST VOYAGE

the danger was great; and the ship's boat would hold only about 20 men, with three times as many on board. But deliverance came. They lightened the ship by taking eight heavy guns and most of the cloves from her; the wind changed, keeping her upright, and as the tide came in they freed her keel, after some 20 hours on the reef. It still remained for them to get clear of Celebes, for they learned that they still were trapped near that long-armed island. For nearly a month more Drake roamed Indonesia, until on February 8 he came to an island called Barativa in *The World Encompassed*, at 7°30′S. Probably it was Timor. Its inhabitants, we are told, were "of handsome body and comely stature, of civil demeanor, very just in dealing, and courteous to strangers," and after the harrowing trip through the coral-infested seas to the north, it was pleasant to enjoy their hospitality. Within a few days they moved on, setting their course for the great island of Java, whose southern shore they reached on March 12.

Java then was divided into a number of native principalities, united mainly in their resistance to Portuguese influence. Along the northern coast the Portuguese were allowed to trade only at the port of Bantam; they met with hostility at such major harbor towns as Djakarta and Surabaya. Drake called at Djokjakarta, which he believed was the capital of the entire island. After sending a shore party to bring gifts to the ruler, he went ashore himself on March 13, "with many of his gentlemen and others . . . and presented the king (of whom he was joyfully and lovingly received) with his music, and showed him the manner of our use of arms." Rajah Donan, the ruler of Djokjakarta, came aboard the next day, as did three lesser princes. They found Drake's musicians endlessly fascinating and on March 21 repaid him for his entertainment with a concert of Javanese music, apparently given by a *gamelan* orchestra. "Though it were of a very strange kind," says *The World Encompassed*, "yet the sound was pleasant and delightful." The seafarers purchased such victuals as goats, coconuts, plantains, and hens, and with great difficulty cleansed their ship's hull of the barnacles that had fastened to it. There was much feasting and jollity, although Hakluyt's chronicler remarks, "The French pox [syphilis] is here very common to all." The treatment, he adds, is "sitting naked in the sun, whereby the venomous humor is drawn out."

On March 26 they took their leave of Java. The course now was west-southwest into the Indian Ocean, and the sailing was fast and easy: they continued without sight of land until May 21, when the African mainland came in view. They passed the Cape of Good Hope three weeks later, coming within gunshot range of the shore, and, says the Hakluyt account, "finding the report of the Portugals to be most false, who affirm, that it is the most dangerous cape of the world, never without intolerable storms and present danger to travelers, which come near the same. This cape is a most stately thing, and the fairest cape we saw in the whole circumference of the earth."

Now they swung out into the Atlantic, not falling in with the land again until July 15 on the coast of Guinea. A week later they stopped in Sierra Leone and spent two days taking on fresh water and observing "great store of elephants" and "oysters upon trees of one kind, spawning and increasing infinitely, the oyster suffering no bud to grow." Through August the *Golden Hind* moved through the Canaries and Azores, and, says *The World Encompassed*, "the 26 of September (which was Monday in the just and ordinary reckoning of those that had stayed at home in one place or country, but in our computation was the Lord's Day or Sunday) we safely with joyful minds and thankful hearts to God, arrived at Plymouth, the place of our first setting forth, after we had spent 2 years 10 months and some few odd days beside, in seeing the wonders of the Lord in the deep, in discovering so many admirable things, in going through with so many strange adventures, in escaping out of so many dangers, and overcoming so many difficulties in this our encompassing of this nether globe, and passing round about the world, which we have related."

11

Drake's first question, before he cast anchor, was whether Queen Elizabeth was alive and well. She was, but she did not quite know what to make of the success of her bold and gallant buccaneer, and it seemed at first as though she might even disown him for his piracies. There was hesitation at court, and Drake got news of it, so that he was not sure whether he would be rewarded or imprisoned for his voyage.

The attitude of the ordinary Englishman was less equivocal. To him, Drake had carried out the grandest voyage ever achieved, eclipsing Magellan's because it was the first circumnavigation successfully carried through to completion by the original commander. The fact that Drake had come home with his holds bulging with Spanish treasure made the occasion all the more delightful. True, there had been heavy losses of men—only 58 out of the 164 who had set forth completed the circumnavigation, though others had come back safely in the deserting *Elizabeth*—but the hazards of naval life were well known. The voyage was beyond doubt a triumph.

The queen certainly admired Drake's achievement as much as anyone in the land, but she had political considerations to deal with. The friends of Thomas Doughty had created an enormous uproar over the execution at Port San Julian; Captain John Winter, upon his return, had attacked

Drake as a tyrant; and Spain had reacted with outrage to his depredations in South America, raising the possibility that there might be retaliatory seizures of English properties in Spain. Philip II had annexed Portugal and, with it, Brazil and the East Indies, and now the might of Spain was something to regard with great caution. Elizabeth listened sympathetically to the protests of Philip's ambassador in England, Don Bernardino de Mendoza.

But a week after his landing Drake came to court bearing his booty, and Elizabeth knew she could not rebuke him. She received him warmly and pacified Mendoza by decreeing that restitution would be made for injuries committed. A good deal of the treasure went into escrow against Spanish claims, and some of it actually was paid out to Spain; this, however, went to pay the Spanish soldiers then suppressing a rebellion in the Netherlands, rather than to the rightful claimants, and there were no further distributions of that sort. The rest of the booty was divided among Drake and his men and their backers, including Elizabeth. The near-contemporary historian William Camden wrote that "some of the chief men at court refused to accept the gold which he [Drake] offered them, as gotten by piracy. Nevertheless the common sort of people admired and highly commended him, as judging it no less honorable to have enlarged the bounds of the English name and glory than of their Empire."

The main geographical result of Drake's voyage was negative: his accidental wind-driven journey to the region of Cape Horn showed that the Atlantic and Pacific oceans were undivided by a *Terra Australis* below South America. And his failure to find the Strait of Anian showed that, if the strait existed at all, it must be much farther to the north than previously supposed. Magellan's voyage, as the first of its kind, had been far more fruitful. Perhaps the most significant result of Drake's circumnavigation was an intangible one: the psychological impetus it gave to England's expanding maritime interests. Now that the flag of England had girdled the world, what barriers to greatness and riches remained? The parallels of the two voyages were interesting: both had started with five ships and come home with one, both captains had dealt with mutineers at the same spot on the coast of Patagonia, both had lost a vessel through desertion in the Strait of Magellan, both had crossed the Pacific in essentially the same path, and both had been to sea about three years. But Juan Sebastian del Cano had limped home with a crew of half-dead men; Drake had breezed to Plymouth in good shape and high spirits, bearing an immense treasure.

Elizabeth could not long maintain her coolness toward such a commander, and on April 4, 1581, six months after his return, she placed her formal blessing upon his accomplishment by going aboard the *Golden Hind* in harbor at Deptford, a borough of London on the Thames. A great crowd attended this visit, so that the bridge laid from shore to the ship collapsed, and 200 people were thrown into the Thames, though none was injured or drowned. After entertainments and dinner, the queen conferred upon Drake the order of knighthood and decreed that his ship be preserved at Deptford as a national shrine. (Eventually, when decayed, the *Golden Hind* was broken up, and a chair made of her timbers and presented to Oxford University.) Drake chose as his new motto that which had previously been granted to Sebastian del Cano: *Tu Primus Circumdedisti Me*, "Thou First Encompassed Me," set upon the globe. But he affixed to the phrase his former motto, *Divino Auxilio*, "By the Help of God."

[5]

IN THE WAKE OF
THE *GOLDEN HIND*

IR FRANCIS DRAKE, AS NOW HE WAS, STILL was less than forty years old, and no less eager than before to harass Spain and to proclaim Queen Elizabeth's glories on the high seas. Soon after the ceremony at Deptford he was involved in a new project, a voyage to the Azores planned for July 1581. Ostensibly its purpose was to help Dom Antonio, the pretender to the throne of Portugal, advance his claim; but in reality Drake planned once more to wound Philip II by intercepting his cargoes of American treasure. That was ever the goal of Drake's private foreign policy: to swell England's power and to diminish that of Spain by diverting the riches of the New World to Queen Elizabeth's coffers.

The project miscarried when the pro-Spanish faction at the queen's court interfered. As a result, the company that had been organized to make the voyage suffered heavy losses, and in an attempt at recouping, a new venture was sent to sea in May 1582. Drake did not go along, but he was among the backers. Edward Fenton, an experienced seaman who had sailed in the Arctic with Martin Frobisher, took four vessels toward the Moluccas via the Cape of Good Hope, planning to raid Spanish and Portuguese shipping on the way. The crew-men were less interested in the Moluccas than they were in piracy, preferring gold to cloves, and off the Atlantic coast of Africa they compelled Fenton to head west instead of east, so that they could duplicate Drake's voyage. After a successful raid at Brazil, though, the enterprise fell apart; Fenton quarreled with his second in command, the younger William Hawkins, and never reached the Pacific at all, turning back to England in dismay with Hawkins a prisoner in irons. One of the other ships, commanded by Drake's cousin John, did attempt to get to the Strait of Magellan, but was captured by the Spaniards near the Río de la Plata.

The dismal end of Fenton's voyage discouraged English ventures to the Pacific for several years. Drake himself was in temporary eclipse, a victim of the machinations of Thomas Doughty's brother, John, and of the intrigues of the Spaniards at Elizabeth's court. But as tensions between England and Spain grew, he returned to influence as the leader of the war party. It was clear now that King Philip planned an invasion of England, and Drake, the national hero, was called to the defense.

His idea of defense was offense. In 1585 he began to assemble the largest privateering fleet yet raised, which he took to sea, after many administrative delays, in June of the following year. He sacked São Tiago in the Cape Verdes, which he had warily bypassed on his circumnavigation, and crossed the Atlantic to raid the Spanish settlement of Santo Domingo on Hispaniola; then, displaying awesome military skill, he looted Cartagena on the Spanish Main and St. Augustine in Florida, stopping on his way back to pick up the survivors of an ill-fated colony Sir Walter Raleigh had planted in Virginia. The devastating campaign disrupted Spain's entire overseas empire and set Philip back in the planning of his invasion; but once again Elizabeth, steering a cautious course, disavowed Drake and avoided an immediate war.

Later, in 1586, a Spanish armada began to assemble at the port of Cádiz. Drake persuaded Elizabeth to name him as her chief admiral and went to sea in April 1587 on his most daring single adventure: an attack on the Spanish homeland. He audaciously entered the harbor at Cádiz, burned 32 Spanish ships, and carried away four more. Next he made for Lisbon, which he threw into terror as he destroyed 24 more of Philip's vessels. By June he was back at Plymouth, having single-handedly wrecked the nucleus of the armada in an action he called "singeing the beard of the King of Spain." He came home, though, to find Elizabeth in a poor temper over domestic political matters, and his only reward was a reprimand. Philip grimly started building a new armada, while deceptively sending negotiators to England to discuss peace. Drake yearned to repeat his raid on Cádiz, but Elizabeth kept him leashed despite his warning that England was losing her advantage by failing to attack Spain in her own waters.

All during the spring of 1588 Elizabeth held back, while news came from Spain of the imminent sailing of the invasion fleet. In mid-May it finally did put to sea, only to be driven back at once by a storm. At this, Drake obtained permission to carry the attack to Spain, to seize what he termed "the advantage of time and place." On May 30 and again on June 24 he attempted to set out, also to be forced back by storm. And on July 12, 1588, the Spanish Armada—the Invincible Armada, it was called—set sail again, forcing a passage through the continuing storms and appearing suddenly in the English Channel a week later. Hurriedly, the admirals of England went to the defense.

And while the conflict between Spain and England was at last erupting into one of history's most famous naval battles, a third voyage of circumnavigation was coming to its conclusion—English once more, for Thomas Cavendish was on his way home after having repeated the feat of Magellan and Drake.

2

Thomas Cavendish, whose name in the Elizabethan books of voyages is commonly contracted to "Candish," belonged, like Drake and Thomas Doughty and so many other voyagers of this period, to the class of gentlemen. Cavendish was of the landed gentry, in fact, coming from a family that held large estates in the county of Suffolk. He went to sea, then, not primarily in search of riches, but out of the love of adventure and in a spirit of patriotism. It seems, though, that he was in some financial embarrassment at the time of his voyage of circumnavigation, owing to his extravagances as a courtier, and embarked on that project in the hope of swiftly recouping his fortunes.

He was born in 1554 or 1555 and attended Corpus Christi College in Cambridge, though he did not take a degree. The lure of the sea was strong for him—perhaps because he was already short of cash—and when he reached his twenty-first birthday he sold part of his lands in order to equip a ship called the *Tyger*, of 120 tons, in which he took part in the 1585 attempt to colonize Virginia. Raleigh was the promoter of that enterprise, though he did not accompany it; the commander was Sir Richard Grenville. The settlement, on Roanoke Island, was in trouble from the beginning, and Cavendish returned to England in October of 1585; this was the colony that Drake rescued the following June. It was a costly experience for Cavendish, but shortly he was planning to recover his losses by a voyage imitative of Drake's and designed mainly to engage in buccaneering. He obtained the support of the influential Lord Hunsdon, Queen Elizabeth's cousin, and through him won royal permission to undertake the voyage. Mortgaging his estate to pay for building and equipping his ships, he readied a fleet in the unusually short time of six months and was ready to sail in the summer of 1586. It may seem frivolous for Cavendish to have gone off around the world at a time when England was threatened by Spanish invasion, but he hoped to make his contribution by draining Spain's American gold, and in 1586 it did not seem at all certain that the long-smoldering war would ever break out into open conflict.

There are only a few firsthand accounts of Cavendish's circumnavigation. One, bearing the initials "N.H.," occupies four pages in the first (1589) edition of Hakluyt's collection of voyages. This sketchy narrative was dropped from Hakluyt's second edition a decade later and replaced by an account ascribed to "Master Francis Pretty lately of Ey in Suffolk, a Gentleman employed in the same action." It is probable that Pretty also was the author of the anonymous account of Drake's circumnavigation published in the same volume of Hakluyt, and, if so, he may have been the only mariner of his era to sail around the world more than once. Aside from the relations of "N.H." and Pretty, there exists a technical paper on latitudes, ocean depths, and other nautical matters, written by Thomas Fuller, the master of one of Cavendish's ships, and published in the second edition of Hakluyt; and Cavendish himself, upon his return, described his voyage in a brief letter to his patron Lord Hunsdon, which Hakluyt also printed.

Though he had gone into debt to furnish his expedition, Cavendish was unstinting. It is said that his sailors were clad in silk, his sails were of damask, and his topmast covered with cloth of gold. Francis Pretty's narrative begins, "We departed out of Plymouth on Thursday the 21 of July 1586, with three sails [ships] to wit, the *Desire* a ship of 120 tons, the *Content* a ship of 60 tons, and the *Hugh Gallant* a bark of 40 tons: in which small fleet were 123 persons of all sorts with all kind of furniture and victuals sufficient for the space of two years." Unlike the voyages of Magellan and Drake, this was intended from the outset to be a circumnavigation, and Cavendish had provisioned accordingly.

Five days after sailing, they met with five Spanish ships off the coast of Spain—fishing vessels, they guessed, coming from the Grand Banks of Newfoundland, but Cavendish ordered an attack anyway. A battle three hours long resulted, but night fell before any of the Spaniards could be taken. Drake, perhaps, would have made a better job of such an encounter. There were no further incidents as the fleet passed through the Canary Islands and ran for the coast of Africa, and on August 26 the ships anchored at Sierra Leone. The next day two Negroes came aboard the *Desire* and informed Cavendish by sign language that a Portuguese ship lay up the river. He sent the little *Hugh Gallant* to search for it, but after a voyage of three or four leagues the ship turned back, her captain fearing to explore farther without a pilot who knew the river. On the 28th some of the English went ashore and "played and danced all the forenoon among the Negroes" while trying to find out more about the Portuguese vessel. They spied a Portuguese seaman named Manoel hiding in some bushes, seized and bound him, and questioned him about his ship, learning from him that the river was too dangerous to attempt and that his ship was stranded upriver. Evidently Cavendish chose to take this at face value, and there was no attempt to find and attack the enemy vessel.

The next day, despite the seeming good relationship thus far between the English and the natives, Pretty inexplicably says that "our General landed with 70 men or thereabout, and went up to their town, where we burnt two or three houses, and took what spoil we could, which was but little. . . . They shot their arrows at us out of the woods, and hurt three or four of our men; their arrows were poisoned, but yet none of our men miscarried at that time, thanked be God. Their town is marvelous artificially [artfully] builded with mud walls, and built round, with their yards paled in and kept very clean as well in their streets as in their houses." What provoked this assault we do not know, although N.H.'s account says, "We burned some 150 of their houses because of their bad dealings with us and all Christians." A few days afterward, while some of Cavendish's men were washing shirts by the shore, they were ambushed by the blacks, and a soldier named William Pickman was struck in the thigh by an arrow, "who plucking the arrow out, broke it, and left the head behind; and he told the surgeons that he plucked out all the arrow, because he would not have them lance his thigh; whereupon the poison wrought so that night, that he was marvelously swollen, and all his belly and privy parts were as black as ink, and the next morning he died, the piece of the arrow with the poison being plucked out of his thigh."

On September 6 they departed from Sierra Leone to make their Atlantic crossing to Brazil. By now such crossings were routine, and their journey was unremarkable, bringing them within sight of the South American mainland on the last day of October. They landed on an island named São Sebastião, about 120 miles down the coast from Rio de Janeiro, and set up a forge on shore so that they could make hoops for water casks. They assembled a pinnace and collected fresh water. During this time a canoe rowed by six Indian slaves appeared bearing 8 Portuguese bound from Rio de Janeiro to another coastal town. The English intercepted it, telling the Portuguese that they were merchants and wished to buy provisions. He promised to return with food to sell if they would let him go, and they released him but never heard from him again. By November 23, tired of waiting and finished with their other duties at São Sebastião, they weighed anchor and started down the coast, remaining some distance off shore until they were past 47°S. On December 17 Cavendish led the way into a harbor near the 48th parallel. He named it Port Desire, but quite likely it was identical with the Seal Bay where Drake had spent 15 days in 1578. In the harbor, wrote Pretty, "is an island or two, where there is wonderful great store of seals, and another island of birds which are grey gulls. These seals are of a wonderful great bigness, huge, and monstrous of shape, and for the fore-part of their bodies cannot be compared to anything better than to a lion: their head, and neck, and fore-parts of their bodies are full of rough hair: their feet are in manner of a fin, and in form like unto a man's hand. . . . Their young are marvelous good meat, and being boiled or roasted, are hardly to be known from lamb or mutton. The old ones be of such bigness and force, that it is as much as four men are able to do to kill one of them with great cowl-staves: and he must be beaten down with striking on the head of him: for his body is of that bigness that four men could never kill him, but only on the head." The ships were careened here, and it proved an easy matter to clean their hulls, the rise and fall of the tides being so great. The only deficiency of Port Desire was its water supply; all the water found was brackish, except in "a very fair green valley at the foot of the mountains, where was a little pit or well which our men had digged." While a man and a boy of Cavendish's crew were washing linens at that well, they were attacked by Indians and wounded with arrows. Cavendish and some 20 men drove them off. "We followed them," said Pretty, "and they ran from us as it had been the wildest thing in the world. We took the measure of one of their feet, and it was 18 inches long." More evidence on the Patagonian giants—this time from a footprint.

They left Port Desire on December 28, pausing on an island three leagues to the south to take and salt penguins; by January 2 they had reached a cape in 51°, and a day later attained Cape Vírgines, "another great white cape, which standeth in 52°45': from which cape there runneth a low beach about a league to the southward, and this beach reacheth to the opening of the dangerous Strait of Magellan." They entered the strait's wide mouth on January 6 and, anchoring in the first narrows that night, saw lights on the north shore, as though someone were sending signals. Cavendish had answering lights set up. In the morning he went by boat to the northern side of the strait, where three men had appeared on the shore, waving a white flag. When the boat drew near, the men on the shore called out in Spanish, asking the name of the country to which the ships belonged. Cavendish knew who these Spaniards were: they were survivors of a garrison placed there in 1584 to guard the Strait of Magellan against further English intrusions. Before leaving England, Cavendish had learned that this garrison was in great distress, and now he had one of his men who spoke Spanish reply that his ships were English and that, if they chose to accompany him, he would carry them peacefully to Peru.

This Spanish settlement in the strait was one of the less successful projects of that ambitious and ingenious man Pedro Sarmiento de Gamboa. He had persuaded Philip II that the only way to protect the Pacific against England was to control the strait, and after some years of delay he arrived in Patagonia in 1584 and set up two towns. One, on the north side near the entrance, he called Nombre de Jesus. He left 150 men there, but the main colony was 15 leagues deeper into the strait, in the narrowest part, at 53°18'S. Here he built Ciudad del Rey Felipe, a well-fortified town occupied by 400 men and 30 women. The town was completed in midwinter; at one time snow fell without a break for 15 days. Sarmiento and his people had arrived with only eight months' provisions, and in May 1585 he left Rey Felipe, planning to pick up some of the settlers in Nombre de Jesus, bring them to Rey Felipe, and go on through the western end of the strait to Chile to obtain food. But when he anchored off Nombre de Jesus, a violent storm drove the ship from her anchors and forced her out into the Atlantic, leaving the colony without a vessel. Sarmiento went to Brazil for provisions; the colonists, meanwhile, feeling that he had betrayed them, planned to assassinate him if he returned. While sailing the Brazilian coast in winter, Sarmiento's ship was wrecked; he purchased another vessel, loaded it with food, and departed from Rio de Janeiro in January 1585, only to run into so fierce a tempest that he had to dump the cargo into the sea and put back to Brazil. Several other attempts at getting food to the colonies in the strait failed; Sarmiento met obstructions from the Brazilian authorities and finally, in despair, set out for Spain in April 1585 to raise funds for a relief expedition. En route he was captured by the English, who brought him before Queen Elizabeth. She treated him courteously and sent him on to Spain, but by then it was much too late to do anything for the starving settlers of the Strait of Magellan outposts.

The three survivors whom Cavendish encountered did not trust his offer to take them to Peru. They feared some trick and shrugged off Cavendish's protestations that he would treat them in a Christian manner. At length he ordered his boat from shore, leaving the Spaniards to debate among themselves whether they wished to be rescued. They held a brief consultation and evidently decided that it was better to risk being murdered by the English than to endure further hardships in this grim and wintry land; they called

Cavendish's boat back, and one of the Spaniards, Tomé Hernandez, entered it. Cavendish asked him how many Spaniards remained, other than the two still on shore. Fifteen, said Hernandez: 12 men and three women. Cavendish told the other two Spaniards to summon the others and invite them on board the English ships; they went to do so, and he returned with Hernandez to his flagship.

The wind, which had been contrary, now changed, becoming favorable for advancing through the strait. Cavendish was placed in a painful dilemma: if he waited for the 17 Spaniards, he might miss the wind and waste weeks or even months. Conceivably he would be delayed into the approaching winter. The strait was difficult to negotiate, and sixteenth-century sailing vessels had to make the most of every opportunity. So, leaving the Spaniards to their fates, he had the anchors taken up, and the ships immediately went forward. No doubt Cavendish expected that a rescue mission would be sent by the Spaniards in a short while, or he might have waited the two or three hours more for the ragged survivors; but no rescuers came, and Tomé Hernandez was the only member of the garrison to be picked up at all, except for one man who lived on to be found by another English ship in 1589.

On September 8 Cavendish halted at an island he called Penguin Island, where the English took aboard great stores of birds, and on the 9th he reached the narrow part of the strait where Rey Felipe stood. "They had contrived their city very well, and seated it in the best place of the straits for wood and water," Pretty wrote. "They had builded up their churches by themselves; they had laws very severe among themselves, for they had erected a gibbet, whereon they had done execution upon some of their company." From Hernandez the English learned of the tragic last days of Sarmiento's colonists. "Their whole living for a great space was altogether upon mussels and limpets: for there was not anything else to be had, except some deer which came out of the mountains down to the fresh rivers to drink. . . . During the time that they were there, which was two years at the least, they could never have anything to grow or in any wise prosper. And on the other side the Indians oftentimes preyed upon them, until their victuals grew so short . . . that they died like dogs in their houses, and in their clothes, wherein we found them still at our coming," said Pretty, "until that in the end the town being wonderfully tainted with the smell and the savor of the dead people, the rest which remained alive were driven to bury such things as they had there in their town . . . and so to forsake the town, and to go along the seaside, and seek their victuals to preserve them from starving, taking nothing with them, but every man his arquebus and his furniture that was able to carry it . . . and so lived for the space of a year and more with roots, leaves, and sometimes a fowl which they might kill with their piece." They had hoped to go somehow by foot to the Río de la Plata, but that proved impossible, and by the time of Cavendish's arrival, less than two dozen remained alive out of the original complement of 580. Cavendish somberly renamed Rey Felipe "Port Famine," and they moved on after digging up six artillery pieces and taking them aboard.

Winds from the west delayed the fleet as it passed through the strait. Cavendish had to stop for six days at a bay on the south side of the strait, and then was held up again on the north side ten leagues farther on. Here Cavendish took a boat to investigate a river which he ascended for three miles through a fertile-looking valley that contrasted sharply with the "craggy rocks and monstrous high hills and mountains" seen elsewhere in the strait. Here he encountered Indians. "They were men-eaters," said Pretty, "and fed altogether upon raw flesh, and other filthy food: which people had preyed upon some of the Spaniards before spoken of. For they had gotten knives and pieces of rapiers to make darts of. They used all the means they could possibly to have allured us up farther into the river, of purpose to have betrayed us, which being espied by our General, he caused us to shoot at them with our arquebuses, whereby we killed many of them."

Near the western mouth of the strait they were forced to lie in harbor nearly a month, until February 23, "by reason of contrary winds and most vile and filthy foul weather, with such rain and vehement stormy winds which came down from the mountains and high hills, that they hazarded the best cables and anchors that we had for to hold." Each day in the rain they scrabbled along the shore for mussels, limpets, and such birds as they could take. The weather abated sufficiently on the 24th to allow them to enter the Pacific; and turning north after the fashion of Magellan and Drake, they made for the Spanish ports of Chile and Peru.

3

A storm separated the small *Hugh Gallant* from her two companions on March 1. Pretty, who was aboard the little bark, says that it became so leaky that they expected it to sink at any moment, and they went without sleep for three days and three nights to keep it pumped dry. It was two weeks before she caught up with the *Desire* and the *Content* at Isla Santa Maria, near the Chilean port of Concepción. The other two ships had called previously at the island of Mocha, where they had been mistaken for Spanish vessels and were attacked, as Drake had been at the same place, by the Indians. They had arrived at Santa Maria only a few hours ahead of the *Hugh Gallant*.

Cavendish landed on Santa Maria with some 80 men. The Indians, who were subject to the Spaniards here, came forth to welcome them, taking them for their masters and offering them the tribute of wheat, barley, potatoes, and fruit that had been set aside for the Spaniards. Cavendish entertained some of the chiefs on board his ship, "and made them merry with wine: and in the end perceiving us to be no Spaniards, made signs, as near our General could perceive, that if we would go over unto the mainland unto Arauco, that there was much gold, making us signs, that we should have great store of riches." The Indians of the mainland belonged to the Araucanian stock, and were among the fiercest in South America; they had halted the southward expansion of the otherwise invincible Inca empire and were just as successfully resisting the Spanish conquest. As Pretty noted, "This place which is called Arauco is wonderful rich, and full of gold mines, and yet could it not be subdued at any time by the Spaniards, but they always returned with the greatest loss of men. For these Indians are marvelous desperate and careless of their lives to live at their own liberty and freedom." Rather than try to conquer an unconquerable tribe, Cavendish decided to seek his gold from the Spaniards up the coast.

But his was the second buccaneering raid in these waters, and the Spaniards were better prepared than they had been when Drake came by. Moreover, Cavendish was not the same kind of charismatic leader who could paralyze the Spaniards merely by presenting himself to them. Thus the takings were meager as Cavendish began his maraudings. He got nothing at Concepción and missed Valparaiso altogether, making his next stop at the port of Quintero on March 30. As the ships anchored, a shepherd sleeping on a hillside overlooking the bay awoke, saw them, mounted a horse, and rushed off to sound an alarm. Cavendish went ashore with 30 men, hoping to carry out a quick raid, but within an hour three armed horsemen rode up. Cavendish sent two of his men toward them, with the Spaniard Tomé

Hernandez as an interpreter; the horsemen made signs that only one of the three could come forward, and so Hernandez approached them, with the two Englishmen standing back. After a conference, Hernandez returned to say that he had negotiated with the Spaniards for a supply of provisions, which they had agreed to furnish. He was sent back alone with another message; this time he stood at a greater distance from the two Englishmen, and abruptly he leaped up behind one of the horsemen and rode off with them at full gallop. It does not seem very surprising that Hernandez would have taken this opportunity to escape, but Francis Pretty records the general shock and anger at his trick, in view of "all his deep and damnable oaths which he had made continually to our general and all his company never to forsake him, but to die on his side before he would be false." Cavendish spent the rest of the day cautiously supervising the collecting of fresh water, and at night the English returned to their ships.

The next morning about 60 men landed under command of an officer named Havers and marched seven or eight miles inland, looking for the Spanish town. The country was fruitful, with many rivers and an abundance of wild game, but they found no town, and turned back when they reached the foot of the mountains. The Spaniards, meanwhile, had dispatched 200 horsemen who circled around the shore party and took up positions near the harbor, well concealed. The next day, April 1, while the English were filling water casks a quarter of a mile from the shore, the Spaniards rushed down from the hills in a sudden attack. According to an account dictated by Tomé Hernandez, 12 Englishmen were killed and nine taken prisoner, without a single Spanish casualty. Francis Pretty admits the 12 English deaths, but claims that 24 Spaniards were slain in a counterattack.

In one skirmish, then, Cavendish had lost six times as many men as had been killed by Spaniards in all of Drake's voyage—and Cavendish still had no gold to show for his losses. He remained at Quintero until April 5, taking on water and having no further contact with the Spaniards, and continued up the coast. On April 23 they reached Arica, Chile's northernmost port, and the *Hugh Gallant* met with a small bark which the English captured, her Spanish crew escaping in a boat. Rechristened the *George*, the bark joined Cavendish's fleet. The pinnace of the *Content* entered Arica's harbor and found a large ship, which was seized; but the cargo had been unloaded a short time before. The shore defenses opened fire, forcing the English to pull back. The *Content* had lagged behind to make prize of a ship some 14 leagues south of Arica bearing a cargo of wine, and so was unable to aid the other vessels. She arrived shortly; but Cavendish had realized "that the town had gathered all their power together, and also conveyed all their treasure away, and buried it before we were come near the town: for they had heard of us." He abandoned a plan to land and ransack the town; the *Content*'s pinnace ventured daringly under the harbor guns to capture another ship, but it, too, contained little. Cavendish sent a boat ashore under flag of truce to ask the Spaniards if they cared to pay a ransom for their big ship —he was thinking of trading it for the nine Englishmen captured by the horsemen at Quintero—but the Viceroy of Peru had strictly forbidden such dealings, and on the morning of the 26th, Cavendish set the great ship afire in the harbor, sank some of his smaller prizes, and left, taking the *George* with him.

The next day the English captured another bark out of the Chilean port of Santiago, which was heading north to Lima to give news of the English raid on the coast. The messengers had thrown away their letters to Lima before being overtaken, but Cavendish put three Spaniards and a man of Flanders to the torture to learn the purpose of their voyage:

"He was fain to cause them to be tormented with their thumbs in a winch. . . . Also he made the old Fleming believe that he would hang him; and the rope being about his neck he was pulled up a little from the hatches, and yet he would not confess, choosing rather to die, than he would be perjured. In the end it was confessed by one of the Spaniards, whereupon we burnt the bark, and carried the men with us." If Cavendish had known that his nine imprisoned seamen had been hanged as pirates in Santiago he might have been less charitable still to his captives.

The unfruitful cruise continued, yielding little better than some bread, wine, bananas, and hens at a small coastal town, and from time to time the ships were separated. The *Hugh Gallant*, sailing alone from May 10 to May 16, seized 400 bags of cornmeal from a Spanish bark on the 11th, and on the 16th took a 300-ton ship, the *Luis*, laden with timber and victuals. Of her 24 men, they retained a pilot named Gonsalvo de Ribas and a Negro named Emanuel, and left the others aboard the leaky vessel after removing her sails. Later that day the *Hugh Gallant* rejoined the fleet; the *Content*, in the interval, had taken two ships, one laden with flour and marmalade, the other with sugar, molasses, corn, hides, and a thousand hens. All this was very far from the golden harvest of Francis Drake.

Cavendish invaded the port of Paita on May 20 with 60 or 70 men, drove the inhabitants into the hills, and set fire to the town, but the loot amounted only to 25 pounds of silver. Five days later they came to the island of Puná, where they sank a 250-ton Spanish ship and went on land. Puná was governed by an Indian married to a Spanish woman; he had, said Pretty, "a sumptuous house marvelous well contrived with very many singular good rooms and chambers in it," with a storehouse nearby in which the materials for the island's chief product, ship's cables, were kept. The chief and his lady lived in opulent style; the Indians regarded her almost as a queen, and she was never permitted to touch the ground with her feet, but always was carried about by four men in a special litter, veiled to protect her complexion from the sun and the wind. Cavendish learned these things from the two or three Indians he found on Puná; all the rest had fled at his approach, the chief supposedly taking with him a treasure worth 100,000 crowns. Cavendish went over to the mainland to look for him and discovered from the Indians there that a garrison of 100 men was stationed at Guayaquil, a short distance to the north, and that reinforcements of 60 Spaniards were on their way to meet the English threat. Nevertheless, Cavendish ordered the *Desire* careened at Puná, though he posted guards by day and night against a Spanish attack.

For more than a week the *Desire*'s hull was scraped and repaired while Cavendish made himself at home in the chief's mansion. During this time the English diverted themselves by burning the island's church and carrying off the bells. By June 2 the flagship was afloat again, and Cavendish relaxed his guard, allowing all the watchmen to leave their posts to collect hens, sheep, and goats on the island. During the night the Spaniards and the natives of Puná had slipped onto the island with their weapons, and the slave Emanuel, who had escaped from the English a few days earlier, now led them toward Cavendish's men. Caught by surprise as at Quintero, the English fought bravely but in vain and were driven from the shore with the loss of 12 out of 20 men. (Among those who got away safely was the chronicler Francis Pretty.) Undaunted, Cavendish sent 70 men ashore that same day for a fresh skirmish, and, says Pretty, "drove them to retire, being an hundred Spaniards serving with muskets, and two hundred Indians with bows, arrows, and darts. This done, we set fire on the town and burnt it to the ground, having in it to the number of three hundred houses: and shortly after made havoc of their fields, orchards, and gardens, and burnt four great ships more which were in building on the stocks."

They left Puná on June 5. Stopping for water a little to the north, they scuttled the *Hugh Gallant*, for they no longer had enough sailors to man her. On June 12 they crossed the equator and left the South American coast behind with very little to show for their efforts. The coast of Mexico came into view on July 1, and eight days later they fell in with a new ship of 120 tons with no cargo and only seven men aboard. Cavendish appropriated the vessel's sails, ropes, and firewood, made her crew prisoners, and set the ship on fire. Among those captured was one Michael Sancius of Marseilles, an experienced pilot who gave them the welcome news that a large and richly laden ship, the *Santa Anna*— this year's Acapulco galleon—was expected soon to arrive in Mexico bearing gold and silk from the Philippines.

On June 27 they anchored at the port of Guatulco. The inhabitants fled, and they burned the town and its church. In the customs house they found 600 bags of valuable dyes and 400 bags of cacao beans. The English knew very little of cacao, or of the bitter drink called *xocolatl* that the Indians of Mexico made from the ground beans, but Pretty was aware that the beans did circulate as currency in Mexico, valued at 150 to the silver real. "They are very like unto an almond," he wrote, "but are nothing so pleasant in taste: they eat them, and make drink of them."

They proceeded up the coast, capturing and destroying a number of Spanish ships and experiencing the usual maddening failure to find gold or silver on any of them. Through an oversight they missed the port of Acapulco altogether, which saved it from the burning that they administered to most of the other small towns along Mexico's Pacific shore.

In the Bay of Santiago they dragged for pearl-bearing shell-fish and found some; at a small island to the north they killed a number of seals for food, and also iguanas, which Pretty described as "a kind of serpents, with four feet, and a long sharp tail, strange to them which have not seen them; but they are very good meat." By late September they were at Mazatlán, anchoring at an island in the harbor for more than a week to take on water.

Cavendish now concluded this most unsatisfactory tour of the coast and on October 9 departed for the tip of Baja California, where he proposed to wait for the galleon from the Philippines. He had just two ships now, the *Content* and the *Desire*, having abandoned his prize bark, the *George*. They made the Cape of San Lucas on the 14th and cruised here, growing ever more fretful and frustrated, until the 4th of November. Between seven and eight that morning, the *Desire*'s trumpeter climbed the rigging and spied a sail head-ing for the cape, "whereupon he cried out with no small joy to himself and the whole company, A sail, A sail!" Cavendish at once ordered his men to give chase, for it was the *Santa Anna*, bound for Acapulco. "In the afternoon," Pretty wrote, "we got up unto them, giving them the broadside with our great ordnance and a volley of small shot." The ship was of 700 tons burden, far larger than the *Desire*. Cavendish had only some 60 men in his ship, and as he prepared to board the rich galleon, her crew, which had taken refuge behind barri-cades, began to hurl "lances, javelins, rapiers . . . and an in-numerable sort of great stones, which they threw overboard upon our heads and into our ship so fast and being so many of them, that they put us off the ship again, with the loss of two of our men which were slain, and with the hurting of four or five. But for all this we new trimmed our sails, and fitted every man his furniture, and gave them a fresh encoun-ter with our great ordnance and also with our small shot, raking them through and through, to the killing and maiming of many of their men. Their captain still like a valiant man with his company stood very stoutly . . . not yielding as yet. Our general encouraging his men afresh with the whole noise of trumpets gave them the third encounter with our great ordnance and all our small shot. . . . They being thus discomforted and spoiled, and their ship being in hazard of sinking by reason of the great shot which were made, whereof some were under water, within five or six hours' fight set out a flag of truce and parleyed for mercy, desiring our general to save their lives and take their goods."

The *Santa Anna* carried 122,000 pesos of gold and a cargo of silks, satins, damasks, musk, and other merchandise of the East Indies, along with fine victuals and wines. Cavendish, savoring the pleasures of piracy, most graciously pardoned the Spaniards and took their officers aboard the *Desire*. The *Santa Anna*'s complement, some 190 men and women, most of them passengers, he set free on shore, giving them provisions and wine, and the sails of their ship so that they could make tents while awaiting rescue. Then the English set to work transferring their haul to their own ships and allotting individual portions of the booty; some of the men of the *Content* were displeased with the shares they received, and for a few days there was talk of a mutiny against Cavendish, but the tensions subsided.

On November 17—the anniversary of Queen Elizabeth's coronation—Cavendish staged a fireworks display, greatly to the awe of the Spaniards; then he made ready for departure. He took with him a number of the *Santa Anna*'s passengers, thinking they might be useful to him in the Orient: "Two young lads born in Japan, which could both write and read their own language, the eldest being about 20 years old was named Christopher, the other was called Cosmus, about 17 years of age. . . . Three boys born in the isles of

Manila, the one about 15, the other about 13, and the youngest about 9 years old. . . . He also took from them one Nicholas Roderigo a Portugal, who hath not only been in Canton and other parts of China, but also in the islands of Japan being a country most rich in silver mines, and hath also been in the Philippines." Another of Cavendish's captives was a Spaniard, Tomás de Ersola, a pilot who knew the route from Mexico to the Ladrones and the Philippines.

At three in the afternoon on November 19 Cavendish had the *Santa Anna* burned, though she still contained 500 tons of goods that could not be loaded aboard his own vessels; then, firing a jubilant salute from their heavy guns, the English "set sail joyfully homeward toward England with a fair wind." The *Santa Anna* was still burning as they departed, although soon the fire freed her from her anchors and she was cast ashore, where the Spaniards were able to extinguish the blaze and repair the crippled ship so that she was strong enough to take them to Acapulco with their tale of woe.

4

At last Cavendish had the rich haul that had been denied him in South America, but as he commenced his Pacific crossing, his voyage was marred by unexpected and inexplicable catastrophe. The *Desire* led the way into the ocean, and Francis Pretty, who had gone with the flagship since the scuttling of the *Hugh Gallant*, relates that "we left the *Content* astern of us, which was not as yet come out of the road. And here thinking she would have overtaken us, we lost her company and never saw her after." The fate of the *Content* was never known.

Alone now, the *Desire* held to a southwesterly course until she reached the latitude of 12° to 13°N., and following that track reached the Ladrones on January 3, 1588, after a crossing of only 45 days. Cavendish passed close to Guam; some 70 native canoes came out to trade, bearing fruit, vegetables, and fresh fish, which the islanders exchanged for small pieces of scrap iron, crowding so thickly about that several canoes were overturned by striking the *Desire*'s sides. Pretty spoke of the natives as "of a tawny color and marvelously fat, and bigger ordinarily of stature than the most part of our men in England, wearing their hair marvelously long"; he expressed admiration also for their canoes, which were equipped with masts and sails and could move forward into a wind. The islanders followed the ship so long and became so troublesome that Cavendish ultimately had to have them driven off with muskets.

By the middle of January the *Desire* was in the Philippines. Cavendish hesitated to attack Manila, which Pretty says "is well planted and inhabited with Spaniards to the number of six or seven hundred persons," and, instead, passed to the south of the main island of Luzon, on which Manila is situated. They halted at a small island off Luzon, where a native chief traded them vegetables for linen, and afterward—reflecting a sophistication learned from the Spaniards—sold hens and hogs for pieces of silver. On January 15, 1588, Cavendish was visited by Nicolas Roderigo, the Portuguese taken from the *Santa Anna*, who told him that the Spanish pilot Tomás de Ersola, also captured in that raid, was planning treachery. Ersola had written a letter to the Spaniards at Manila which he planned to have carried there by the natives: it told the story of Cavendish's piracies, gave his present location, and asked for help. Cavendish summoned the Spaniard and asked him about the letter; he denied the story at first, but weakened, probably under torture, and was hanged the next morning.

They spent nine days at this island, which was Capul, in

the San Bernardino Strait. Pretty found one custom remarkable, though it had been commented on by Pigafetta before him: "Every man and man-child among them hath a nail of tin thrust quite through the head of his privy part, being split in the lower end and riveted, and on the head of the nail is as it were a crown: which is driven through their privities when they be young, and the place groweth up again, without any great pain to the child: and they take this nail out and in, as occasion serveth. . . . This custom was granted at the request of the women of the country, who finding their men to be given to the foul sin of Sodomy, desired some remedy against that mischief, and obtained this before named of the magistrates. Moreover all the males are circumcised. . . . These people wholly worship the devil, and often times have conference with him, which appeareth unto them in most ugly and monstrous shape."

On January 23 Cavendish presided over a gathering of chiefs from many islands, accepting a tribute of hogs, hens, and coconuts, and making it known that he was no Spaniard but an Englishman. He raised his flag and "sounded up the drums, which they much marveled at: to conclude, they promised both themselves and all the islands thereabout to aid him, whensoever he should come again to overcome the Spaniards." Cavendish consummated this illusory treaty by giving the chiefs money in return for their tribute, "which they took marvelous friendly, and rowed about our ship to show us pleasure marvelous swiftly."

The next day the *Desire* left, running northwest along the coast of Luzon and taking the time to chase a Spanish frigate up a river. Cavendish deftly guided his ship through the archipelago and to the south, and by February 8 the Moluccas came into sight. Cavendish did not call there, despite Drake's successes in dealing with the Sultan of Ternate. Many of his men were growing ill from long exposure to the tropical weather; one died on February 17, and another, an officer, was the victim "of a most fervent and pestilent ague" four days later. "Moreover," says Pretty, "presently after his death myself with divers others in the ship fell marvelously sick, and so continued in very great pain for the space of three weeks or a month by reason of the extreme heat and untemperateness of the climate."

Cavendish went swiftly on to the southern shore of Java, where he sent a slave taken from the *Santa Anna* ashore to arrange for the purchase of provisions. For a week they waited, collecting water and firewood, and on March 8 came several canoes bearing eggs, hens, fresh fish, oranges, and limes, and inviting Cavendish to come closer to the main town. The *Desire* moved to another bay, and an emissary came from the local ruler, accompanied by a halfbreed who spoke Portuguese. Through this interpreter, Cavendish struck a friendly deal for victuals, and soon came nine or ten royal canoes, "deeply laden . . . with two great live oxen, half a score of wonderful great and fat hogs, a number of hens which were alive, drakes, geese, eggs, plantains, sugar canes, sugar in plates, cocos, sweet oranges and sour, limes, great store of wine and aquavitae, salt to season victuals withal, and almost all manner of victuals else." Two Portuguese traders also showed up, declaring themselves supporters of Dom Antonio, the pretender to their country's throne. Cavendish "used and entreated them singularly well, with banquets and music. They told us that they were no less glad to see us, than we to see them, and enquired of the estate of their country, and what was become of Dom Antonio their king, and whether he were living or no: for that they had not of long time been in Portugal, and that the Spaniards had always brought them word that he was dead. Then our general satisfied them in every demand; assuring them, that their king was alive, and in England, and had honorable allowance of our queen, and that there was war between Spain and England, and that we were come under [permission of] the King of Portugal into the South Sea, and had warred upon the Spaniards there, and had fired, spoiled, and sunk all the ships along the coast that we could meet withal, to the number of eighteen or twenty sails. With this report they were sufficiently satisfied."

The Portuguese described the customs of Java, and the account of N.H. in the 1589 Hakluyt says, "The king of this country was reported to be very near 150 years old. This old king's name was Rajah Bolamboam." Pretty, probably more accurately, declares simply, "the king himself is a man of great years, and hath an hundred wives, his son hath fifty." All these wives, he adds, must slay themselves upon the rajah's death. His subjects, too, were fanatically loyal: "If their king command them to undertake any exploit, be it never so dangerous or desperate, they dare not nor will not refuse it, though they die every man in the execution of the same. . . . It maketh them the most valiant people in all the Southeast parts of the world: for they never fear any death."

This agreeable visit was concluded on the 16th of March, and now this most impatient of circumnavigators sped onward toward the Cape of Good Hope. "The rest of March and all the month of April," wrote Pretty, "we spent in traversing that mighty and vast sea, between the isle of Java and the main of Africa." Through wind and tempest they pushed westward; Africa was in view by May 11, but for the next two days they were becalmed, "and the sky was very hazy and thick," so that they did not round the Cape of Good Hope until May 16. Cavendish observed that although by the Portuguese charts it was 2,000 leagues from Java to the Cape, "it is not so much almost by an hundred and fifty leagues, as we found by the running of our ship. We were in running of these eighteen hundred and fifty leagues just nine weeks."

On June 8 they came to the South Atlantic island of St. Helena, then used by the Portuguese as a way station for voyages to India by the eastward route. The only permanent settlement was a small one, and Cavendish, by pointing out the great advantages of the island's location in an otherwise almost empty part of the ocean, stimulated its seizure first by the Dutch and then by the English in the middle of the following century. "This island," Pretty wrote, "is very high land, and lieth in the main sea standing as it were in the midst of the sea between the mainland of Africa and the main of Brazil and the coast of Guinea. . . . We went on shore, where we found a marvelous fair and pleasant valley, wherein divers handsome buildings and houses were set up, and especially one which was a church. . . . This valley is the fairest and largest low plot in all the island, and it is marvelous sweet and pleasant, and planted in every place either with fruit trees, or with herbs. There are fig trees, which bear fruit continually, and marvelous plentifully: for on every tree you shall have blossoms, green figs, and ripe figs, all at once: and it is so all the year long: the reason is that the island standeth so near the Sun. There be also great store of lemon trees, orange trees, pomegranate trees, pomecitron trees, date trees, which bear fruit as the fig trees do, and are planted carefully and very artificially [artfully] with very pleasant walks under and between them . . . and in every void place is planted parsley, sorrel, basil, fennel, aniseed, mustard seed, radishes, and many special good herbs: and the fresh water brook runneth through divers places of this orchard, and may with very small pains be made to water any one tree in the valley." He remarked likewise upon the "great store of partridges which are very tame, not making any great haste to fly away though one come very near them," and the pheasants, "which are also marvelous big and fat," the turkeys, and the wild goats, which roamed in flocks of hundreds and even thousands.

The only inhabitants of this ocean paradise at the time were three black slaves who informed Cavendish that if he had come three weeks earlier he would have had the opportunity to attack the India fleet, returning to Lisbon "all laden with spices and Calicut cloth, with store of treasure and very rich stones and pearls," five large ships in all. The reason for the island's fertility, Pretty observed, was that the Portuguese "suffer none to inhabit there that might spend up the fruit of the island," leaving only slaves as caretakers, and sick men who would not survive the last leg of the voyage to Europe; thus St. Helena remained always bountiful when the ships from India stopped for provisions on their way home.

The *Desire*, itself well provisioned, left St. Helena on June 20 bound for England. Now becalmed, now sped along by a good wind, she moved north to the Azores by late August and turned northeast for home. On September 3 she encountered a Flemish ship out of Lisbon; the two captains exchanged greetings and Cavendish received some welcome news: Spain had invaded England during the summer just past, and her grand armada had been utterly overthrown and destroyed by the valor of Sir Francis Drake, Sir John Hawkins, Sir Martin Frobisher, and the other great captains. The circumnavigators rejoiced. And then, Pretty concludes, "the 9th of September, after a terrible tempest which carried away most part of our sails, by the merciful favor of the Almighty we recovered our long wished port of Plymouth in England, from whence we set forth at the beginning of our voyage."

It was the fastest circumnavigation of the three yet made: two years and fifty days. It was the least productive in geographical knowledge, for Cavendish had done little more than follow Drake's path and could offer as his own discovery only Port Desire in Patagonia, which Drake most likely had found ahead of him. In terms of financial return, the voyage was far less productive than Drake's, although the taking of the *Santa Anna* had averted a complete fiasco. Cavendish had shown himself to be an able commander—the first circumnavigator not to be afflicted with mutiny or serious dissension —though he was not an inspired leader, and he often exposed himself and his men to needless risks through a lack of caution. On the day of his arrival at Plymouth he told of his voyage in a letter to his patron, Lord Hunsdon, which unavoidably stresses the sackings and burnings that were his most conspicuous achievements: "It hath pleased the Almighty to suffer me to circompass the whole globe of the world, entering in at the Strait of Magellan, and returning by the Cape de Buena Esperanza [Good Hope]. In which voyage I have either discovered or brought certain intelligence of all the rich places of the world that ever were known or discovered by any Christian. I navigated alongst the coast of Chile, Peru, and Nueva España [Mexico], where I made great spoils: I burnt and sunk 19 sails of ships small and great. All the villages and towns that ever I landed at, I burnt and spoiled: and had I not been discovered upon the coast, I had taken great quantity of treasure."

5

Drake had spent the summer of 1588 in more stirring matters. The Spanish Armada came to the English coast on July 19, and the next day the English went out to meet it, 90 ships against Spain's 130. The Spaniards were amazed by the speed and power of the English fleet and, after preliminary skirmishing, drew back. Inconclusive probings followed, but on the night of July 28 the English drew near the anchored Spanish fleet and sent fire ships into it—unmanned hulks ablaze from stem to stern. The Spaniards panicked, cutting cables and heading to sea in the dark. By morning they were scattered all up and down the French side of the English Channel, and the full English fleet swept in for the attack. A desperate Spanish retreat followed, with Drake giving chase. The wind pattern forced the Spaniards to take the long way home, up the eastern coast of England, around Scotland, and down through the Atlantic west of Ireland; Drake abandoned pursuit off Scotland, with provisions running low and ammunition gone, but the gods of the storm finished the job of shattering the Invincible Armada, driving most of the large ships to wreck on the shores of Ireland. Of the magnificent fleet that had set out in July, only a battered fragment reached Spain again by mid-September, and England was saved. Though Spain was far from destroyed as a naval power, her prestige was wounded, and England's was given a great increase, opening the way for further maritime expansion.

Another English voyage to the Pacific was one of the first projects to follow the defeat of the Spanish Armada. In August 1589 three vessels left Plymouth under the command of John Chidley: the *Wild Man*, the *White Lion*, and the *Delight*, bound for the Strait of Magellan. The ships were separated off the coast of North Africa, and little is known of the fates of the *Wild Man* and the *White Lion*, though evidently they returned to England; but Andrew Merick, the captain of the *Delight*, resolved to carry out the enterprise alone, hoping to meet with his companions on the Brazilian coast or at Port Desire. By the time he reached Patagonia he had lost 16 of his 91 men through sickness and accident. He entered the strait on January 1, 1590, and paused at an island to kill and salt penguins, which, says William Magoths of Bristol, whose account of the voyage was published by Hakluyt, "must be eaten with speed, for we found them to be of no long continuance." At this island

Merick sent out a boat with 15 men, which was lost in a storm, and seven more men were slain by natives. At Port Famine, Merick picked up the last survivor of Sarmiento's garrison and moved on toward the western mouth of the strait; but his ship was stopped by a wind out of the west that blew without cease for six weeks, and, having lost all his boats, three anchors, and most of his sailors, Merick was compelled to turn back without attaining the Pacific. Lacking a boat, he could not pick up provisions at Brazil and had to go all the way to Europe in a state of extreme distress, lacking fresh food. Only six men remained alive when the *Delight* reached Cherbourg on August 30. Here the last anchor was lost, and a storm drove them onto the rocky coast of Normandy. Merick himself died on the crossing; the six survivors of this most unhappy voyage were four Englishmen, a Breton, and a Portuguese, as well as the Spaniard who had been rescued at Port Famine.

Drake, in 1589, had gone on a voyage nearly as dismal. First, he led a fleet toward Portugal, planning to restore Dom Antonio to that country's throne, but he received only half-hearted support from Queen Elizabeth and even less from the Portuguese themselves, and the project came to nothing. Later that year he slipped into the Spanish port of Coruña and successfully destroyed a new armada under construction, and then, disregarding Elizabeth's orders, went southwards to Lisbon with Dom Antonio. He made a landing, but the Portuguese seemed not very interested in the restoration of their former dynasty, and the expedition failed. Afraid to go home to face Elizabeth's rage—she was angry both at his defiance of her wishes and at his failure to carry out what he had begun—he went first to the Azores, then raided the Spanish coast again, and finally, oppressed by perpetual bad weather, came home to face court martial and some years of royal disfavor.

Cavendish, having more or less successfully encompassed the globe in 1586–88, proposed to duplicate the feat in 1591. It was a singularly catastrophic venture, as though, by offering himself as the first two-trip circumnavigating captain, Cavendish had asked too much of fate. As usual, his extravagances had left him short of cash, and, as on his last voyage, he hoped to replenish his coffers at the expense of Spain. Three accounts of this expedition have come to us; one written by Cavendish himself as he lay in his final illness, one the work of a seaman named John Jane, and the last and longest a grotesque and fantastical narrative full of astonishing exaggerations, set down by a crewman named Anthony Knyvet. Jane's account was published in Hakluyt's collection, and those of Cavendish and Knyvet in the collection of Hakluyt's successor, Samuel Purchas.

Five ships sailed from Plymouth on August 26, 1591. Cavendish's flagship was the *Leicester Galleon*. John Davis, a veteran mariner who had made three Arctic voyages in search of the Northwest Passage, was second in command aboard the *Desire*, with which Cavendish had previously circumnavigated the world. The third ship was the *Roebuck*, commanded by a Mr. Cocke; in addition, there were two small barks, the *Black Pinnace*, under Randolfe Cotton, and the *Dainty*, commanded by Robert Tharlton. The first four of these had been outfitted by Cavendish; Tharlton's bark belonged to a Devonshire gentleman named Adrian Gilbert, who had actively promoted the quest for the Northwest Passage in the past.

The fleet arrived off the coast of Brazil at the end of November. On December 15 Cocke and Davis took the *Desire* and the *Black Pinnace* to the town of Santos, which they invaded and seized in a surprise attack. Cavendish had wanted Santos captured for the provisions it held, and at first all went well, for the attack came when the inhabitants were at Mass, and everyone was kept prisoner in the church. John Jane says, "But such was the negligence of our governor Master Cocke, that the Indians were suffered to carry out of the town whatsoever they would in open view, and no man did control them: and the next day after we had won the town, our prisoners were all set at liberty, only four poor old men were kept as pawns to supply our wants. Thus in three days the town that was able to furnish such another fleet with all kind of necessaries, was left unto us nakedly bare, without people and provision."

When Cavendish reached Santos, about Christmas, he learned of these blunders and compounded them with a worse one of his own: for he ordered that the fleet remain in Santos while trying to persuade the Indians to bring food. Five weeks were foolishly consumed this way, and on January 22, says Jane, "we departed out of the town through extreme want of victual, not being able any longer to live there . . . so that in every condition we went worse furnished from the town, than when we came unto it." Not only had Cavendish wasted his dwindling provisions without gaining a new supply, but by his delay he had missed the season for passing through the Strait of Magellan. As he lamented in his doleful deathbed narrative, "Such was the adverseness of our fortunes, that in coming thither we spent the summer, and found in the Straits, the beginning of a most extreme winter, not durable for Christians."

En route to the strait, the fleet was separated by storm on February 8. Jane says that Cavendish had neglected to select a port of rendezvous for such an eventuality; Anthony Knyvet asserts that he had ordered his captains to meet him at Port Desire. The *Desire* and the *Roebuck* met in the storm and proceeded together to Port Desire, arriving on March 6. Ten days later the *Black Pinnace* got there, and on the 18th Cavendish himself brought the *Leicester Galleon* into the harbor. Only Adrian Gilbert's bark, the *Dainty*, did not appear; her captain had lost heart and taken her back to England.

Cavendish had had the worst time of all. He had lost his ship's boat in the storm, and also a pinnace built at Santos. He had also been threatened with mutiny, so that, he wrote, "had not my most true friends been there . . . I had been constrained either to have suffered violence, or some other most disordered mishap." So bitter were these attacks that, at Port Desire, Cavendish took the strange step of leaving his own ship to sail with John Davis aboard the *Desire*. John Jane relates, "Being aboard the *Desire* he told our captain of all his extremities, and spake most hardly of his company, and of divers gentlemen that were with him, purposing no more to go aboard his own ship, but to stay in the *Desire*." The tides at Port Desire were so savage that Cavendish dared not remain there, and on March 20, two days after his arrival, he gave orders to sail on to the Strait of Magellan. This was another error, but an unavoidable one; the crews of the other ships had had from five days to two weeks to rest and reprovision, but the *Leicester Galleon*'s men were exhausted, and so all four ships departed, wrote Cavendish, "they being fresh, and infinitely well relieved with seals and birds . . . and my company being grown weak and feeble, with continual watching, pumping, and bailing."

They came to the strait on April 8, after enduring storms more terrible than those past. Forcing their way in despite the grim winter weather, they passed the first narrows, but then were compelled to seek shelter in a small cove from April 18 to May 10, "in all which time," Cavendish wrote, "we never had other than most furious contrary winds. And after that the month of May was come in, nothing but such flights of snow, and extremities of frosts, as in the time of my life, I never saw any to be compared with them." He had returned to his own ship by this time. In a single week, he says, 40 men of the *Leicester Galleon* died of the cold, and 70 sickened, "so that there were not fifty men that were able to stand upon the hatches." This time of hardship inspired Anthony Knyvet to some of his most remarkable flights of prose. Soaked by freezing spray, "the next morning I was numbed, that I could not stir my legs, and pulling off my stockings, my toes came with them, and all my feet were as black as soot, and I had no feeling of them. . . . Here one Harris a goldsmith lost his nose: for going to blow it with his fingers, cast it into the fire."

In despair, Cavendish called his officers together and told them that he regarded a passage of the strait impossible at this time; he wished to go back into the Atlantic and sail to the East Indies by way of the Cape of Good Hope. John Davis strongly opposed this. They had been in the strait only a month, Davis said; perhaps the weather would change soon and allow them to enter the Pacific, where they would soon have access to the Spanish towns. To sail eastward across the Atlantic in these latitudes was something no one had ever done, Davis argued, and they were in no shape to attempt such an adventure now. Jane tells us that Davis asked Cavendish "to consider the great extremity of his estate, the slenderness of his provisions, with the weakness of his men. . . . We have no more sails than masts, no victuals, no ground-tackling, no cordage more than is overhead. . . . Therefore it will be a desperate case to take so hard an enterprise in hand." If Cavendish would not agree to wait in the strait for better weather, then let us go back to Brazil for provisions, said Davis; but it would be madness to head at once for the Cape of Good Hope.

Cavendish could abide the Patagonian winter no longer and sensed that he would face a mutiny if he insisted on an immediate sailing for Africa, so reluctantly he admitted that they would have to go back to Brazil, a place that he regarded as the source of all his woes, after the bungling at Santos. On May 15 the ships sailed, and they reached the eastern mouth of the strait three days later. Turning north, they were in the latitude of Port Desire on May 20 when the fleet was separated again at midnight. The *Leicester Galleon* and the *Roebuck* together tacked and stood toward the land 30 leagues away, but the *Desire* and the *Black Pinnace* continued running to the north all night and all the next day.

What actually happened became a matter for painful controversy. John Davis of the *Desire* later testified, "By what occasion we were severed we protest we know not, whether we lost them or they us. In the morning we only saw the *Black Pinnace*." John Jane, who was with Davis, wrote, "In the night the general altered his course, as we suppose, by which occasion we lost him: for in the evening he stood close by a wind to seaward, having the wind at Northnortheast, and we standing the same way, the wind not altering, could not the next day see him: so that we then persuaded ourselves, that he was gone to Port Desire to relieve himself, or that he had sustained some mischance at sea, and was gone thither to remedy it." Cavendish, on the other hand, regarded the separation as Davis' deliberate and villainous attempt to destroy him by robbing him of the pinnace, the only vessel small and agile enough to enter Brazil's harbors. He wrote of "that villain that hath been the death of me, and the decay of this whole action, I mean Davis, whose only treachery in running from me, hath been an utter ruin of all. . . . [It was] Davis' intention ever to run away. This is God's will, that I should put him in trust, that should be the end of my life, and the decay of the whole action."

Angered and despondent, Cavendish made for the coast of Brazil with his two remaining vessels, but they were struck at about 36°S. by what he called "the most grievous storm, that ever any Christians endured upon the seas to live," and he lost sight of the *Roebuck*. He brought the unwieldy *Leicester Galleon* to anchor off São Vicente, just south of Santos, and sent two dozen men ashore to obtain food. The shore party apparently intended to desert at this point and dwell comfortably in Brazil, but they were ambushed and slain by a party of Indians and Portuguese, leaving only one man, a friendly Brazilian Indian who had been serving as their guide, to escape and bring the tale to Cavendish. Now he had lost not only some of his best men, but also his last boat; luckily he came upon an old boat of the Portuguese, which he sent off to look for the *Roebuck*. It returned without success eight days later, but nine days afterward the *Roebuck* appeared, all but one of her masts gone, her sails blown away.

With the aid of the *Roebuck*'s boats the voyagers finally got provisions from shore, though not enough, and Cavendish now hatched a bit of trickery of his own, which he confesses quite candidly in his narrative. He would abandon the crippled *Roebuck*, a drag on his resources, and, combining both crews into one, go to a nearby island to refit for a new attempt at the Strait of Magellan. He kept this plan secret and told the crews of both ships that they would sail, after repairs, for St. Helena to raid Portuguese vessels. But first he needed fresh fruit and other victuals, and each time he sent men ashore a few were killed, so that the Brazilian stay turned into a nightmare of steadily dwindling forces. Cavendish lost all control not only over his men but over events, and every move he made turned out more disastrous than the last. The climax came when the men of the *Roebuck*, realizing that Cavendish meant to expose them to the furies of the Strait of Magellan if he ever got safely free of Brazil, patched their battered ship together and slipped away in the night, heading for England. "In running from us

[Cavendish wrote], they not only carried away our surgeons, and all their provision, but also our victual, wherein consisted all our relief and comfort: having in them at their departure but six and forty men, carrying away with them the proportion for six months' victual of one hundred and twenty men at large. I leave you to consider of this part of theirs, and the miserable case I was left in, with so many hurt men, so little victual, and my boat being so bad, as six or seven men continually bailing water, were scant able to keep her from sinking."

With the determination of madness, Cavendish had his remaining men collect food and water, rig the ship anew, and prepare for sailing. They would go to the Strait of Magellan, he said, "which words were no sooner uttered, but forthwith they all with one consent, affirmed plainly, they would never go that way again. . . . I sought by peaceable means to persuade them, showing them that in going that way, we should relieve our victuals, by salting of seals and birds. . . . And further, if we got through the strait (which we might now easily perform, considering we had the chiefest part of summer before us) we could not but make a most rich voyage." This dream did not impress them, sore and weary and hungry as they were, in their dilapidated ship. Even though it was 600 leagues to the strait, and 2,000 to England, they would run for home, despite all Cavendish's appeals to their pride as English mariners. Only Cavendish's own cousin and one other man supported him. One sailor defied Cavendish to his face. "I took this bold companion by the bosom, and with mine own hands put a rope about his neck, meaning resolutely to strangle him, for weapon about me I had none," Cavendish wrote. This so startled the men that they momentarily yielded and agreed to follow Cavendish wherever he would take them. Again he sent men ashore for provisions and to build a new boat; again they were ambushed by Indians and Portuguese; again there were treacheries and blunders, and desertions to the Portuguese by men who had come to fear their gaunt, obsessed captain. Cavendish had fewer than 30 sailors left, hardly enough to haul the heavy anchors. Once more they refused to go to the strait, and this time Cavendish had to give in, but when they begged him to head for England, he replied that he "was then determined, that ship and all should sink in the seas together," if they did not follow his course. "Upon this, they began to be more tractable, and then I showed them, that I would beat for St. Helena, and there, either to make ourselves happy by mending, or ending." Though displeased, they followed him. The broken, disappointed Cavendish set a course for St. Helena, though his crew was hardly sufficient now to raid any sort of vessel. They came within two leagues of the island, and then, with that fair place of fruit and herbs and fat partridges so close, they were swept to the north by the winds, and Cavendish let them have their way and make for England. As his strength ebbed, he wrote his account of the voyage in the form of a letter to his friend and executor, Sir Tristram Gorges. This tragic document ("Now I am grown so weak and faint, as I am scarce able to hold the pen in my hand") related all of Cavendish's mishaps and torments and told how he wished himself "upon any desert place in the world, there to die, rather than thus basely to return home again." With his last strength he listed his bequests, hopelessly, for the voyage had bankrupted him, and death came to him somewhere at sea. The *Leicester Galleon* struggled home with the somber tale.

6

Among the mariners Cavendish lost in Brazil was Anthony Knyvet. He claims that he fell ill and lay belowdecks "lame, sick, and almost starved," and finally was put ashore on a barren island, left for dead. But he was spared to write one of the most entertaining, if least reliable, of the Elizabethan maritime narratives. Awakened by noon heat, he looked about him and saw the bodies of 20 of his dead companions, and gave thanks for his own deliverance; the ship was gone, but he lived on crabs until his strength returned, and began to explore the island. Now begins a tale of wonders, for he had not spent 15 minutes beside a river "but I saw a great thing come out of the water, with great scales on the back, with great ugly claws and a long tail, this beast came towards me, and I had not the power to shun it, but as it came towards me, I went and met it, when I came near it, I stood still amazed to see so monstrous a thing before me. Hereupon this beast stood still and opening his mouth, and thrust out a long tongue like a harping-iron [harpoon]. I commended myself to God, and thought there to have been torn in pieces, but this beast turned again, and went into the river."

On Knyvet went, now dining for a fortnight on the flesh of a beached whale, now captured by Portuguese, now a prisoner of the Indians; he tells of cannibals, Amazons, mermaids, pygmies, and other monsters; he is condemned to be hanged as a Protestant in Rio de Janeiro, and is saved by a merciful band of Jesuits; he works as a slave in a sugar mill for nine months, with hoops of iron weighing 30 pounds round his legs; he escapes; he strikes fast friendship with a cannibal named Quarasips-juca, and they brave a desert together in which are found leopards, lions, crocodiles, "and divers other serpents." He is tried before a senate of savages; he lives among them in their own costume; he is in a canoe overturned by a whale; he embarks on a Portuguese ship for Africa, hoping to make his way from Angola to Prester John's country and thence to Turkey and Europe; he is imprisoned and shipped back to Brazil; he reaches Lisbon; and after a decade of wanderings, he returns to England to set down his amazing narrative. Not the least of Knyvet's tales is his contribution to the growing myth of the Patagonian giants, for, in a kind of ethnological appendix to his lengthy account, he writes, "At Port Desire, which is the next haven to the Straits of Magellan, inhabited giants of fifteen or sixteen spans of height [11 or 12 feet]. I affirm, that at Port Desire I saw the footing of them, by the shore side, that was above four foot of one of our men's in length; and I saw two of them that were buried newly, the one of them was fourteen spans long. . . . I saw another of these in Brazil, that was taken by Alonso Dias a Spaniard, that with foul weather was driven out of Saint Julians; this was but a young man, yet above thirteen spans long." To balance these, Knyvet told of pygmies at Port Famine in the strait, "a kind of strange cannibals, short of body, not above five or six spans high, and very strong and thick made: their mouths are very big, and reach almost to their ears." He saw four or five thousand of them there, a fact unrecorded by any of his companions, or by any other visitors to that part of the world.

7

John Davis, whom Cavendish considered so treacherous, had notable adventures of his own after the separation of Cavendish's fleet off Port Desire on May 20, 1592. Thinking Cavendish had gone to Port Desire, Davis went to seek him there. The *Desire* and the *Black Pinnace* made harbor on May 26, did not find Cavendish, and, says John Jane, "being most slenderly victualed, without sails, boat, ores, nails, cordage, and all other necessaries for our relief, we were strooken into a deadly sorrow." But they found a pool of fresh water and filled their casks; they took an abundance of mussels at low tide and fished for smelts with hooks made of bent pins. Davis, mystified by Cavendish's disappearance, began to consider the possibilities of waiting out the southern-hemisphere winter and returning to the Strait of Magellan.

This determination produced an incipient mutiny which Davis quelled, and they spent the rest of the winter making nails, bolts, spikes, and ropes to refit their ships and laying in a supply of seal and penguin meat. Cavendish still had not appeared, and the men now thought he might be waiting for them at the Strait of Magellan. On August 6 the ships set out for the strait. Three days later a storm struck in which they took in all their sails to save them, for they were too badly worn to stand against bad weather, and the vessels drifted for several days. On the 14th, Jane writes, "We were driven in among certain isles never before discovered by any known relation, lying fifty leagues or better from the shore east and northerly from the straits: in which place, unless it had pleased God of his wonderful mercy to have ceased the wind, we must of necessity have perished." Davis gave these islands no name; but they are known today as the Falkland Islands and were the major discovery of the voyage.

They entered the strait on August 19 and traversed it quickly, though harassed by Indians who "threw stones at us of three or four pound weight an incredible distance." By the 25th they were in Long Reach near the Pacific mouth of the strait; here the loyal Davis chose to anchor in the hope that Cavendish might yet arrive. "After we had stayed here a fort-night in the deep of winter," Jane wrote, "our victuals con-suming, (for our seals stunk most vilely, and our men died pitifully through cold and famine, for the greatest part of them had not clothes to defend the extremity of the winter's cold) being in this heavy distress, our captain and master thought it the best course to depart from the straits into the South Sea." Davis planned to go to the isle of Santa Maria, off the Chilean coast, and wait in relatively warm climate for Cavendish. On September 13 they entered the Pacific for the first time, but immediately were driven back into the strait by high winds. A second entry the next day also failed. They sought shelter in a cove three leagues inside the strait and somehow were not wrecked even though all they had to hold them were broken anchors and spliced cables. Davis was determined to go forward, though, and urged his reluctant men on: "For at the Isle of Santa Maria I do assure you of wheat, pork, and roots enough. Also I will bring you to an isle, where pelicans be in great abundance . . . besides all our possibility of intercepting some ships upon the coast of Chile and Peru. But if we return there is nothing but death to be hoped for: therefore do as you like, I am ready, but my desire is to proceed." On October 2 they entered the Pacific a third time and reached the open water; but another storm came up, and they did not know what to do, for the condition of their anchors and cables made a return to the strait unwise, and the condition of their sails made it even more risky to stay at sea. The *Black Pinnace* reported that she was in great difficulties, but the *Desire* could do nothing to help her, and on the night of October 4 the *Pinnace* disappeared and was not seen again.

The *Desire* kept to the sea, her men mending one sail with the scraps of another, "the storm continuing without all reason in fury, with hail, snow, rain, and wind . . . the seas such and so lofty . . . that many times we were doubtful whether our ship did sink or swim." On October 10, with the weather at its worst, the end seemed inevitable; but, says Jane, after a particularly eloquent prayer by Captain Davis, the sun broke through, allowing a calculation of latitude, and the next day the *Desire* fought her way once more into the strait. Davis now admitted defeat. The sails were ribbons, the hull was a sieve, his men were at the limits of their endurance. Just as Cavendish had tried too late in the season to pass the strait, they had tried too early; and having emerged three times and been thrust back three times, Davis knew he could not reach the Pacific. They gave up and, after many perils and hardships, rethreaded the strait to the Atlantic, anchoring at Port Desire on October 30. Several days afterward, Davis sent nine men to hunt penguins, and they did not return, presumably being slain by the Indians. Included in the group had been several of the most mutinous men, and John Jane saw in this "the just judgment of God."

The weather gradually improved, and they lived well on the eggs and flesh of penguins and on "an herb called scurvygrass, which we fried with eggs, using train oil [penguin fat] instead of butter. This herb did so purge the blood, that it took away all kind of swellings, of which many died, and restored us to perfect health of body, so that we were in as good case as when we came first out of England. We stayed in this harbor until the 22 of December, in which time we had dried 20,000 penguins. . . . Thus God did feed us even as it were with manna from heaven." With 14,000 of their dried penguins aboard, they headed for Brazil. Davis rationed the food so that it would last six months, the time he estimated it would take to reach England: five penguins for each four men a day, six quarts of water for four men a day, penguin oil three times a week. They stopped at an island off the Brazilian coast to gather fruits and edible roots, despite strange dreams that many of the men had, warning of disaster; and while they rested after eating well and loading the ship, they were attacked by Indians and Portuguese, and 13 men were slain. Of the *Desire*'s original complement of 76 men, 27 now remained.

More woes awaited them at sea. They were caught in crosswinds in the Atlantic which held them idle for three weeks, while the water supply ebbed, until they seriously discussed landing in Brazil and surrendering to the Portuguese. Then came rain, which saved them from death by thirst, but as they passed into the warm latitudes the dried penguins began to rot, and, Jane says, "there bred in them a most loathsome and ugly worm of an inch long. This worm did so mightily increase, and devour our victuals, that there was in reason no hope how we should avoid famine. . . . There was nothing that they did not devour, only iron excepted: our clothes, boots, shoes, hats, shirts, stockings: and for the ship they did so eat the timbers, as that we greatly feared they would undo us, by gnawing through the ship's side." All attempts at exterminating these vermin failed, and they continued to multiply, "so that at the last we could not sleep for them, but they would eat our flesh, and bite like mosquitos." The sailors sickened and swelled and died in terrible pain. Davis and a cabinboy alone remained in good health; three others were still able to move about; 11 more were ill, and the rest were dead. The five able men did the work of all the crew, but could not manage the sails, so that they remained set in all weather, and were torn to pieces. "Thus as lost wanderers upon the sea," Jane declared, "the 11 of June 1593, it pleased God that we arrived at Bear-haven in Ireland, and there ran the ship on shore. . . . In this manner our small remnant by God's only mercy were preserved, and restored to our country, to whom be all honor and glory world without end."

8

The shattering failure of Cavendish's second voyage warned the too-confident Englishmen that the South Sea held great challenges and that the Strait of Magellan was not an easy gateway to fortune. But there was one further attempt to follow in the wake of the *Golden Hind*.

Sir Richard Hawkins, the only son of Sir John, led this venture, which was designed as much as a scientific expedition as a buccaneering cruise. "I resolved [Hawkins wrote] on a voyage to be made for the Islands of Japan, the Philippines and Moluccas, the Kingdom of China, and the East Indies, by way of the Straits of Magellan and the South Sea. The principal end of our designments was, to make a perfect discovery of all those parts where I should arrive, with their longitudes, latitudes, the lying of their coasts, their ports, cities, and peoplings; their manner of government; with the commodities which the countries yielded, and of which they have want." Thereby he hoped to lay the foundation for an Elizabethan empire in the Pacific and to finance his research by raiding Chile and Peru.

Hawkins sailed from Plymouth on June 12, 1593. He commanded a fine new ship called the *Dainty;* he was accompanied by the *Fancy* and the *Hawk*, two much smaller vessels, one of them captained by Robert Tharlton, who had sailed in Cavendish's ill-fated fleet. They headed for the strait in the usual way and with some of the usual events: in a storm off the Río de la Plata, Tharlton took his ship back to England, deserting Hawkins as he had earlier deserted Cavendish. "I was worthy to be deceived," Hawkins said, "that trusted my ship in the hands of a man who had before left his general in the like occasion." The *Hawk* had been scuttled by prearrangement off Brazil, so Hawkins went on alone to the strait. En route he rediscovered the Falkland Islands and, unaware that Davis had found them a year and a half earlier, gave them the name of Hawkins' Maiden-land, in honor of the Virgin Queen. Passing through the strait, Hawkins stopped at the island of Mocha for provisions and headed north, planning to make no stops on the coast until Lima. His men, hungry for booty, prodded him into raiding Valparaiso first—a tactical error, for though the raid was profitable, it warned the Spaniards of their approach. A fleet of six Spanish warships set out from Callao, headed the *Dainty* off, and forced her into a bay near Atacames, Ecuador. A battle of heroic proportions followed, lasting three days; the *Dainty* did not surrender until she was ready to sink and 60 of her 75 men had been wounded, including Hawkins himself. At the end of June 1594 Hawkins was taken to Lima—the first English commander captured by the Spaniards in the Pacific since Oxenham, two decades before—and ultimately he was sent to Spain, where he remained a prisoner for many years before returning to England.

After this, the English turned away from the Strait of Magellan and from the Pacific, which seemed too vast and too hostile to merit further exploration. There were other and better ways to reach the Orient. Three English ships had sailed by the eastern route in 1591, led by two veterans of the Armada battle, George Raymond and James Lancaster. Though the venture was generally unsuccessful—Raymond and his ship went down off Africa—Lancaster did round the Cape of Good Hope to Zanzibar, reach Ceylon and the Malay Peninsula, and raid Portuguese shipping off Malacca before the threat of mutiny forced him to struggle back into the Atlantic. Finally, there was mutiny when Lancaster was stumbling about in the West Indies, and he was marooned with 19 other men, eventually reaching England on a French vessel. A second eastward venture to the Orient in 1596 under George Wood brought English ships to the mainland of India for the first time; Wood plundered the Portuguese from Goa to Malacca, losing men to scurvy and ships to storms, and finished his voyage as a shipwreck victim on the Indian Ocean island of Mauritius, where he was rescued by a Dutch ship in 1601. Despite these two discouraging ventures, England continued to seek the Orient by way of Africa, especially after the founding of the British East India Company in 1600, a corporation which, designed to foster England's trade with Asia, eventually evolved into an empire within an empire, ruling India and surrounding lands in England's name. As a substitute for their raids on Spain's Pacific ports, the English buccaneers intensified their attacks on the West Indies, and in one of these privateering ventures the careers of Sir Francis Drake and Sir John Hawkins ended. Emerging from years of obscurity and disfavor, Drake persuaded Elizabeth to let him cross the Atlantic once more, and he set out in 1595 in the company of the old slaver John Hawkins. The expedition was poorly managed, for Hawkins was cautious with age and Drake more impetuous than ever; they disagreed over strategy and, in their quarrels, brought the attention of the Spaniards upon them. Hawkins fell ill during a fruitless attack on a treasure ship at San Juan, Puerto Rico, and died in mid-November; Drake went on to the Spanish Main, where he found the Spaniards heavily fortified and ready for him, and then to Central America, where the wind was against him and a pestilence swept his crew. Drake contracted dysentery and died on January 28, 1596, closing a brilliant career whose final years had been darkened by controversy and difficulties. It was the fate of all three circumnavigators of the sixteenth century to find death far from home.

Spain, which had done little in the Pacific in the second half of that century but send galleons shuttling between Mexico and the Philippines, turned again to discovery in 1595. Philip II had suggested to the Viceroy of Peru that a voyage of exploration might be a useful way to rid that land of idle, restless, overambitious gentry, and the viceroy, seeing the wisdom of that, appointed Álvaro de Mendaña to found a colony in the Solomon Islands. Mendaña had helped to discover the Solomons in 1568, serving as nominal commander of an expedition actually led by Pedro Sarmiento de Gamboa. He had been a very young man then; now he was fifty-three, wealthy, something of a dreamer and idealist who had sought permission to make this voyage for more than 20 years. The ships were well equipped but had been stocked with every superfluous ruffian in Peru, and to make things worse, Mendaña brought along his wife, an aggressive, ferociously ambitious woman whose selfishness and arrogance greatly disrupted the enterprise. Most notable among the 378 members of the expedition was a Portuguese pilot, Pedro Fernandez de Quiros, who became the hero of the debacle that followed.

Mendaña sailed from Callao in April 1595. Three months later he reached the Marquesas Islands and by September he was in the Solomons, where—over Quiros' objections—the Spaniards commenced a wanton butchery of the natives that soon led to equally murderous disputes among themselves. Mendaña's wife drove the men on to new barbarisms; Mendaña died of a fever in October; illness and the determined resistance of the islanders cost hundreds of Spanish lives. At last Quiros took charge, guided the survivors through uncharted seas, and brought them to Manila. Quiros later returned to Mexico by Urdaneta's Passage, possessed now by a vision of finding *Terra Australis* and converting its natives to Christianity. Half mad with his passionate scheme, Quiros sought and obtained support and in 1605 sailed from Callao on the last great Spanish voyage of exploration. Burning with a religious zeal reminiscent of Magellan's in the Philippines, Quiros returned to the Solomons, turned south to discover the New Hebrides (mistaking an island of this group for the southern continent he sought), and, finding the natives hostile, mysteriously returned to South America after a stay of only three weeks. His ship, he later declared, had been blown from harbor by a sudden squall and could not regain her anchorage. Quiros' second in command, Luis Vaez de Torres, was astounded by his commander's unexpected departure and regarded it as a desertion. After waiting awhile for Quiros to return, Torres set out for the

Philippines, in the course of which journey he sailed completely around the huge island of New Guinea and thereby proved it was no part of a southern continent. In this way he discovered the Torres Strait which separates New Guinea from Australia, the real and yet undiscovered *Terra Australis;* he may have been the first European explorer to sight Australia itself.

The voyages of Mendaña, Quiros, and Torres added to man's knowledge of the South Pacific, which the three circumnavigators had bypassed. They marked the end of Spain's great century of discovery—a century in which the most important expeditions had been led by foreigners like Columbus and Magellan, but in which the kingdom of Charles and his son, Philip, had done more to reveal the nature of the globe than in all previous millennia. Portugal had had her century and had found India; Spain had had her century and had found America; now the time of the Dutch had come.

[6]

THE DUTCH

IN THE ORIENT

THE DUTCH WERE A MERCANTILE PEOPLE, and they knew more than a little about the sea; furthermore, they had been active in the spice trade since the beginning of the sixteenth century, when the Fuggers made Antwerp the distribution center for King Manoel's cargoes. Yet few would have predicted that the stolid Dutchmen would shoulder aside Spain and Portugal and England and seize the East Indies for themselves, so that for the first time one nation controlled the spice trade from plantation to retail market.

There was not even a Dutch nation during the years of Spanish and English domination of the sea. Among the many crowns inherited by the boy who was to become the Emperor Charles V was that of the Low Countries, Flanders and Holland, today Belgium and the Netherlands. These were 17 loosely federated provinces comprising hundreds of quasi-independent city-states, French-speaking in the south, Flemish-speaking in the north. Charles had been born in the Netherlands and was well liked there, and his efforts to incorporate the provinces into his immense empire were relatively successful. Since he was also King of Castile, Charles was able to grant the Dutch the same privileges in Spanish ports

VOYAGE OF SCHOUTEN + LE MAIRE 1615–1617

that were enjoyed by the merchants of Spain, and they participated in the prosperity stemming from the Americas. However, Charles also taxed his subjects heavily to finance his ambitious enterprises, which created such discontent in his own native city of Ghent that he was forced to invade and subjugate it in 1540. Another complicating factor blocking the union of the Low Countries with Spain was the rapid spread of Protestantism in the Netherlands, but on the whole the reign of Charles V was a period of relatively little friction between Spaniards and Dutch. Both were equals in one vast empire.

The Dutch had a long maritime history. In the eighth century they were trading in England and France for wool, honey, and wine; during the time of Charlemagne they began to send their ships to the Rhine and the Baltic. For two centuries the turbulent Vikings interrupted this commerce, but the Dutch slowly resumed their position in Western European trade afterward. An accident of geography in the thirteenth century reshaped their homeland: the sea swept inward, apparently through a subsidence of the land, to create the great salt-water body known as the Zuider Zee. Towns that had been far inland found themselves transformed into ports; tiny fishing villages became major commercial centers. The Dutch prospered, although they were hampered in their attempts to exploit Baltic trade by the competition of the Hanseatic League, a federation of German city-states that controlled the northern waterways. Such newly important Zuider Zee towns as Amsterdam and Hoorn challenged the Hanseatic League with considerable success. As the Dutch merchant and fishing fleets expanded, Dutch seafaring skills grew rapidly, until by 1500 the cities of the Zuider Zee had one of the world's strongest and soundest navies. Nevertheless, the Dutch stayed close to home, capitalizing on the steady decline of their Hanseatic competitors and ignoring the temptation to seek the Indies or the New World. Let the Portuguese and the Spaniards bear those risks; the Dutch financial capital of Antwerp thrived by offering banking and mercantile services to those adventurous but commercially backward nations.

In the fifteenth century the many provinces of the Low Countries had come under the rule of the Dukes of Burgundy through purchase, force, and advantageous marriages of nobility. One of those marriages linked the House of Burgundy to the House of Habsburg in 1477, and six-year-old Charles of Habsburg inherited the Burgundian properties a decade before the death of his grandfather, King Ferdinand, gave him the thrones of Spain's two kingdoms of Castile and Aragon. Charles spent his long reign wearily trying to consolidate his immense and poorly joined empire, and by the time he was fifty-five, he began to put down his responsibilities, abdicating piecemeal and dividing his realm between his brother, Ferdinand, and his son, Philip. It was Philip who became sovereign of the Netherlands in 1555, and the following year King Philip II of Spain, as Charles retired to a monastery to spend his last two years of life in peace.

Philip was a dark-souled, harsh, deeply religious man, quite unlike his tolerant and amiable father, and his rule fell bitterly upon the Netherlands. The Protestant merchants of Holland wanted no part of Philip's zealous Catholicism. They could look upon Charles as one of their own, but Philip was wholly Spaniard, alien by language, culture, temperament, and religion. Such Netherlands nationalists as William the Silent, Prince of Orange, and the Counts of Egmont and Hoorn sought to break their homeland free of what had ceased to be confederation with Spain and had become dominion by Spain. Philip had brought the Counter-Reformation to the Netherlands—the Inquisition, with its thumb-screws and rack, its fanatic persecution of heresy. Calvinist rioters responded by sacking Catholic churches; dissension turned into insurrection, and, with anarchy threatening, Philip sent the Duke of Alva into the Netherlands at the head of 10,000 men to restore order.

Alva swiftly and brutally repressed the rising national-ism of the Netherlands. In January 1568 he decreed William of Orange an outlaw and confiscated his estates; he de-feated an army William had raised; he captured the Counts of Egmont and Hoorn and had them beheaded at Brussels in June, thus creating two martyrs to freedom and marking the beginning of a war that would last for 80 years. From 1568 to 1573 Alva was master of the Netherlands through a course of merciless butchery, but the Dutch could not be sub-jugated. Gradually the northern provinces fought free of the Spaniards, though the Catholic south remained loyal to Spain. The division of north and south was made formal early in 1579, when the seven provinces of the north, com-prising approximately the modern Netherlands, joined in the Union of Utrecht. The provinces remained sovereign, but agreed to send delegates to a national administrative body, the States-General, in which the city of Amsterdam and the province of Holland held the dominant roles. An unusual po-litical structure evolved—an oligarchic republic, ruled by the burghers, or merchants, which also maintained in an anoma-lous position a hereditary quasi-monarch, the Prince of Or-ange. The United Provinces bickered among themselves, and the two strongest, Holland and Zeeland, looked warily upon each other while the other five, Friesland, Groningen, Over-ijssel, Gelderland, and Utrecht, were jealous and suspicious of both. Only William of Orange, revered by all the prov-inces, served as a unifying figure.

Philip II did not lightly accept the revolt of the Dutch, who had formally renounced their allegiance to him in 1581. From bases in the south he directed a reconquest of the United Provinces, taking all but Holland and Zeeland; and after the assassination of Prince William in 1584 a return to Spanish domination seemed certain. The States-General turned for help to King Henri III of France, who seemed sympathetic to the Protestant cause but was too busy with domestic problems, and the Dutch went next to the most powerful Protestant monarch in Europe, Queen Elizabeth of England.

To Elizabeth the rebels were repugnant because they were commoners who had thrown off allegiance to a rightful king; and since she was endeavoring to keep out of war with Philip II herself, she was understandably wary of offending him by backing his Dutch enemies. However, she knew that the security of England depended on limiting Spanish power, and a Spanish Netherlands, facing England across the North Sea, represented a troublesome threat. In August 1585 Philip II's army took Antwerp, and it appeared that a Spanish Netherlands would soon be reality, so, after much temporizing, she sent the Earl of Leicester with 5,000 men that December to aid the Dutch. Leicester came to rule and not merely to aid, but his attempt to take the place of William of Orange was a failure, and he left within two years. Another noted Englishman who came to Holland at this time was Francis Drake, who called there in 1586 to collect ships for his "beard-singeing" raid on the Spanish fleet in Cádiz. His mission indicates the high regard in which Dutch shipping was held, and from Drake the Dutch learned something of the Moluccas, which he had visited on his circumnavigation. They were far more interested in those isles than he had been—when his ships needed to be lightened on the reef, Drake had jettisoned cloves, not gold—and some Dutch merchants began to look past the war toward a time when they, and not King Philip, would reap the profits of the Spice Islands.

2

Occupied on two fronts, making war on England and the Dutch Netherlands simultaneously, Philip was overextended, but not yet in real difficulties. Despite the defeat of his armada in 1588, he was ready to invade the Low Countries the following year, and only a political convulsion in France diverted his attention and led to the cancellation of the attack. The Dutch put their reprieve to good use. New leaders had emerged to fill the gap left by the assassination of William of Orange: Jan van Oldenbarneveldt of Holland now guided the States-General, and his protégé, Prince William's young son, Maurice of Nassau, had taken command of the Dutch army. In 1591 and 1592 Maurice struck repeatedly, taking back the towns that had been lost to the Spaniards, until the United Provinces again were free. The war with Spain would proceed, in fits and starts, until ended by the Treaty of Münster in 1648—signed on the eightieth anniversary of the execution of the Counts of Egmont and Hoorn—but the Spaniards had been permanently dislodged from the seven northern provinces, and, with independence won though not yet assured, the Dutch turned to the sea.

It was a necessary step. The prosperity that had come from serving as bankers to Spain and Portugal was ended, for those two countries now were joined under the rule of Philip II, and Philip had put an embargo on Dutch trade. If the Hollanders wanted spices and silks and ivories—or even salt, which came then mainly from the Cape Verde Islands— they would have to go out and get these themselves, pushing the Portuguese aside in the process. They had sturdy ships; they had skilled seamen; they had unsurpassable self-confidence. All that remained was to learn the art of making long voyages.

The new Dutch maritime enterprise differed in many important ways from what the Spaniards, Portuguese, and English had been doing. In Portugal and later in Spain, trade with America and the Indies had been a royal monopoly, and private merchants were compelled to pay a heavy licensing fee to the crown; among the Dutch, all voyages were sent out by private entrepreneurs on their own account and at their own risk. The Portuguese, digging in at Goa and Malacca, had been willing to depend on a network of Moslem middlemen; the Dutch wished to gain control over every phase of the spice trade. As for the English, they were mere pirates, building no empire, simply raiding the treasure ships of King Philip; the Dutch had no objections to raiding those ships themselves, but they planned to create a substantial and permanent presence in the Orient and looked upon the English activities as shallow and of little long-range benefit.

They moved carefully, learning what must be learned, for the cautious merchants were newly come from a devastating war and had to conserve their limited capital. They studied maps and travelers' journals and somehow came into possession of vital and secret Spanish and Portuguese sea charts. A young man named Jan Huyghen van Linschoten of Haarlem was immensely valuable to his countrymen, for he was the first Hollander actually to see the Orient. In 1579, when he was sixteen, he went to Spain to learn of foreign trade, moving on to Lisbon after the Spanish annexation of Portugal. He boarded a ship for Goa in April 1583 and spent five years in Portuguese India, listening, studying, and taking notes. Although he never went east of Goa, he learned a great deal about Malacca, Sumatra, Java, the Moluccas, and the rest of the East Indies, and when he came home to Holland in 1592 he wrote it all down in an immense book, the

Itinerary, which was to have great influence on his countrymen. It was virtually a handbook for eastern trade, telling
which spices grew where, describing the best routes to the
Indies, commenting on the shortcomings of the Portuguese
as mariners and as administrators, and—of greatest historical importance—recommending Java as the keystone of any
projected Dutch empire in the East Indies. Pepper, cloves,
nutmeg, and mace were available there; the Portuguese did
not go there; it could be reached from Africa via the Soenda
Strait, without running the risk of approaching the Portuguese outpost on the Straits of Malacca.

The first Dutch expedition to the Indies repeated an old
English error: it tried to go by way of a Northeast Passage.
In theory such a voyage, north of Scandinavia, Russia, and
Siberia and down through the Bering Strait into the Pacific,
is possible, but the Dutch could no more get their wooden
ships through the ice of the Polar Sea than they could get
them to the moon. The English had been stopped near Novaya Zemlya; the Dutch squadron sent out in June 1594 got
little farther. It was led by the great Arctic navigator Willem
Barents; Linschoten went along, for he would be useful if the
fleet got to the Indies. Barents went to the northern tip of
Novaya Zemlya but could not find a passage through the ice
that lay ahead; another ship of the squadron took a slightly
more southerly route into the Strait of Vaigatz and found
clear water, turning back only because it was too late in the
season to go on. This led to a second voyage by Barents in
1595, but the strait was impassable because of unusually severe weather, and a third the following year, in which he
tried to go across the North Pole and discovered the island of
Spitsbergen before meeting impenetrable ice. On this voyage
Barents perished, and there were no further Dutch attempts
to find the Northeast Passage to the Indies.

During Linschoten's involvement with the first of the

Barents voyages, some of his countrymen, tempted by the tales of spices in his *Itinerary*, were organizing at Amsterdam a trading company to sponsor Indies voyages by the Portuguese route. This Company for Far Lands, as it was called, was founded by nine merchants in March 1594 with a capital of 290,000 guilders. Four ships were built, three of them (*Mauritius*, *Hollandia*, and *Amsterdam*) of 300 to 400 tons, the fourth a 50-ton yacht, the *Duifke* ("Little Dove"). They sailed from the island of Texel at Holland's northernmost point in April 1595, with 230 men and 18 officers, bound for the Cape of Good Hope and the East Indies. The fleet carried democracy to a fault: there was no supreme commander, and major decisions had to be made by a council of delegates from all the ships, though several of the officers were regarded as first among equals and could break ties.

Calm weather slowed the southward voyage, the unfamiliar stars made navigation difficult, and scurvy was a constant problem. By the time the fleet had rounded Africa and paused at Madagascar, 71 men were dead, and the rest so ill that months of rest were needed. By the time they set out again—in February 1596—it was the wrong season for crossing the Indian Ocean, and they did not reach the Strait of Soenda for four months. Though fierce disagreements were splitting the leadership of the fleet, they reached the port of Bantam on Java in the fifteenth month of the voyage and began to trade for spices. At first they were well received, but matters soon deteriorated as Cornelis Houtman, a hot-headed young merchant-captain who had emerged as the leader of this leaderless expedition, tried to beat down the going rate for pepper. When one party of Dutch went off to investigate the rest of the Java coast, Houtman and the others who remained in Bantam were imprisoned, and the local ruler entertained an offer from the Portuguese of Malacca to buy them for slaves. Eventually the Dutch prisoners were released, and after lengthy negotiations a commercial treaty was signed giving the Dutch trading rights in Bantam. Houtman torpedoed this, though, by seeking revenge for his imprisonment in acts of piracy; he ordered the seizure of some junks arriving from Banda with spices, and then took the fleet toward the Moluccas, intending to show Bantam that he could get along without its merchandise. Bantam passed word along the Java coast, and near Surabaya a Javanese attack took twelve Dutch lives; at another town, a friendly prince came out to meet them in the royal *prau*, and the edgy Hollanders opened fire, killing the prince, a priest, and a number of his subjects. This rendered further landings on Java impossible. The ships still had not taken on any important cargo; 150 men were now dead, including the ablest officers, and the others could not agree on the conduct of the voyage; Houtman wished to go on to the Moluccas, the weary sailors did not. When Houtman's chief opponent died mysteriously, the crew accused him of poisoning the man, and put him in irons, though he was subsequently freed. The Molucca voyage was dropped and the ships headed for home, after one, the *Amsterdam*, was scuttled as unserviceable. On the way back, the Dutch visited Bali, which had no spices to offer but whose women were so attractive that two crewmen deserted. The fleet arrived at Texel on August 14, 1597, after a sour voyage lasting more than two years.

Just 89 men—little more than a third of the complement—had survived, the cargo holds of the three returning ships were nearly empty, and the Dutch had needlessly acquired a bad name in Java on their first venture. Yet Houtman had managed to bring home 245 bags of pepper, 45 tons of nutmeg, 30 bales of mace, and some porcelain plates originally from China, and the proceeds of the sale of this modest cargo more than covered the expenses of the expedition. Even a bungled and mismanaged voyage could show a profit, the Dutch merchants realized. Immediately the Company for Far Lands began to plan a second expedition that would avoid the errors of the first. And soon the States-General was besieged with petitions from other investors wishing to form their own syndicates for exploitation of the East Indies. The Dutch rush to the Orient was on.

Among the companies founded at that time was a second Amsterdam group, the New Company for Voyages to East India. The merchants of Zealand, unwilling to let the burghers of the province of Holland get too far ahead of them, organized two companies; two more were founded in Rotterdam. Then the Company for Far Lands and the New Company for Voyages merged to form a supercompany in Amsterdam, so that in 1598 there were five rival Dutch trading firms in all, which sent a total of 22 ships to the East Indies.

The consolidated Amsterdam group, now known as the Old Company, sent eight ships from Texel on May 1, 1598, under the command of a merchant named Jacob von Neck who took special lessons in navigation for the expedition. Like the 1595 fleet, they went by way of the Cape of Good Hope in defiance of the Portuguese, who now were unable to protect their old monopoly of this route. Storms separated the ships soon after they rounded Africa; Neck went on with three vessels to Madagascar and then to Bantam, completing the outward voyage in only seven months. To his surprise he found that Hollanders were welcome there, since the Portuguese had recently tried to invade the town in retribution for Bantam's having allowed the earlier Dutch fleet to land there. The Bantamese had driven the Portuguese away, destroying three of their ships, but they expected them to return some day and shrewdly decided to ally themselves with the Dutch against that eventuality. Neck cheerfully promised to aid the

Bantamese, and with good will reestablished he swiftly purchased enough spices to fill his ships.

On the last day of 1598 the five other vessels arrived at Bantam. Prevented by the storm from making rendezvous at Madagascar, they had landed instead at a small, uninhabited island in the Indian Ocean which they named Mauritius in honor of Maurice of Nassau, though it had been visited 91 years earlier by a Portuguese who called it Ilha do Cerne. Mauritius was a fertile, agreeable place, well suited for a way station for ships bound to the East Indies; it had wood, fresh water, and an abundance of wildlife, including huge flocks of a queer, waddling flightless bird no one had ever seen before. Two of these birds were taken along and ultimately reached the Netherlands. They were the first dodos to get to Europe, and very nearly the last, for Dutch settlers on Mauritius hunted them so efficiently that none was seen alive after 1681.

Neck loaded a fourth ship with spices, took one of the dodos, and headed for home early in 1599. It was agreed that the four other vessels, commanded by Wybrand van Warwyck and Jacob van Heemskerck, would go east to explore the Spice Islands first. Neck was in Amsterdam in July 1599, having completed the round trip in a shorter time than it took the 1595 fleet to reach Bantam; he brought 600,000 pounds of pepper, 250,000 pounds of cloves, and lesser amounts of other spices. A contemporary chronicler noted, "For as long as Holland has been Holland, such richly laden ships as these have never arrived." The cargo provided a 100-percent profit over all expenses for the Old Company. Meanwhile, the rest of the fleet had divided again, Heemskerck taking two ships to the Banda Islands, Warwyck going to Ternate. Banda was then the only place in the world that produced nutmeg and mace—both spices coming from the same fruit—and Heemskerck took on a valuable load, though he commented about the Javanese traders with whom he had to deal, "A man needs seven eyes if he does not want to be cheated." Warwyck did well in Ternate, too. As usual, the Sultan of Ternate was engaged in war with Tidore, where the Portuguese were still established, and he was also undergoing attack from the Spaniards of the Philippines. Since the English, despite Drake's vows of friendship, had never returned, Ternate turned to the Dutch as protectors against Spain and Portugal and invited them to set up a factory there. Thus Neck's voyage was wholly successful: not only did it bring great profit to the Old Company, but it gave the Dutch trading posts at Bantam, Banda, and Ternate.

The two Zeeland companies had not done so well with their expeditions, both of which went to sea some weeks ahead of Neck's. The first, which departed in March 1598, was led by the unfortunate Cornelis Houtman, who hired as pilot John Davis of the unhappy second Cavendish voyage. Houtman did not dare to go to Bantam after the events of 1596, and he made for Sumatra instead, taking so long to get there that Neck, who had set out after him, was nearly home before Houtman got to the East Indies at all. At Sumatra, Houtman succeeded in buying some few hundred tons of pepper in Atjeh, but then got into a dispute with the natives and was slain with many of his men. Davis saved one ship and wandered with it along the Malay coast, enduring many hardships, before bringing it back to the Netherlands in July 1600. The other Zeeland expedition left in April 1598; one of its three ships capsized in the English Channel, the other two required a year to get to Bantam, and when they arrived they found that Neck had cleaned out the entire pepper crop. They had to wait eight months for the new harvest and paid an exorbitant price for what they got. Though they returned safely to their home port, their profits were small.

All three of the 1598 expeditions—the two from Zeeland and the one of the Old Company of Amsterdam—took the traditional route to the Indies, via the Cape of Good Hope, as the ships of the Company for Far Lands had done in 1595. The remaining two ventures of 1598, sailing from Rotterdam, were conceived in bolder fashion. They chose to go by the western route, to go through the Strait of Magellan. It was an ambitious and, in the end, unwise experiment, but out of it the Dutch got their first circumnavigation.

3

One of these Rotterdam companies was organized by refugees from Spanish-occupied Antwerp, which may explain their choice of a route. To go by way of Magellan's strait was to trespass on the territory of Spain; it was an expression of contempt for King Philip II. The leaders of the syndicate were Pieter van der Hagen and Johan van der Veken. They chose as their commander one Jacques Mahu and provided him with five ships, whose names can be translated as *Hope*, *Faith*, *Charity*, *Fidelity*, and *Good News*. The vessels were furnished both for trade and for war, the intention being to amortize the cost of reaching the Indies by looting the Spanish coastal settlements of Chile and Peru.

They sailed from Rotterdam on June 27, 1598. Progress was slow; it took two months simply to reach the Cape Verde Islands; en route to the coast of Guinea late in September, Mahu died and was succeeded as commander by Simon de Cordes, captain of the *Faith*, in accordance with the instructions of the syndicate. Cordes moved from his ship to the flagship, the *Hope*, and there was a general reshuffling of the other officers. Attempts to pick up provisions in Guinea were frustrated by the Portuguese and by hostile natives, and 30 men were dead of scurvy before Cordes reached the New World. In the Strait of Magellan, which they entered on April 6, 1599, Cordes erred by not making a quick passage while he had the opportunity; though the winds were favorable until April 20, he wasted valuable time in a too-leisurely period of taking on water and firewood, and then the wind came from the west, so that the fleet could not leave. The ships were forced to lay up for the winter in a bay that Cordes named for himself. Even during occasional spells of good weather in the months that followed, Cordes refused to quit his bay; William Adams, the Englishman who was his chief pilot, wrote, "Many times in the winter we had the wind good to go through the Strait, but our general would not." It was a time of great suffering, and 120 men died, chiefly of starvation, though three perished from Indian attacks. (The natives were said to be of great stature, ten or 11 feet tall.) On August 23, Cordes at last gave orders to move on, and the half-frozen men, all but starved, who had stood in snowstorms to hear their pious but iron-souled commander deliver long sermons, staggered to their duties. The fleet emerged from the strait on September 3 into a turbulent sea, and four days later the mast of the *Good News* was disabled in a gale. She fired a gun as a distress signal, and the other vessels went to her aid, except for Cordes' *Hope*. The flagship, cut off from the rest of the fleet by a thick fog, continued sailing after the others had halted and soon left them far behind. When he discovered that he had lost his fleet, Cordes proceeded toward the planned rendezvous point at the island of Santa Maria on the Chilean coast.

The *Good News* was repaired and, with her three companions, went in search of the *Hope;* but another storm on September 10 dispersed the fleet. The *Good News*, commanded by Dirck Gherritz, was carried far south of the strait, to a latitude Gherritz calculated at 64°S. If he was correct, he came closer to the South Pole than any man before Captain Cook, and he reported seeing "a high country, with mountains, which were covered with snow like the land of

Norway." On this account Gherritz has been credited with the discovery of the sub-Antarctic island group later known as the South Shetlands, but few modern authorities believe he actually saw them or even that he reached so high a latitude. When he recovered control of his vessel, Gherritz made for Chile, but he missed Santa Maria and was captured by the Spaniards at Valparaiso.

The *Charity* came safely out of the storm and started north. On October 9 she caught up with Cordes and the *Hope*, which had been driven south by the storm to 54°30′; they sailed together for eight or ten days toward Chile, then were separated again. The *Charity* stopped at the island of Mocha, where her captain and 27 men were killed by the natives, and went on to Santa Maria, reaching that island early in November. Four days later the *Hope* arrived. After losing sight of the *Charity* the second time, Cordes had spent nearly a month ashore in 46°S., resting and purchasing sheep and potatoes for bells and knives; then he had sailed for Santa Maria, but chose to make a second mainland stop on the way. He led a shore party to obtain provisions and was killed, with 23 of his men, by the Indians at the instigation of Spaniards.

Since both ships had lost so many sailors, the new captains of the *Hope* and the *Charity* discussed combining crews at Santa Maria and scuttling one ship, but they could not agree on which ship to destroy so both were kept. They left Santa Maria on November 27, having waited a decent time for the other three vessels of the fleet. Since their complements were so weakened, the *Hope* and the *Charity* had to forgo the project to raid the Spanish ports, but instead of going to the Spice Islands, as might be expected, they sailed for Japan, where the woolen cloth that was their chief cargo was thought to have a good market. They traveled together across the Pacific until February 23, 1600, when they lost sight of each other. The *Hope* was never heard of again, but the *Charity* did reach Japan in mid-April with 24 men on board, 17 of them sick. Among the survivors was William Adams, the English pilot. The Japanese, thinking they were pirates, imprisoned them at first, but they were freed by royal order, and Adams was taken to Osaka for presentation to the emperor. "He viewed me well [Adams wrote], and seemed to be wonderful favorable. There came one that could speak Portuguese; by him the King demanded of what land I was, and what moved us to come to his land, being so far off. He asked me divers other questions, as, what way we came to his country. Having a chart of the whole world, I showed him through the Straits of Magellan, at which he wondered, and thought me to lie. Then, from one thing and another, I abode with him till midnight. Two days after, he sent for me again, and enquired of the qualities and conditions of our country, of wars and peace, of the beasts and cattle; and it seemed he was well content with my answers to his demands."

So began Adams' remarkable career as the first and only English samurai. The Japanese ruler refused to let him go home, but put him to work building ships and advising on nautical matters; Adams became a court favorite and was granted a pension, "about 70 ducats by the year, with two pounds of rice a day also. Now being in such grace and favor, by reason I learned him some points of geometry, and the mathematics, with other things, I pleased him so well, that what I said could not be contradicted." After five years he applied for leave to go home, "desiring to see my poor wife and children, according to conscience and nature," but he was politely and firmly ordered to remain. Adams lived on in Japan until his death in 1620, enjoying great prestige and wealth, and occasionally sent letters to England describing his adventures. He succeeded in procuring important commercial privileges for the Dutch in Japan, and also in winning permission for the other survivors of his voyage to depart on a later Dutch ship.

The last two members of the Rotterdam fleet, the *Fidelity* and the *Faith*, remained together when the ships were hit by the storm of September 10, 1599. They were thrust back toward the Strait of Magellan, entering it from the western side on September 27. They anchored just within the entrance until December 2, when they tried again to reach the Pacific. They did not succeed and returned to their anchorage, but six days later the *Fidelity* was blown from her harbor and driven into the Pacific. She went up the South American coast, raided some Spanish vessels, failed to find any of the other ships, and turned her course to the Moluccas. She was the only ship of the expedition that actually reached the Spice Islands, but not to any great success, for she made the mistake of landing at Tidore instead of Ternate and was captured by the Portuguese.

The *Faith*, left alone in the strait, did not attempt to continue the westward voyage. Her captain, Sebald de Weert, yielded reluctantly to the insistence of his men and agreed to return to Europe. On December 15 he sailed eastward to the Bay de Cordes, losing the ship's only boat when the rope by which it was being towed broke; as he approached the bay, Weert had a gun fired in case the *Fidelity* was nearby, and the faint sound of an answering cannon was heard. On the morning of the 16th a boat came toward them in the bay from the east which they thought must be from one of the ships of their fleet, but it proved to belong to the second Rotterdam expedition to the Indies, commanded by Olivier van Noort, which was on its way westward through the strait on what was to be the first Dutch circumnavigation. The *Faith* fell in with Noort's fleet and followed it for a few days, but could not keep up with it, since she was storm-damaged and had lost nearly two-thirds of her company since leaving Rotterdam. Once more left by herself, the *Faith* returned to the Bay de Cordes at Christmas, and on the first day of 1600 two boats from Noort's fleet appeared, bearing Noort himself with the news that his ships were held up by contrary winds a little farther on in the strait. After a brief conference Noort went back to his stranded fleet, and on January 8 Weert sent him a message asking for a two-months' supply of bread so that he could proceed on his way. Noort, who was not notable for generosity, replied that he had a long voyage of his own to make and had scarcely enough bread for himself.

Three days later the *Faith* moved toward the eastern entrance of the strait. When some of Weert's seamen went ashore on a small island to hunt penguins, they found a Patagonian woman in hiding, "of large stature, and strong in proportion." She had been injured and seemed stunned by some great tragedy, but Weert could not communicate with her and, giving her a knife, let her go in peace. Later he learned that she was a survivor of a tribe that had been virtually exterminated seven weeks earlier by Noort's men in a barbarous reprisal for the deaths of three Hollanders killed by other Indians.

Weert left the strait on January 21. On his way north in the Atlantic he became the third to discover the Falkland Islands, after John Davis and Richard Hawkins, and afterward they were sometimes called Sebald de Weert's Islands, or the Sebaldines. (Their present name, which seems quite undeserved, was given them in 1690 in honor of Viscount Falkland, an English naval official.) The *Faith* arrived in the Netherlands on July 13, 1600, having been gone two years and 16 days, of which nine months had been spent in the Strait of Magellan and only 24 days in the Pacific. She was the only one of Jacques Mahu's five ships to come back; the only accomplishment of the expedition was the compiling of an excellent chart of the strait by one of Weert's mates; the promoters of the voyage lost their capital, and one, Pieter van der Hagen, was forced into bankruptcy.

4

The fifth of the 1598 Dutch voyages to the Indies was the circumnavigation of Olivier van Noort. Noort was scarcely an admirable character, but he was an enterprising one: a Rotterdam tavernkeeper who personally raised the money for his expedition, appeared before the States-General himself to win approval for the venture, nominated himself as his own commander, and took his ship all the way around the globe in a voyage lasting more than three years. His motives for going, apparently, were a mixture of greed and the lust for adventure. He was forty-four years old when he set out, and if he had any previous experience at sea we do not know of it. Perhaps decades of hearing sea stories from the customers of his tavern led Noort at last to go in quest of Moluccan spices and Spanish gold.

Apparently Noort was also his own chronicler. A journal of his expedition was published at Amsterdam in 1602 in Dutch, German, and French, with a Latin translation following in the same year in De Bry's collection of voyages. It was anonymous and references to Noort were in the third person, but from internal evidence the journal appears to be Noort's. It was entitled *Description of the Toilsome Voyage made round the World by Olivier van Noort, in which are related his strange adventures, and portrayed to the life in various plates, many strange things which happened to him, which he has therein met and seen.* This is our only source for details of this circumnavigation.

There were four ships, two of them financed by Noort, two by an Amsterdam syndicate; he had openly invited outside capital, to such an extent that even the Spaniards knew of the projected intrusion on their South American domain. Noort's flagship was the *Mauritius*, a large vessel of unknown tonnage; the "vice-admiral," or second ship, was the *Hendrick Frederick*, commanded by Pieter Claesz. Two small yachts accompanied them: the *Hope*, commanded by Jan Huydecooper, and the *Eendracht*, led by Pieter Esias de Lindt. (The last was a common Dutch ship's name in the seventeenth century; it meant "Unity" or "Concord.") Through confusion at the outset, the departure of the fleet was delayed for many weeks; the *Hope* and the *Hendrick Frederick* were late in preparation, and Noort sailed without them on August 1, 1598, and waited for them off the English coast for some weeks, at last returning in annoyance to Holland to get them. It was an inauspicious beginning.

On September 13 Noort set out again, with all four ships, from the Dutch port of Goeree. Six days later he put in at Plymouth and hired an English pilot named Melis, a veteran of Cavendish's circumnavigation. Six sailors from the *Hendrick Frederick* deserted during the two-day stay at Plymouth, taking with them the ship's boat, but the wind was strong from the east, and Noort, desperately eager to be on his way, refused to lose time recovering either the men or the boat. The fleet hurried toward North Africa, and on September 27 Noort tried his hand at piracy for the first time, boarding two Biscayan vessels encountered in passing.

Early in October they passed the Canary Islands; on the eighth, the *Hendrick Frederick* lost a second boat, which she was towing, and lost the man in the boat as well, as night came on. The next day Noort nearly found himself aground on the coast of North Africa when his men misunderstood the instructions of the English pilot; Melis told them to steer southwest, but they held a southerly course and were within half a mile of shore before anyone noticed.

They sighted the coast of Guinea on November 3; Noort

rounded the continent's entire bulge, coming on December 11 to the Portuguese island of Principe, where he sent a group of officers ashore to parley for provisions. The Portuguese seemed to honor their flag of truce, but only as a ruse to decoy more of the Dutchmen ashore. In a sudden attack they slew Melis, Noort's brother, Cornelis, and three others, the rest barely escaping alive. Noort sent 120 men—half his entire complement—to attack the Portuguese fort, but it proved impregnable, and two more Hollanders were killed and 16 wounded. Noort had to content himself with burning the plantations of sugar cane around the fort and left on the 17th, having obtained a supply of fresh water but nothing else.

Noort followed the coast southward. Evidently there was some disagreement about the point at which the fleet should make for South America, for on December 25, after calling a "council of war," Noort marooned a pilot named Jan Volkersz on the shore of what is now Gabon for alleged mutinous practices. (To Noort, as we will see, any serious opposition to his plans was mutiny.) While this was taking place some Dutch ships came by, and Noort learned from them that Jacques Mahu's fleet had stopped here a few months earlier, and that Mahu and many of his men had died of scurvy and other diseases. Noort resolved to get quit of the African coast at once. He turned westward, crossing the Atlantic in five weeks and making Brazil on February 3, 1599. Six days later he anchored off Rio de Janeiro, but the Portuguese, warned to expect Dutch ships, shelled them from their shore batteries and drove them off. Several further attempts to land and obtain fresh fruit and other necessary provisions also failed, and storms did great damage to the *Eendracht*.

On March 20, in 31°S. on the Brazilian coast, a gloomy Noort called another council and presented a bleak account of their prospects. Winter was coming on, and many of the men were down with scurvy; it seemed suicidal to go toward the Strait of Magellan or even to seek winter shelter at Port Desire, and Noort had decided to wait out the season at the island of St. Helena, whose virtues had been so eloquently praised in the narratives of Cavendish's voyage. But St. Helena is a small isle in a great sea, and Noort's navigational skills were limited; he sailed east, missed St. Helena, and was almost back to Africa before he realized it. After wandering the South Atlantic until the end of May, Noort came to what he thought was the island of Ascension, which lies almost exactly midway between Africa and Brazil in 8°S. His reckoning turned out to have been off by some 12 degrees of latitude and a thousand miles of longitude, for he was actually at Brazil once again in 20°21′S. On June 1 the ships anchored near the mainland and were again driven off by Portuguese; a day later Noort was able to halt at an island called Santa Clara, where the sick men were taken ashore. There were five deaths from scurvy, but the others recovered upon eating the "sour plums" found on the island, and there was no Portuguese harassment.

Noort decided here to abandon the leaky and unsafe *Eendracht;* she was unloaded, dismantled, and burned. Two more mutineers were brought before Noort's "council of war" and were sentenced to be marooned. A third man, Gerrit Adriaensz, had wounded a pilot in a knife fight and was condemned to a cruel but common punishment of the time: he was pinned to the mast by a knife through his hand, there to remain until he should release himself by pulling the hand away.

On June 21 the three ships headed south, stopping at the Island of São Sebastião to catch fish and take on fresh water, and after a stormy passage in the worst season of the year they came to Port Desire on September 20. Thus it had taken a year and seven days merely to get from Holland to

[*406*]

Patagonia. Noort's *Toilsome Voyage* declares, "In an island three miles from thence southwards, they furnished themselves with store of penguins and fishes. Of those fowls they took fifty thousand, being as big as geese, with eggs innumerable, which proved very refreshing to the diseased. Here they careened their ships and set up a smith's forge. They went up the rivers the fifth of October, and going on land, found beasts like stags and buffalos [!], and multitudes of ostriches; in one nest they took nineteen eggs which the hen had forsaken." That day Captain Huydecooper of the *Hope* died of scurvy. Pieter Esias de Lindt, who had been captain of the *Eendracht*, replaced him, and the *Hope* was renamed for Lindt's former ship.

Indians were seen on shore for the first time on October 20. Noort went toward them into two boats, but they disappeared; landing, he took 20 men on an inland march in search of them, leaving five men in the boats with orders not to stir from them. The weather was cold, and the five soon went ashore to keep warm by walking about. Some 30 natives came upon them, "tall in stature, their looks fierce, their faces painted," and killed three of the men with stone-tipped arrows. Noort, returning from an unsuccessful exploration, learned of the calamity from the two survivors and vowed grimly to take revenge.

He left Port Desire on October 29 and by November 4 was at Cape Vírgines, the headland guarding the approach to the Strait of Magellan. Wind, rain, hail, and snow assailed them here; three times they entered the strait, only to be driven back into the Atlantic each time. Noort's *Mauritius* lost three anchors in this process, and he sent word to Captain Claesz of the *Hendrick Frederick* to furnish him with an anchor at once. Claesz refused and a hot exchange of messages followed, with Noort demanding an anchor and the other captain ignoring the order. Finally, says *The Toilsome*

Voyage, Claesz replied to an outright command by saying "that he was as much master as Olivier van Noort himself; which answer terribly angered the Admiral; but he deferred taking notice of it till a more convenient opportunity."

They entered the strait a fourth time, on November 22. While passing through the first narrows, they saw a man on the southern shore running toward them; he wore a cloak and seemed to be a European. A boat was sent to him from the *Mauritius*, and as it drew close, it became obvious from his painted face and his dancing and jumping that he was a native. He was of ordinary stature, says the journal; the Dutch greeted him with a volley of rifle fire, but he escaped unharmed.

Deeper in the strait, the fleet halted at the two small islands known as the Penguin Islands, and two boats went out when more natives were seen ashore. About 40 Patagonians gathered on a high cliff and, as though believing the Dutch had come merely to collect penguins, threw down some birds to them in the hope it would induce them to leave. Noort's men were bent on vengeance, though. They ascended the cliff; the Indians shot arrows at them, but were met with a fusillade of musketballs and fled in disarray, taking refuge in a hillside cave where they had previously left their women and children. This they attempted to defend with their bows and arrows, and they succeeded in wounding three or four of the Dutch, but the attackers did terrible destruction with their guns, not ceasing until the last of the tribesmen lay dead. Noort's journal relates the details of this massacre in a calm, matter-of-fact tone as though it were quite unexceptionable to slaughter 40 innocent men as reprisal for the deaths of three Dutch sailors in another part of the country.

Within the cavern Noort's men found frightened, naked women huddling over their children; many of the mothers and some of the children had been slain by the gunfire. There was no further bloodshed, but four boys and two girls were carried off as trophies to the ships. One of the boys later learned to speak a little Dutch and gave Noort some information about his people, which found its way, probably in highly garbled form, into *The Toilsome Voyage.* The boy said that his own tribe was named Enoo, and that Noort had killed every adult male in it; he named four other tribes, of which three, like the unfortunate Enoo, were of normal stature; the fourth, who were known as Tirimenen, were "great people like giants, being from ten to eleven feet high; and they came to make war against the other tribes, whom they reproached for being eaters of ostriches." Obviously Noort was hearing what he wished to hear, but these scraps of unlikely ethnology were the only benefits gained from the extermination of the tribe of Enoo. Sebald de Weert, seven weeks later, came upon one surviving woman of the tribe when he stopped at the same island.

Noort moved westward, looking for the ruined Spanish town that Cavendish had renamed Port Famine, but he could find no trace of it. Early in December he anchored at a good-sized bay which he named for himself; here a forge was set up and carpenters went to work building a 37-foot boat, which took 12 days. Sebald de Weert and his *Faith* were encountered in mid-December, and Weert told the somber tale of the Mahu fleet: the death of many men, the months wasted in the strait, the scattering of the ships in the Pacific. Weert joined Noort's fleet, but when Noort got under sail on December 18, the dilapidated *Faith* was quickly left behind. The next day, when Noort anchored a little to the west, his second in command, Captain Claesz, did not, but, taking advantage of a fair wind, sailed on, firing signal guns as though he were commander in chief. Not until Christmas Day did Noort catch up with him.

The fleet now was anchored near the western end of the

strait, and here Noort struck at last against Claesz: another "council of war," dominated by Noort, ruled that the vice-admiral's independent and insubordinate conduct had a tendency to arouse mutinous feelings in the fleet. It was ordered that Claesz be seized and kept as a prisoner aboard Noort's flagship to await trial; he was given three weeks to prepare his defense. So firm was Noort's authority that he had no difficulty in removing Claesz from the *Hendrick Frederick* and imprisoning him on the *Mauritius*.

Strong winds from the west prevented Noort from leaving the strait, and he fell back to the east as far as an anchorage that he named Mauritius Bay, where he saw 1599 out. From this bay many channels led to the southeast, and Noort found lakes of fresh water in which ice floated, though it was then "the heart of summer" in the southern hemisphere. He conjectured that broken islands and not a continuous mainland must lie south of the strait. Rain fell daily now, and there was little to eat except mussels, but Noort's crew was in surprisingly good health, with only four men sick out of 151. He had lost 97, though, since leaving Holland.

On January 8, 1600, came a melancholy letter from Sebald de Weert, who was anchored in a bay to the east. Weert asked for a supply of bread, and Noort refused, making a reply that became notorious in the Netherlands: this was not a part of the world, he told Weert, where bread could easily be bought.

Noort now went westward again against storms and contrary winds. The trial of Captain Claesz was held on January 24 in a small bay near the mouth of the strait. His defense failed to sway Noort and the other officers, and Claesz was condemned to be put ashore. *The Toilsome Voyage* declares that the deposed captain was given "some bread and wine, but there was no place for him to go on that wild coast. He would either starve to death or be eaten by the natives.

After this was done the General [Noort] ordered a prayer to be said in the whole fleet, and every one was warned to take this example to heart."

Unfavorable winds held the fleet trapped only a short distance from the Pacific for more than a month. Noort did not wish to follow the example of Simon de Cordes and pass a winter in the strait, and so. at a meeting of officers it was decided that they would wait only two months more for an opportunity to enter the South Sea. If by May they had not succeeded, they would swing about and make for the East Indies by way of the Cape of Good Hope. However, this resort was unnecessary; on February 29,* 1600, this maladroit but determined commander was at last able to lead his fleet into the Pacific, nearly a year and a half after leaving home.

5

More skillful admirals than Noort had suffered separations of their fleets coming out of the strait, and in anticipation of this he had selected the Chilean island of Santa Maria as the rendezvous point. The seas were rough, storms were frequent, and in a thick fog on March 12 the *Hendrick Frederick* disappeared. The *Mauritius* and the new *Eendracht* continued to the island of Mocha, the customary first stop for ships leaving the strait. Drake and Cavendish had both been attacked by natives there during their circumnavigations; and less than five months previously, 28 Dutch seamen of Simon de Cordes' fleet had been slain there. Noort knew nothing of that last event, but he was wary of the island's reputation and sent a man ashore as an envoy, bearing knives, beads, and other trinkets. He was Jan Claesz, one of the two men who had been sentenced to marooning at the island of

* By the Gregorian calendar system employed today, February of 1600 would not have had a 29th day; but the Gregorian calendar was not adopted by Protestant countries until the eighteenth century, and Noort used the old Julian reckoning.

Santa Clara off Brazil; possibly he was a relative of the castaway vice-admiral, Pieter Claesz. He and his fellow mutineer, Gerraert Willem Prinz, had been condemned "to be abandoned in any strange country where they could hereafter be of service," a far milder penalty than had been meted out to Captain Claesz, and Noort had been carrying them both as prisoners ever since. Now he offered to pardon Jan Claesz if he returned safely from his dangerous mission to the Mochans.

Claesz succeeded in winning the islanders' favor, and the next day Noort was able to purchase sheep, fowls, and fruits for hatchets and knives. Two native chieftains came aboard the *Mauritius* and stayed all night, and some of the Hollanders visited the village and were treated to a drink made of fermented corn. On March 24 Noort sailed north toward Santa Maria and at noon the next day, nearing the island, saw a ship lying at anchor there; he thought it might be the missing *Hendrick Frederick*, but it proved to be a Spanish ship, the *Buen Jesus*, which he pursued all night and captured the following morning. The Spaniard had been stationed on that part of the coast expressly to watch for foreign ships coming from the Strait of Magellan, and Noort was pleased to have intercepted her before she could give alarm of his presence. In the course of the chase, he had gone well to the north of Santa Maria, and he learned now from the Spanish captain that prevailing southerly winds would make it impossible to get back to that island. Though by prior agreement he was supposed to wait there two months for the *Hendrick Frederick*, Noort bowed to necessity and kept going north, putting a prize crew aboard the *Buen Jesus* and taking her with him. (Sailing alone, the *Hendrick Frederick* raided Spanish shipping as far as the coast of Nicaragua and then crossed the Pacific safely, only to be wrecked on the coast of Ternate.)

Noort's next stop was Valparaiso, where he raided some Spanish ships in the harbor, taking provisions from them but finding no treasure. He found out here that Simon de Cordes had lost his life, and received letters from Dirck Gherritz of Cordes' fleet, telling of his captivity in Lima. On April 1 Noort released the captain of the *Buen Jesus* and most of his men, hoping to bring about Gherritz' release, but in this he was unsuccessful. He took the Spanish ship with him and kept her pilot, Juan de San Aval, along with two Indians and two Negroes.

The northward cruise was unsatisfying, for the Spaniards had had months to prepare for Noort's coming, and he found the pickings slim. On April 6 he had one of his own seamen shot for stealing provisions; on the 20th, near Arequipa, the fleet was enveloped in a dry fog of white sand, and Noort lost sight of the *Eendracht* and the *Buen Jesus* for two days. As they neared Callao, united again, Noort learned from his Spanish pilot that three large ships of the King of Spain were waiting for him in that port, and so he ordered a wide detour out to sea to avoid them. Emanuel, one of the Negroes taken from the *Buen Jesus*, declared about this time that the ship had been carrying some five tons of gold when Noort had sighted it and that her captain had thrown it all overboard during the chase. San Aval and the other Negro denied this, but Noort had them tortured until they admitted the truth of the story. It is difficult to understand what satisfaction this interrogation could have brought him.

After a fruitless chase of two Spanish ships encountered some 90 miles off shore, Noort steered toward the coast again; then, still worrying about those three warships at Callao, he thought better of it and decided to end his attempts at piracy along the South American coast. Before crossing the Pacific, he proposed to stop for provisions at Cocos Island, west of Panamá. But finding remote islands was not Noort's

specialty, and he missed Cocos through inaccurate calculations of latitudes. On May 20, having searched three weeks
for it, he held a council and declared his intention to sail at
once for the Philippines by way of the Ladrones.

Not until the middle of June did the fleet pick up the
trade winds and begin to make much westward progress. On
June 30 Noort dispensed with the services of Juan de San
Aval. *The Toilsome Voyage* declares, "The General, with
the advice of his council of war, ordered the Spanish pilot to
be cast into the sea: for although he ate in the cabin, and the
General showed him entire friendship, he had nevertheless
the effrontery to say, because he found himself ill, that we
wanted to poison him; which he not only said in presence of
all the officers, but afterwards maintained; for which reason,
the General with the said officers found good to dispatch
him; and therefore we threw him into the sea, leaving him to
sink, to the end that he should not ever again reproach us
with any treachery."

The rudder of the *Buen Jesus* broke on August 15, and
since the Spanish prize had become very leaky anyway, she
was abandoned. The *Mauritius* and the *Eendracht* went on
together to Guam in the Ladrones, arriving in mid-September. More than 200 canoes came to the ships, bearing fish,
coconuts, bananas, and gourds of water to trade for iron,
"crying Hiero, Hiero, that is, Iron, Iron, with greediness
overturning their canoes against the ship's side, which they
regarded not, being expert swimmers, and could easily recover their boats, goods, and selves. They were subtle deceiv-
ers, covering a basket of coconut shells, with a little rice in
the top, as if they had been full of rice; and upon fit opportunity snatching a sword out of the scabbard, and leaping into
the sea, where with deep and long diving they secured themselves from shot." Noort's Pacific crossing had been remarkably swift, considering his usual tendencies—less than two

months—but nevertheless many of his men were ill with scurvy, and they benefited greatly from the fresh fruit obtained on Guam. After a few days Noort sailed on, well supplied with water by frequent rainstorms, and on October 15, in the second month of the third year of his voyage, he came to the island of Luzon in the Philippines. He sent a boat ashore to purchase fruit from the natives. The next day a large boat came out from the island with a Spaniard aboard. Noort thoughtfully had a Spanish flag hoisted and ordered one of his men to don a friar's robe; thus the Spaniard was persuaded to come aboard. Receiving him courteously, Noort declared that his ships were French and wished to go on to Manila to purchase provisions, but had lost their way owing to the death of their pilot. The Spaniard took this blandly delivered tale at face value, told Noort of his exact position, and commanded the islanders to bring rice, hogs, and poultry to sell to the "Frenchmen."

Several days later, while still engaged in taking these goods aboard, Noort had less gullible visitors: a Spanish officer and a priest. The officer sternly informed Noort that, while friendship existed between Spain and France, it was none the less the strict policy of the King of Spain to forbid strangers to trade at Spanish ports overseas or to purchase provisions there. He asked to see Noort's royal commission, and, greatly enjoying himself, Noort produced a document in Dutch, signed by the Prince of Orange. The hoax was exposed; the chagrined Spaniards were ushered to shore, and Noort, having obtained all the victuals he needed, sailed on.

On October 21 he seized a small Spanish-owned bark laden with rice and fowls. The crew escaped; the Dutch took the cargo and sank the ship. Shortly they came close to going to the bottom themselves, for a storm struck them in the San Bernardino Strait and nearly took off their sails and masts. At night on the 24th they anchored off the island of Capul, whose inhabitants promptly fled their homes, so that Noort could obtain no provisions from them; here a Londoner named John Caldway, "an excellent musician," strayed from the shore party and was slain from ambush. Expecting a full-scale attack, Noort mounted all his guns, but the natives did not appear. He burned their villages to repay them for Caldway's death. On the 29th, Emanuel, one of the Negro slaves, escaped, "contrary to the great professions he had made." The other black, Bastien, admitted under close examination that he had known of Emanuel's plan and would have done the same himself if he had had the chance. "The General seeing by this confession the pure villainy of these Negroes," says *The Toilsome Voyage*, "commanded this one to be shot."

In a leisurely manner Noort advanced toward Manila, looting every vessel that came his way. On November 6 he took and sank a Spanish bark. A day later he made prize of a Chinese sampan bound for Manila with a cargo of rice and lead. A short time afterward, he took two more barks, carrying 250 fowls and 50 hogs. Noort sent some of his own men aboard the sampan as a prize crew, leaving five of the Chinese on her as well. Several of the Chinese who spoke Portuguese he brought to the *Mauritius* and learned from them the pleasing news that 400 Chinese vessels called at Manila every year between Christmas and Easter, and that two Japanese ships were expected there shortly with a cargo of iron and other metals. The Moluccas and their spices could wait; Noort resolved to intercept as many of these Manila-bound freighters as he could find.

The sampan slipped away in the night on November 21, taking six of Noort's men along; he supposed that they had kept a negligent guard and had had their throats slit by the five Chinese. Three days later he arrived at the Bay of Manila, coolly intending to station himself at the entrance to the harbor until February, picking off all incoming ships. One of the Japanese vessels arrived on December 3. She was a 50-ton ship of strange form, "the forepart like a chimney, the sails of reed or twisted mat, the anchors of wood, the cables of straw," carrying flour, fish, hams, and irons. Noort helped himself to some provisions and a wooden anchor, although with curious politeness he chose to pay the Japanese a small sum for their goods. "These Japanese are people of brown complexions," says *The Toilsome Voyage*, "and have manly voices. Their captain presented to the General a boy of his country." Noort observed that they "make themselves bald, except a tuft left in the hinder part of the head," and was much taken by the sharpness of Japanese swords: "They told us that there were scimitars in Japan which would, with one stroke, cut through three men, and that in selling these scimitars, they made the proof on certain slaves."

On the 9th, the Dutch took a Spanish ship laden with palm wine, and on the 12th, a sampan carrying rice. Both vessels were stripped of their cargoes and burned. The Spaniards of Manila, meanwhile, outraged by the presence of a buccaneer at their front gate, were hurrying to outfit a pair of elderly galleons of war. The ships, the *San Antonio de Zebu* and the *Almiranta*, were not in fighting condition, for no one had anticipated a foreign pirate in the Philippines, and Noort had the run of the harbor for three weeks. On December 14, finally, the counteroffensive began.

Noort's two ships lay cozily at anchor just to the north of the entrance to the bay. The Spanish attackers came upon them so suddenly that there was no time to take up the *Mauritius'* anchor, and the cable had to be cut. Then the battle was joined. There were just 55 men on the *Mauritius*, 25 on the *Eendracht; The Toilsome Voyage* claims that each Spanish vessel carried 400 to 500 men, which is probably an exaggeration, but not an extreme one. As the Spaniards approached, the Dutch guns began firing. The Spaniards could not return the fire because the wind was strong, and to keep from being swamped by high waves they were forced to keep their gunports shut on the side facing Noort's ships. The Spanish commander, Antonio de Morga, braved this broadside and brought the *San Antonio de Zebu* up along the *Mauritius*. Dozens of Spaniards swarmed onto the deck of Noort's flagship, and the Dutch, giving way before greater numbers, were driven to take refuge belowdecks. When they had possession of the deck, the Spaniards dropped the *Mauritius'* sails and rigging and lowered the Dutch flag. When the men of the *Eendracht* saw the flagship striking colors, they assumed that Noort had surrendered, and tried to escape to the open sea; the *Almiranta* gave chase and soon captured her.

But Noort had not surrendered. For six hours the Spaniards were masters of his ship's deck, while he raged at his men, telling them to leave the cabins and go above to fight. Finally he cried that he would thrust a torch into the powder magazine and blow up the ship if they did not come forth. This threat was effective; the Dutch rushed upon the Spaniards with such vigor that they were driven back to their own vessel, taking with them Noort's flag. The ships separated and bombarded each other with heavy artillery for a short while; the *Mauritius* caught fire, but the *San Antonio de Zebu*'s forequarters were blown open, and she began to take in water rapidly and go down.

Paying no heed to the plight of the hundreds of Spanish sailors in the water, Noort's men extinguished the fire on their own ship, "our Lord God most mercifully saving us from these imminent perils." When Spaniards swam to the *Mauritius* and begged for help, they were clubbed or speared in the water. *The Toilsome Voyage* relates with quiet pride how the Dutch "steered through the midst of the Spaniards swimming all together in the sea, stabbing and killing many of them with pikes in passing, and firing great guns among them." Many of the Spaniards, however, were rescued by boats from the shore; Morga, in his account of the battle, estimated that he lost 50 men altogether in the fighting and by drowning. Noort, as soon as he could hoist sail, headed for the sea; he had lost five men, and 26 had been wounded. However, he had also lost the *Eendracht* with her entire complement, for he did not judge that he had enough strength to rescue her from her captor, the *Almiranta*. While Noort sailed toward Borneo, the *Eendracht* was brought into Manila, where her captain and all her crew were summarily executed as pirates.

The *Mauritius* reached Borneo on December 26. A Chinese pilot whom Noort had captured at Manila warned him to be on his guard at the great port of Brunei, where, as Magellan's men and many others since had discovered, foreigners were often treated treacherously. Noort sent the Chinese ashore bearing gifts and requesting leave to purchase pepper and provisions. He returned a day later accompanied by a native official, who first satisfied himself that the newcomers were not Spaniards before allowing Noort to do business. Some trading followed; Noort found that the linens he had brought from Holland had little appeal in Brunei, but he did well selling the Chinese textiles he had taken from the vessels looted off Manila. The bare-breasted Bruneian women proved to be tough bargainers, quick-witted and shrewd; they guarded their virtue well, too, as one Hollander found out when he fondled one, only to have her thrust a javelin at him with near-fatal effect. Noort remained cautious during these few days of commerce, and when, on January 1, 1601, he saw a hundred *praus* assembling near his ship, he had his men make ready to defend themselves. The islanders attempted to get on board, pretending that they bore gifts from their ruler, but were not permitted entry, and Noort gave orders for a speedy departure. The *Mauritius* was still in port two days later, though, when four natives slipped up to the ship in a *prau* to cut the anchor cable in the dark so that they would be hurled against the shore; but they were seen and fired upon, and swam away before doing any harm. Noort took possession of their *prau*, for he had lost his ship's last boat in Manila, and on the morning of January 4 he set sail.

Outside the harbor he encountered a Japanese junk whose captain was a Portuguese dwelling at Nagasaki. Noort hailed him, and there was an exchange of news by which the Dutch learned that a ship of the Mahu fleet had reached Japan and that William Adams had won favor at court. Noort asked the Portuguese to carry his good wishes to his countrymen in Japan and gave him a safe-conduct to protect him against any Dutch pirates he might meet.

Noort's hope now was to reach Java and pick up a load of pepper at Bantam, but he was without a pilot and had no charts of the area, and would have been helpless if he had not captured a Malayan ship and appropriated her pilot. With the Malay's help, Noort came around the western side of Borneo, but as he headed for the trading ports of Java's north shore he was caught by the west monsoon and carried eastward through the Java Sea, past Bantam and the other familiar towns. Since the *Mauritius* now had but one anchor left, with a weak, worn cable, Noort had no choice but to run before the wind, which took him finally into the Bali Strait, after he had called at one Javan town and taken on a cargo of mace. His skills were not equal to the task of getting back to Bantam, and so on February 11, when he was well south of Java in 13°S., he made his course toward the Cape of Good Hope and home.

Calms and crosswinds slowed the voyage, and at one point water had to be rationed; but on April 24 they saw land, and fires blazing on it, and knew they were near Africa.

They passed the Cape of Good Hope without coming close to shore and headed for St. Helena, which this time Noort was able to find, though he had searched in vain for it in May of 1599. On May 26, 1601, they called at St. Helena and refreshed themselves with fresh water, fish, and goat's meat. They departed on the 30th, crossed the equator on June 14 for the fourth time in their wanderings, and two days later met six ships from Amsterdam, commanded by Jacob van Heemskerck, that had set out in April for the East Indies by way of Africa. Noort proudly announced that he had spanned the world via Magellan's strait, but he had little else of note about which to boast. Through most of July he was becalmed in the weedy Sargasso Sea, so that the bread, worm-eaten though it was, was doled out in reduced allowances. But by August they were in the Azores, where Noort fired upon a Portuguese ship and had his mainmast shattered by return fire; on the 18th of that month he encountered three German ships out of Emden, which gave him bread and meat in exchange for pepper and rice and told him that he was farther from Europe than he thought he was; and on August 26 he anchored at Rotterdam after a voyage of three years. Noort, the only merchant-promotor to lead his own voyage to the Indies, had come home with but one ship out of four, 45 men out of 248, and no cargo of any consequence. His bungled venture had been the slowest of the four circumnavigations, had yielded nothing at all in the way of geographical information, had achieved nothing commercially, had not even been particularly notable as an enterprise of piracy. It had, furthermore, been marked by shameful cruelties in Patagonia and elsewhere. Yet the Dutch were well satisfied with Noort's expedition. Its value to them was purely symbolic, yet immense: it showed the world that a Hollander could be a circumnavigator, and by placing himself in the company of Magellan, Drake, and Cavendish, the tavern keeper Olivier van Noort gave his newly independent, still insecure little country a claim to be the equal of Spain and England on the seas.

6

The impact of Noort's achievement—such as it had been—was considerable, but the Netherlands could not prosper on symbolism alone. The burghers who comprised the trading syndicates demanded tangible profits. Noort, who had wiped out his own investment and that of his many backers, published his book and then presumably went back to his tavern, and the various spice companies, taking heed of the disaster of the Mahu fleet and the failure of Noort's, sent no more expeditions by way of the Strait of Magellan for a long time.

The East Indies boom continued, though. The Old Company of Amsterdam still led the way, but other syndicates proliferated. Even before the great success of Jacob van Neck's 1598–99 voyage was known, the Old Company had sent three more ships eastward in April 1599, under Steven van der Hagen. Hagen reached Bantam to find that his company's rivals from Zeeland had bought all the spices on the market, but he was able to take on a full cargo of cloves at Amboina. The repeated success of the Old Company inspired imitators, so that by 1601 there were ten companies in existence which in that year sent out 14 fleets totaling 65 ships. Competition was harsh as the Dutch vessels clustered about Ternate, Amboina, Banda, and Bantam, each scrabbling for special trade arrangements with the local merchants. The bitterness of this rivalry is indicated by a letter of instructions issued by the directors of the Old Company in 1601 to the captains of its Indies fleets: "You know as well as we do what losses it would cause us if the Zeeland ships were to arrive before ours are fully loaded. Therefore, buy! Buy everything you can lay your hands on, and load it as quickly as possible. Even if you have no room for it, keep on buying and bind it to yourselves for future delivery. You must see to it that we shall not suffer in the least at the hands of the Zeelanders."

The sixteenth century, which had begun with Portuguese ships uncertainly following the newly discovered sea route to the Indies, thus came to its close with Dutch companies embroiled in a sordid fight over commercial exploitation of the Spice Islands. The entire shoreline of South America had been discovered and examined minutely in that century; Magellan had found his strait and the Philippines; the Pacific had been explored from 40°N. to 10°S.; and, though everything below New Guinea and Java was still a mystery, the romance had otherwise departed from that great ocean. The Portuguese, demoralized by the absorption of their country into Spain, had failed to take advantage of their early start; the Spaniards seemed unable to make headway in the East Indies at all; the English appeared to prefer piracy to trade, though they would soon change that policy. By default, the Dutch were moving into the spice trade, but their advance was hampered by the divisiveness of their rampant free-enterprise system.

The logical solution to that was a monopoly, and in the summer of 1601 the Old Company of Amsterdam volunteered modestly for the position. "For many and various reasons," it told the States of Holland, which was that province's legislative body, "it is advisable that this commerce must be conducted by one administration, because if it is left in the hands of a number of companies, then this promising trade will come to naught." Pointing out that it was by far the most successful of the companies, having sent more than half of all the Indies ships—eight in 1598, three in 1599, ten in 1600,

13 thus far in 1601—the Old Company requested exclusive rights to trade east of the Cape of Good Hope for a period of 25 years.

The States of Holland decided that it could not grant so one-sided a request, even though some sort of consolidation was clearly desirable. It asked the States-General, the national legislative body, to consider the question. The States-General called a meeting of the Indies shippers at The Hague in December 1601, at which the general idea of an amalgamation was approved and an agreement quickly reached that Amsterdam should supply half the capital for the new company, Zeeland one-fourth, and the remaining provinces the rest. Zeeland, however, held out for an equal voice with Amsterdam in the company's management, which was obviously unacceptable to the representatives of the Old Company, and intricate negotiations followed, resulting in a major compromise: the company would have 17 directors, eight from Amsterdam, four from Zeeland, four from the other provinces, and one chosen in rotation from the smaller regions. Thereby Amsterdam would dominate the board but would never have a majority on it. These directors quickly became known as *De Heeren Zeventien*, "The Lords Seventeen," or simply as "The Seventeen."

After further haggling among the touchy, chauvinistic merchants, final papers were drawn and approved by the States-General, which on March 20 awarded a 21-year charter to the new United Dutch East India Company, the *Vereenigde Oost-Indische Compagnie*, known simply as the V.O.C. to the Dutch and to the islanders they were destined to rule for three and a half centuries. The company was granted a monopoly on all navigation east of the Cape of Good Hope or west of the Strait of Magellan; The Lords Seventeen were empowered to conclude treaties of peace and commercial agreements with native rulers, to build fortresses

and strongholds overseas, and to wage defensive war. Dutch
citizens who infringed on the V.O.C.'s monopoly were subject to the penalty of forfeiting their ships and cargoes. In the
46 clauses of the East India Company's charter, the Dutch
not only created the world's first modern publicly owned corporation, but laid the foundation for their astonishing Asian
empire.

7

The Lords Seventeen sent out their first fleet 11 days
after the incorporation of the V.O.C. Sebald de Weert took
three ships to the Indies on March 31, 1602, and Wybrand
van Warwyck followed with a dozen more on June 17. Weert
went to Ceylon, where the Maharajah of Kandy was looking
for an ally against the Portuguese; Warwyck's destination
was Atjeh on Sumatra. The Atjenese, who had stood off the
Portuguese very nicely for decades, gave Warwyck a cool
welcome, while Weert, after an initial good start in Ceylon,
involved himself in a civil war on that island, angered the
Maharajah of Kandy through unintentional breaches of etiquette and other blunders, and finally was murdered, with 46
of his men, while he sat as a guest at the maharajah's table,
in June 1603. Warwyck, though, moved on from Atjeh to
Bantam on Java and established small shoreside forts there
and at Surabaya. Next, he went to China, where he failed to
gain trading permission and lost 18 men to the Portuguese at
Macao, and he returned to the Netherlands in 1607, after an
absence of five years. His only accomplishment of significance
was the acquiring of a permanent foothold in Java.

Meanwhile, a second V.O.C. fleet, of 13 vessels and
1,200 men, had gone forth in December 1603 under Steven
van der Hagen. His orders called for him to try to drive the
Portuguese from Goa and Malacca, then to force the Spaniards from the Moluccas and even the Philippines. It was an

ambitious schedule; but when he reached Goa, he saw that the fortress was obviously impregnable, and he made no attempt to attack it, though he did strike up friendly relations with the Zamorin of Calicut and give the Dutch their first wedge on the Malabar Coast. By December 1604 he was at Bantam, where he left a garrison and some merchants; then he sailed on to Amboina, compelled the small Portuguese force there to surrender without a battle, and negotiated a treaty in which Amboina pledged allegiance to the Dutch States-General. That, with previous Dutch success at Ternate, gave the Netherlands a good grip on the chief sources of cloves. The squadron's next stop was Tidore, where a Spanish garrison was defeated, but the Dutch failed to leave an adequate garrison of their own behind and so did not achieve permanent control. At Banda another favorable treaty was obtained. Hagen did not try to invade Malacca, though, and returned to the Netherlands in July 1606, having accomplished a good deal even while falling far short of The Seventeen's grandiose plans.

Two small pinnaces in his fleet had carried out important voyages of their own. The *Delft* had gone to India's hitherto unexploited Coromandel Coast—its eastern shore—and obtained large quantities of cotton textiles, which it brought to Bantam. These were in demand in the Spice Islands and gave the Dutch a commodity with which spices could be purchased. The other pinnace, the *Duifke*, "Little Dove," which in 1595 had been part of the first Dutch fleet to go to the East Indies, sailed from Bantam in November 1605 under Willem Janszoon, followed the southern coast of New Guinea for a thousand miles, and came to the opening of the strait that Luis Vaez de Torres would discover two months later. Not realizing that the strait gave him clear passage, Janszoon turned south instead of entering it and sighted a low desert coast, Australia's Cape York Peninsula.

Janszoon is the probable discoverer of Australia, then, but he did not know that he had found *Terra Australis* at last, thinking that the land he saw was merely part of New Guinea. He came back to Bantam in June 1606, unaware of what he had done.

The third V.O.C. fleet sailed in May 1605, consisting of 11 ships headed by Cornelis Matelief, a former director of the company. He blockaded Malacca for four months, driving off a Portuguese relief fleet from Goa, but failed to take the town, so that Dutch ships plying the Bantam-Coromandel route had to continue to go the long way around the west coast of Sumatra instead of using the Straits of Malacca. At Bantam he learned that the Spaniards had overrun the small Dutch garrison on Tidore and, for good measure, had seized Ternate, taking the sultan, who favored the Dutch, as a captive to Manila. Matelief carried reinforcements to Amboina, which might next be threatened; then he sailed to the Moluccas with eight ships. Though he did not succeed in driving the Spaniards from Tidore and Ternate, he managed to set up a Dutch fort on Ternate in the face of Spanish opposition. He sailed for home early in 1608, shortly after a fourth V.O.C. squadron had reached Bantam.

The fluctuating fortunes of the Dutch East India Company were reflected in the price of its shares on Amsterdam's informal stock market. Issued at 100, they rose to 125 when the first cargoes of spices returned, to 140 upon the capture of Tidore and the treaty with Amboina, and above 200 by 1606. Then came news of the Spanish resurgence in the Moluccas, while the repeated failures to take Goa and Malacca indicated that Portuguese strength there had been underestimated; a further problem was the glut of pepper as a result of the early voyages' success, and shortly company shares were going at 60. The activities of a dissident director, Isaac Le Maire, did not improve the company's fortunes. Le Maire, a

restless, tempestuous merchant of enormous energy and ambition, was a refugee from the south, having been driven out
of Brabant by the Spaniards. In 1599 he had organized the
New Brabant Company, a syndicate of investors formerly
from the southern provinces, which had sent six ships to the
Indies. This was among the firms later absorbed into the
V.O.C., and Le Maire became a member of the United Company's executive board. He quarreled noisily with his fellow
directors, opposing them particularly on their choice of a
route. Despite the sad experiences of Mahu's and Noort's
fleets, Le Maire believed the Dutch should use the westward
path. He envisioned capturing and fortifying the Strait of
Magellan, driving Spain out of South America, and turning
the Pacific into a Dutch lake; ultimately, he maintained,
every nation bordering its waters would be a tributary of the
Netherlands. When the company rejected his plan, Le Maire
sold his stock, getting out in 1605 when the market was near
its crest. Then, hoping to win control, he initiated the first
bear raid in the history of capitalism, selling V.O.C. stock
short and spreading false rumors that drove the price to a low
point of 48. It seemed for a while as though the company
might have to liquidate; The Seventeen turned for help to the
States-General, which prohibited further short sales and ordered delivery within 30 days of all shares that had already
been sold short.

Le Maire's next recourse was to turn to Jan van Oldenbarneveldt, the country's most influential political leader,
and ask permission to send ships through the Strait of Magellan. Although the V.O.C. held an exclusive franchise for
such navigation, Le Maire said, it had thus far not sent a
single vessel by that route and deserved to be stripped of that
portion of its monopoly. Oldenbarneveldt disagreed. The only
possibilities Le Maire now saw were the Northeast and
Northwest Passages, for which the V.O.C., regarding them as

mythical, had not bothered to seek franchises. With the secret backing of France, Le Maire hired the English navigator Henry Hudson to search for a northern route. Hudson had already made voyages in 1607 and 1608 on behalf of England's Muscovy Company, trying to reach China by the Northeast Passage; but The Seventeen thwarted Le Maire's plans by hiring Hudson away from him. They sent him off in the *Half Moon* in 1609 on the voyage that, after many detours, brought him to the river that now bears his name, and led eventually to the settlement of the Dutch colony of New Amsterdam.

Le Maire subsided for a few years, and the United Company concentrated on strengthening its shaken position. One tactic it advocated was the limiting of Spain's power in the East Indies by destroying her ships in their home waters, and in 1606 and 1607 the States-General authorized raids against Spanish shipping in the Atlantic. Philip II of Spain had died in 1598, and his successor, Philip III, had little stomach for war; in 1604 he had ended one old enmity by making peace with the new King of England, James I, and as the Dutch started to harass his ships he let it be known that he favored a truce with the Netherlands, whose people were in theory still deemed rebellious subjects of Spain. Negotiations began secretly in 1607 for an agreement to end the state of war that had existed for the past 40 years. While these talks were going on, a Dutch fleet of more than two dozen warships was roving the coast of Portugal under the veteran commander Jacob van Heemskerck. When Heemskerck learned that a large Spanish fleet, including some of Spain's most valuable galleons, was gathered at Gibraltar, he went to the attack. The Dutch swept down on Gibraltar on April 25, 1607, and from early afternoon to dusk the battle raged. At the end of it, the entire Spanish fleet of 21 ships was destroyed, with the loss of thousands of men; no Dutch ship had gone down, and only about 100 men were killed, unfortunately including Admiral Heemskerck. The Gibraltar battle administered a permanent injury to Spanish naval strength, and by 1609 great Spain was forced to sign a 12-year truce with the tiny Netherlands, under the terms of which the Spaniards promised not to interfere with Dutch trade in the Orient.

Much still had to be done before the V.O.C. had the true monopoly it desired. The Spaniards hung on by a precarious grip to their strongholds on Ternate and Tidore, and the Portuguese maintained their control of Goa and Malacca. The Dutch, whose main bases in the East Indies were at Bantam on Java and at Amboina, did not care about Goa, but they coveted Malacca for its strategic position and wanted the Moluccas for their spices. They also were concerned with keeping a grasp on Banda, the prime source of nutmeg and mace, for despite several treaties with the Dutch, the Bandanese were stubbornly retaining their independence. In 1609 the V.O.C. outpost on Banda was wiped out by the natives, which led to a bloody reprisal and a new treaty on August 10, 1609, by which the Bandanese grudgingly agreed once more to permit Dutch trade and acknowledged the conquest and annexation by the Dutch of Neyra, one of the islands in their group. This was the first outright acquisition of territory in the East Indies by the Dutch, as distinct from mere commercial agreements. With Banda subdued, the V.O.C. expanded its foothold on Ternate and threw a blockade around the Spaniards on Tidore without succeeding in forcing their surrender.

A new factor in this troubled region was the return of the English. They had belatedly begun to found their overseas empire, starting in North America in 1607 with John Smith's Jamestown settlement, and now they also had an East India Company of their own which planned to replace

piracy with commerce. It had been chartered by Queen Elizabeth on the last day of 1600, with a capitalization much
smaller than that of the similar Dutch company that came
into being 16 months later; its first voyage to the East Indies
was made in April 1601, when James Lancaster brought
home four ships full of spices and captured a heavily laden
Portuguese vessel as well. Lancaster had done most of his
buying at Atjeh on Sumatra; he had taken the Portuguese
ship in the Straits of Malacca with the help of a Dutch captain, Joris van Spilbergen. The Dutch were less cooperative
when Lancaster set up a small English trading post near
Bantam. When the second English East India Company expedition, under Henry Middleton, got to Bantam in 1604, it
heard a bitter tale of Dutch opposition from the Englishmen
there; but Middleton was able to load two ships with pepper
and send two more to Amboina and the Moluccas for cloves.
The company's third fleet, sent out in 1607, was well received in India—foreshadowing the much later British conquest of that subcontinent—but reached Banda to find the
Dutch firmly in control. The ships of the fourth voyage, in
1609, were wrecked on the Arabian coast; the fifth got to
Banda and did some trading despite the Dutch, but the sixth,
which also reached Banda under Henry Middleton, failed
when the flagship caught fire and was destroyed there. The
English East India Company's ventures, then, were sporadic
and generally feeble, but to the Dutch they represented a potential threat to their own growing power in the East Indies,
and they took what steps they could to keep the English shut
out of the spice trade.

The V.O.C. strengthened its position through treaties
with native rulers, through armed conquest, through the construction of a network of forts, and through well-timed
thrusts at the Spanish, Portuguese, and English bases in the
region. Nevertheless, the Dutch were far from secure, and

there were frequent grave setbacks, even at their headquarters in Bantam, where the natives burned down the company's warehouses in February 1613. In more than a decade of hard work, the V.O.C. had built a trading empire that insured a steady flow of spices, but there still were European rivals all about, and the danger of concerted native uprisings threatened to destroy everything overnight. What seemed appropriate at this stage was the dispatch of a strong Dutch military fleet which would cruise the Pacific and the East Indies, strike terror into the V.O.C.'s rivals, and reinforce the Dutch position in the Orient. Command of this enterprise was given to the able and experienced Joris van Spilbergen, and he was instructed to sail not by the customary route, but via the Strait of Magellan. The reason was twofold. The V.O.C., stung by Le Maire's charges that it had been ignoring the westward route, would thereby stake a claim to it; and the Netherlands, which was running into difficulties with Spain despite the supposed truce, wished once more to raid the Spanish settlements of South America's western coast as a reminder of Dutch naval might. This was a voyage, then, planned to have a largely symbolic effect, and to underscore the symbolism it was to be another circumnavigation: the first of the seventeenth century, the fifth ever made, and the second engineered by the Dutch.

8

We know little about Spilbergen except that he was an admirable leader, a courageous warrior, and a skillful seaman. Probably he was the most professional of the early circumnavigators, for by comparison Magellan was too much the dour fanatic, Drake too mercurial, Cavendish too hasty, Noort too clumsy; and none conducted himself quite so deftly as Spilbergen in his voyage round the world. Spilbergen—whose name has also variously been spelled Spilberg,

Speilberghen, Speilbergen, and more—probably was born no later than 1570, for when we first hear of him he is already the captain of an important expedition to the East Indies sent out in May 1601 by a merchant-promoter of Zeeland. With three vessels, the *Ram*, the *Sheep*, and the *Lamb*, Spilbergen rounded the Cape of Good Hope and arrived on May 28, 1602, at the port of Batticaloa on the eastern coast of Ceylon. The local rajah did not dare open trade with him, fearing the wrath of the Portuguese on the one hand and the displeasure of the powerful maharajah of the inland city of Kandy on the other. The Maharajah of Kandy had been educated by the Portuguese and was a Christian who had taken the name of Dom João, but he had turned against his mentors and was eager for the friendship of another European power. Boldly marching inland with only ten men, Spilbergen—the first Dutchman to visit Ceylon—called upon Dom João, introduced himself as a special ambassador from Maurice of Nassau, and presented the maharajah with a life-sized portrait of Maurice on horseback and in full armor. Dom João, duly impressed, bade the Dutch be welcome to Ceylon and invited them to build a fort there, offering to carry the stone and cement on his own shoulders. (He was just as friendly to Sebald de Weert, the next Dutch visitor to Ceylon, but did not hesitate to murder Weert in 1603 when his affections cooled.)

After a highly successful stay on Ceylon, Spilbergen sailed for Sumatra on September 2, 1602. Here he conspired with James Lancaster of the English East India Company to attack a richly laden Portuguese ship that was passing through the Straits of Malacca on its way from India; after dividing the spoils of this raid, he went on to Bantam in April 1603, returning to the Netherlands the following March. Nothing further is known of Spilbergen's doings until April 1607, when he took part in Heemskerck's destruction of the

Spanish fleet at Gibraltar. He must have remained in naval service until he was picked to lead the circumnavigation of 1614–17, but nothing is recorded of his deeds.

A detailed journal of Spilbergen's voyage was published soon after his return, under the title *Oost ende West-Indische Spiegel*, "The East and West Indian Mirror." Two editions in Dutch and one in Latin appeared in 1619, and versions in German and French followed within two years; the first English edition was a greatly abridged translation in Samuel Purchas' 1625 collection of voyages. The *Mirror* carried no author's name, and all references to Spilbergen were in the third person, but quite clearly Spilbergen himself was the author. (He had earlier written an account of his journey to Ceylon, published in 1604.) The dedication to the first edition seems unambiguous on that account: signed by Spilbergen, it declares, "The pleasure I derived from revealing and describing my previous voyages has served me as an incentive and caused me to omit nothing worthy of mention from this narrative of my last journey." However, this dedication was omitted from later editions, and through a chain of improbable circumstances the authorship of Spilbergen's journal was credited to Jan Corneliszoon May, the master of one of his ships. May's name was signed to a descriptive caption on one of the book's illustrations; an eighteenth-century French editor of the work mistakenly attributed the entire journal to him, and the error was perpetuated by later editors for two centuries, until J.A.J. de Villiers of the British Museum, the editor of the 1906 Hakluyt Society text, exposed the confusion and restored Spilbergen to the authorship of his own narrative.

The journal must have been a close adaptation of Spilbergen's log, for it is set down day by day, and the individual entries show no anticipation of events to come. Thus the book begins, "On the eighth of August of the year sixteen hundred and eighteen, we sailed out from Texel with the help of God with four ships, the wind being south-east: may the same God grant us good fortune and prosperity on this voyage. Amen." There is one error and one inaccuracy in this passage, for Spilbergen sailed in 1614, not 1618, and he had six vessels, not four. Two of them were yachts, though, and he did not consider them technically "ships." Spilbergen's flagship was the *Groote Sonne*, or *Great Sun*, of Amsterdam; his other vessels were the *Halve Maen*, or *Half Moon*, and the yachts *Jagher* (*Huntsman*) and *Meeuwe* (*Sea Gull*), also of Amsterdam; the *Aeolus* of Zeeland; and the *Morghensterre*, or *Morning Star*, of Rotterdam. We do not know the tonnage of these ships, but the four large ones were of good size, and all were furnished both for trade and for war, with merchants and supercargoes aboard as well as military officers. All important matters were to be decided by a council of the principal merchants and officers.

They sailed first toward England, where they were delayed awhile at the Isle of Wight to repair a leak in the *Aeolus*. By October they had passed Madeira and the Canary Islands, and then the Cape Verdes; without wasting much time on the African coast, Spilbergen headed for Brazil, which he reached at dawn on the morning of December 13. A week later they anchored near Ilha Grande, a short distance south of Rio de Janeiro. They set up nets to catch fish, hauling in also some crocodiles "the length of a man," and erected tents on shore to house the men who had fallen ill during the Atlantic crossing. A river two miles from their anchorage seemed like a good source of fresh water, and on the 29th Spilbergen sent a boat and the flagship's barge there, instructing the *Huntsman* to anchor close to shore to protect the water-gatherers from possible attack. Several shore parties collected a supply of water and firewood, and went back for more in the afternoon. This time the boats were caught by low tide and could not return; the men spent the night in an improvised hut ashore, and when they came out on the high tide the next day, they reported they had heard the noise of some men in the bushes.

Nevertheless, three more boats went out for food and water that day, containing nine or ten men who, contrary to Spilbergen's orders, did not bother to carry arms. Soon came the sound of cannonfire from the *Huntsman*. The shore parties had been attacked by five canoes of Portuguese and Indians, and the *Huntsman* had foolishly anchored so far from shore that she could be of little help. The men who had gone ashore were slain or captured, and the boats were taken.

Spilbergen had more troubles on the first day of 1615. Four sailors were brought to him in irons. They were men of the *Sea Gull*, accused of having devised a plan to steal the *Huntsman* and desert from the fleet. "They were very narrowly and separately heard," Spilbergen wrote, "and we learned that the accomplices were fourteen in number." Keeping the ringleaders confined, Spilbergen had the entire crew of the *Sea Gull* distributed among the other ships and a fresh crew put aboard that vessel to break up the plot. The interrogation continued for several days, and on January 5, the *Mirror* declares, "the Admiral had the Broad Council summoned, which found two of the prisoners guilty . . . and sentenced them to forfeiture of life and property, wherefore each was to be hung up at the yardarm and be shot through by six musketeers as he was being hauled up." A chaplain and a merchant spent the night with the condemned men, "in order to exhort them to a state of repentance and remorse for their sins," and on the 6th, "the Admiral had the blood flag of the Company hoisted. . . . The execution was immediately carried out, the bodies being buried on land." Two days later Spilbergen judged that they had taken on a sufficient quantity of water, and they prepared to sail south.

Before departure, he selected the Bay de Cordes in the Strait of Magellan as the rendezvous in case of separation through storm, and decreed that on all other bays and islands thereabouts "a stake should be planted in passing, upon which each ship should hang a hoop or rope with some other direction, in order that the later comers might know which had passed there." Spilbergen was well aware of the confusions that had come upon most of the other fleets to pass through that troublesome strait. Each ship, he said, should wait for the others in the Bay de Cordes only a week, and then pass on to the Pacific and wait again at Mocha.

However, Spilbergen soon realized that his men were not ready to attempt the strait. Many were still sick, and provisions were low. His merchants wished to press on at once, but he convened his council and pointed out to them "how greatly victuals were needed, and how, moreover, sickness, and especially scurvy, was daily increasing, and that, according to human judgment, it was impossible to bring such heavy ships, which have to be tacked, turned, and often brought to anchor, through Magellan's strait, without first having sound and ablebodied crews." His consideration for his men prevailed over the zeal of the businessmen, and he won agreement to spend several weeks more on the coast of Brazil. They moved slowly south and on January 18 came to a populous settlement a little above Santos. A crowd of Portuguese and natives appeared on shore, heavily armed; the *Sea Gull*, flying a flag of truce, ventured close, and the Portuguese cried out that they should send only one man to the beach and not approach with any boats. Thereupon Jan Hendrixszoon, the boatswain of the *Half Moon*, "sprang naked into the sea and swam towards them. . . . Our boatswain, standing on a rock, called out that they should lay down their arrows, and that one of them should speak with him; this was done, and one of them coming forward and making the others draw back, asked our boatswain where we came from, what we wanted there, and whither we wished to go." The boatswain twisted the truth only slightly by saying that they came from Flanders and that they were bound for the Río de la Plata; he asked for provisions, and the Portuguese, though pointing out that they were forbidden by the King of Spain to trade with non-Spaniards, agreed to wink at the law if Spilbergen's men would keep the transaction secret. Through these sly dealings the Dutch voyagers were able to obtain fruits, pigs, fowls, sugar, and some preserves. While this highly unofficial trade was quietly going on, the Portuguese authorities at Santos made contact with Spilbergen and involved him in a lengthy exchange of pointless letters over his request to let his men go ashore. Gradually he realized that they were simply trying to delay him and make him waste valuable time; he took down his flags of peace, ran up the Dutch flag, and sent seven boatloads of armed men into Santos to collect additional provisions. The Portuguese made little resistance.

On January 26 a Portuguese vessel appeared, returning from a voyage to Lisbon and Rio de Janeiro. She had 18 men on board, both crew and passengers; the Dutch seized her easily, but found that "her cargo was of no great consequence, other than a little iron, cotton, oil, salt, and such like." Spilbergen learned from her officers that some of his men who had been captured at Ilha Grande were prisoners in Rio de Janeiro, and he sent word to the officials at Santos that he was willing to arrange an exchange of captives. When this offer was refused, Spilbergen proposed to throw in a stock of religious articles that he had taken from the Portuguese ship: "Many relics, crosses, grants of absolution, indulgences, and such-like foolery; moreover, some very fine written books containing matters of theology and law, a chest full of beautiful prints and paintings, a silver gilt crown and some more silver-work. We also found in the vessel two slaves and some other goods belonging to the Society of the Jesuits established there; all of which—including vessel and crew—our Admiral offered to return to them if we could have had our prisoners back instead, but all was in vain. So it was plain that they preferred to have the life and blood of a Netherlands sailor than much property of which they are otherwise so superstitiously fond."

All negotiations having failed, Spilbergen had the captured ship set on fire on January 30. From letters he discovered in her, he found that the Portuguese of Brazil had been expecting him, "so that it must be true that there are some traitors in our country who give the King of Spain warning of all that takes place." He released some of the Portuguese mariners, including the captain, but kept others who looked as though they would be useful on his voyage. On February 4, the provisioning at last completed, the fleet set sail, having lost four men a few days previously when a watering-party from the *Huntsman* was attacked by savages.

Now the fogs of the far southern latitudes drifted about them; they fired shots from time to time to keep together, but Spilbergen had to halt on March 2 while the *Half Moon* and the *Morning Star* caught up with the others. Toward evening on March 7 they reached Cape Vírgines, but the ships were scattered by storm about midnight and had some perilous hours before the weather cleared and they were reunited. In the morning they attempted to round the cape and enter the strait; the *Huntsman*, the *Sea Gull*, and the *Morning Star* made it, but the others were driven off by storm, and Spilbergen's own ship was swept well out to sea and far to the north. He did not get close to shore again until the 14th, and a week later was still wallowing in heavy seas off Cape Vírgines, unable to go forward.

The *Huntsman* and the *Sea Gull* came back on the 21st,

having left the *Morning Star* safe at anchor within the strait. They bore the grievous news of another mutiny. "A great tumult," the *Mirror* relates, had arisen aboard the *Sea Gull*, "the sailors having made themselves masters of the ship, obtained possession of the gun, and compelled the skipper and ship's clerk to do as they desired, making the clerk their cook; and they would also have murdered him in the cabin had not the skipper interceded for them." The mutineers liberated the ship's stores of wine, and a drunken dispute broke out among them as to who should be captain. This gave the deposed officers a chance to arm themselves and seize the two main conspirators; the other sailors quickly subsided, blaming everything on those two. Once order was restored aboard the *Sea Gull*, the officers quickly deliberated the fate of the two principal mutineers and agreed to throw them overboard, which was done at once. Spilbergen, greatly disturbed to hear of all this, held a formal inquiry but decided to make no shift of officers aboard the troubled ship.

The weather remained hostile, and Spilbergen wandered up and down between 50°S. and 52°S. without obtaining admission to the strait. The capacious eastern mouth was usually accessible, and few navigators had had so much difficulty here before; but on March 25, 18 days after first sighting Cape Vírgines, Spilbergen approached it once more and wrote, "Not withstanding that we cast three anchors, one after the other, it was impossible for them to hold, on account of the softness of the bottom, whereby the whole afternoon was spent in re-weighing them each time; and towards the evening the Admiral, by two shots, gave the signal for setting sail again, directing his course west-nor'-west, but he was followed by none of the other ships." Tacking all day on the 26th, Spilbergen worked back to the cape the following day and proceeded along the coast, "which was low and flat, being very like the shores of England." He came upon the

Sea Gull, which fired a shot to signal him that it was dangerous to run this close to land; after more tacking, he got out to sea and beyond the strait, to the coast of Tierra del Fuego, where he found the *Aeolus*, the *Half Moon*, and the *Huntsmen* at anchor. During this troublesome time many of the merchants and some of the officers had begun to assert that such big vessels would not be able to pass the strait at all, for the winter was advancing. Some spoke of wintering at Port Desire, "where Candis [Cavendish] and Olivier van Noort had been; others said that it would be better to make our way betimes to Cape de Bonne Esperance [Good Hope], and so to the East Indies, and more such like opinions." A merchant named Pieter Buers led a delegation to Spilbergen's cabin and demanded to know what plans the admiral had, in case they failed to make the strait. Spilbergen replied stoutly, "Our orders and charge are to sail through the Magellanes; I know of no other way to show you; take heed to do your best and keep up with us." This ended the muttering, and at daybreak on March 29 Spilbergen led the fleet toward the entrance to the strait. He was perturbed to find that the *Sea Gull*, which had been beside him the night before, was nowhere in sight, and suspected that there had been another mutiny aboard her. In this he was correct, for the *Sea Gull's* men, obeying an impulse familiar to many previous mariners in the vicinity of the Strait of Magellan, had deserted their commander and were on their way home.

9

On April 3, 1615, Spilbergen entered the strait, observed by "a human being of very big stature" who appeared several times, at one point climbing a hill to have a better view. Nearly a century before, Magellan had plunged here into an unknown and intricate maze whose secrets he had solved in a triumph of navigational skill, but now the twists and turns of the strait were familiar, and every cove and isle had its name, some of them two and three names. Spilbergen did not fail to add his own designations to the growing accumulation. A merchant named Cornelis de Vianen went ashore with Spilbergen on April 7 to inspect the terrain; they found two of the ostrich-like rheas, a river, and small trees bearing tasty berries, and Spilbergen named the promontory Cape Vianen. On the 8th they went on to the islands just beyond the second narrows, which had come to be called the Penguin Islands, but which Spilbergen renamed Great Shore Island, Giant's Island, and Cruyck's Island. On Great Shore his men found a stake and a hoop as markers, with a note saying that the *Morning Star* had been there two weeks earlier and gone on.

Spilbergen passed the ruins of Port Famine on the 11th and later that day was startled to see on the south side of the strait "very fine green woods and many parrots," despite the harshness of the climate. Now the land grew high and hilly, with snow on the mountains. Spilbergen went ashore in person at several points, making note of various unusual trees and some Indian burials; and on the 16th the flagship entered the Bay de Cordes to find that the other four ships had arrived there a little while before. He had not been with them for a number of days. "It was a wonderful mercy of God," he wrote, "that such big ships had come with such great trouble, contrary winds and storms, through such narrow channels, various turns, and many whirlpools, at the same time and day to their appointed rendezvous, especially as they had got separated from each other, and had passed the first narrows at different times." They spent eight days here, gathering water and firewood, refreshing themselves on huge mussels "superior in flavor and quality to oysters," and enjoying "much watercress, parsley, salad, and many red berries."

Indians came to them and were given knives and trinkets in exchange for ornaments of mother-of-pearl, "very finely made." The Dutch allowed the Patagonians to sample some Spanish wine, which they indicated by pantomime was very much to their liking. But when Spilbergen's men went ashore to hunt geese and ducks, the sound of their guns frightened the natives away, and they did not return.

To celebrate the happy reunion at the Bay de Cordes, Spilbergen invited his principal officers to dinner on the flagship. "They were well regaled there," he wrote, "with many fresh dishes of meat, pork, poultry, oranges, lemons, candied peel, and marmalades," most of which they had obtained in Brazil, "also with olives, capers, good Spanish and French wine, Dutch beer, and many other things which it would take too long to mention here; and moreover, we enjoyed there a fine concert of various instruments, and music of many voices." After this jolly feast, the voyagers went onward. The weather was unusually mild for the season, and they passed pleasantly through the remainder of the strait without difficulty. Spilbergen gave names to seven or eight islets and, in Long Reach, discovered an opening that seemed to be an outlet to the Pacific other than the one customarily used. With some of his men he climbed a mountain to verify his belief, but he did not venture to attempt the shortcut, declaring stolidly, "Our orders and instructions were always to follow the Strait of Magellan, without trying any other passage." They anchored a little way to the west in a bay which Spilbergen named for himself. Spilbergen sent boats out to scout for the strait's exit, and on the morning of May 6, with a strong wind and drizzling weather, they sailed through the final fearsome walls of the channel and into the Pacific. They had traversed the strait in 34 days, respectable enough in terms of the four months Noort had consumed there, or the two months taken by Cavendish; but Drake had needed only 17 days for the passage, and even Magellan, the pioneer, had come through it in just one month.

Beset by rain and fog, often separated, the Dutch fleet hacked its way north through the Pacific until, on May 23, the Chilean island of Mocha came into view. Though the weather drove them off, they returned and made anchorage on the 25th, half a mile from the shore of this often inhospitable island. Spilbergen sent four well-armed boats to land. By indicating that they were enemies of the Spaniards, his men won the favor of the Mochan Indians, and the reception was so friendly that Spilbergen himself landed, met with the chief and his son, and brought them back to the flagship to entertain them and show them the guns that he planned to use against the Spanish settlements. He staged a deckside parade of his troops, which pleased the Indians very much. Trading commenced the next day. "They received us with every amiability," said Spilbergen, "but they did not permit any of us to come into their houses or near their wives, bringing everything to the boats themselves." The natives were "well-mannered, very polite and friendly, very orderly in their eating and drinking, of good morals, and almost equal to Christians." Spilbergen purchased and brought to his ship a llama, which he described as "a sheep of a very wonderful shape, having a very long neck and a hump like a camel, a hare-lip, and very long legs. . . . Of other sheep we procured here more than a hundred, which were very large and fat, having white wool as in our country, and in addition to these a large number of fowls and other poultry . . . for which the Admiral gave them some hatchets, knives, shirts, hats, and other similar things, so that we parted from each other in great friendship."

With a good wind from the south, the fleet went on to the island of Santa Maria, which was held by a small Spanish garrison. Spilbergen put on a display of might for the benefit of the Spaniards, drawing up his men in battle array; the Spanish commandant, evidently impressed, sent a friendly invitation to dinner, and several of the Dutch officers actually accepted and went ashore. Immediately, though, a boat from the *Huntsman* came after them, bearing news that a troop of armed men had been seen marching toward the place where they were to dine. Upon hearing this, they hurried back to their ships, taking the Spanish messenger with them as a prisoner. The next day, Spilbergen led three companies of soldiers ashore; the Spaniards fled on horseback after a skirmish in which two Dutchmen were wounded and four Spaniards killed, and Spilbergen emptied their warehouses of provisions. On leaving he wrote, "We set fire to all their dwellings, which burn very easily and quickly, since they are made and covered with cane." Their Spanish captive told them that the Viceroy of Peru had known of the coming of the Dutch fleet for several months, that in April three Spanish warships with a thousand men had come to Santa Maria in search of them, and that a larger force was gathered at Callao to attack them. Spilbergen, "with the consent and approbation of the merchants," resolved to carry the offensive to the Spaniards and issued a detailed set of battle orders to prepare his men for the meeting. "In the event of the galleons being found to be higher or bigger than our ships, and seeking to grapple us and board us in large numbers, each commander, captain, or skipper, shall, according as the circumstances demand, take such careful measures as may prevent our soldiers and sailors from being killed where they can do no good, and shall place them in a safe spot under the quarternettings fore and aft, in order to annihilate the boarders by the fittest means, wherewith each ship is well provided in the shape of mortars and other things. . . ."

On June 1 the fleet sailed from Santa Maria. At Concepción the Hollanders landed and burned some houses; at Valparaiso on the 12th they found a Spanish ship at anchor, but her crew set fire to it to keep them from seizing it; on the 13th they stopped in the Bay of Quintero, which Spilbergen describes as "fine and pleasant, having a well-situated anchorage, and in addition to that, one could not find in the world a better place for getting water, the latter being very clear and sweet of taste." Here he released two of the Portuguese that he had been carrying since Santos, and his men threw up an earthen rampart that shielded them from Spanish attack while they were filling their casks. "In this spot," Spilbergen noted proudly, "Mr. Candijs [Cavendish] likewise got in his supply of water, but with the loss of many men. So far as we are concerned, we lost not a single man, nor was anyone injured."

They left Quintero on June 17 and, slowed by calm weather, came to Arica on July 2. This was the chief depot for the shipment of silver from the fabulous Potosí (Bolivia) mines, but Spilbergen found no treasure on hand and went on. It rained on July 10, much to the astonishment of the Spanish prisoner, who reported—correctly—that rain had not fallen in many years along the desert coast of Peru. A speedy Spanish ship now was scouting them; the *Huntsman* tried in vain to overtake her on the 11th. Five days later they encountered a different ship, and Spilbergen sent out four boats of armed men who captured her without resistance. She carried a cargo of olives and "a good sum in copper coin," most of which was distributed among the Dutch soldiers and sailors. When the ship was unloaded, the Dutch knocked a hole in her and sank her, making prisoners of her crew and Juan Baptista Gonzalez, her captain, who had been on his way from Arequipa to Callao.

That evening, eight Spanish ships "of wonderful size" approached, and Gonzalez declared that they were the war fleet out of Callao, coming forth under the command of Don Rodrigo de Mendoza, cousin of the Viceroy of Peru. Mendoza had boasted to the viceroy of the ease with which he would take the Dutch voyagers: "Two of my ships would conquer all England," he said, "let alone those Dutch hens, after so long a journey has spent and wasted them!" His flagship, the *Jesus Maria*, carried 460 men and 24 big guns, and the others, though smaller, were formidably armed.

Mendoza's armada approached the Dutch ships by evening on July 17, but could not get close enough to open fire. The Spanish second in command, a veteran soldier named Pedro Álvarez de Pilgar, warned Mendoza against so unprecedented a tactic as an attack by night, but the impetuous Spanish commander, "with great self-conceit," bore down on Spilbergen's flagship about ten P.M., and "after some words had been exchanged between them, they fired upon each other, first with a salvo of musketry, and afterwards with the guns, which seemed not only strange, but horrible in the hour of night." (The description is Spilbergen's.) The Dutch artillery did such damage that Mendoza quickly sought to withdraw from the fray, but the wind was at a standstill, and the two flagships faced one another a long while, continuing the bombardment amid "continual beating of drums, sounding of trumpets, and . . . the indescribable yelling and shrieking of the Spaniards." At last Mendoza got clear, and the *Great Sun* turned her guns on another Spanish ship, and then on a third, the *San Francisco*, which was so badly riddled that its imminent sinking seemed certain. She drifted away and approached the *Huntsman*, which the desperate Spaniards grappled and attempted to board. The men of the Dutch yacht repulsed this assault, though, and shortly the *San Francisco* went down with most of her men. In the most frantic part of the struggle, Spilbergen sent a boat from the *Great Sun* to aid the *Huntsman*, but the latter's gunners, mistaking its occupants for Spaniards, smashed it with a cannonshot, and one man was drowned. Elsewhere during the fray, several of the Spanish ships attacked the *Half Moon* and were driven off. Spilbergen could not see the *Aeolus* and the *Morning Star*, which had drifted away in the darkness during the prevailing calm; nor was there any sign of the *Santa Anna*, Captain Pilgar's ship, and some of the smaller Spanish vessels.

Morning revealed both fleets spread widely over the quiet sea. The *Aeolus* and the *Morning Star* were far from the *Great Sun*, the *Huntsman*, and the *Half Moon*. The two largest Spanish ships, the *Jesus Maria* and the *Santa Anna*, likewise were well apart from the other five vessels. Those five sent word to Mendoza that they had had enough, as Spilbergen later learned from prisoners; as they withdrew, the Dutch closed in on the vessels of Mendoza and Pilgar. Finding themselves overmatched, those two captains hoisted sails and attempted to flee, but the *Santa Anna* could not keep up with the flagship, and Mendoza halted the *Jesus Maria* to wait for her. The *Morning Star* fell upon the two Spanish vessels, followed shortly by the *Great Sun*, and "a very hot fight ensued between these four ships, the one riddling the other with shot and musket-fire. At last, our *Aeolus* also arrived on the scene, discharging its guns upon the Spaniards, who finally laid their vessels right alongside of each other, and so gave our men a great advantage in being able to attack them from all quarters." The *Santa Anna* was soon in such straits that many of her men, expecting her to sink, sprang across into the *Jesus Maria*. There they found only 40 or 50 men alive out of more than 400 and a struggle going on between those who were trying to hoist a flag of surrender and those who, preferring to fight to the death, kept pulling it down. The deserters from Pilgar's ship returned to their own vessel and fought on. The outcome was inevitable, and in a little while Mendoza turned and ran. The *Great Sun* chased him until sundown, losing sight of his ship then, and sometime during the night the *Jesus Maria* went to the bottom, taking Mendoza with her. The *Santa Anna*, last of the Spanish fleet, remained ringed by Spilbergen's ships, absorbing a bombardment that at last compelled Captain Pilgar to put up a white flag. The captain of the *Morning Star*, Maerten Pieterssen Cruyck, dispatched two boats of armed men as a boarding party, instructing them to bring Pilgar back. But the Spaniard's Castilian sense of honor came to the fore, and he declared "that he wished to remain still that night on his ship unless some [Dutch] captain would remain in his place as a hostage, which was declined. Our men therefore warned him again that he should no longer trust himself in a ship which looked as if it would seek the bottom every hour. But all this notwithstanding, he remained obstinate, finally agreeing to go if the Vice-Admiral [Cruyck] came for him in person, but declaring that otherwise he would rather die with honor in his present capacity, and on his ship, in the service of his king and country." Cruyck had no intention of personally entreating Pilgar to leave the *Santa Anna*, and so the Spaniard remained with his vessel. Night fell, and the Spaniards, aided by a dozen or so Dutchmen who against orders had boarded the *Santa Anna* in hopes of being first at the loot, manned the pumps to keep the ship afloat, "but, seeing that all was of no avail and that they had nought but death to expect, they kindled many lights and torches, and amidst much shrieking, weeping and wailing . . . they finally went down in our presence with all aboard." On the morning of July 19, Spilbergen sent four boats to look for survivors; they found 60 or 70 men drifting on planks and spars, but the stubborn Captain Pilgar had perished with his ship. The Dutch picked up the Spanish pilot and a few other officers, "leaving the rest to the mercy of the waves, although some of our sailors slew a few Spaniards, contrary to the orders they had received."

Spain had lost three major galleons of war. The only Dutch casualties were 16 men who had been killed aboard the *Morning Star* when the waves had carried her between the ships of Mendoza and Pilgar on the night of the 18th, and two dozen men slain in the other four vessels. Spilbergen offered pious thanks for his victory and steered his fleet toward Callao.

10

Fourteen Spanish ships were in harbor at Callao. But when Spilbergen anchored close to land, the shore batteries greeted him with a barrage of 36-pound iron balls, one of which smashed through the *Huntsman* and came close to sinking her. He could discern an ample army waiting for him —eight companies of cavalry and 4,000 infantrymen—and so, Spilbergen tells us pleasantly, "it was, therefore, after mature deliberation, resolved by the Admiral and all his officers . . . to retire a mile or two." For five days Spilbergen lay at the entrance to the harbor hoping to snare some unwary vessel, but the Spanish shipping was too swift for him, and on July 26 he gave orders to sail on. That afternoon the Dutchmen encountered a small ship laden with salt and sugar, which they captured and took along as a tender for the fleet.

On August 3 Spilbergen released a number of Spanish prisoners on the coast, and on the 8th he anchored near the town of Paita. In a preliminary skirmish with the Spaniards the next day, one Hollander was killed and several were wounded; Spilbergen sent the *Aeolus*, the *Morning Star*, and the *Huntsman* up under the shore batteries to blockade the harbor, and on the 10th the three ships "bombarded the aforesaid town so furiously with their cannon that everything around shook." The inhabitants fled to the mountains, taking their possessions with them, and Spilbergen ordered Paita set afire, "so that in a short time the greater part of the aforesaid town lay in ashes." Since the provisions acquired in Paita were scanty, Spilbergen sent the captured Spanish tender out under an officer named Jan de Wit to raid the surrounding coastal region. Wit captured an Indian *balsa*, or sailing raft made of extremely light wood, which was agreeably laden with a two-month catch of fish. Doña Paula, the wife of the governor of Paita, sent gifts of lemons, oranges, cabbages, and other victuals from the town 12 miles away where she had taken refuge, along with a letter interceding for the release of the rest of Spilbergen's Spanish prisoners. The admiral noted that "this Doña Paula is very renowned on account of her beauty, good grace, and discretion. . . . Had we in the beginning been acquainted with her courtesy and kindness, we would, for her sake, have spared the town of Paita." But he politely declined to release more prisoners at this time. Only when it became apparent, a few days later, that he would not be able to feed so many Spaniards did he let the remaining captives go, keeping, however, the pilot, another officer, and some 30 men of the vanquished *Santa Anna*.

The fleet departed from Paita on August 21, heading north "with mild and very fine weather." As Noort had done, Spilbergen proposed to make for Cocos Island to take on supplies; and, as had also happened to Noort, Spilbergen failed to find Cocos, for as he crossed the equator he was "much subjected to all kinds of tempests, whirlwinds, rain, lightning, and the like." Jan de Wit's little tender sprang a bad leak and sank moments after her crew and cargo had been removed. The lack of fresh food caused outbreaks of scurvy as the search for Cocos dragged on through storm and lightning for a second week and a third, and at length Spilbergen had to steer for the coast of Mexico, which came into sight on

September 20. Continuing storms whipped the ships along the coast; one high wind drove the *Huntsman* and the *Great Sun* together, with serious damage to the former, and another stripped away the flagship's mainsail. In vain the mariners beat toward shore, each time to be swept back to sea; not until October 10 were they able to drop anchor "near a tongue of land behind which lay the town of Acapulco, having a fine and well-situated harbor."

The citadel at Acapulco fired ten cannon shots as a token sign of defense, but they did no harm, and when Spilbergen sent out a boat under a flag of truce, the Spaniards were quick to strike an agreement. Two of them who had served in the Netherlands and spoke Dutch came aboard Spilbergen's ship and negotiated an agreement: in return for the release of all his Spanish prisoners, the Dutch commander would be given 30 oxen, 50 sheep, and a quantity of fowls, fruit, and vegetables. Both sides remained armed and ready to take action against a violation of the truce, but all went well; Dutch and Spanish officers mingled freely, Spilbergen's son went ashore to be entertained by the governor, the prisoners were set free, and a cousin of the Viceroy of Mexico came to the flagship to inspect with awe the fleet that had conquered the royal armada of Don Rodrigo de Mendoza. More than 60 men were ill on the *Great Sun* alone, and so it was with "incredible joy and recuperation among our men" that the Dutch accepted the promised oxen, sheep, and fruit from Acapulco. In the privacy of his journal Spilbergen admitted that it would have been difficult for him to storm the town, which was well armed and had had eight months to get ready for his arrival; his reputation for invincibility had saved him a great deal of trouble here.

On October 18 the voyagers moved on up the Mexican coast. They captured a pearl-fishing vessel on the 26th, taking her along as a tender, and after calling several times along the shore for supplies—losing two men to a Spanish ambush at one point—Spilbergen began his westward crossing of the Pacific on November 20, 1615. His original intention was to make for Cape San Lucas at the tip of Baja California and wait for galleons from the Philippines, but the winds were unfavorable, and on December 2 he decided to go straight to the Ladrones.

As usual, only a few barren rocky islands were encountered during the voyage. They had a good wind and made excellent time, though many men suffered from scurvy and several died. The Ladrones were reached on January 23, toward evening: "This land was very low and flat, wherefore, since night was approaching, and we feared we might be nearer the land than we indeed thought, we lowered all the sails, drifting all night without making any progress." In the morning they found themselves near one island of the group, and native canoes hurried out, bearing fruits and herbs. At noon on the 25th Sybrant Cornellisen, the supercargo of the *Morning Star*, "whilst seated at table in good health, was suddenly seized with a fainting fit from which he presently died, to the great astonishment of all who were present," and he was buried the next day to the accompaniment of "many rounds of big guns and muskets, which frightened the Indians so, notwithstanding that they had been previously warned for what reason it would be done, that they dispersed themselves with their skiffs, one here, the other there, and durst not come back." Since this appeared to put an end to chances for further trade, the fleet sailed on; but the ships were becalmed at night and got nowhere, and the islanders, their confidence returning, came out in their canoes again, "bringing with them all kinds of fruit and other necessaries, until the wind began to rise, and it became impossible for them to follow us further."

Sailing without a halt until February 9, the Dutchmen

reached the Philippines, stopping at the outer islands to get provisions and directions from the natives. Toward the end of February they arrived at Luzon and traveled along the big island's coast for more than a week, until they entered the harbor of Manila. Rich trading vessels from China were due to arrive there in mid-April, and Spilbergen planned to lie in wait for them. In the first week of March, the Hollanders indiscriminately raided small ships belonging to Spaniards, Chinese, and Japanese, taking from them rice, poultry, cattle, and other goods; their cargoes were distributed among the fleet, the Chinese and Japanese seamen released, the Spaniards made prisoner. This program of piracy was interrupted when Spilbergen learned from some prisoners on March 6 that the Spaniards had sent a large armada from the Philippines to the Moluccas four weeks previously with the intention of driving the Dutch from the Spice Islands. This fleet, under Don Juan de Silva, consisted of "ten galleons of wonderful size, two yachts, four galleys, and two thousand Spaniards, in addition to the Indians, Chinese, and Japanese, also in great numbers." Though it was painful to leave Manila before the rich junks from China had arrived, Spilbergen deemed it necessary to go to the aid of his countrymen, and on March 10 the five Dutch ships set sail for the Moluccas.

Progress was slowed by contrary currents and troublesome winds; Spilbergen was forced to stop several times in the Philippines, and the natives, upon learning that he was an enemy of the Spaniards, provided him with victuals and even offered to accompany him in their own small vessels to do battle against Spain. Declining these offers, Spilbergen nevertheless was pleased by these signs of native friendship. He reached the Moluccas on March 29, arriving at Ternate and anchoring opposite Malayo, the fort the Dutch had built a decade earlier. Officials of the East India

Company came on board to welcome them, led by Laurens Reael, the Governor-General of the Dutch East Indies. From Reael, who was a poet and astronomer as well as an administrator, Spilbergen learned that the threatened armada under Don Juan de Silva had not yet made its appearance in the Moluccas and was believed to have called first at Malacca. Spilbergen also corrected his calendar at Ternate, noting that he had lost a day, "since in sailing to the town we had shaped our course from east to west, whilst those who sail from west to east gain a day, as many others have experienced before."

The main purposes of Spilbergen's voyage had largely been accomplished: he had demonstrated Dutch naval might in the Pacific and he had brought five of his six ships safely across the great ocean, a feat of captainship unmatched by previous voyagers. It remained now for him only to proceed through the other Dutch islands of the East Indies and complete his circumnavigation. For the time being, though, he stayed at Ternate holding consultations with Governor-General Reael, while the *Huntsman*, commanded by the merchant-captain Cornelis de Vianen, sailed to Banda early in April. In May, Spilbergen toured the other islands of the Moluccas and successfully negotiated with the Spaniards on Tidore to trade five Spaniards he had taken in the Pacific for seven Dutchmen who had been captives more than four years. Apparently there was some thought of invading the Spanish fort on Tidore, and at one point 17 Dutch warships collected at Ternate for that purpose; but nothing came of the plan, and on July 18 Spilbergen was ordered to go on to Java with two of his vessels, the *Great Sun* and the *Half Moon*.

Bantam, long the chief Dutch outpost on Java, was then beginning to lose precedence to a newer Dutch factory 50 miles to the east at Djakarta, which Europeans called Jacatra. The architect of the Dutch presence at Djakarta was a young, exceptionally forceful man named Jan Pieterszoon Coen, who was born in 1587, was sent off to Italy at the age of thirteen as an apprentice to a house of merchant bankers, and in 1607 joined the United East India Company as a humble submerchant. Farsighted, fiercely ambitious, a devotee of empire-building for its own sake, Coen was witness to the early development of Dutch power in the East Indies and by 1613 had privately picked Djakarta as Bantam's successor, arguing that it was a good spot to found a "rendezvous and headquarters, provided we build a stronghold there to guard our merchandise and where [Dutch] colonies should be planted to be no longer at the mercy of the perfidious Moors."

Coen by that time had risen to be bookkeeper-general for V.O.C. in the East Indies, and this remarkable and headstrong young man bombarded The Lords Seventeen with memoranda on the expansion of the company's activities in Asia. More clearly than anyone else, Coen saw that the company could not be content merely to be a trading firm sending ships to call at armed forts on generally hostile islands, but would have to transform those islands into Dutch settlements and preside over a full-fledged empire in which colonists of Dutch blood prevailed and dominated. Trading concessions were not enough; Coen envisioned Dutch civilization transplanted to the East Indies in wholesale lots, good sturdy burghers rearing huge families on every island. It was a vision that was realized, and in it lies the explanation for the ability of the Dutch to hold the East Indies for more than three centuries, where Portuguese, Spaniards, and English had failed to gain more than a foothold. Coen chose Djakarta as the key to this empire, much as Albuquerque had chosen Goa for Portugal a century earlier; the native

ruler of Djakarta had been unwilling to tolerate Dutch in-
roads beyond the founding of a factory, but at the end of
1614 Coen persuaded the monarch to accept a trifling payment in return for the right to build a stockade-protected
stone warehouse. From this tiny nucleus, Coen expanded rapidly. At twenty-eight he was now the second highest V.O.C.
official in the East Indies, and, without consulting much with
Governor-General Reael or the home office, Coen began
transferring men and goods from Bantam to Djakarta. By
1618 Coen would replace Laurens Reael as Governor-General of the Dutch East Indies; in 1619 he would order the
armed seizure of Djakarta; by 1620 the new Dutch city of
Batavia, future capital of the Netherlands' empire in Asia,
would be rising on the ruins of the native town.

It was to Djakarta that Spilbergen came when he arrived off Java on September 15, 1616. He presented himself
to Coen, and doubtless their meeting was congenial, for both
were fanatic devotees to duty and to their company. The invasion fleet of Don Juan de Silva was still at Malacca, Spilbergen learned, and on September 30 came news of Silva's
death there, allegedly from poison. His fleet had begun to return to Manila; there would be no confrontation between
Spain and the Netherlands in the East Indies. A number of
Dutch ships arrived at Djakarta during Spilbergen's stay,
most of them from the Moluccas and Banda, carrying spices
for the account of V.O.C. But on October 20 there came an
unexpected vessel. Spilbergen writes of the arrival that day of
"the ship named the *Eendracht*, of Hoorn, under the command of Jacques le Maire, having set out from the Netherlands on the 15th July, 1615, and come south of the Strait of
Magellan, and whereas it was found that the said vessel was
not associated with the General Company [V.O.C.] and that
she had set out on this voyage without their orders, the Presi-

dent, Jan Pieterszoon Coen, confiscated the said ship on behalf of the General Company and transferred her crew to our
vessels."

For the first time, two voyages of circumnavigation had
intersected.

11

Isaac Le Maire of Amsterdam continued to be one of
V.O.C.'s most persistent and determined enemies. Still seeking some loophole through which he might thrust a spice expedition of his own, Le Maire and some fellow merchants
organized a company in 1614 and petitioned the States-General for the right to seek the East Indies through some route
yet undiscovered. This new firm, which Le Maire called The
Australian Company, claimed to be seeking *Terra Australis*,
although actually its primary goal was the Moluccas. On
March 26, 1614, the States-General issued an ambiguous decree by which Le Maire was enabled to form an expedition:
"All persons, inhabitants of the United Provinces, who
should make discoveries of new passages, harbors, or lands,
should be permitted and entitled to make the first four voyages to the places by them discovered," and all other inhabitants of the Netherlands were forbidden, under penalty of
confiscation of ships and goods and a fine of 50,000 ducats,
from navigating or trading in such places until the said four
voyages were completed.

The V.O.C., secure in its exclusive control of the Cape
of Good Hope and Strait of Magellan routes to the Spice Islands, regarded Le Maire's new enterprise as no real threat.
But Le Maire had conferred with a veteran seaman, Willem
Corneliszoon Schouten of the Dutch maritime city of Hoorn,
and was confident of finding a passage that did not infringe
on the V.O.C. franchises—a passage *below*, not through, the
Strait of Magellan. Of course this passage had already been

discovered, and not recently; it was Francis Drake in 1578 who had been driven by storm far to the south of land's end, into open sea. But *The World Encompassed by Sir Francis Drake*, with its explicit description of the ocean to the south of the strait, had not yet been published, and the accounts of Drake's voyage in Hakluyt's collection made no mention of the Drake passage. Though many navigators believed it was possible to pass south of the strait, either through an archipelago or in open water, the generally accepted geographical theories still clung to the notion of another continent on the far side of the strait. Schouten and Le Maire felt otherwise.

They raised money for an expedition without giving any of the investors knowledge of the proposed route, and outfitted two ships, the 220-ton *Eendracht*, with a crew of 65, and the 110-ton yacht *Hoorn*, with a crew of 22. Isaac Le Maire was too old to attempt the voyage himself, and in his place went his son Jacob as supercargo and general commander aboard the *Eendracht*. Schouten also sailed on the *Eendracht* as her captain, and his brother Jan was skipper of the *Hoorn*. The officers and crew were engaged without receiving any notice of their destination or route and signed on with the understanding that they would go wherever their captain and commander decided. In this mysterious fashion, preparations for the voyage were completed, and on May 25, 1615, the *Eendracht* sailed from Hoorn, arriving at Texel on the 27th. She was joined there on June 4 by the *Hoorn*, and on June 14 the Schoutens and young Le Maire began their voyage, a gallant challenge to the power of the United East India Company.

Several accounts of this voyage, the sixth and last of the early circumnavigations, were published, and distinguishing among them is a vexing matter for bibliographers. The first to appear was *The Journal of the Wonderful Voyage of Willem Schouten of Hoorn*, which in 1618 was printed in a variety of Dutch editions and in a French translation. Within a year this version existed in several Latin translations and also in an English rendering, an 82-page quarto of 1619 that in abridged form was included six years later in Samuel Purchas' vast collection of travel accounts, *Purchas his Pilgrimes*. It is noteworthy that the 17 editions of this work issued in 1618 and 1619 make no reference in their titles to Jacob Le Maire and describe the voyage as solely that of Willem Schouten—with one exception. That exception is the 1619 *East and West Indian Mirror*, published in Dutch and then in Latin, and, as we have seen, the primary source for details of Spilbergen's voyage; as a sort of appendix to this narrative, the *Mirror* included a section entitled *The Australian Navigations of Jacob Le Maire*. The numerous subsequent editions of the *Mirror* continued to include this account, ascribing the voyage entirely to Le Maire, and it was published separately as well. The text of this journal, supposedly Le Maire's, is virtually identical to that previously published under Schouten's name. An intricate controversy, with which we need not be concerned in detail, raged for decades between partisans of Schouten and partisans of Le Maire over the authorship of the rival books; since Le Maire did not live to the conclusion of the voyage, he was unable to state his own claim, and Schouten maintained silence. It appears that the 1618 volume actually was the work of Schouten, with Le Maire's name unfairly suppressed, and that the 1619 work credited to Le Maire was merely an adaptation of Schouten's journal concocted by Le Maire's family; but it has also been alleged that Schouten fraudulently published the dead Le Maire's journal as his own. In any event, the narratives' true authors are not likely now to be known, and the two works are the same in substance, though they differ oddly and bewilderingly on minor details of latitudes and dates. An additional authority is the journal of Aris Claesz, supercargo of the *Hoorn*, which was published for the first time at Amsterdam in 1754.

The voyagers' first stop was Dover, where on June 17 Schouten went ashore to hire an English gunner. From there they went to Plymouth to take on a carpenter, and at the end of June they headed south into the Atlantic. An announcement of the ration of food that each man was to receive was made on July 4: a tankard of beer a day, four pounds of bread and half a pound of butter per week (with allowance for melting), and five cheeses for the whole voyage. Fresh fruit and meat would have to be obtained as they went. To this end they anchored off Cape Verde on July 23, but were unable to obtain a hoped-for supply of lemons, and by mid-August, after a long delay on the African coast in calm weather, many of the men were down with scurvy. Schouten and Le Maire therefore put in at Sierra Leone for provisions, landing on August 22 and finding the country, says Le Maire's account, "uninhabited by human beings, though we saw numerous footprints of big wild beasts; the country was desolate, full of wildnesses, low swamps and high mountains." Le Maire went three miles up a broad river and "found no people here either, but saw three wild oxen and numbers of marmosets, as well as some birds that barked like dogs." On the 24th two of the boats entered two other rivers, and one returned with lemons. Gradually they realized that they were in the wrong part of the coast, though, and on August 30 they found their way to the inhabited region and, at a village of blacks, obtained "by barter, at a guess, some 25,000 lemons, all for a few beads and some poor Nuremberg knives. We could have got a hundred thousand, had we desired them, for there were whole forests full of them. In the evening we also bartered with the Negroes for a quantity of fish." Le Maire's account also tells of coming upon "a small white animal called an *antilop*" which some of his men found in a trap set by the natives.

They sailed from Sierra Leone at the beginning of September, but calms and variable winds pinned them close to Africa almost to the end of the month, and it rained heavily for whole days and nights together. By October 5 they were still some 4° north of the equator. On that day a great noise was heard about the *Eendracht*, and Schouten, rushing forward to see what was the matter, looked over the side and "saw that the sea was quite red with blood, as if a large quantity of blood had been poured out, whereat he was astonished, not knowing what it could mean. But afterwards we discovered that a great horned fish or sea-monster had struck the ship with his horn with most wonderful force, for when we reached Port Desire [in Patagonia] and beached the vessel in order to clean her, we found sticking in the ship, forward in the bow, about seven feet below the water-line, a horn, very similar in shape and thickness to the end of an ordinary elephant's tusk. . . . It pierced through three sheathings of the vessel, to wit, through two stout fir planks, through another of stout oak and partly through another rib, where it was finally stopped, to our great good fortune, for if it had penetrated between the ribs into the interior of the ship it would possibly have made a larger hole and have endangered the safety of the vessel with all aboard. This horn was sticking in the ship's side to the depth of quite half a foot, with nearly half a foot protruding, where it had been broken off short with great violence, this having caused the monster to bleed so profusely." Almost certainly they had been struck by a great swordfish.

Late in October they crossed the equator at last, and on the 28th Schouten and Le Maire publicly announced the scheme of the voyage to all officers and crewmen, revealing now that "we should try to get by a way other than the Strait of Magellan into the South Sea in order to discover there certain new countries in the south [*Terra Australis Incognita*] where it was thought great wealth could be got, or, if that did not succeed according to desire, that we should then sail along the great South Sea to the East Indies. There was great joy among the crew that day concerning this declaration, for they now knew whither they were being taken, and each one hoped to get something on his own account out of a prosperous voyage and to profit by it." Some of the men, to remember the name *Terra Australis*, wrote it in their caps with chalk.

The Atlantic crossing was uneventful, and on December 6 they saw the South American coast at about 47°30′S. They made for the harbor known as Port Desire, using Noort's journal as their guide, but the tide was high and some rocks near the entrance that Noort had described were not visible, so they ran past the port. When they realized their error, they anchored just south of the harbor in 33 feet of water. Now the tide was running out, until to their dismay they were at a depth of only 14 feet, and the *Eendracht's* stern was firmly aground on the rocky bottom. Luckily, the wind was blowing from the land, "for had we had an east wind blowing at all freshly we should certainly have lost the ship." At daybreak the tide came in and they got clear, entering Port Desire and anchoring in 20 fathoms. But the anchors did not take hold, for the bottom was of slippery stones, and both vessels drifted against the shore. "The big ship," says Le Maire's journal, "lay side on upon the rocks and as the tide fell she slipped down a bit at intervals, but remained tight; the yacht, however, settled upon the rocks in such a manner that the ebb left her dry, and at low tide it was possible to walk under her keel near the mainmast without wetting one's feet. The keel stood more than a fathom out of the water, a thing terrible to behold." Only a strong gale kept her from toppling over. "This was evident from the fact that when the gale abated she fell to windward from the shore upon her side, with her deck three feet lower than her keel, whereat we were all very terrified, thinking that the yacht was quite lost to us, but the tide rising and the weather remaining calm, she floated again, at which we were not all a little glad."

Spared despite these mishaps, Schouten and Le Maire got their ships into a safe anchorage, the same one Noort had used, and celebrated their escape with a feast of penguins and penguin eggs. At a nearby island the men dug wells up to 14 feet deep but found only brackish water, and on December 11 a short party searching for fresh water or native camps had no success on either account. "We saw some ostriches and animals almost like deer, with very long necks, which were very shy of us," says the Le Maire account. "On the summit of the mountain we found some graves, consisting of a few heaps of stones, and as we did not know what these meant we overturned one heap and found under it the bones of human beings 10 and 11 feet in stature." This new contribution to the tale of the Patagonian giants was received with excitement when it reached Europe, and most of the early editions of Le Maire's *Australian Navigations* included a plate of the uncovered grave and its gigantic skeleton, with sailors of normal stature shown looking on in awe.

The mariners beached their ships deliberately on the 17th to clean them. It was at this time that the swordfish spear was discovered. Two days later, while the *Hoorn*'s hull was being cleansed of barnacles by fire, "the flames unexpectedly and very quickly flew up as far as the rigging and took hold of her, so that in an instant there was no more chance of putting them out, especially as the yacht was beached some 50 feet from the water; and we were therefore compelled to see her totally burnt before our eyes without being able to do aught to prevent it." The gunpowder took fire, causing an explosion that scattered merchandise and tools over a great distance, and the unfortunate ship burned all night. In the days that followed she was broken up and her guns, anchors, ironwork, and salvageable timbers were taken aboard the *Eendracht*.

A happier event was the discovery, on Christmas Day, of an abundant supply of water in pits of white clay; in a single day the Dutch seamen were able to load ten tons of water. The solitary *Eendracht* resumed her voyage on January 13, 1616, after she had been prepared for entry into tempestuous high latitudes by putting the guns and everything else that could be spared from the decks into the hold. Evidently there was some quarrel between Schouten and Le Maire at this time, but none of the accounts gives a comprehensible explanation of the point of disagreement.

On January 18 they passed the Falkland Islands, which they called the Isles of Sebald de Weert, and, at noon on the 20th, calculated that they now were crossing the latitude of the Atlantic entrance of the Strait of Magellan. They reckoned their position as some 20 leagues out from Tierra del Fuego. On the afternoon of the 23rd they sighted land in the west and southwest and, shortly afterward, in the south as well, as though perhaps an unknown continent did indeed block their path. But they kept on and, early on the morning of the 24th, sighted land to starboard—that is, to their right, or on the west—about a mile away. "The land ran east by south with very high mountains," says Le Maire's account, "which were all white with snow. We continued to sail along the land, and about noon we came to the end of it and saw more land east of the last, also very high and dangerous looking." A channel some eight miles wide separated the land to the west—Tierra del Fuego—from this newly found land mass to the east, and a strong current to the south ran between them. They put the latitude at 54°46'S. at noon. As they entered the channel they saw immense numbers of penguins and "whales by the thousands, so that we were compelled to be constantly on our guard . . . in order to avoid the whales and not run into them." On the morning of the 25th they sailed through, having land to either side of them and a clear sea ahead. They gave the name of Staten Land to the eastward land, in honor of the states of the Netherlands, and called the land to the west after Prince Maurice of Nassau. Staten Land appears on modern maps as Staten Island, for its insular nature was determined many years later; and the passage is called Le Maire Strait.

As they emerged from the southern end of Le Maire Strait, they could feel great waves rolling in from the southwest, as though this were certainly the place where Atlantic and Pacific met in a clashing of the waters, and they "were certain that we had open and deep water on the weather-side, not doubting that it was the Great South Sea, whereat we were very glad, holding that a way had been discovered by us which had until then been unknown to man, as we afterwards found to be the truth." Now they proceeded in a southwesterly direction past some small rocky islands and, on the evening of January 29, came to land again. It lay northwest of them, and they knew it to be "the land south of the Strait of Magellan, which stretches away to the south. It consisted entirely of high mountains covered with snow, and ends in a sharp corner, which we called the Cape of Hoorn, and which lies in latitude 57°48'." What Drake had discovered by accident, Schouten and Le Maire had found in deliberate search. The terminating point of South America was named in honor of Willem Schouten's native city of Hoorn; and as Cape Horn it still is known. More significantly, the Strait of Magellan, with all its mazy intricacy, had been relegated to history; for now the open sea route from ocean to ocean was known, and thereafter virtually all traffic in these parts would go round Cape Horn, not through the strait, until the cutting of the Panama Canal made such southerly voyages unnecessary.

12

The basic purpose of the voyage had been accomplished, for here indeed was a route to the Indies over which the United East India Company held no franchise. The land fell away, and on the last day of January the voyagers began to sail north in what they knew to be the Pacific. Through storm and mist they moved along, and when, on February 12, they reckoned themselves again in the latitude of the Strait of Magellan, but on the western side, a triple ration of wine was distributed to the seamen in celebration. On that day at a council of officers Le Maire formally requested that the new strait be named for him, "to the end," says the *Australian Navigations*, "that the glory of the action which he had so courageously undertaken and so happily executed, should remain to him perpetually." This was the most troubled point of contention between the seventeenth-century supporters of Schouten and of Le Maire; for the *Australian Navigations*, which purports to be Le Maire's own work, clearly states that he requested the designation in his own honor, and not for his father Isaac. No one would have objected had he named the strait for the elder Le Maire, the instigator of the voyage, but as it was, he gave offense to Schouten, and the pro-Schouten account of the expedition declares, "At the instance of the Commissary Jacob Le Maire, the Council ordered that the new passage should be named *the Strait of Le Maire*, although of good right it would have been better named *the Strait of Willem Schouten*, our ship master, by whose industry, good management, and knowledge in navigation the discovery was principally effected." Certainly the veteran Schouten, and not the inexperienced Jacob Le Maire, was responsible for the successful attainment of the new strait; on the other hand, Le Maire was Schouten's superior officer and had the legal if not the moral right to claim the strait for himself. It was the most significant achievement of discovery in this area since Magellan's own voyage, though, and it would have been more proper, surely, to have called the strait after both Le Maire and Schouten.

It was not done that way; and there was little opportunity to debate the point or to celebrate the feat, for the weather was harsh, and all the month of February they beat onward to the north without touching land. On March 1 they came to the Juan Fernández Islands, with many men suffering from scurvy, but by mistake approached the islands from the west, found no anchorage, and were unable either to reach shore or to get around to the side where a landing could be made. The sick men looked longingly at "a fine verdant valley" in which pigs and goats could be seen, but they had to be content with fish, which were taken by the ton. One boat did reach shore and collected water; her men tried to hunt the animals, but were hampered by underbrush and caught nothing. On the third day the breeze carried the ship four miles from the islands, and they spent all day trying to get back to them, "which at last began to vex us, seeing that it was impossible to make them. It was therefore then agreed and decided by the Council that we should leave the islands and pursue our course in the prosecution of our voyage, since we had a very favorable wind each day which we were neglecting to use—this to the very great pain and sorrow of the sick, who thereby saw all their hopes of life lost, but God gives relief." To Jan Schouten, Willem's brother, the only relief granted was death on April 9, after a month of suffering "from a very grievous malady."

The Dutch in the Orient

By then the *Eendracht* was more than 2,000 miles west of Peru, and Schouten and Le Maire were searching the empty Pacific perplexedly for some trace of *Terra Australis*. Their course had taken them northwest in a month's time from Juan Fernández, in 33°40′S., by their reckoning, to 15°S. But on the day after Jan Schouten's funeral, a small low island appeared to the northwest. Le Maire suspected, probably correctly, that this was the island Magellan had named San Pablo, in the group he called the Desaventuradas. Quite likely it was Pukapuka of the Danger Islands. Landing a boat proved impossible on account of rough surf; Le Maire, who led a shore party, had to anchor his boat and swim with his men to the beach, using ropes to keep everyone together. "In the evening," Schouten's account declares, "they returned on board, without having done anything, except that they brought some herbs, which tasted very much like cresses. They also said they had found three dogs, which could not bark or make any noise." Le Maire's account adds the gratuitous information that these were "Spanish" dogs, presumably descendants of some left behind by Magellan a hundred years earlier. On their account, the Dutchmen named the place Honden Eyland, "Island of Dogs."

It held no refreshment for them, and they went on, sighting another island on April 14. The *Eendracht* headed for it, and, says the Le Maire account, "Towards the evening, when our vessel was still quite a mile from the land, a canoe came to meet us containing four Indians, who were quite naked and red of color, with very black and long hair. They kept a good way off the ship all the time, calling us and making signs that we should come ashore, but we could not understand them nor they us, although we called to them in Spanish, Malay, Javanese, and in our Dutch language." This was probably Takaroa Atoll. The natives eagerly beckoned the Dutch ashore, at one point overturning a canoe in their excited gestures, but the mariners could not find a place to anchor. The *Eendracht* circled the island, which was nothing more than a narrow ring of sand enclosing a large salt-water lagoon, but the bottom was far beyond the reach of their lines. The natives continued to signal, shouting, climbing trees, waving their skimpy garments. Three islanders approached the ship in a canoe and accepted gifts of knives and beads but would not come aboard. Finally one man overcame his timidity and boarded the ship, where he grew bolder at the sight of iron, pulling some nails from the portholes in the cabins of Schouten and Le Maire and hiding them in his hair. "They were very greedy after iron," Le Maire says, describing how they attempted to steal a boat-hook, refused to return a metal pannikin in which they had been served wine, and "pulled at and thought they could drag out the bolts in the ship." When a shore party of eight musketeers and six seamen with swords went to the beach under Aris Claesz, 30 natives with clubs attacked them, evidently wishing to do nothing more serious than ransack their pockets for bits of metal; the musketeers opened fire, and the islanders, who were armed with nothing more deadly than spike-tipped sticks, fled, leaving several of their number dead. After this inauspicious episode the Dutch departed, giving the island the name of Sonder Gront, "Bottomless," from their failure to secure an anchor.

On the 16th at daybreak they discovered another island to the north, uninhabited and again rising so steeply from the sea that it was impossible to attain anchorage. Men went ashore and found water, four casks of which were taken to the ship with great difficulty by swimming them through the heavy surf; they also collected lobsters, crabs, snails "of very good flavor," and the cresslike herb which, when boiled, was an excellent scurvy remedy. This island, which may have been Manihi Atoll, they called Waterlandt on account of the fresh water obtained there.

The sea had been calm on this journey from atoll to atoll, with scarcely any waves, leading them to hope they were near the desired southern continent. They proceeded westward, coming on April 18 to the next island in the group, once again a narrow, ringlike atoll with no access for their ship. A shore party managed a landing, frightening off half a dozen natives, one of whom seemed to be holding a bow and arrow—uncommon weapons for the Pacific region at that time. Schouten wrote, "Our people returning aboard from the island were entirely covered with flies, so that we could not see their faces or hands; besides the boat and oars, as far as they were out of the water, were wholly covered and black with flies; a very strange thing to see, these flies came aboard with them, and, without ceasing, they kept flying about the bodies and faces, that we did not know by what means to get rid of them, so much that when we ate or drank all was full of flies, we slapped our faces and hands without ceasing, made instruments to kill them as fast as we could; this lasted two or three days with great plague, then arose a fresh wind, by the aid whereof, and our continually chasing them away, they vanished in three or four days." They called the island, accordingly, Vliegen Eyland, "Island of Flies."

Now they were through with the Tuamotus, and after leaving the fly-plagued island (perhaps Rangiroa), they proceeded westward toward an unhappy incident that took place late in April, according to Le Maire, or on May 8, according to Schouten—for at this point a serious discrepancy develops in the dates of the two narratives. Both accounts agree that in latitude 15°20′S., at a distance computed to be "1,510 German leagues" from the coast of South America, a sail was seen in the south, coming rapidly toward the *Eendracht*. At first it was thought to belong to a Spanish ship, but shortly it must have become apparent that the sail was of no European design. The other vessel was, in fact, a large double native canoe. Schouten had a shot fired across her bows to make her strike sail and wait to be identified; why he thought this international signal would be intelligible to the occupants of the canoe is hard to say, but it was unknown to them, and in their terror they reacted logically and prudently by making all the speed they could in an attempt to escape. Whereupon, says Le Maire, "we therefore launched our shallop with ten musketeers to take her, and whilst these were rowing towards her we again sent a shot abaft her, but all without intention of striking or damaging her, but still she would not haul down, seeking rather to outsail us as much as possible. . . . The shallop, which was too smart for her, overtook her, and when our men were about half a musket shot off they fired four times with a musket. When we approached her, and before our men boarded her, some of her crew sprang overboard from fright; amongst others there was one with an infant and another who was wounded, having three holes in his back, but not very deep, for they were caused by a grazing shot, and this man we got out of the water again. They also threw many things overboard, which were small mats, and amongst other things, three hens. Our men sprang on board the little vessel and brought her alongside of us without the least resistance on the part of her crew, as indeed they had no arms. When she was alongside of us we took on board two men who had remained in her and these immediately fell down at our feet, kissing our feet and hands. One was a very old gray man, the other a young fellow, but we could not understand them, though we treated them well. And the shallop immediately rowed back to the aforesaid men who had jumped overboard, in order to rescue them, but they got only two who were floating on one of their oars and who pointed with their hands to the bottom, wishing to say that the others were already drowned. . . . In the vessel were some eight women and three young children, still at the breast, as well as some who were perhaps nine or ten years old, so that we thought they must have been in all quite twenty-five strong; both men and women were entirely naked and wore only a bagatelle over their privy parts."

Schouten and Le Maire did their best to undo this tragic, blundering collision of cultures, restoring the survivors to their vessel and giving them beads and knives, for which they received coconuts and finely made mats in return. Le Maire reports his astonishment at seeing these people drink salt water from the sea, and give it to their infants as well; Schouten, commenting on the vessel, described it as strange in form and construction, "for it was in effect a platform on two little canoes, separated from each other about a fathom and a half, and upon these across were laid thick sticks and beams, upon which was built the said platform, well fastened together, and above it a little shed of mats, wherein were the women and children; they steered the boat before and abaft with oars pretty broad and thick. The mast was in the forepart of the ship, fastened in a step with thick ropes. They had a long yard in the manner of mizzens, and good ropes of several kinds and of different stuff, a hatchet of black touchstone, which they would not on any account sell; the sail was made with mats; the whole, in short, very well made, and they well experienced in the navigation to benefit of all winds, like good sailors, but they do not use the compass, sailing in uncertainty." This was one of the first encounters between Europeans and the oceangoing seafarers of Polynesia whose nautical feats of sailing out of sight of land far excelled anything accomplished in the Christian world before the era of Columbus and Magellan.

The two vessels parted, and the native canoe headed

toward the southeast, with one of the widowed women lamenting bitterly. This was not the course on which they were bound when they had the ill luck to meet the *Eendracht*, and perhaps they now were off to report the event to some island authority. Still looking for *Terra Australis*, the Dutch ship pursued its westward track, and on April 21 by Le Maire's journal, May 10 by Schouten's, two more islands came into view, one mountainous, the other, two miles to the south, long and low. A day later they anchored by the high island whose cliffs were covered with coconut palms, on which account the Dutch named it Cocos Island. (It should not be confused with the Cocos Island off the coast of Panamá; this was actually Tafahi, in the Tonga Islands.) Native canoes swarmed about them, and the islanders willingly traded coconuts and yams to the Dutch for nails and beads at a ratio of four or five coconuts for one nail or a small string of beads. While this was taking place, the ship's shallop was sent to the flat southern island to search for a safer harbor, and there found itself surrounded by dozens of canoes occupied by natives armed with spears of sharpened wood. They boarded the shallop and began to pilfer things, and one of the seamen was forced to fire his musket several times, "whereat," says Le Maire, "they first laughed and made fun, thinking it was child's play, but the third time one was hit in the chest, the bullet coming out at the back." The islanders fled with their wounded comrade, and the shallop returned to Cocos Island. Trade was almost uncontrollably brisk there. The Dutch had won the friendship of the natives with a demonstration of fiddle playing, "at which they took great pleasure, laughing and talking amongst themselves: our sailors who were most of them good drolls, began dancing, which the savages also did, who showed them delighted and joyful beyond measure, making very soon a great acquaintance with us." The Schouten account continues, "This done we gave them to understand that they should bring us coconuts, bananas, yams, hogs, and fowls, or other goods and fruits of the country for nails, and such like merchandises, which they understood very well, and promised to do so, saying that all these and more things were there in abundance. Then they went ashore and immediately brought us at least 200 coconuts, and afterwards came so thick on board of us, that we did not know how to turn ourselves for the multitude of people; they came to us swimming, having the coconuts round their neck, and all of them were so terribly given to pilfering that one could not guard against it. They attempted to pull out the nails of the ship with their teeth and nails; they took the balls of the cannon; one took a knife out of the hand of a kitchen boy, by which his fingers were all cut, and he threw himself immediately overboard. One took a brass inkholder, one a mattress, one a pillow, another a coat, others pushed their noses into the gunner's cabin; in short more than 100 eyes were requisite to guard our goods."

The next morning the canoes returned laden with coconuts, yams, roots, fresh water, and some small pigs; the Dutch acquired so many coconuts that a dozen could be given to each of the *Eendracht*'s 85 men. The natives, says Le Maire, "were greatly surprised at the size and strength of the vessel; some climbing down aft, near the rudder right under the ship, knocked against the bottom with a stone to see how strong it was." A little later came a messenger from the king of the flat southern island, bearing a young wild pig as a gift, and in the afternoon the monarch himself arrived in a big *prau* accompanied by 35 smaller canoes. "This king or chief was called *Latou* by his people," Le Maire's journal notes. "We received him with drums and trumpets, whereat they were greatly astonished. . . . They showed us much honor and amity, according to appearances, bowing their heads, beating their foreheads with their fists and performing

[*475*]

other strange ceremonies. When he was still a little way off the king began to call aloud and to rave as if he were offering up prayer in his fashion, and all the other people did the same, without our knowing what it meant, but we presumed it was their welcome. Shortly afterwards the king sent us a mat by his servants to whom we gave in return an old hatchet, a few beads, some old nails and a piece of linen, which he received with gladness, laying the same three times upon his head and then bowing his head low, as a sign of reverence and gratitude or respect." The latou would not board their ship, but his son did and, by gestures, invited the Dutch to come to their island.

On the following day the natives returned in great numbers, once more trading coconuts for nails, and again the latou's son pressed the Dutch to cross from Cocos Island to the other. When the morning's barter was done, the *Eendracht* hoisted anchor and set sail to go over. Suddenly it became apparent that some two dozen of the largest canoes were forming into something suspiciously like a battle formation; then a drum began to beat, and angry shouts were heard. One canoe sped toward the Dutch ship with great swiftness, deliberately colliding at full force, which did no harm to the *Eendracht* but shattered the canoe and sent her crew leaping into the water. "The others," wrote Le Maire, "began to throw stones at us most bravely, thinking to frighten us thereby, but we fired amongst them with muskets and three cannon loaded with musket balls and old nails, so that all who were alongside threw themselves into the sea." Though nearly a thousand natives now were trying to attack, the Dutch easily eluded them and put out to sea, giving the flat island the appellation of Verraders Eyland, "Traitor's Island."

Still following a course far to the south of the routes taken by most other Pacific voyagers, the *Eendracht* came on May 14 (Le Maire: April 24) to a small island about a hundred miles farther west, in 16°S., which they named Good Hope Island. Here they gathered water and slew two natives of a 14-canoe attacking party. This was the island of Niuafoo, lying between the Tonga and Fiji groups. Though they had no very clear idea of where they were, the voyagers realized they must be nearing the vicinity of New Guinea, and, Schouten's account declares, on May 18 "we assembled our grand council" to discuss their course. Schouten pointed out "that we had already sailed full 1,600 leagues from the coast of Peru and Chile, and had not yet discovered the *Terra Australis* as had been expected, and that if we advanced farther to the west in this latitude, we should undoubtedly fall in with the south side of New Guinea, where it was uncertain whether any passage would be found; and if there should not be one, the ship and merchandise would be lost, as it was impossible to return to the east against the constant trade wind." Of course a passage south of New Guinea did exist— the Torres Strait—for, ten years before, Luis Vaez de Torres had sailed the whole length of New Guinea's southern coast, proving it an island and continuing thence to the Moluccas. But the report of Torres' historic voyage was buried in the archives at Manila and would not become known until 1762; and the only other ship that had then ventured south of New Guinea, Willem Janszoon's *Delft* in 1605, had not traversed the strait. Both Janszoon and Torres, apparently, had had glimpses of the authentic *Terra Australis* south of New Guinea—the continent of Australia—but had not approached it closely, and now Willem Schouten forfeited a great role in geographical history by recommending to the council of the *Eendracht* that, for safety's sake, they change their course and turn north, "that they might be able to pass by the north of New Guinea to the Moluccas. Which advice, being maturely considered by each person, appeared to be well founded; and it was unanimously, and with one voice, concluded to sail to the north to avoid falling to the south of New Guinea." So goes the Schouten version. The version prepared by the Le Maire family insists that Jacob Le Maire wished to keep going due west, at least for another 150 miles, but that Schouten's views prevailed, preventing them from making the discovery of the *Terra Australis*. (Actually they would have had to continue some 1,300 miles on their present course, not 150, to reach the eastern coast of Australia.) Northward they turned; the reality of the Moluccas was more compelling than the dream of *Terra Australis*.

13

Two islands appeared on May 19, the day after the taking of this decision. Two days of contrary winds intervened before a landing could be made, but on the 21st the *Eendracht* approached, greeted by islanders in three-man canoes who set up shouts of welcome. There was an exchange of fish for beads, and some natives came on board in seeming friendship. One, though, crept into the galley and stole one of Le Maire's shirts, which was hanging up to dry. The supercargo, Aris Claesz, saw the theft and demanded the return of the shirt; the thief began to hurl stones at him, which Claesz scooped up and threw back. On deck another native made a menacing gesture at a seaman with his spear, leading some of the sailors to think they were to be attacked; muskets and cannon were fired, and the natives took alarm and leaped into the sea, abandoning the stolen shirt. But soon more friendly relations were established and trade was begun. The shallop went out and found an excellent harbor in a gulf near the native village, which pleased Schouten so much "that he said here was the true *Terra Australis;* seeing that here was found a river of fresh water, many hogs seen ashore, and plenty of other things. He even proposed to stay there the space of five weeks."

The native king invited the Dutch to his village, which consisted of a number of circular huts 25 feet in circumference and ten or 12 feet high, pointed at top and covered with leaves. On the morning of the 24th Aris Claesz and two other men went ashore, with six natives delivering themselves to the *Eendracht* as hostages. Claesz found the *ariki*, or king, seated on a mat in an open shed, his hands joined and his forehead nearly touching the ground. He maintained this posture for nearly half an hour, showing evident signs of perplexity toward the end, while Claesz, equally perplexed, stood by wondering what to do. At length it occurred to Claesz to adopt the same position, which the ariki had been waiting for him to do; and the chief, greatly relieved, rose now and kissed his hands and feet. "Another man of great quality, who was seated near the king, did not do less," says Schouten, "weeping and crying like a child, wishing to say and show many things, putting Claesz' foot upon his neck, whom he made sit down on a little mat, and he himself on the ground, humbling himself before him like a reptile." All was well: a sword that had been taken from the Dutchmen was returned and the thief beaten in their presence, four small pigs were given them, and at the ariki's request the guns of the *Eendracht* were fired, which threw the islanders into panic even though they had been warned there would be a great noise.

On the 25th the natives offered in trade more coconuts than the Dutch could use, and the next day, as a token of the growing harmony, Le Maire himself went ashore with Claesz, taking along a trumpeter and such gifts for the ariki as beads, gold thread, a mirror, and a magnifying glass. The king welcomed them with deep prostrations, escorted them to his shed to wait out a rainstorm, and listened in joy and amazement to the sound of the trumpet. He and his son removed their headdresses of plaited feathers and placed them on the heads of Le Maire and Claesz, which act is considerably amplified in the Le Maire account into a ceremony of submission in which the ariki was "crowning them king and viceroy of the island, as a due recompense to their great labors, care, and diligence which they had bestowed in the enterprise and execution of so troublesome a voyage." Le Maire attempted to purchase hogs, but these proved to be in short supply.

In the days that followed, the mariners and the natives mingled both on shore and on the ship. "Our men danced with the savages," says Le Maire, "who were very pleased thereat, being surprised that we treated them so familiarly and with such kindness. We got to be as free and easy there as if we had been at home." Still hoping to obtain hogs, Le Maire went ashore again—to the sound of trumpets—and managed to purchase two, but at a very high price. During this visit he presented some newly caught fish to the ariki, "which he received very willingly, and ate them immediately, heads, tails, entrails, and all, with a good appetite." The king of the neighboring island came over, and Le Maire watched the two monarchs greet each other elaborately and then fall into a loud dispute, apparently because the second king had proposed a plan to seize the Dutch ship, which the friendly ariki feared to do.

Le Maire and Claesz, with some other men, made a journey inland on May 29. The king's son and brother were their guides; they went up into the mountains, spanning valleys rendered bare by heavy rains, until the path became too difficult. On the way back the king's son showed how coconuts were harvested: he "tied a bandage round his feet or legs and climbed with great dexterity and swiftness up a

straight tall tree, and in a moment brought down ten coconuts, which he opened very easily in a moment by a peculiar
knock with a small piece of wood." Toward noon the entire
group returned to the *Eendracht* to dine. Despite Schouten's
wish to prolong the island idyll for five weeks, Le Maire had
decided to depart in two days' time, and at lunch he conveyed this news to the king's son, "whereat the young king
was so glad that he immediately jumped up from the table
and went into the gallery shouting out that we intended to go
in two days." His delight was a reaction to his distress over
the quantity of provisions that the Dutch were draining from
a none too wealthy island; for beads and knives and nails, no
matter how interesting they might be, were less useful to the
natives than the coconuts and yams that the mariners were
acquiring in such huge amounts.

The ariki himself came aboard later in the day, inspect-
ing the ship and giving special attention to the big guns, and
in the evening the Dutch officers went to the king, whom
they found being entertained by a bevy of naked dancing
girls. "One of them," wrote Le Maire, "played upon a piece
of hollow wood like a pump that gave forth some sound,
whereupon these maidens danced very prettily and entertain-
ingly and with much grace to the measure of that music, so
that our people were surprised to see the like amongst these
savage folk." During the feast that followed, two natives
stole some fish, which so enraged the king that he had them
beaten almost to death.

The following morning, May 30, the ariki sent two
small hogs as gifts, no doubt to encourage the speedy departure of his revered but expensive guests. That afternoon the
king of the neighboring island returned, accompanied by 300
of his men, and "when that king had almost come up to the
other he began to bow and to bend before him from afar with
strange ceremonies and homage, falling with his face to the

earth and praying incessantly, with much shouting and raving, and with very great zeal, so it seemed to us." A feast was held at which the chief delicacy was *kava*, a beverage which Le Maire, Claesz, and their companions, like many explorers in Polynesia since their day, found to be no temptation. It was prepared, said Le Maire, from a green herb, which they began to chew to a pulp, then "they took it out of their mouths and put it all together in a great trough or platter of wood, poured water upon it, stirred and kneaded it together, and gave it to the kings, who drank thereof with the nobles. They also offered it to our men, but these had more than enough at the sight of it." The main course was roast pork, since the other king had brought 16 hogs; Le Maire was not delighted by the method of cooking them, for they "merely had the entrails taken out, and all bloody, without washing them, threw some hot stones into them to roast them within," yet the flavor of the nearly raw meat was quite acceptable. At the conclusion of the feast, the Dutch received "eleven small live pigs and a few of medium size. We presented them in return with three small copper pails, four knives, twelve old nails and some beads, wherewith they were well satisfied."

The visit was drawing to its end. On the 31st, as the *Eendracht* made ready to sail, both kings came aboard, presenting six more pigs, and the common folk brought great quantities of yams, bananas, and coconuts. Schouten and Le Maire toasted the monarchs with wine, displayed a portrait of Maurice of Nassau to them, attempted to explain a map of the world, and offered more beads and knives. When Le Maire escorted them to shore he received three more pigs, which he brought on board. Now it was time for farewell, much to the relief and satisfaction of the islanders, "since as long as we were there," said Le Maire, "they were in constant fear that we should kill them and take their land." He summed up his impression of the people by saying that the men were strong, agile, intelligent, and handsome, the women ugly, slack-bosomed, immodest, and unchaste. He admired the abundant hair of the men, which some wore curled, "others beautifully crimped, others again had it tied up in four, five, and six plaits," and some had standing on end to a great height; but the hair of the women was cut as short as that of men in Holland. "We could not perceive that this people worshipped any god or gods or that they cultivated any religion, small or great, living only a life free of care, like the birds in the forest. They know naught of buying or selling, but by fits they presented us with something and we them. They neither sow nor mow nor do they perform any kind of work; the earth of itself gives them all that they need to support life. . . . On leaving we gave these islands the name of the Hoorn Islands, after our native town of Hoorn, and the bay in which we had lain that of Eendrachts Bay, after our ship." They still are known on our maps as the Hoorn Islands, though to their inhabitants they remain Futuna and Alofi.

The Dutch put to sea on the first of June, losing two anchors in the process, and followed a northwesterly course. Le Maire, who seems to have had something romantic in his spirit, still regretted the decision not to have gone further in the quest for *Terra Australis*, but the more businesslike Schouten had his way, creating continued disagreement between the two leaders. Making brief calls at a number of islands, they came by June 25 to a high, rugged land which they took to be the eastern coast of New Guinea; it was in fact New Ireland, an island east of New Guinea. It was inhabited by naked savages, very black of skin, who wore rings in their nostrils and came out to pelt the Hollanders fiercely from slings. They took flight when fired upon. Next day there was another battle farther along the coast in which the Dutch killed a dozen of the primitive islanders and took three

[*483*]

prisoners. One of these they ransomed for ten pigs; another died, and the third was so badly wounded that they set him ashore.

The *Eendracht* left New Ireland on July 1 and anchored at a smaller island, where 25 canoes commenced an attack and were driven off with heavy losses. One Dutchman was wounded, "being," says Le Maire, "the first that was hurt in all our voyage." A young native of about eighteen was captured and named Moses, after the wounded man. They sailed on, now coasting New Britain, not at all clear about the proper location of the huge island of New Guinea, and hoping every day to find themselves in the Moluccas, which they knew lay just west of that island. They were able to obtain water, coconuts, and hogs, not without frequent combat; the natives here seemed more civilized, "for they covered their privy parts with small leaves and had a handsomer kind of canoe, adorned fore and aft with a little carved work. They are very proud of their beards, which they powder with chalk as well as the hair of their head." On July 5 a "burning island" came in view, "emitting flames and smoke from the summit," and Schouten guessed that they might have arrived in the Banda Islands, where a volcano of about the same height was found; but on a close approach they saw land beyond the volcano, extending so far to the east and west that no end could be seen on either side, with three or four more mountains rising from it, and they knew they had reached New Guinea at last.

All of July they followed the northern coast of New Guinea, bothered by rain and lightning and wondering if the island would ever come to an end. All the peas, beans, and barley had been consumed, as had the meat, bacon, and fish; they were rationed now to bread, oil, Spanish wine, and a glass of brandy per day, and for other provisions they would have to trust to the natives. These folk, the Papuans, struck

Le Maire as "a funny kind of people, having short hair, which was curled, and wearing rings through their noses and ears, with certain small feathers on their head and arms, and hog's tusks around their neck and on their chest as ornaments." At one village, the Papuans were glad to trade coconuts for linen, but at another they "pelted us very fiercely with darts so that some sixteen of our men were severely wounded, one being shot right through his arm, another through his leg, a third in his neck, hands, or other parts." Relations improved on the following days, and they were able to purchase coconuts, bananas, and green ginger for old nails, rusty knives, and beads. On July 23 they encountered some natives of a different race, taller and lighter-skinned, who clearly had dealt with strangers before: in their ears they had rings of green, blue, and white glass, seemingly of Spanish origin, and brought a few saucers of Chinese porcelain to trade. Civilization was nearer, obviously.

The voyage now was enlivened by an earthquake, by "terrific thunder and lightning," and "such heavy rain that we had never in our life seen the like of it," and frequently the mariners found themselves sailing into time-consuming cul-de-sacs. They crossed the equator on July 31, 1616, ending a continuous sojourn of nine months in the southern hemisphere, and on August 3 New Guinea came to an end after they had followed its coast for 280 miles. The problem now was to find the Moluccas, for no one except Torres had ever entered the East Indies from the southeastern side as they were doing, all other European voyages having been made via the Philippines. Some islands appeared on the 5th, inhabited by people who met them under a flag of peace; they spoke a few words of the language of Ternate, and there was one among them fluent in Malay, a language that Aris Claesz understood. Some also spoke a little Spanish, and they wore bright-colored clothes, silk breeches, turbans, one a hat of

Spanish felt. "They exchanged their wares with us for small beads and were shy and afraid of us," Le Maire's account declares. "We asked them what their country was called, but they would not tell us, for which reason partly and also from other circumstances we opined that we were at the eastern end of Gilolo . . . and that they were natives of Tidore, friends of the Spaniards, as indeed we found to be so." From August 6 to 18 the voyagers attempted to get around the northeast corner of Halmahera, the largest island of the Moluccas, but they were bedeviled by calms, currents, and difficult winds. At a village farther up the coast they anchored and found it inhabited by men of Ternate, whose language they could speak; they learned here that some 20 Dutch ships were cruising in the East Indies and felt great joy at the thought of meeting countrymen again—without stopping to consider that all of those countrymen would be in the service of the United East India Company, whose monopoly on the spice trade they had come to break. The *Eendracht* remained here until September 5 and then resumed her endeavor to round Gilolo; Ternate was only 25 miles away, but they lay becalmed for days, and when they sailed they could make little more than three or four miles a day. On September 17, though, they encountered at sea the *Morning Star* of Rotterdam, learning that she was one of the ships that had passed through the Strait of Magellan under Spilbergen, and that Ternate lay nearby. (Spilbergen himself, with two other ships of his five-ship fleet, had gone from Ternate to Java the previous week and had landed at Djakarta on September 15.) The *Eendracht* made for Ternate, reaching it later in the day on September 17, and anchored before the Dutch fort of Malayo.

They had come safely to the isles of cloves with every man in good health, for scurvy was much less of a problem for the Dutch than it was aboard the generally overcrowded

Spanish ships. They had discovered the Le Maire Strait, had been the first mariners to sail around Cape Horn, and had added a number of islands to the map of the South Pacific. Remarkably, the *Eendracht*'s entire crew had come through the voyage alive, and just two men of the ill-fated *Hoorn* had died at sea, a sailor off the coast of Portugal early in the journey and Jan Schouten in the Pacific. With some satisfaction, then, Schouten and Le Maire went ashore that evening to present themselves to the high officials of the East India Company at Ternate. Le Maire carried with him a letter of introduction from his father to the Governor-General of the Dutch East Indies, Gerhardt Reynst, but upon landing he discovered that Reynst had died nine months before and had been succeeded by Laurens Reael. Reael welcomed the adventurers warmly, responding to the glamor of their achievement and tactfully choosing to overlook the fundamentally anti-V.O.C. purpose of the voyage. In the following week Schouten and Le Maire sold some spare anchors, guns, cables, lead, and other items that no longer would be required, as well as both shallops of the *Eendracht*, and when 15 of their seamen requested permission to transfer to the service of the East India Company, the necessary discharges were quickly given. On September 26 Le Maire and Schouten breakfasted on shore with Laurens Reael and formally took their leave, after which the governor-general and his staff escorted the voyagers to their ship with a color guard and a parade of armed troops. When these amiable ceremonies ended, the *Eendracht* sailed for Java, accompanied part of the way by Spilbergen's *Morning Star*, which was bound for the Moluccan island of Motir.

The pathetic final moments of this grand voyage of discovery were at hand. The *Eendracht* reached Java in mid-October, and on either the 20th or the 28th—the accounts are contradictory—anchored off Djakarta, where three

Dutch ships and three English vessels were taking on cargo. On the night of October 29 the *Eendracht* suffered her first fatality since leaving home when a sailor died; and two days later that grim and dedicated man, Jan Pieterszoom Coen of the Dutch East India Company, arrived from Bantam to look into the matter of this intrusion on the company's territory. To Coen, the company was indistinguishable from the nation, and in his patriotic zeal he regarded the arrival of the *Eendracht* with much the same warmth that the appearance of a Spanish galleon off Java would have produced in him.

On November 1 Coen ordered Schouten and Le Maire ashore to appear before a meeting of the V.O.C. Council. Brusquely he asked them why they had dared to infringe on the lawful rights of the East India Company. They replied that they had come to the East Indies neither by the Cape of Good Hope nor by the Strait of Magellan, but rather through a newly discovered passage, and so had committed no violation of the company's franchise. Coen was scornful of these claims. He refused altogether to believe that Schouten and Le Maire had sailed south of the Strait of Magellan, and he made harsh remarks about captains who deliberately went out of their way for the glory of finding new lands, thus dismissing the *Eendracht*'s adventures in the South Pacific. It made no difference to him that Schouten and many of the backers of the voyage came from his own native city of Hoorn; ignoring their insistent assertions of having found a new route, he found them guilty on the spot of having trespassed on the territory of the East India Company and ordered their ship and all the goods it contained confiscated for the use of the company. If they thought themselves wronged, he said, they were free to bring suit when they returned to the Netherlands. By nightfall on November 1 this cruel sentence had been carried out: two company officials had taken an inventory of everything on board the *Eendracht*, the seizure was consummated, and Schouten and Le Maire, with all their men, were compelled to quit the sturdy ship that had borne them halfway around the world. In his report to the directors of the East India Company, Coen declared that he had taken possession of the *Eendracht* because old Isaac Le Maire was "an opponent to the common good."

Deprived of their ship and the fruits of their discoveries, the men of the *Eendracht* suffered no other punishment and were free to make what arrangements for themselves they could. Most of the crewmen enrolled at once in the service of the East India Company. The rest, including Schouten, Le Maire, Aris Claesz, and many of the other officers, were put aboard Spilbergen's two ships, the *Great Sun* and the *Half Moon*, which shortly were to depart for Europe on the final leg of their own voyage of circumnavigation. Jacob Le Maire, his brother Daniel, Willem Schouten, and ten more of the *Eendracht*'s company were placed aboard Spilbergen's flagship, the *Great Sun*. Aris Claesz and another ten *Eendracht* veterans found berths on the *Half Moon*.

Spilbergen, a good company man himself, with a professional officer's disdain for irregular procedures, looked coldly upon these newcomers at first. He accepted at face value Coen's belief that they were lying about their newly found passage, writing in his journal at the beginning of November, "These people had not in so long a voyage discovered any unknown countries, nor any place for new commerce, nor anything which could be of benefit to the public, although they pretended that they had discovered a passage shorter than the usual passage: which is very improbable, inasmuch as it took them fifteen months and three days to make their voyage to Ternate, and that, too (according to their own admission) with a favorable wind and only one ship, which is not called upon to wait for others, as happens in a whole fleet." But the contact he had with the unfortunate voyagers during the next few weeks caused him to mellow this sharp evaluation. He was an excellent judge of men, able to see that Schouten and Le Maire both were strong of character, energetic, trustworthy. If they said they had come around South America a new way, he decided, it must be so. From his conversations with them he learned the details of their voyage and knew them to be authentic, and thereafter Spilbergen held both captains in high regard, giving them full credit for their important discovery.

On December 14, 1616, Spilbergen sailed from Djakarta for home. Le Maire, who had been in a dark, brooding mood since the loss of his ship at what should have been his moment of triumph, fell ill almost at once, and little more than a week after leaving Java he died—of a broken heart, it is said. He was only thirty-one years old. Spilbergen noted that Le Maire's death was a cause of grief to all on board, "since he was a man endowed with remarkable knowledge and experience in matters of navigation."

Spilbergen's two ships were separated at the beginning of January 1617. The *Great Sun* stopped at Mauritius on January 24 to take on provisions and water, passed around the Cape of Good Hope without seeing it, and on March 30 came to the island of St. Helena, where Spilbergen was relieved to find the *Half Moon* waiting for him. They went on together, and, Spilbergen wrote, "On the 1st day of July, through the mercy of the Almighty, we reached, with these two richly-laden vessels, the harbor of our country in the province of Zealand, to which we had so long looked forward, wherefore we all thanked and praised God Almighty for the mercy shown us and for bringing us back from so long and not less perilous a voyage." The fifth and the sixth circumnavigations thus ended together, with the core of the Schouten–Le Maire expedition coming home in Spilbergen's ships. Spilbergen's voyage around the world had lasted 37 days less than three years; two years and 17 days had elapsed since the departure from the Netherlands of Schouten and Le Maire. For Spilbergen, it was the culmination of a mission well fulfilled, although he had discovered nothing of consequence to geography; for Schouten, who had played his part in pioneering the vital Cape Horn route, the outcome had been financial disaster. Evidently Schouten struck some sort of agreement for recompense from the East India Company, and there is some likelihood that the company even helped to sponsor the publication of the account of the voyage that appeared in 1618. (As the price of its cooperation, it seems, it insisted that the role of Le Maire be suppressed in Schouten's book, for the company had no real quarrel with Schouten but entertained the deepest hostility toward the family of Le Maire.) As for old Isaac Le Maire, who had lost both his ship and his son, his only recourse was to the courts, and after two years he won a judgment from the Supreme Court of Holland and Zealand under which The Lords Seventeen of the East India Company were directed to return the confiscated vessel and its cargo and to pay all costs with interest from the date of seizure. But the V.O.C. chose to ignore the verdict, and Le Maire could not enforce it. In the end his only profit from the venture was the name of Le Maire on the new strait at South America's uttermost point.

[7]

THE WORLD
ENCOMPASSED

HE FIRST GREAT EPOCH OF CIRCUMNAVIGA-
tion was over. Magellan had shown the
world that man could encompass it by sea;
Drake, Cavendish, Noort, and Spilbergen
had demonstrated, with varying degrees of
skill and gallantry, that Magellan's feat
could be repeated; Schouten and Le Maire
had found a superior waterway that opened the Pacific to
regular commerce with Europe. There was no longer any
real reason that a voyage from Europe to the East Indies had
to be a circumnavigation, for it now was as feasible to sail
from west to east in the Pacific as from east to west, and
after six circumnavigations had been performed between
1519 and 1617, no more such voyages were executed until
the eighteenth century. The last attempt at an expedition in
the old manner was made in 1623, when the Dutch sent out
11 ships under the command of Jacob l'Hermite in an endeavor that met dismal fortunes. Some 42 men died when the
fleet had got no farther than Sierra Leone, and l'Hermite
himself contracted a disease there that took his life in less
than a year. The fleet passed through Le Maire Strait, made
the customary voyage up the western coast of South America

—where l'Hermite died—crossed to the Ladrones early in 1625, and arrived in the Moluccas, greatly reduced by hardship and illness, in March of that year. There the expedition was broken up, and though a few of the voyagers returned to Holland in the summer of 1626, their journey was a circumnavigation only in the narrowest technical sense, since the expedition had officially terminated in the Moluccas.

A time had come for consolidation of present gains, rather than continued questing after new empires. The Dutch had emerged as the chief beneficiaries of the era of the circumnavigations, for they held the tightest grasp on the Spice Islands, which had been the main goal of European voyagers since the time of Prince Henry the Navigator. That grasp was made more secure by the implacable Jan Coen, who, before his death in 1629—of an apoplectic stroke, at the age of forty-two—saw to it that the islands Magellan had coveted became the private property of the Dutch East India Company. To give the Netherlands their empire, Coen first found it necessary to force out his superior, Governor-General Reael, whom he regarded as indecisive and overly genteel—contrast Reael's treatment of Schouten and Le Maire with Coen's—and by 1618 Coen was master of the Dutch East Indies. A year later he destroyed the native town of Djakarta and soon was building on its site the new Dutch city of Batavia as his capital. (He wished to call it New Hoorn, but was overruled by The Seventeen.) The Dutch now had a firm hold on Java and also controlled the Banda, Amboina, and Molucca Islands, giving them a virtual monopoly of the sources of cloves, though for the time being a Spanish outpost on Tidore and an English factory on Amboina still remained. The Portuguese held on at Malacca, giving them control over the Sumatran pepper trade, but that too fell to the Dutch in 1641 when, after a blockade lasting many years, they expelled the Portuguese from the strategic port they had held so long. Thereafter, only a mop-ping-up operation was needed; the Dutch pushed Portugal out of Ceylon, eliminated most English trade in the East Indies, and finally got the Spaniards out of Tidore in 1663. The centuries-long struggle for control of the spice trade thus ended. At the peak of its power, about 1669, the V.O.C. possessed 150 trading ships, 40 vessels of war, and 10,000 soldiers, and was able to pay a dividend of 40 percent on its capital. After that its strength gradually ebbed, but not until after the Second World War did the Netherlands lose her Indonesian empire.

2

That other goal of early voyages to the Pacific, *Terra Australis*, remained a puzzle well into the eighteenth century. Even after Australia was discovered and its continental na-ture recognized, men continued to search for still another southern continent. As we have seen, the first explorers to sight Australia were probably Janszoon and Torres in 1606, though they got, at best, glimpses of one outlying peninsula. In 1611 the Dutch found an improved route to the East Indies via the Cape of Good Hope, which cut the average time of a journey from 18 months to six by swinging much farther to the south than previously to catch favorable winds; taking this route in October 1616, Dick Hartogszoon of Am-sterdam descended to 25°S. before beginning his northward curve and came upon the western coast of Australia. In 1618 another Dutch ship touched much the same part of Australia, but her skipper had no idea whether he beheld a new continent or merely a series of islands. The following year Frederick Houtman, bound for Batavia, came to the Austra-lian coast near the present site of Perth, followed it north for 400 miles, and persuaded himself that he had found Locach, the rich, fertile southern continent described by Marco Polo.

During the next two decades, the Dutch made sporadic attempts to find out more about this great territory south of New Guinea, with the major contribution that of Abel Tasman in 1642.

Tasman sailed from Java to Mauritius, then doubled back through the Indian Ocean and passed along the southern side of the new land mass without ever sighting its coast. Emerging near the island now known as Tasmania, he continued on into an unexplored part of the South Pacific until he came to a body of land that he thought might be the Staten Land of Schouten and Le Maire. That, however, lay east of Tierra del Fuego; Tasman, who was still in the Pacific, had discovered New Zealand. His voyage south of Australia severed that continent from the supposed *Terra Australis*, which was thought to extend to the South Pole. Australia, as it would later be called, had proved to be *a* southern continent, but not *the* southern continent, and for nearly a century and a half geographers would continue to urge efforts to find it. A typical attitude was that of John Callander, who, publishing in 1756 a collection of voyages to the Pacific, asked, "Who can doubt that this vast tract must furnish objects innumerable, both of commercial advantage and curiosity, equal to any that were found in America by the first discoverers? Numbers of people, entirely different from us, and from each other, in their figure, customs, manners, and religion; their animals, insects, fishes, plants, medicinal herbs, fruits, metals, and fossils entirely of another species. . . . Here too we are sure to find an advantageous market for all our wares. . . ." The continent whose discovery Callander and many like him advocated actually did exist, as Captain James Cook was destined to show late in the eighteenth century— but the real *Terra Australis Incognita*, when it was found, turned out to be frosty Antarctica, no advantageous market at all.

There was little Pacific exploration in the generation after Tasman. "It were to be wished," said the directors of the Dutch East India Company in 1645, "that the said land [*Terra Australis*] continued still unknown and never explored, so as not to tell foreigners the way to the Company's overthrow." The Dutch did send some ships to explore the coast of Australia, usually only to have them strike reefs and go down; but their time of oceanic supremacy was ending, and now the English were returning to the Pacific. After 1670 many English buccaneers raided the Spanish settlements of South America's western shore, some of them cutting across the Isthmus of Panamá to build ships on the far side, others traversing the Strait of Magellan or Le Maire Strait. One of them, the ingenious and widely renowned William Dampier, completed a private circumnavigation of a kind between 1684 and 1691, with many detours and changes of ship, in the course of which he was part of the first group of Englishmen to land in Australia. Dampier made a more orthodox voyage around the world between 1703 and 1706 as a privateer, and from 1708 to 1711 he went around again as pilot to an expedition led by Captain Woodes Rogers. This was again purely a pillaging enterprise, notable chiefly for the rescue from the Juan Fernández Islands of a castaway mariner named Alexander Selkirk, whose story became the inspiration for Defoe's *Robinson Crusoe*.

These post-Elizabethan piracies proved so profitable that in 1718 two separate circumnavigations began, both for the same ignoble motive. Their captains, George Shelvocke and John Clipperton, set out together but lost sight of each other's vessels after six days. Clipperton went through the Strait of Magellan, ransacked the Spanish ports of South America and Mexico for several years, and met Shelvocke off the coast of Mexico in 1721. The captains were cool to one another and soon parted again, Clipperton going on to the Ladrones and then to China, losing most of his booty there, and coming home in June 1722, to die within a week of his arrival. Shelvocke, who had taken Le Maire Strait and rounded Cape Horn, achieved a place in literary history late in 1719 when, as he tells us in his own narrative, "a disconsolate black albatross" followed his ship for several days south of Le Maire Strait, "till Hatley (my second captain) observing, in one of his melancholy fits, that this bird was always hovering near us, imagined, from his color, that it might be some ill omen. That which, I suppose, induced him the more to encourage his superstition, was the continued series of contrary tempestuous winds, which had oppressed us ever since we had got into this sea. But be that as it would, he, after some fruitless attempts, at length shot the albatross, not doubting (perhaps) that we should have a fair wind after that." Samuel Taylor Coleridge was to make literary capital of the incident.

Shelvocke reached England by way of China and Africa in July 1722, and this second group of circumnavigations— those of the English buccaneers—came to an end. The Dutch meanwhile had spanned the world again, in 1721–22, under Jacob Roggeveen, who hoped to find *Terra Australis* but discovered instead Easter Island and its strange stone images. Next, in 1740, after the outbreak of war between England and Spain, Commodore George Anson led six ships of the Royal Navy around the globe to raid Spanish ports, coming home in 1744 with only one vessel remaining, but that one bearing £400,000 in treasure. Like most of the circumnavigations of the first half of the eighteenth century, Anson's voyage was geographically sterile.

A new phase of world-girdling travel began in the latter half of that century: officially sponsored government exploring expeditions, most of them British. The conviction that

Terra Australis could be found and would prove to be a rich prize was then at its strongest. In 1764 the British Admiralty sent John Byron—grandfather of the poet—to find the unknown continent, and also to locate the Northwest Passage across the top of North America. Ignoring that part of his assignment, Byron made for the Pacific and tried to explore the untouched region of the ocean between Chile and New Zealand. Wind conditions made a westward voyage in that latitude impossible, so he moved north into the islands of the South Pacific, called at Batavia, and came home quickly by way of the Cape of Good Hope. An expedition of 1767–68, led by Samuel Wallis and Philip Carteret, failed, as Byron had done, to find *Terra Australis*. At this time the French made their first circumnavigation, under Louis Antoine de Bougainville, who sailed at the end of 1766, paid a celebrated call on the isle of Tahiti, performed valuable scientific observations at sea, and returned to his homeland in 1769.

The greatest of all eighteenth-century circumnavigators, and probably the only captain whose achievements can be ranked beside Magellan's, began the first of his three major voyages while Bougainville was still at sea. He was Captain James Cook, who sailed from Plymouth in August 1768 aboard *H.M.S. Endeavour*, rounded Cape Horn, made astronomical observations at Tahiti, charted New Zealand, went up the east coast of Australia and discovered the Great Barrier Reef, and visited New Guinea and Java, before returning to England in 1771. Cook had seen no sign of a new southern continent and expressed his belief that no such thing existed except, possibly, in the vicinity of the South Pole. A geographical propagandist named Alexander Dalrymple took the opposite view, declaring in 1772, "The number of inhabitants in the southern continent is probably more than 50 millions." Envisioning a territory stretching from Chile to Australia, Dalrymple stirred such fantasies of trade and exploitation that Cook was sent out again by the Royal Navy in July of that year with two small, sturdy ships, the *Resolution* and the *Adventure*. On this voyage, which lasted until 1775, Cook became the first mariner to cross the Antarctic Circle, penetrating as far south as 71°10′, where he was stopped by the fringes of the polar ice pack. He thereby demolished the old fantasy of a warm, inhabited southern continent, opening the way for the discovery of Antarctica in the nineteenth century. On his third voyage, begun in 1776, Cook went northward into the Pacific, and two years later met his death on a Hawaiian beach, dying as Magellan had died at the hands of the natives of a Pacific isle. With his passing an epoch closed. Cook had completed the work of the early circumnavigators, and no longer could expeditions go forth in the hope of finding vast tracts of unknown land. The outlines of the Earth's continents now were known; it was the job of those who followed after to fill in the details.

3

Traffic was heavy along the shores of Patagonia in the eighteenth century, and the many mariners who passed through the Strait of Magellan and around Cape Horn devoted themselves to the great biological mystery of the Patagonian giants, an enigmatic heritage bequeathed by Magellan's Pigafetta. The baffling colossi had been reported in *The World Encompassed by Sir Francis Drake;* Pedro Sarmiento, looking for Drake in the Strait of Magellan in 1580, had seen giants, according to the untrustworthy historian Argensola; Anthony Knyvet, of Cavendish's crew, claimed to have observed giants in the strait in 1592; Sebald de Weert in 1598, Noort in 1599, and Spilbergen in 1615 noticed men of great stature there, and Schouten and Le Maire, later in 1615, uncovered a grave containing the bones of men eleven feet long. Such a weight of evidence seemed unanswerable. Pigafetta was perhaps too fond of a good story; *The World Encompassed* appeared to have plagiarized its tale of giants from Pigafetta, and Knyvet was plainly a spinner of tall tales, but how could one argue away the reports of those stolid Hollanders? Dismissing the accounts of such men as Weert and Spilbergen was not easy.

Sir John Narborough, who spent ten months on the Patagonian coast in 1670, found nothing to indicate the existence of giants there. "The natives," he declared, are "not taller than generally Englishmen are," and one of his captains wrote in his journal that the Patagonians he had seen "were very well set men of no such extraordinary stature as is reported by Magellanes and other Spaniards; to be 10 or 11 foot high none of these being above 6 at the most but I suppose they did imagine none would come here to disprove them." This seemed almost a paraphrase of the words of Edward Cliffe's account of the Drake circumnavigation: "These men be of no such stature as the Spaniards report, being but of the height of English men. . . . But peradvanture the Spaniard did not think that any English men would have come thither so soon to have disproved them in this and divers others of their notorious lies. . . ." The skepticism that Narborough awakened was reinforced in 1741 when John Bulkeley and John Cummins, two of the officers of George Anson's circumnavigation, wrote, "The Indians we saw in the Straits of Magellan are people of a middle stature and well shaped," and in a later edition of their book, "The Patagonian Indians, at least those in that part of the country where we resided, were tall and well-made, being in general from five to six feet high."

One of the purposes of Commodore John Byron's circumnavigation of 1764–66 was to secure more information about the size of the Patagonians. In this he was successful, and Byron, "Foul-Weather Jack," depicted by his famous grandson as that "certain relative of mine," acquired a measure of international notoriety as a result of his Patagonian investigations. Byron's *Dolphin* anchored at Cape Vírgines near the Strait of Magellan on December 21, 1764, and shortly some natives appeared on the shore. Surprisingly, they were on horseback, a sign of European encroachment, for no horses were found in the Americas after remote prehistoric times until the Spaniards reintroduced them. The natives waved to Byron, inviting him to come ashore, and he landed to parley with their chief, while some 500 others remained at a distance. The first account of this meeting to reach England was in a letter from Bryon to his patron, Lord Egmont, written at Port Famine on February 24, 1756, and received the following June. Byron said of the Patagonians that they were "people who in size come the nearest to giants of any people I believe in the world," but he provided no precise measurements. This letter was not made public, but on May 9, 1766—two days after the *Dolphin*'s return to England—this notice appeared in the *Gentleman's Magazine:* "Commodore Biron [*sic*], in his Majesty's ship *Dolphin*, arrived in the Downs from the East Indies. She has been out upon discoveries and the papers say, has found out a new country in the East, the inhabitants of which are eight and a half feet high."

Since Byron had found no "new country," the other statement was equally suspect; but Byron himself made no immediate comment on the report, and soon every British journal was speculating on the size of the Patagonians. The *London Chronicle* declared on July 12, "We are informed that the giants found by Commodore Byron measured from 8 feet and ½ to 10 feet in height, and every way stout in proportion. The men's feet measured 18 inches." These tales caused great excitement in France, which had replaced Spain as

England's bitterest foe, and the official French position was that the story of giants was a fable deliberately concocted to create confusion and to conceal the real motives for the new British expedition under Wallis and Carteret then being organized; though Wallis and Carteret planned to look for giants, too, the French alleged that they really were going to Patagonia to exploit a rich mine discovered by Byron.

It was Admiralty policy then to impound the journals of British officers and turn them over to professional writers to be prepared for publication. Byron's own account had thus been given to Dr. John Hawkesworth, a disciple of Samuel Johnson, who proceeded to embellish Byron's plain and serviceable prose with Johnsonian flourishes. Hawkesworth's edition of Byron's voyage did not appear until 1773, which heightened the mystery over what Byron actually had seen in Patagonia, but another report on the circumnavigation did appear in 1767. This was an anonymous account by one of the *Dolphin*'s officers, who had failed to heed the Admiralty's request for the surrender of his manuscript. His book enjoyed great popularity, since it was the only firsthand narrative of the voyage available during the seven years of Hawkesworth's labors over Commodore Byron's manuscript. It provided a nine-page account of the giants, declaring that they averaged eight feet in height with "an extreme of nine feet and upwards," and offered a much-admired frontispiece showing a Patagonian man and woman holding a colossal baby and looming over an English seaman.

The excitement over Byron's giants continued all through 1767, with French scientists claiming a hoax, various English mariners coming forth with new corroborative details about the titans, and Byron maintaining silence. By now the *Dolphin* was on her way around the world again, in the fleet of Wallis and Carteret, and in May, September, and November of 1767 the *London Chronicle* printed three let-

ters written in Patagonia by crewmen who claimed to have
seen the same giants encountered by Byron in 1764. One
letter spoke of 300 giants; another, "some thousands." Their
heights were given as ranging from seven to eight feet. And
in 1768 Charles Clarke, who had sailed as a midshipman
with Byron, published a brief account of the voyage in which
he said of the Patagonians, "Some of them are certainly nine
feet, if they do not exceed it. The commodore, who is very
near six feet, could but just reach the top of one of their
heads, which he attempted, on tip-toe; and there were several
taller than him on whom the experiment was tried. . . .
The women, I think, bear much the same proportion to the
men as our Europeans do; there was hardly a man there less
than eight feet, most of them considerably more; the women,
I believe, run from 7½ to 8." On the French side was offered
Bougainville's statement about his voyage to Patagonia:
"We made contact with these so-famous Patagonians and
found them to be no taller . . . than other men." But two of
Bougainville's officers reported meeting seven Patagonians,
the least of whom stood a quarter of an inch less than six feet,
while "the others were much taller," and British critics observed that these, while not necessarily eight or ten feet high,
were nevertheless much bigger than the average European
and might represent some degenerate branch of the Patagonian race.

The giants figured in satiric literature and in an infinity
of journalistic rehashes over the next few years, but no further new material was available until the release in 1773 of
the three big volumes that Hawkesworth had fashioned from
the impounded journals of the recent British circumnavigators. Here at last were the official accounts of Byron, Wallis
and Carteret, and Cook, withheld so long. The public expected revelations about the giants and was not disappointed.
This was Byron's account, as polished by Hawkesworth, of

the meeting he and Lieutenant James Cumming had had with the giants in 1764: "One of them, who afterwards appeared to be a chief, came towards me: he was of a gigantic stature, and seemed to realize the tales of monsters in a human shape: he had the skin of some wild beast thrown over his shoulders. . . . I did not measure him, but if I may judge of his height by the proportion of his stature to my own, it could not be much less than seven feet." This is close enough to Byron's account in his unpublished manuscript journal in which he described the Patagonian chief as "one of the most extraordinary men for size I had ever seen till then," but the admission in Byron-Hawkesworth that he had not actually measured the giant is significant. In his journal Byron also had written, "Mr. Cumming . . . was as much astonished at the size & figure of these people as I was, for though he is very tall himself he appeared comparatively speaking a mere shrimp to them." Hawkesworth produced this passage: "Mr. Cumming came up with the tobacco, and I could not but smile at the astonishment which I saw expressed in his countenance, upon perceiving himself, though six feet two inches high, become at once a pigmy among giants; for these people may indeed more properly be called giants than tall men; of the few among us who are full six feet high, scarcely any are broad and muscular in proportion to their stature, but look rather like men of the common bulk, run up accidentally to an unusual height; and a man who should measure only six feet two inches, and equally exceed a stout well-set man of the common stature in breadth and muscle, would strike us rather as being of a gigantic race, than as an individual accidentally anomalous; our sensations, therefore, upon seeing five hundred people, the shortest of whom were at least four inches taller, and bulky in proportion, may be easily imagined."

This was a major deflation of the earlier accounts.

Clearly the Patagonians were large, brawny men, but Byron said nothing about eight-footers, let alone the eleven-footers reported by the first circumnavigators, and made the important point that the giants might appear taller than their actual heights because of their unusually broad and muscular frames. The narrative of Wallis, also published in Hawkesworth's 1773 collection, was even more explicit: "As I had two measuring rods with me, we went round and measured those that appeared to be tallest among them. One of these was six feet seven inches high, several more were six feet five and six feet six inches; but the stature of the greater part of them was from five feet ten to six feet."

Hawkesworth's own editorial conclusion was that the Patagonians were indeed immense, and that "the concurrent testimony of late navigators, particularly Commodore Byron, Captain Wallis, and Captain Carteret,* gentlemen of unquestionable veracity, who are still living, and who not only saw and conversed with these people, but measured them, will put an end to all the doubts that have hitherto been entertained of their existence." Nothing more was heard, however, of tribes whose average height was eight, nine, or a dozen feet, except in the transient publications of journalists who chose to revive the old stories for sensation's sake.

What, then, had Pigafetta, Fletcher, Knyvet, and the other early visitors to the Strait of Magellan really seen?

Undoubtedly they saw very tall men, verging on seven feet in height and proportionally massive. To a child, all adults are colossal; and to Europeans of the sixteenth and seventeenth century, when the average height of an adult male was only slightly over five feet, the giants of Patagonia may have seemed incredibly huge. Then, too, an element of understandable human exaggeration must have entered these

---

* Cook, who had not bothered to enter the Strait of Magellan but had gone straight around the Horn, had had no contact with Patagonians.

accounts of men who had traveled so far and endured so much; and the natural wish not to be outdone by one's predecessors helped to produce the repeated fantasies of Goliaths ten feet or more in height. Thus the Patagonian giants seem to have been the product of awe, poor judgment of heights, and, to some extent, deliberate fabrication. Of the existence of tall men in Patagonia we need have no doubt, for nineteenth-century anthropologists found that the men of one tribe, the Tehuelches (numbering several thousand then, but exterminated in 1880), had an *average* height slightly over six feet, considerably greater than the mean even for modern men of the United States. One account of these people whose reliability cannot be questioned is that of Charles Darwin, who visited Patagonia in 1834 during his five-year round-the-world voyage of scientific research aboard *H.M.S. Beagle.* Darwin wrote, "We had an interview . . . with the famous so-called gigantic Patagonians, who gave us a cordial reception. Their height appears greater than it really is, from their large guanaco mantles, their long flowing hair, and general figure: on an average their height is about six feet, with some men taller and only a few shorter; and the women are also tall; altogether they are certainly the tallest race we anywhere saw."

4

In Darwin's day, circumnavigations had ceased to be remarkable events; nearly every nineteenth-century mariner found himself making a cruise around the world at some stage in his career, and those two landmarks of the longest voyage, Cape Horn and the Cape of Good Hope, were busy way stations. The cutting first of the Suez Canal and then of the Panama Canal removed both southern capes from the standard route by the beginning of the present century, however.

Today, voyages of circumnavigation—performed by jet plane, not by bobbing wooden vessels—are commonplace things, offered at special rates to patrons of commercial airlines seeking novel vacation ideas. In our own day, though, two extraordinary and unusual journeys about the globe have been performed that surely would have wrung gasps of astonishment from Magellan or any of his immediate successors who went forth on the most arduous of human adventures in search of the spices of the Moluccas or the gold of Peru. The first of these was a circumnavigation performed entirely underwater by the nuclear-powered submarine *U.S.S. Triton*, under the command of Captain Edward L. Beach. The *Triton*, 448 feet in length, with a displacement of 6,000 tons surfaced and 8,000 tons submerged (with her main ballast tanks filled), dwarfed any of Magellan's ships and carried a crew of 183 as she left New London, Connecticut, on February 18, 1960. She set her course for St. Peter and St. Paul's Rocks, midway between Africa and Brazil, and there, on February 24, began her formal attempt to duplicate Magellan's voyage without breaking the surface. Across the Atlantic, down past Cape Horn* by March 7, into the Pacific toward Easter Island, which Magellan had missed and whose eerie stone statues the men of the *Triton* admired through their periscope, then on toward Guam, where the weary Spaniards had halted after their harrowing Pacific crossing. By the last day of March the *Triton* reached the Philippines, Magellan's great gift to Spain, and lifted her periscope again in Magellan Bay on the island of Mactan, to view the monument that marks the place where the first circumnavigator perished. Then on to Borneo and Indonesia, to the Indian Ocean, back into the Atlantic, attain-

* Since the Strait of Magellan lies within Chile, it was impossible to use it without requesting Chilean permission, which would have broken the secrecy in which the voyage was performed.

ing St. Peter and St. Paul's Rocks once more on April 25, 1960, completing the submerged circumnavigation of 26,000 miles in 60 days and 21 hours, unseen by any human being other than a Filipino who had been paddling his canoe off Mactan when the submarine's periscope rose above the water. Continuing north, the submarine paused at Tenerife in the Canary Islands, Magellan's last port of call in the Old World, and then went on to Cádiz, where Spanish officials were given a bronze plaque to place on the Magellan monument at San Lucar. The legend on the plaque read, *Ave, Nobilis Dux—Iterum Factum Est:* "Hail, Noble Captain, It Is Done Again."

Magellan could perhaps have comprehended the achievement of the *Triton*, which was, after all, a ship of the seas, larger and faster and more complex than his own, and wondrously able to travel beneath the waves, but not fundamentally different in its essential nature from the little wooden tubs he sailed so ably. What would he have made, though, of the circumnavigation performed one year after the *Triton*'s and some 440 years after his own—the adventure that transformed man's longest voyage into one of man's shortest and opened a new era as surely as Magellan had done? It was a circumnavigation performed by a single man, 27-year-old Yuri Alekseyevitch Gagarin, who on April 12, 1961, climbed into a strange metal capsule, rode it a hundred miles into the sky atop a Soviet rocket, and completed a journey around the world in ninety minutes.

Bibliography

Primary Sources

Arber, Edward (ed.). *The First Three English Books on America.* Westminster: Archibald Constable, 1895. Contains sixteenth-century translations of works by Spanish, German, and Italian geographers, and extracts from Pigafetta.

Callander, John (ed.). *Terra Australis Incognita.* 3 vols. Edinburgh: Donaldson, 1766–68. Contains accounts of the voyages of Magellan, Loaysa, Drake, Sarmiento, Cavendish, Richard Hawkins, Spilbergen, Schouten and Le Maire, etc.

Chapman, Walker (ed.). *Antarctic Conquest.* New York: Bobbs-Merrill, 1965. Extracts from various voyagers.

Dalrymple, Alexander. *Voyages and Discoveries in the South Pacific Ocean.* 2 vols. London: 1770–71. Includes accounts of the voyages of Magellan, Mendaña, Quiros, Schouten and Le Maire, Tasman, etc.

[Drake, Sir Francis, Bart.] *The World Encompassed by Sir Francis Drake.* London: Nicholas Bourne, 1628. Modern edition, London: Argonaut Press, 1926.

Hakluyt, Richard (ed.). *The Principal Navigations Voyages Traffiques and Discoveries of the English Nation.* 12 vols. London: 1598–1600. Modern edition, Glasgow: James MacLehose and Sons, 1903–05. Contains the narratives of Edward

Cliffe, Nuno da Silva, and Francis Pretty concerning the Drake and Cavendish voyages.

Markham, Albert Hastings. *The Voyages and Works of John Davis*. London: The Hakluyt Society, 1880.

Markham, Sir Clements (ed.). *Early Spanish Voyages to the Strait of Magellan*. London: The Hakluyt Society, 1911.

Nuttall, Zelia (ed.). *New Light on Drake: A Collection of Documents Relating to His Voyage of Circumnavigation 1577–1580*. London: The Hakluyt Society, 1914.

Pigafetta, Antonio. *First Around the World: A Journal of Magellan's Voyage*. Edited by George Sanderlin. New York: Harper & Row, 1964.

Purchas, Samuel (ed.). *Purchas His Pilgrimes*. 20 vols. London: 1625. Modern edition, Glasgow: James MacLehose and Sons, 1906. Contains accounts of the voyages of Magellan, Drake, Cavendish, Noort, Spilbergen, and Schouten and Le Maire.

Stanley of Alderley, Lord (ed.). *The First Voyage Round the World by Magellan, 1518–1521*. London: The Hakluyt Society, 1874. Narratives of Pigafetta and others concerning the Magellan voyage.

Stevens, Henry N. (ed.). *New Light on the Discovery of Australia*. London: The Hakluyt Society, 1930.

Villiers, J. A. J. de (ed.). *The East and West Indian Mirror*. London: The Hakluyt Society, 1906. The circumnavigations of Spilbergen and Schouten–LeMaire.

Secondary Authorities

Adams, Percy G. *Travelers and Travel Liars, 1660–1800*. Berkeley and Los Angeles: University of California Press, 1962. Section on Patagonian giants.

Anonymous. *An Historical Account of the Circumnavigation of the Globe*. Edinburgh: Oliver & Boyd, 1837.

Beaglehole, J. C. *The Exploration of the Pacific*. London: Adam & Charles Black, 1966.

———— (ed.). *The Journals of Captain James Cook*. Volume One: *The Voyage of the Endeavor*. Cambridge: The Hakluyt Society, 1955.

Benson, E. F. *Ferdinand Magellan*. London: John Lane the Bodley Head, 1929.

Boxer, C. R. *The Dutch Seaborne Empire, 1600–1800*. London: Hutchinson, 1965.

Burney, James. *A Chronological History of the Discoveries in the South Sea or Pacific Ocean*. 5 vols. London: 1803–17.

Chapman, Walker. *The Golden Dream: Seekers of El Dorado*. New York: Bobbs-Merrill, 1967.

————. *The Loneliest Continent: The Story of Antarctic Discovery*. Greenwich, Conn.: New York Graphic Society, 1964.

Dibner, Bern. *The Victoria and the Triton*. New York: Blaisdell, 1964.

Friis, Herman R. (ed.). *The Pacific Basin: A History of Its Geographical Exploration*. New York: American Geographical Society, 1967.

Gallagher, Robert E. (ed.). *Byron's Journal of His Circumnavigation*. Cambridge: The Hakluyt Society, 1964. Includes "The Patagonian Giants," essay by Helen Wallis, and relevant material.

Gould, Rupert T. *Enigmas*. New York: University Books, 1965. Material on Patagonian giants.

Guillemard, F. H. H. *The Life of Ferdinand Magellan*. London: G. Philip and Son, 1890.

Hart, Francis Russell. *Admirals of the Caribbean*. Boston: Houghton Mifflin, 1922.

Herrmann, Paul. *The Great Age of Discovery*. New York: Harper & Brothers, 1958.

Kirkpatrick, F. A. *The Spanish Conquistadores*. London: Adam & Charles Black, 1963.

Lach, Donald F. *Asia in the Making of Europe*. Volume One: *The Century of Discovery*. Chicago: University of Chicago Press, 1965.

Masselman, George. *The Cradle of Colonialism*. New Haven, Conn.: Yale University Press, 1963.

Mitchell, Mairin. *Elcano: The First Circumnavigator*. London: Herder, 1958.

Newton, Arthur Percival (ed.). *Travel and Travellers of the Middle Ages*. London: Routledge & Kegan Paul, 1926.

Nunn, G. E. *Geographical Conceptions of Columbus*. New York: American Geographical Society, 1924.

Parks, George Bruner. *Richard Hakluyt and the English Voyages*. New York: American Geographical Society, 1928.

Parr, Charles McKew. *Ferdinand Magellan, Circumnavigator*. New York: Thomas Y. Crowell, 1964.

Parry, J. H. *The Age of Reconnaissance*. London: Weidenfeld & Nicolson, 1963.

Penrose, Boies. *Travel and Discovery in the Renaissance*. Cambridge: Harvard University Press, 1952.

Prestage, Edgar. *The Portuguese Pioneers*. London: Adam & Charles Black, 1933.

Sanceau, Elaine. *Henry the Navigator*. New York: W. W. Norton, 1947.

Unwin, Rayner. *The Defeat of John Hawkins*. London: Allen & Unwin, 1960.

Winsor, Justin (ed.). *Narrative and Critical History of America*. 8 vols. Boston: Houghton Mifflin, 1886.

Wright, John Kirtland. *Geographical Lore of the Time of the Crusades*. New York: American Geographical Society, 1925.

Index

Andreque, Francisco, 298
Andrew of Bristol, 129, 180
Angel, Miguel, 297, 305
Anson, George, 497, 500
Antarctica, 148–50, 158, 166–
    167, 284, 495, 499
Anton, San Juan de, 300–3
Antonio, Dom, 357, 363
Antony, Nicholas, 279
Arabia, 12, 26
Arabs
    trade, 16–17, 24, 26–7, 31,
        49, 53–4
    ships, 17–19
    navigation, 18–19, 91
    travelers, 19–21
    war with Portugal, 57, 61
Aranda, Juan de, 107–10, 113,
    119–20
Arauco, 346
Archimedes, 21
Argensola, Leonardo de, 83,
    319, 499
Arica, 348, 446
Aristotle, 7, 8, 11, 15, 20, 21,
    29
Arriata, Juan de, 225
Arucete Island, 221
Ascension Island, 406
Asia, 13, 22–4
Atacames (Ecuador) sea battle,
    378–9
Atjeh, 322, 425, 431
Augustine, St., 13, 15–16
Australia, 382, 478, 498
    discovered by Janszoon, 426–
        427, 477
    Dutch explorers, 494–6
    See also Terra Australis In-
        cognita
Australian Company, The, 458
Australian Navigations of Jacob

Le Maire, The, 460,
    464, 467
Azores, 28, 320, 360, 421
    and Drake, 329, 333, 363

B

Baabullah, Sultan, 322–5
Babylonians, 6, 14
Bachan Island, 218
Bacon, Roger, 21
Balboa, Vasco Núñez de, 92,
    100
Bali, 393, 420
Banda Islands, 25, 322, 431,
    455, 484
    and Dutch, 395–6, 422, 426,
        430–1, 454, 493
Bantam Island, 392–6, 420,
    422, 425–7, 430–2,
    455–7
Barativa Island, 328
Barbosa, Diogo, 93, 101, 106–
    107, 118–20, 136–7,
    228
Barbosa, Duarte
    and Magellan, 101–2, 105,
        118–19, 121, 128,
        141, 144, 146–7,
        200–1
    Easter mutiny, 153–4
    captain of the Victoria, 164,
        166, 172, 177, 187
    private trade, 195
    removed as captain, 198
    after Magellan's death, 206–9
Barents, Willem, 391–2
Barlow, Roger, 240
Basil, St., 14
Batavia Islands, 457, 493, 498
Bay of Parting Friends, 287
Bay of Toil, 150
Beach, Edward L., 507–9

Index

Index

Index

[527]